CHICKEN SOUP FOR THE TWEEN'S SOUL COLLECTION

CHICKEN SOUP
FOR THE
TWEEN'S SOUL
COLLECTION

Jack Canfield
Mark Victor Hansen
Patty Hansen
Irene Dunlap

Health Communications, Inc.
Deerfield Beach, Florida

www.hcibooks.com
www.chickensoup.com

We would like to acknowledge the following publishers and individuals for permission to reprint the following material. (Note: The stories that were penned anonymously, that are in the public domain, or that were written by Jack Canfield, Mark Victor Hansen, Patty Hansen or Irene Dunlap are not included in this listing.)

Where in the World Is Carmen? Reprinted by permission of Marieta Irwin. ©1998 Marieta Irwin.

Trash Bags Are for Trash. Reprinted by permission of Makenzie Snyder and Margie Snyder. ©2000 Makenzie Snyder.

Run with It. Reprinted by permission of Susan B. Overton. ©2000 Susan B. Overton.

The Back of David's Head. Reprinted by permission of Mary Ellyn Sandford. ©1998 Mary Ellyn Sandford.

(Continued on page 532)

**Library of Congress Cataloging-in-Publication Data
is available from the Library of Congress**

©2005 Jack Canfield, Mark Victor Hansen, Patty Hansen and Irene Dunlap
ISBN 0-7573-0386-2

Publisher: Health Communications, Inc.
3201 S.W. 15th Street
Deerfield Beach, FL 33442-8190

Cover re-design by Larissa Hise Henoch
Inside typesetting by Lawna Patterson Oldfield

Contents

v

3. ON FAMILY

4. ON LOVE

5. ON CRUSHES

6. ON DEATH AND DYING

7. ON ATTITUDE AND PERSPECTIVE

8. OVERCOMING OBSTACLES

9. ON CHOICES

13. LIFE HAPPENS

14. BUSTIN' DOWN WALLS

1

ACHIEVING DREAMS

If it were all up to me
The poor would have riches
And the blind man would see
The hungry would eat
And the weak would be strong
And the people with hatred would all get along
The ones who are greedy would start to share
And unfriendly people would start to care
The thirsty would drink
And the deaf person hear
And sorrow and sadness would all disappear
And that is how the world would be
If it were all up to me.

Sara Alfano, eleven

Where in the World Is Carmen?

My mother always told me, "Seize the moment of excited curiosity." In other words, go for it.

Michael Thomas

What can you learn from a teddy bear, a little bit of stuffed fluff that can't talk? One summer, my oldest daughter and the rest of our family learned a lot.

We had seen a program on television about a reporter who had hitchhiked across America. My daughter Ashley's first comment was, "I wish I could do that!" Of course, as far as my ten-year-old hitchhiking across America—that wasn't going to happen. But I wanted to encourage that spirit of adventure in her just the same.

Three years earlier, Ashley had been diagnosed with cancer. Ever since her surgery, she was shy and distrustful of new situations and new people. Although she is cancer-free now, the tests and scary procedures had made her reluctant to take risks or to venture outside her known world. I began trying to think of a way for her to "hitchhike" across the country without leaving home. That's how Carmen was born.

Carmen is a teddy bear that Ashley had received as a gift while she was in the hospital. We decided that sending Carmen in Ashley's place was a good compromise. So we purchased a notebook to serve as a travel journal and a bag for Carmen to travel in, and Carmen was ready to begin her trip. Ashley wrote this letter in Carmen's journal:

My name is Ashley and I am ten years old. One time on TV, I saw this story about how these kids sent a bear on a trip on a plane. Then I saw another story about how this reporter guy walked across America. Well, we don't live very close to a big airport, and Dad and Mom won't let me walk across America. Carmen can't walk, so will you please help her?

This is my bear, Carmen. She is a special bear. I got her when I had to go to the hospital. She wants to go to all fifty states if she can. But, she will need your help. (Maybe she can even go to Disneyland.) Mom says we can't go until she won't have to carry my little sister. Please let her ride with you and keep her safe. Tell her about yourself so she won't be lonely. I will miss her. So please take very good care of her. I let her wear my guardian angel pin to help keep her safe.

Write a little about yourself and then introduce her to someone new. She wants to meet as many new people as she can. If you keep her for more than one day, please try to write in the journal every day. Where are you going? Where did you pick Carmen up? Which roads did you take? Where are you from? How old are you? Do you have kids? Do you have sisters? I do and sometimes I don't like them. (Mom says I can't say "hate," but I can say that I don't like them, and some times I don't like them a lot!)

I think by about September she will be ready to come

*home. In her coin purse is $5.00. Please put her in a nice
sturdy box with her journal and bag and send her to Sac
City State Bank, Attention: Caretaker of Carmen Bear.*

*Someone there will keep her safe for me until I can
pick her up. If you would like to hear from Carmen
after she gets home, please leave your address in her
notebook and we will send you a note and let you know
when she gets home safely.*

*Thank you for taking care of Carmen, and thank you
for taking the time to write in her notebook.*

*Your new friends,
Carmen and Ashley*

Our family friend is a highway patrol officer. We asked
him if he would be willing to start Carmen on her trip by
taking her on his route for a day. That afternoon, he spotted a driver from out of state that wasn't wearing a safety
belt. After pulling her over and letting her off with only a
warning, Phil asked the driver to take Carmen on the next
part of her journey. Naturally, she agreed. That's how
Carmen began her tour of the United States.

Summer passed with a flurry of activities, family vacations, visiting grandparents and summer fun. Each day
Ashley would ask if any packages had come for her. Each
day the answer was, "Not today, Ash." By the middle of
September we thought that the chances of Carmen
returning home were slim.

Then on September 24, Carmen came home in a ten-
inch-square box that had a postmark from Hawaii! The
box was packed with mementos of all of the wonderful
places and people that Carmen had met. A straw hat from
Wisconsin, to keep the sun out of her eyes. An Indian
beaded necklace from Cherokee, Oklahoma. An autograph from Mickey Mouse when she went to Disneyland.

A picture of her celebrating the Fourth of July in St. Louis. Another picture of her floating in a swimming pool "catching some rays" while she was in Arizona. Carmen made it to sixteen states, including Hawaii. Not too bad for five months of travel!

But Carmen came back with much more than just "things." She came back with friends whom a ten-year-old living in rural Iowa wouldn't have had a chance to meet. Ashley wrote letters to all of the people who helped Carmen along in her travels. She thanked every one of them for their help and friendship to Carmen and her.

Pretty soon, word traveled around our small community about the traveling bear, and Ashley was asked to give a program about Carmen to a group of over one hundred people. Ashley ended her talk by saying, "Be kind to traveling bears! And if you need a traveling companion, let me know because Carmen still has thirty-four more states to go!"

Since Ashley's presentation, Carmen has become a world traveler. Once again, we are awaiting her return. She was expected home some time ago, and we very much hope to see her again.

I never would have dreamed that a little bit of stuffed fluff could have taught so many things: patience to see what things can happen if we are just willing to wait, the ability to imagine what wonderful things might happen, courage to take the chance and allow those things to happen, and faith to believe in people and in the goodness in their hearts.

My favorite part of the story? After reading the journal, looking at the pictures and tracing the roads that Carmen had traveled, I opened the zippered coin purse that Ashley had sent with Carmen. Inside, folded in half, was the five-dollar bill that Carmen had left with five months ago.

Marieta Irwin

Trash Bags Are for Trash

What do we live for if not to make life less difficult for each other?

George Eliot

I walked through the den on my way to get ready for bed and looked once again at the amazing mountain of duffel bags. Each bag had a stuffed animal, a luggage tag and a note from me inside of it. The pile of bags went from floor to ceiling, more than five thousand bags, enough for each and every foster-care kid in three states. My dream was coming true—big time.

After I went to bed, right before I went to sleep, I closed my eyes and thought back to when it all started . . . when I got the idea for my dream. . . .

I had been in second grade when I went with my two brothers and my parents to Paris, France. My brothers, Brock and Cory, and I had entered an essay contest about what we were going to do to change the world to make it a better place to live. We won and were chosen as three of ten kids who would represent the United States at the Children's World Summit. Nine hundred kids from around the world were chosen to meet with each other and talk about world issues. We exchanged ideas on solving the problems in our world today and had lots of fun during the days we were together.

While I was there, I met two foster-care kids. They were two boys, and after getting to know them, I learned a lot about what foster-care kids go through. They told me that when kids go into the foster-care system, they don't just lose their parents and their home, sometimes they are also separated from their brothers and sisters. Not every foster-care home wants to care for an entire family of kids. Foster-care kids also lose most of their toys and clothes. They told me that when the kids are picked up from their home by a social worker, they are given only a trash bag to put their few belongings into. This trash bag is what foster-care kids carry with them when they are moved from home to home.

I felt really sad when I heard this. I couldn't even imagine what life would be like without my family and home—much less what it would be like to have to live out of a trash bag. Trash bags are for trash, not for kids to carry their belongings in.

After I came home from France, I saw an after-school movie that was about a girl living in foster care. It was just like what the boys had described to me at the Children's World Summit, and it made me cry. Right then I decided that I wanted to help foster-care kids. These kids needed my help, because they were not being respected like they should be.

My whole family is into volunteering. Brock and Cory had started a project after they saw a show on television about some kids who died in a fire. The kids had died because the fire department didn't have this special camera that can see through smoke to find people in a burning house. My brothers began Project Rescue Vision in

1996 to raise needed money for our town's fire department. Of course, I helped too. I was only four years old,
and I was the "President of the Art Department." My job
was to hand-color all of the information envelopes that
were given out. I helped them until I was seven. Then I
began my own project for foster-care kids.

I started by asking my mom to stop at garage sales
when I saw suitcases or duffel bags for sale. I would tell
the person who was having the garage sale what I wanted
to do with the bags, and most of the time they gave me
the bags for free. I tried to put myself into the mind of a
foster-care kid, and I decided that the kids should have a
stuffed animal in the bag, too. I figured that if I was in that
situation I would want a cuddly friend to hug when I was
sad and felt lonely for my parents. People often gave
those to me for free, too.

In October 1998, I helped organize a luggage drive during
our local "Make a Difference Day." Some congresspeople
and senators showed up to give their support, and I came
up with this idea for everyone to get their hand painted
and then put their handprint on a big banner to show that
they had made a difference that day. I got all these kids to
help paint people's hands. It was really funny to watch
these important people have their hands painted.

The senators and congresspeople went back to
Washington and told other people about my project, and
then a company named Freddie Mac set up a grant for me
and donated fifteen thousand dollars. I am the youngest
person they have ever granted money to. Because of this
grant, I had a story about my project and me on the cover
of the *Washington Post*. Then the most amazing thing
happened. President and Mrs. Clinton read about me and
wanted to meet me. I was really excited! They were so
nice, and I gave the president one of my bags with a
Beanie Baby in it to give to any foster kid that he may

meet. A few days later, he sent some bags to me from his own collection to give to foster-care kids, so I did.

My project really started growing because of all the media attention. Radio stations called me for interviews about what I was doing and some TV shows had me on. More people then heard about me from the TV and radio interviews and from word-of-mouth, and they called me to offer help.

Every week I called my friends and family to see if they wanted to come and put together bags. I always had help from many people. My class even helped, too. My teacher announced to my class what I was doing, and everybody started bringing stuffed animals and duffel bags to school. One of my friends brought in ten big bags full of stuffed animals!

On each bag, I put a luggage tag designed by me. On the front of each luggage tag is a picture of a girl and a suitcase with wheels on it. In each bag, I put a cuddly stuffed animal and a special note I wrote, letting them know that I love and care about them. My mom helped me type this note:

> *Dear Friend,*
>
> *Hi, my name is Makenzie Snyder. I am nine years old, and I'm in the third grade. I collect suitcases and duffel bags as an act of kindness for those who are in need of them. God told me you could use a duffel bag and a cuddly friend so I sent this with love to you. I want you to always know that you are loved, especially by me. And, always remember to be positive, polite and never give up.*
>
> *Love, your friend,*
> *Makenzie Snyder*

After the bags are stuffed, I call social workers to tell them they can come and pick up the bags to hand out to the foster-care kids. I have had a lot of support from several big companies, schools, churches, organizations and individuals who have donated money, or sent me bags and stuffed animals. I've even been on the *Rosie O'Donnell Show!* Several thousand bags have been sent out so far, and right now I have five thousand more ready to go, sitting in my den. Those bags will go to kids in Maryland, Washington, D.C., and Virginia.

I have had a lot of help from a lot of people, but most importantly from my parents and my brothers. My brother Brock came up with the name for my project. He said I should call it "Children to Children" since it was all about kids knowing what other kids want and helping them get it. My brothers have also given me good advice about always sending thank-you notes to the people who help me. They told me I had to work hard, call tons of people and to never give up . . . and I haven't.

I know that this is just the beginning. There are 530,000 foster-care kids in the United States. My dream is for all the foster-care kids in the entire United States to receive a duffel bag and a cuddly friend. I know it can be done if everyone helps out. It is a lot of work but I never get tired of it. I remember the girl in the movie that I saw. If she had been given one of my duffel bags, she would have known that someone out there cared about what happened to her. I don't want any kid, anywhere, to go through what she or the two boys did. Kid to kid, Children to children— that's what it's all about.

Makenzie Snyder, nine

[EDITORS' NOTE: *If you would like more information about Children to Children, go to Makenzie's Web site at* www.children tochildren.org.]

Run with It

Do what you can, with what you have, where you are.

Theodore Roosevelt

The first time I saw Jeff was when my best friend, Brian, and I were in the fourth grade. When our teacher introduced Jeff to the class she explained that he was sick and that he might not be able to be in class all of the time.

Jeff was completely bald from cancer treatments, and he wore a hat. That was one reason that he and I bonded right away. Being the tomboy that I was, I liked wearing a hat—only I wasn't allowed to wear one in class. Jeff was allowed to wear his hat all of the time. Other than that, he was a normal friend to both Brian and me. Some things he couldn't do as well as the other kids because he had tubes in his chest for his treatments, but we never thought of him as sick because he didn't act that way.

The only time that we would realize that Jeff was sick was when he went for his chemotherapy treatments. We'd notice the difference, but we'd just sort of think, *Yeah, Jeff's not feeling really well now,* and then it would pass and things would be back to normal. Jeff, Brian and I were really sports-oriented, and we became best buds. We would swim, run and jump on the trampoline. As fourth grade progressed, Jeff got better and better. By the end of the school year he went into remission; the cancer was all gone.

Brian, Jeff and I spent tons of time together during the summer between fourth and fifth grades. We loved being outdoors, running everywhere and staying over at each other's houses. Before school started, Jeff went away on vacation with his family for a few weeks.

Then came the night that I will always remember. We were eating dinner when the phone rang. It was Jeff's mom, calling to say that Jeff was in the hospital. The cancer had come back. My reaction was, *Wait a minute. What's going on?*

Jeff and I talked on the phone the next day and he sounded like his normal self. I couldn't really imagine him being back in the hospital. Then, a few days later, my mom took me to visit him. When I walked into his room, Jeff looked really weak. His mom was talking about a trip to California for a bone marrow transplant operation, and how important it would be for Jeff. Even though everyone looked very serious and sad, the thought of losing Jeff never crossed my mind. I just thought he would get better.

During the next few weeks, before the operation, Jeff was allowed to play with Brian and me but he had to wear a surgical mask because he had to be careful of infections. I realize now that his parents wanted him to experience as much of life as possible while he could. One night, they took Jeff and me to this really fancy restaurant up in the mountains, and it felt sort of like a date. We both dressed up—which was weird for me, because I never wore anything but shorts and hats.

When Jeff left for California to have his operation I told

him, "Bye, see you in a month or so," as if nothing much was happening. I wrote to him while he was there, and the letters that he sent to me talked about the things that we would do together when he returned home. It didn't even cross my mind that I might never see him again.

Then, one night, I went to a skating party. Brian was supposed to be there but I couldn't find him. When I got home, my dad was out in the garage working on a project. When Dad spotted me, he opened the door to the house to let my mom know that I had arrived. I walked into the house, and Mom said, "I need to talk to you alone in your bedroom, Susie." I grabbed some chocolate chips off the counter and bounded off to my room. "Jeff's mom called . . ." was all she had to say. I knew. The chocolate chips turned sour in my mouth, and I cried as my mom held me tightly. I've never been an emotional person, but my heart just sank and I felt empty. It was too hard to believe. Brian had heard about it just before the skating party, and that's why he hadn't been there.

That evening, Brian and I talked for hours. We had never talked much on the phone before, because we had always been doing things, but that night we talked and talked, reminiscing about Jeff. We started worrying about Jeff's parents and if they could handle the medical expenses. And that was the beginning of our idea. We wanted to do something, but we didn't know what.

When we figured out that Jeff's parents didn't need the money, we started thinking instead about something that would help everybody remember Jeff, something to honor him. Brian and I thought about the time the three of us did a run together. Jeff had loved running, but it had been hard for him to finish the run. He was really happy when he was able to cross the finish line, and so were we. *Why not do a run for Jeff?*

It seemed like a good idea. We knew that we would

have to advertise in order to have enough runners, and that we'd have to get sponsors for food and drinks. We even thought we knew what the forms needed to look like for sign-ups.

I know now that all of this planning was part of our grieving process. All through it, we told each other stories about Jeff. Right around that time, his parents donated a tree to the school and we all planted it in Jeff's memory. It was tough on his parents, but it really helped all the kids. Everyone got to shovel some dirt around the tree, and Jeff's parents held hands with each other and cried.

If we'd been old enough to know what was really involved, we probably wouldn't have started it. But we were just some kids with a great idea, so we went for it. We took the phone book and started calling Coors, Pepsi and Mile-High Yogurt—anything we could find. "We want to do a run, and we're looking for sponsorship," we would say to whoever answered the phone. "Who can we talk to?" I wonder if the people on the other end could tell that we were only fifth-graders!

Then one day, Mom came to me all excited. "A man from Pepsi called and asked to talk to you. What's going on?" I guess we'd been persuasive enough! After I called him back and got his pledge of support, I told my parents about the run and they promised to help. The vice-principal got involved and he brought the plans for the run to the gym teacher, who was a runner. All of the adults in our lives were encouraging us.

We started writing letters to lots of companies, which was pretty funny because Brian has the worst hand-writing in the world. I don't know how anyone ever read what he was trying to say. But somehow it worked because we started receiving all kinds of gifts. The yogurt place gave us five hundred free yogurts, and other companies donated money.

The plans for the run were growing so big that we needed a professional organizer. Someone came along and donated this service for free, and that's when things really started to roll. The entire community became involved: stuffing packets, raising money, writing numbers on racing bibs, holding meetings. Pretty soon, the whole city knew what was going to happen.

The day of the run finally came, and it was huge! Tons of people ran, ReMax donated T-shirts and there were awards for anyone who could beat the gym teacher's time. The park where the run was held was near Jeff's house, which was where the processional had gone after his funeral. Because of where it was held, the run had even more of a special meaning to Brian and me. And, we raised ten thousand dollars! We donated the money to the Leukemia Society in Jeff's name.

Even now, I think about Jeff quite a lot. If something's going on in my life that feels bad, I tell myself, *Come on, get over it. Stop feeling sorry for yourself. If Jeff were still alive, he would be glad just to have the opportunity to deal with this.*

The run made such an impact on my life. The biggest thing was (and I credit the adults for this) that no one ever told us "No." We kept hearing, "If you want to do it, you can do it!" It has helped me in everything I've done since, and I've had a "Go for it!" attitude about things.

There's a big bike ride I've heard about that goes from Los Angeles to Orlando, and I'm thinking about riding in it. Some of my friends think I'm crazy and they ask me, "Is that even possible?" Of course it is! *You're alive, you're here—so run with it!*

Susan Overton

The Back of David's Head

Have a belief in yourself that is bigger than anyone's disbelief.

August Wilson

I couldn't stand fifth grade. I didn't like the milk that was warm by lunchtime from sitting near the radiator all morning. I didn't like recess because I could never get a turn on the swing. But most of all I didn't like my teacher, Mrs. Kelly, because I was sure that Mrs. Kelly didn't like me.

Mrs. Kelly never let me pass out books or collect papers. Mrs. Kelly made me sit in the last seat of the sixth row behind David Abbot, the biggest kid in the whole class. David was bigger than most of the eighth-graders, and he never, ever took a bath. The only thing I could see all day was the back of David's head.

At the beginning of fifth grade, Mrs. Kelly had explained all the classroom rules including the one about being excused for the rest room. She told all the students that they had to raise their hand with one or two fingers when they wanted to be excused. Then she would know what they were going to do in the restroom, and how long they would be gone from the classroom. The whole class would laugh whenever anyone held up two fingers to be excused.

One Monday in October, Mrs. Kelly said, "Clear your desks and take out your composition books. Today I want you to write a composition called 'Something Interesting' about something you have personally seen. Do not repeat any topics."

"Can we write about Disneyland?" Maureen Murphy asked. Everyone in the class knew that Maureen had been to Disneyland more than anyone else in the whole school.

"That would be perfect, Maureen," Mrs. Kelly answered with a smile.

I opened my black and white composition book. I tried to ignore the huge red U for "unsatisfactory" that partly covered the title, "My Summer Vacation." I remembered Mrs. Kelly's comments without even looking at them.

> *It has been brought to my attention that this composition is about your last year's summer vacation, and you have already written about the same trip for a composition last year during the fourth grade. Therefore, this assignment is unsatisfactory. Your penmanship is also unsatisfactory.*

I didn't care about the penmanship comment. That was on every assignment I turned in. What bothered me was that Mrs. Kelly would not accept my composition about my train trip to Denver. The only trip I had ever gone on in my whole life had been the trip to Denver. In the fourth grade, my composition had been about all the things I had seen from the train windows on the way to Denver. For the fifth grade, I wrote a whole new composition about the hotel in Denver with the glass elevators.

Mrs. Kelly wrote an outline on the blackboard. One

paragraph for an introduction, then three paragraphs to describe the topic in detail. A final paragraph for a conclusion. I knew that Maureen Murphy had a composition book filled with E's for excellent and even S's for superior while my best grade had been an F. In spite of Mrs. Kelly's red marks, I really liked to fill the pages of my composition book with words and ideas. I frowned and stared at the back of David's head.

That's when I noticed that the back of David's head looked like a brown forest with a long, brown, hairy trail that ran down his neck. He had three big brown freckles peeking out from the forest. The top of his head looked like a cartoon porcupine with brown hairs sticking up all over. David's ears were reddish tan with pudgy lobes that flapped against his neck when he raised his hand with only one finger. Looking at the back of David's head, I decided this composition could be different. It could be full of imagination instead of boring and embarrassing because I had never had the chance to see anything interesting, outside of the trip to Denver.

I opened my composition book and began to write. I wrote and wrote until Mrs. Kelly said, "Mary Ellyn, this is the third time I've called your name. It is time to line up to go home. However, you will stay after and write 'I will pay attention in class' one hundred times before you are excused."

On Wednesday, Maureen tiptoed around the room in her fancy shoes passing back everyone's composition notebooks. I ignored her snotty smile and opened my book, paging past all the F's and U's. I couldn't wait to see a beautiful letter at the top of my composition, entitled "The Back of David's Head."

By the time I found the page, my whole body was so tense with excitement I almost fell off my seat. But what I saw made my breath stop in a gasp. Across the whole composition Mrs. Kelly had scrawled a huge red U. It was the biggest and reddest U I had ever seen. The red words in the margin swam in a blur from the tears that filled my eyes. A huge tear plopped onto the page, splashing over the comment about penmanship. I slapped the book shut and raised my hand with two fingers. I didn't care who laughed.

In the bathroom, I sat on the edge of a toilet and cried for a long time. After a while I heard the restroom door swish open.

"I know you're in here, Mary Ellyn," Maureen Murphy's voice oozed under the green painted metal door. "Mrs. Kelly says you'd better get back in class, right now."

I waited for the sound of the door swishing closed. "You just wait and see, Mrs. Kelly," I said in a low scary voice. "Someday I'll show you. Someday I'll write lots of stories and SELL them for lots of money. Someday my stories will be in books! Just you wait and see."

And when I grew up, that's *exactly* what I did.

SO THERE, MRS. KELLY!

Mary Ellyn Sandford

[EDITORS' NOTE: *Mrs. Kelly and readers might be interested to know that Mary Ellyn's work has been published in several magazines as well as* Chicken Soup for the Kid's Soul.]

Going to the Dogs

If we all did the things we are capable of doing, we would literally astound ourselves.

Thomas Edison

One day my mom and I were sitting in her office looking at a magazine called *Humane Society News.* We read a very sad story about a New Jersey police dog named Solo that had been sent into a building to catch an armed suspect. The last thing Solo did before entering the building was to lick his owner's face. A few minutes later, Solo was shot and killed in the line of duty. I knew how sad that officer must have felt because my own dog, Kela, had recently died. I felt like my world had ended when I lost Kela. She had been my best friend since I could remember.

The article went on to tell about a fund-raiser that was going on in New Jersey to help buy bulletproof vests for the police dogs there. I thought, *Every police dog should be protected just like the police. I may be a kid, but why can't I do a fund-raiser to help save the dogs in our area?*

Then I found out that a bulletproof vest for a police dog costs $475. My mom thought it was a lot of money for an eleven-year-old girl to raise, but she told me to go ahead and try anyway.

We called our local Oceanside Police Department and found out that their dogs needed bulletproof vests. At that point, I realized that I needed a name for the fund-raiser and thought since I was trying to protect just one dog's life, I would call my program Vest A Dog.

I decided that veterinarian offices and pet stores would be really good places to go with donation boxes and Vest A Dog flyers. I used little green Chinese take-out boxes, decorated with a picture of Tiko, the dog I chose to vest, and me. I wrote on each box "Help protect the life of a police dog by donating a dollar."

One afternoon, after all the boxes had been distributed throughout our community, I got a call from a local news-paper reporter who had seen one of my fliers. The reporter decided to do an article about Vest A Dog. *That ought to spread the word,* I thought. I asked K9 Officer Jim Wall, who is Tiko's partner, if they would have their pic-ture taken with me for the article and they did.

After the article came out, I waited for a few days before checking to see if there were any donations. I was really nervous when I finally went to collect the money. *Would there be anything in the boxes?* I wondered. I really wasn't sure that I could raise enough to buy the vest. But when I collected the first box, I couldn't believe my eyes. I real-ized that there are many generous animal lovers out there. The box was practically overflowing with dollar bills! I kept checking back to collect the donations every few days. After about three weeks, I counted the money from all of the boxes. It totaled over three thousand dollars! I was so excited and totally amazed at the amount of money that I had raised. Not only was there enough money to buy Tiko's vest, but Vest A Dog had raised enough to buy vests for the other five unprotected dogs on the Oceanside Police Department. I couldn't believe it!

When the officers from the K9 unit found out that they were going to be able to protect all six of their dogs, they couldn't stop thanking me. They decided to put together a presentation ceremony where I would give the six vests I was donating to the department's dogs. That's where I got to meet all of the other police dogs and their handlers. I was actually a little scared of them, but the officers assured me that the dogs were very friendly. I learned that these were not just police dogs, but also the officers' family pet. Again, I thought of my dog Kela and also about Solo. I wanted even more to make sure that these police dogs didn't die while trying to protect people.

Once I began presenting the vests at the ceremony, I kept seeing television reporters come in and set up cameras. I never expected to see so many news stations there! I was excited to talk with them about what I was doing. When they asked me if I was going to continue my Vest A Dog program to help protect the other fifty dogs in San Diego County, where we live, I replied, "Yes! We need to protect these dogs because they protect us every day."

Soon the phone was ringing off the hook! Each day, reporters from newspapers and television stations called with interview requests. They wanted more information about my Vest A Dog program and also wanted to know where donations could be made. The media is so powerful! People began to mail donations to Vest A Dog!

Looking back, the success of Vest A Dog totally surprised me at first. Then I realized that it wasn't unusual that a lot of other people felt the same way I did about these dogs. They just didn't know how to help before Vest A Dog got started.

So far, Vest A Dog has raised more than twenty-five thousand dollars and has supplied *all* of the law enforcement dogs within San Diego County with a protective vest! Then, just when I had achieved what I thought was my highest goal, people from all over the country began to call me to find out how to raise funds to vest dogs in their areas. So now my fund-raiser is continuing nation-wide, and I have a Web page to tell other people how to organize a fund-raiser like the one that I did.

Knowing that more and more dogs are being protected is really rewarding. It has made all my efforts more than worth it.

Then, one day after school, my mom told me that the Society for the Prevention of Cruelty to Animals (SPCA) wanted to honor me for the work that I had done to pro-tect police dogs. They invited my mom and me to New York so that I could receive an award and a check for five thousand dollars! That vested another ten dogs!

I'm so proud and happy that the money I have raised is all going to the dogs. I'm still amazed that I have vested so many dogs when I really wasn't sure if I could vest even one. Even though some days I was tired from schoolwork, I knew it was important to continue fund-raising to help save these special dogs. It was a lot of hard work but I learned that if you just keep going, you can accomplish anything. Don't think that just because you are a kid that you can't make a difference. Even if you think something is impossible, it can be done.

Stephanie Taylor, eleven

[EDITORS' NOTE: *For more information on how to start a Vest A Dog program in your area, log on to* www.dogvest.com.]

If I Could Change the World
for the Better, I Would . . .

Eliminate every manmade weapon and all war. I would make sure that everyone treats each other equally.

Lance Bass, *NSYNC

Find one positive thing that everyone in the world could believe in. Prove to everyone there is a common ground in all people, no matter what race, color, sex, faith, rich or poor. Bring people a little closer together, and remind them we're all the same. Just try to make it through life as human beings, and remember that every life is just as important as the next.

J. C. Chasez, *NSYNC

Have free ice cream breaks for everybody. I would have children have more say-so in the world, and ban all guns and drugs.

Joey Fatone Jr., *NSYNC

Put a smile on everyone's face.

Chris Kirkpatrick, *NSYNC

End racism and make equality for men and women. I would teach life through music.

Justin Timberlake, *NSYNC

Melt every cold heart and mold them into new warm ones.

Scarlett Kotlarczyk, eleven

Help people realize that people like me who learn and do things differently than them are still really the same underneath it all. We want to be liked and smiled at.

Wilson Cook, nine

Find another way to test drugs instead of using them on animals.

Brandon Barger, thirteen

Make it so every kid would have a warm meal, and no one would go starving.

Timothy Blevans, eleven

Open a house for all of the orphans of the world. I would get lots of people to help me take care of them.

Stacey Bergman, fifteen

Stop kids from making fun of other kids. Prejudice is just what we don't need. Kids hate being ridiculed.

Rachel Force, eleven

Make people realize that it's not what other people think of you, but what you think of yourself. You shouldn't put yourself down when people say cruel things about you or do things to you, because they're the ones that need a little *Chicken Soup* for their soul.

Sarah Hampton, fourteen

Travel back in time, and make sure the people who invented drugs and smoking never discovered or invented them.

Lisa Cline, eleven

Find a cure for diabetes. My little brother's friend has juvenile diabetes. Every year my family "Walks for the Cure." I wish there wasn't such a disease because he has to take shots and stuff.

Kristin Boden, thirteen

Want everyone to keep an open mind about everything, because with an open mind, you can accomplish anything.

Annemarie Staley, fourteen

Make everything solar powered including factories, vehicles and all types of machinery. By doing this, there wouldn't be as much air pollution and people could breathe easier.

Tracye Paye, thirteen

Give every child a grandmother like mine. She may not be rich and famous, but she has enough love in her heart for her twenty-one grandchildren and great-grandchildren, and plenty more to spare. How many millionaires can say that?

Casey Singleton, eighteen

Make it so that kids don't have to go through child abuse.

Kristen Hamilton, eleven

Make every capable person do one hour of community service per month. This would include cleaning up rubbish, bathing and feeding homeless people, and planting trees.

Trevor Burton, nineteen

Make sure that no one in the world is harmed because of their religion.

Pratima Neti, eleven

Stop child labor, which is unfortunately still going on in this world. Children deserve the right to live, and working at a very young age will not give you that freedom.

Jessilyn Yoo, twelve

Pay teachers more, because teachers are the foundation of all learning. Without teachers, the world would just be a useless space full of useless people.

Angela Rotchstein, fourteen

Make sure that everybody in the world is able to read. Reading is the world's greatest gift for the mind and imagination.

Jessica Behles, fourteen

Have everybody just agree to disagree instead of fighting. After all, we are all different, and have our own ways; this is the spice of life.

Jill Ananda, fourteen

Plant the rainforests back all over the world, so that the trees will grow and the rivers will flow. I would bring back the animals that have died out, but without the dinosaurs!

Kyla Cangemi, ten

Make the world a happier place with no bombings or school shootings.

Chap Arst, thirteen

Show everyone the love that my adoptive mother showed me. I was angry at the world because I thought no one loved me or could ever love me. No one wanted a thirteen-year-old girl, but she came along and showed me that people could and do care about me. I would definitely give that to any person in this world. Love is all the world needs.

Mia Sifford, seventeen

Give every child a blanket, not only to keep them warm, but to snuggle with. We each need something to hold onto, and a fuzzy blanket would help keep away the problems of the world, if only for a moment or two.

Steve Hayden, thirteen

Let all the kids in the whole world know that they can succeed in anything that they put their heart into. There is always a solution for problems; you just have to look in your heart to find them.

Alysia Escalante, thirteen

Fix that hole in the ozone layer so the heat of the sun won't kill us.

Nikole Pegues, eleven

Ask everyone in school to say one nice thing to another person every day. Have every family tell each other they love one another.

William Baun, twelve

Have people talk to each other and listen more, and make sure that everybody would have enough play time.

Neil Gogno, nine

Stop all the violence that is on TV, which is where people get the idea that it is okay to hurt or kill someone. When we were channel surfing, my stepmom and I saw seven guns and three acts of violence all in one minute; even my dog got scared!

Bethany Hicks, twelve

Want everyone to have at least one best friend that they could count on.

Andrea Hawsey, eleven

Create vehicles that would run on natural resource waste material to stop the pollution.

Rosie Huf, eleven

Get more clubs and activities going so that people would stay away from gangs, drugs and crimes.

Stacy Luebbe, fourteen

Bring back all our lost loved ones for a day.

Rita Koch, ten

Make sure that all children in the world can go to school, and have *Chicken Soup* books so they know that they aren't alone.

Allison Opsitnick, twelve

A Run to Remember

Thirteen can be a challenging age. Not only did I have to adapt to my changing body; I also had to deal with my parents' bitter divorce, a new family and the upsetting move from my country home to a crowded suburb.

When we moved, my beloved companion, a small brown pony, had to be sold. I was trashed. Feeling helpless and alone, I couldn't eat or sleep, and I cried all of the time. I missed my family, my home and my pony. Finally, my father, realizing how much I missed my pony, purchased an old red gelding for me at a local auction.

Cowboy was without a doubt the ugliest horse in the world. He was pigeon-toed and knock-kneed. But I didn't care about his faults. I loved him beyond all reason.

I joined a riding club and endured rude comments and mean snickers about Cowboy's looks. I never let on about how I felt, but deep down inside, my heart was breaking. The other members rode beautiful registered horses.

When Cowboy and I entered the events where the horse is judged on appearance, we were quickly "shown the gate." No amount of grooming, vitamins or unconditional love would turn Cowboy into a beauty. I finally realized that my only chance to compete would be in the timed-speed events. I chose barrel racing.

One girl named Becky rode a big brown thoroughbred mare in the race events. She always won the blue ribbons. Needless to say, she didn't feel threatened when I competed against her at the next show. She didn't need to. I came in next to last.

The stinging memory of Becky's smirks made me determined to beat her. For the whole next month I woke up early every day and rode Cowboy five miles to the arena. We practiced for hours in the hot sun and then I would walk Cowboy home. On the way home I would be so tired, those five miles seemed twice as long.

All of our hard work didn't make me feel confident by the time the show came. I sat at the gate and sweated it out while I watched Becky and her horse charge through the pattern of barrels, acing the course with ease.

My turn finally came. As I nudged Cowboy forward he stumbled, and almost fell, much to the delight of the other riders. I jammed my hat down on my head, stroked Cowboy's big red neck and entered the arena. At the signal, we dashed toward the first barrel, quickly whipped around it and with perfect precision rounded the second and thundered on to the third. We tore around the final curve and shot for the finish line.

No cheers filled the air. The end of our run was met with surprised silence. With the sound of my heart pounding in my ears, I heard the announcer call our time. Cowboy and I had beaten Becky and her fancy thoroughbred by a full two seconds!

I gained much more than a blue ribbon that day. At thirteen, I realized that no matter what the odds, I'd always come out a winner if I wanted something badly enough to work for it. I can be the master of my own destiny.

Barbara L. Glenn

Shining Down

You must be the change you wish to see in the world.

Gandhi

One dark morning while driving to work, my dad, Clayton Kavalinas, swerved to avoid a deer in the road. His car skidded on black ice, hit a guardrail and spun into an oncoming truck. He died in the crash. He was only thirty-five years old. Streetlights could have helped prevent the accident, but there were no lights on that stretch of highway called the Marquis of Lorne Trail on the outskirts of Calgary, Canada.

I was only eleven when he died. I was devastated over the loss of my father, especially when I realized that his death could have been avoided. In a two-year period, my father and one other driver were killed, and twenty-nine accidents happened on that area of the highway. Time and again I thought, *How could I find a way to make my dad's short life really count?*

I felt triumphant when I figured out what I could do. I decided that I would try to get some lights put up in that area to help other drivers see better.

Once I figured out what I had to do, I fought as hard as I could to get new lights on that road. But I didn't realize what a big deal that would be! I was determined and very motivated. I didn't want what happened to my father to happen to anyone else.

I was studying government in school, and I tried to find a way to increase public pressure on city hall to install lights. With help from my classmates, I handed out flyers at homes and shopping malls, and obtained over three hundred signatures on the petition needed to grab the attention of the politicians in charge of road safety issues. I contacted them, too, and told them what I was trying to do. I was pretty amazed when some of the politicians actually listened to a kid! Finally, there was a meeting at city hall about the need for new lights.

Before the meeting, the local media found out what I was trying to do and reported on the problem. The reporters helped people in the area "see the light" and acknowledge the danger on Marquis of Lorne Trail.

With TV, radio stations and newspapers covering it, more people understood why lights were needed. They also learned what it was like for a child to lose a father. A lot of people told me they were touched and they decided to help. The public pressure began to rise and within four months from the morning my dad lost his life on that highway, the city council agreed to spend $290,000 for new lights.

Sometimes, going through the accident over and over, in order to make a point, was a hard thing to do emotionally. At times, I had hard nights and I cried. But at other times, I'd be really happy and proud that my dad's life was the one that made the difference in helping to save many other lives from fatal accidents.

I was never so proud in my life as I was on September 16, 1996, nearly a year after I lost my dad. Speaking through a walkie-talkie at the side of the road, I gave a city worker instructions to turn on the lights for the first time. During the same lighting ceremony, I was given a plaque from the City of Calgary honoring me for my public service efforts. Since then, the number of collisions on Marquis of Lorne Trail has been drastically reduced.

While helping many people I'll never even meet, I think I also helped my mother, my younger brother, Shaun, and my little sister, Kaitlin, become more determined to continue to enjoy life. I helped lift their spirits, and they were there to support me. We all cried together. We all laughed together. We all thought about life together. My dad's death brought us closer together as a family, making something positive come out of the situation and helping to ease our grief.

But it was really my dad who ended up teaching me a lot about determination, courage and faith. In his own way, through this project, he helped me grow up. I learned that if you're determined, if you put your heart into something, you can overcome any obstacle. You can accomplish anything.

Life goes on now. The cameras have stopped filming and the civic leaders focus on other problems. But the streetlights will always be there to help me get through difficult times.

I know that I'll always be reminded of the terrible accident and I'll still suffer grief from losing my dad, but I gain comfort knowing that area of the highway is now a safer place. I feel my dad's presence there. I'll always have the comfort of knowing that every night, a little bit of Dad is shining down.

Michael Kavalinas, sixteen
As told by Monte Stewart

Dreams

They say a person needs just three things to be truly happy in this world. Someone to love, something to do and something to hope for.

Tom Bodett

When I was three years old, I slept on a very small bed in a large room with twenty-five other boys and girls in an orphanage in Hungary. Being the youngest boy in the building, I got picked on often because I was the smallest. My sister, Kristin, protected me when she could, but the older boys were really mean to me. Kristin and I had been taken from our birth mother when we were only babies because she couldn't take care of us.

When I was about one year old, Kristin and I were taken in by a lady who became our foster mom. We thought we'd found a home and had really grown to love her, when about a year and a half later, she decided she couldn't afford to keep us any longer. She told us that she was taking us to the orphanage for a visit, but she never came back to pick us up.

We had lived in the orphanage again for about six

months by the time Christmas came. None of us got any presents at all. I had only a few clothes of my own and no toys. We got two meals a day but the bread was hard and the food was terrible. I had one good friend at the orphanage named Attila, and we used to talk a lot about what it would be like to have somebody come and take us away from there. Our dream was to have a real family and do things that most other kids did. I had never even gone swimming or seen a movie in my life. Sometimes Attila, Kristin and I watched the only show they had on television, which was *Teenage Mutant Ninja Turtles*.

Two or three times, people came to the orphanage and talked to my sister Kristin and me, but they never came back to see us again.

One day, this pretty lady with big hair and a big man with glasses came to see Kristin and me. We couldn't understand what they were saying, but the Hungarian girl who was with them told us that they had come from a faraway place called America. We spent a lot of time with them that day, and I told Attila what a good time I had.

They came back to see us every day for a week and took us for ice cream and long walks. The Hungarian girl told us that the man and lady wanted to adopt us and take us back with them to America. We were so excited and happy.

When I told Attila what was going to happen, he was very sad and didn't want us to leave him there. I told him he should ask the big man if he would take him so that he could come to America and be my brother. The next time the man and lady came, he jumped up into the man's lap and asked him if he could come with us. But, since the man didn't speak Hungarian, he didn't know what Attila wanted and just smiled at him.

Kristin and I flew on a great big jet plane to America. Things look very different but wonderful here. All the food tastes great, and I have my own room with a big bed and lots of clothes. I got a stuffed animal of my very own: my first toy.

Everyone was really nice, and our neighbors even gave each of us something called a bicycle. It didn't take long for me to learn to ride. Christmas came and there were lots of boxes under the tree for Kristin and me. America is a great place and I am very happy here.

After a year, we went with a group of kids to a special ceremony where we were made citizens of the United States! After the ceremony, two men with a TV camera came and asked us questions about what life was like in Hungary. That night we were on television like the Ninja Turtles!

I hope that Attila got to see us and I wonder if he knows that dreams really can come true.

Ryan Kelly, ten

Head-Butting the Wall

Every action we take, everything we do, is either a victory or defeat in the struggle to become what we want to be.

Anne Byrhhe

I grew up in a small town in New Jersey where I felt bored and trapped. My family life was all about, "Mom works, Dad works and kids are expected to go to school." My parents didn't have the money to buy me stuff I got interested in, and we didn't have any time to spend together except during meals. That didn't cost anything or take up any extra time.

I was angry and frustrated most of the time—it seemed that no matter what I did or said, I felt like I was head-butting the wall and getting nowhere. No one could get through—not my parents, my teachers or my guidance counselor. No one could help me.

Then I started high school, and a lot of the people I knew began using drugs and alcohol. Because I wasn't interested in that, I found myself on the outside of my peer group. I was totally alone and I hated the world.

I started roaming the streets looking for trouble. I fought older, tougher guys around town and gained a reputation for being crazy. I'd take any dare. If someone said to me, "Smash your head on this rock for five bucks!" I would.

I was well on my way to prison or the morgue when I stumbled on punk rock music. The whole idea of a punk lifestyle sounded cool. So, I spiked my hair and took on a whole new identity until, one day, some *real* punkers came up to me in the hall at school.

"Hey, man, are you punk?"

"Yeah, yeah, man, I'm punk," I fumbled.

"Oh, yeah? What bands do you like?"

I didn't know any bands—none.

"Who do you listen to?" I didn't know one band from the other. Then my eyes landed on their band-logo T-shirts.

"Dead Kennedys, Black Flag, The Misfits . . ." I thought I had them fooled. But I was pretty much busted.

"Stop looking at our shirts. You don't really know any punk bands, do you?"

Totally busted. *Where do I go with this?* I thought to myself. Before I could come up with a strategy, one of them dared me to come home with them to his house. We went down into his basement and they shaved my spikes off. Then they said I was really punk. The next thing I knew, I was meeting up with them after school and hanging out.

Some of my new friends would occasionally get a hold of a skateboarding magazine, and they'd show me pictures of some decks. When I saw the boards, I connected. I became obsessed. I wanted to get my hands on a board and more of those magazines. One kid, the younger brother of one of my friends, had a stash. I cruised over to his house and knocked on the door.

"Hey, man, can I take a look at some of your skateboard magazines?" I asked.

This guy was hardcore. He wasn't about to let me *touch* his prized possessions, but he let me stand on his back porch and look at them through his screen door as he turned the pages, one by one. That's when I saw an article about street skating and a photo of a guy jumping off a car.

"I can do that! I can totally do that," I tried to convince him. He looked at me, doubting every word, but he got his board out and challenged me right then and there. I took the dare, grabbed the board and got up on his grandpa's car. Slam! I hit the ground. I got back up. I went through the same thing over and over—biting dust every time. Then finally . . . I landed it!

He screamed, "You did it! You're a skateboarder!"

I was hooked, rushing on adrenaline. I wanted to experience it again and again.

I began to follow a group of guys in my neighborhood that had boards. I'd beg them to let me skate. They treated me like dirt, but because they had boards, I took it.

I *had* to figure out how I could get my own board. I finally conned my mom into giving me money for a board by promising her that it would be my one and only Christmas present. I ordered a board and when it arrived, I was totally stoked. Then my mom made me hand it over. Her words, "Sorry. You can't have it until Christmas, Mike," were torture.

Weeks later, Christmas came and *finally* I got my board. I skated every spare second I could. I went from skating a few minutes a day to hours a day. I'd skate to and from school, after school, after dinner and after homework. When I started trying to skate the half pipe, I'd get nothing but grief about my style. I was doing everything I could just to gain the speed needed to get up the other side of the ramp. I'd flap my arms to get momentum. "Look at the chicken-man," guys would taunt. I didn't care—whatever it took, I'd try it. I lived and breathed skateboarding. It was my sanctuary and my salvation; it was my "thing."

I easily navigated the traps and pitfalls of high school and adolescence by just getting on my board and riding. But it wasn't just the physical act of skateboarding that made an immediate and lasting impact on me; it was the entire subculture of doing your own thing. Instead of following the crowd, I had discovered my individuality. My small town that once felt full of dead-end streets suddenly opened up. I found a wide-open country of possibilities. At fourteen, that's some vital stuff.

I truly believe everyone needs to find something to help them discover their identity and give them a sense of purpose, meaning and direction. For me . . . it just happened to be skateboarding. Skateboarding saved my life. It gave me the ability to express myself, connect to a passion and offer something unique back to the world. Now, as a professional, I travel the world, skateboarding and sharing my life story.

I'm still head-butting the wall, the difference is that now I'm fighting to keep the sport of skateboarding open to everyone and anyone—regardless of how good they are, what they look like or where they live. I want everyone to know that if they just believe in themselves and have a passion for the sport, anything is possible.

Mike Vallely

[EDITORS' NOTE: *To find out more about Mike, log on to* www.mikevallely.com.]

No Place I'd Rather Be

All our dreams can come true, if we have the courage to pursue them.

Walt Disney

Growing up, I always dreamed of being a professional figure skater. After years of hard work, support from my family and good coaching, I am living proof that dreams can come true.

When I was born, my parents immediately noticed something wrong. My feet were deformed, pointing inward and curling under. I wore casts and foot braces my first two years to correct the problem. My casts were changed every two weeks. I teetered at first, yet I learned to balance and walk in casts. Soon after the last set of casts came off, Mom enrolled me in dance classes as therapy for my feet.

I, however, quickly decided to try something else. Not far from my house was an ice rink in the mall. There, local skaters would perform ice shows. I remember seeing the glittery costumes, the dazzling spotlight, and their graceful movements. I wanted to try skating.

I started taking group skating lessons, but I'd cry before class because going into a group scared me. Performing on ice came naturally, but I have always been shy and afraid to speak in group settings.

One thing I've never been afraid of is competition. I get nervous, like everyone else, but never fearful. For me, skating has never been about beating others. It's been about being my personal best. I progressed through various levels rapidly and gave my first ice performance at age seven. Soon I started winning local and regional competitions. That's because being on the ice has always been the one place I can truly express my emotions. The ice is like home.

I began seriously training when I was nine years old. Mom and I would wake up at four o'clock in the morning, six days a week. I'd skate for five hours. Then I'd go to school. Since education has always been important in my family, I had to find creative ways to fit in school studies throughout my amateur career.

Twenty-four hours after graduating from high school, I moved to Canada. Saying good-bye to my family and friends made me homesick before I even left, but I knew deep down that I had to leave and train full-time to give my dreams a chance at reality.

I went to compete in the Olympic Games in 1992. No one, not my coach or even my family, ever talked to me about winning a gold medal. In fact, I wouldn't even allow myself to think about it. I thought that would jinx me. So, I went with the attitude that I wanted to enjoy the Olympic spirit.

My practice sessions felt great leading up to the competition. Finally, the day arrived. I remember stepping onto the ice and thinking, *I can't do this. How am I going to keep myself from freaking out?* I took a deep breath and eased into a solid performance that placed me first going into the finals.

Two days later, I was the first of the final six skaters on the ice. My long performance started well, but I slipped while landing one of my easiest triple jumps, and my hand touched the ice. I didn't want to make two mistakes in a row, so next I did a jump with just two spins to play it safe. As I neared the end, I had one more jump, the triple Lutz. *Okay, this is it. You have to do this,* I told myself. I landed it perfectly.

When medals were awarded, I found myself on the top step, the gold hanging around my neck and America's national anthem playing. Words can't describe the overwhelming mixture of emotions I felt.

Little did I know how much that one night would change my life. Interviews. TV shows. Magazine covers. Dignitaries. Celebrities. Parades. Fans. Endorsements. My big dream came true when I signed a contract to skate professionally with the Stars on Ice tour. I thought life as a pro would be easy. It's not. It takes as much training now as before.

Throughout the tour, special children visit us at practice. Their courage in the face of incredible challenges teaches so much to all who meet them. It has helped me see that we all have the opportunity to make a difference in someone's life. That's why I started the Always Dream Foundation. Our goal is to make a positive difference in the lives of children.

How can anyone love ice? Frozen water can be so painfully hard and oh so cold—just as life can be. Ice doesn't care who skates across its surface. It doesn't care who loses balance and falls on its slippery back. Still, when the lights go on and the crowd roars its welcome, there's no place I'd rather be.

For me, the ice is a warm world of beauty and grace. Being on the ice is being alive. I encourage you to pursue the things that make you feel alive. And, as you glide your way along life, remember . . . always dream.

Kristi Yamaguchi

[EDITORS' NOTE: *To find out more about the Always Dream Foundation, log on to* www.alwaysdream.org. *Check out* www.positivelyforkids.com *for cool books featuring the life stories of star athletes and celebrities.*]

2

ON
FRIENDSHIP

When you are sad I will dry your tears
When you are scared I will ease your fears

When you are worried I will give you hope
If you want to give up I'll help you cope

When you're lost and can't see the light
I'll be your beacon shining so bright

This is my oath that I pledge to the end
Why you may ask?

Because you're my friend.

Nicole Ritchie, fifteen

The Forgotten Friend

*Friendship without self-interest is one of the
rare and beautiful things of life.*

James Francis Byrnes

It was my tenth birthday—double digits—and I would
have the biggest party ever. The guest list, which I kept at
the back of my homework assignment folder, began with
a few close friends. But in the two weeks before that special Friday night, it had quickly grown from seven girls to
a whopping total of seventeen. Nearly every girl in my
fifth-grade class had been invited to sleep over at my
house for a big celebration. I was especially happy when
each guest I invited excitedly accepted the invitation. It
would be a night of scary stories, pizza and lots of presents. But as I later realized, I would truly treasure only
one gift I received that night.

The family room was a flurry of shouts and bursts of
laughter. We had just finished a game of Twister and were
lining up for the limbo when the doorbell rang. I hardly
paid attention to who might be at the door. What did it
matter, really? Everyone I liked from school was there, in

my family room, preparing to lean under the stick held by my two sisters.

"Judy, come here for a minute," Mom called from the front door.

I rolled my eyes and shrugged to my friends as if to say, *Now who would dare bother me at a time like this?* What I really wanted to say was, *It's tough being popular!*

I rounded the bend toward the front door, then stopped. I know my mouth dropped open and I could feel my face turning red, for there on the front porch stood Sarah Westly—the quiet girl who sat next to me in music class—and she was holding a gift.

I thought about the growing list in the back of my assignment folder. *How had I forgotten to invite Sarah?*

I remembered that I only added a name to the list when someone had shown an interest in me (like kids do when they know someone is having a party and they don't want to be left out). But Sarah had never done that. Never once had she asked me about my birthday party. Never once did she squeeze into the circle of kids surrounding me at lunch time. And once she even helped me carry my backpack while I lugged my science project to our third-floor classroom.

I guess I had forgotten to invite her simply because she wasn't pushing to be invited. I accepted the gift from Sarah and asked her to join the party.

"I can't stay," she said, looking down. "My dad's waiting in the car."

"Can you come in for a little while?" I nearly begged. By now I felt pretty bad about forgetting to invite her and really did want her to stay.

"Thanks, but I have to go," she said, turning toward the door. "See you Monday."

I stood in the foyer with Sarah's gift in my hands and an empty feeling in my heart.

I didn't open the gift until hours after the party had ended. Hours after the games, the food, the ghost stories, the pillow fights, the pranks on those first to fall asleep and the snores.

Inside the small box was a ceramic tabby cat about three inches tall with its tail in the air. In my mind, it was the best gift I had received, even though I was never really into cats. I later found out that the figurine looked exactly like Sarah's cat, Seymour.

I didn't know it then, but now I realize that Sarah was my one true childhood friend. While the other girls drifted away, Sarah was always there for me, ever loyal and supportive. She was an unconditional friend who stood by me, always encouraging and understanding me.

Although I'll always feel bad about forgetting her, I also realize that I might not have discovered Sarah as a friend had I remembered to invite her to that unforgettable tenth birthday party.

Judith Burnett Schneider

Backfire!

Actions, not words, are the true criterion of the attachment of friends.

George Washington

It was spring at last. The sun was high in a cloudless sky. Birds sang. Flowers bloomed. Best of all, it was Saturday—a perfect day to be out playing with friends. The problem was, we'd only been in town two months so I hadn't made any friends. My family moved a lot. It's hard when you're always the new kid on the block.

So, here I was, stuck with my baby brother John and Mary, the new sitter, while Mom and Dad were out of town on business. It was not going to be a fun day!

Just as we started lunch, the phone rang. I hopped up to answer it. "Hello, Morrell's residence. Lou speaking."

"Hi, Lou. It's Alicia."

My heart did a rapid pit-a-pat-pat. "Alicia Whitman?"

She giggled. "You know another Alicia?"

"No." There was only one Alicia: the most popular, prettiest, richest girl in my class.

"I called to invite you over to my house this afternoon. We can ride my horse."

"Hang on. I'll ask." Heart racing, I ran to the kitchen. "Mary, can I go play with my friend Alicia this afternoon?"

Mary was trying to scoop peas off the floor faster than my brother dropped them. "Where does she live?"

"Only a few blocks from here," I said, picturing the fancy brick house that we passed on our way home from school. I held my breath.

"Would your mom let you go?"

"Sure, she would. Please, Mary. Please, please, please."

John dumped the whole dish from his highchair.

"Oh, all right," Mary said with a sigh.

I rushed back to the phone. "Alicia, I can come. What time?"

"One o'clock?"

"Great. See ya then."

I was so excited I could hardly breathe. I was going to hang out with Alicia Whitman! Ride her horse. Every girl in class wanted to be Alicia's friend.

"Come eat your lunch," Mary called.

"I'm not hungry. I have to get ready."

I chose my outfit very carefully: my best shorts, clean T-shirt and brand-new shoes. I even washed my face and combed the tangles out of my hair. When I was satisfied, I called, "I'm going now, Mary."

I set off. The sun beat down on my back and bounced off the sidewalk. Cars and trucks swished by on the highway. I didn't care about the heat or the noise. I was too busy daydreaming about the possibility of becoming good friends with Alicia. I'd liked Alicia from the first day. We were a lot alike. We both loved to read. Our hands were the first up to answer questions. We mostly got A's. We both liked to play sports, although Alicia was always picked first and me last. And we both were horse-crazy. I just knew we could be best friends—if we had a chance.

The sidewalk stretched on forever and ever. It hadn't seemed this far in the car! My shirt was getting sweaty and one heel in my new shoes hurt like crazy. I stopped and pulled down my sock. A big, fat blister had bubbled up. *Youch!* I kept going, walking on my tippytoes. *It couldn't be that much farther now, could it?*

Several blocks later, across the highway, I saw the meadow with Alicia's horse, Buttercup, in it. Now all I had to do was cross four lanes of traffic. I sure hoped I wasn't late!

Cars and trucks whizzed past me. I waited the longest time for a break. When it came, I made a mad dash to the other side. *Whew! I was there.*

The Whitman house was surrounded by big, old trees. The cool shade felt wonderful. I smoothed my hair and my shorts. My mouth was dry. I hoped Alicia would offer me a cold drink right away. I walked up to the front door and rang the bell.

No one answered.

I rang again, then knocked. No one came to the door.

Maybe they were out back? I walked around on the brick walk. There were no cars in the driveway. No one on the fancy rock terrace either. I knocked on the back door.

Nobody came.

Alicia's tree house was empty, too. I climbed up to check. Except for Buttercup, the whole place was deserted!

I couldn't believe it. *Had I heard Alicia wrong? Didn't she say today? Why would she invite me and leave? Maybe she'd gone to pick me up?* That was it! Alicia didn't walk to school or ride the bus. A shiny black car brought her and was waiting when school was out. She wouldn't expect me to walk all the way out here. We'd just missed each other.

Happily, I went back and sat on the front steps. I waited

and waited and waited. It got later and later. No Alicia. No Whitmans. Nobody came.

I sat there with my head in my hands, growing more disappointed and confused by the minute. I finally decided that Alicia wasn't coming, so I got up and trudged home. I was ashamed of myself. I'd been so hungry for a friend that I'd fallen for her mean trick.

By Monday morning my shame had turned to anger. Being pretty and popular didn't give someone the right to trick people! I spotted Alicia on the playground, surrounded by the usual group of girls. I pushed my way into the circle. "What you did was mean, Alicia Whitman. I don't want to be your friend, now or ever!" I stomped away.

"Wait!" Alicia cried. "What did I do?"

Right there, in front of God and all her friends, I told her.

Alicia was shaking her head. "I didn't call you, Lou. It wasn't me. We were out of town all weekend."

Someone giggled and said, "Miss Brainiac got fooled."

I ignored the name-caller. "Then who called me, Alicia? Who played that dirty trick?"

Alicia looked around the group. Her gaze stopped on Morgan, who was trying to hide the fact that she was laughing to herself. "It was a dirty trick, Lou. I don't know who did it—for sure. But that person's no friend of mine."

Morgan turned bright red. "It was just a joke. Can't you take a joke, Lou?"

"Some jokes aren't funny. Right, you guys?" Alicia said, taking my arm.

Everyone nodded and closed in behind Alicia and me. Morgan's hurtful joke backfired. We all walked away, leaving *her* standing alone on the playground.

Lou Kassem

Best Friends

I thought she was my best friend
The best one I've ever had
Instead I found out the truth
And what I learned was sad.

We still call each other friends
But I feel we're far apart
Though we see each other every day
I have a broken heart.

She has made new friends
And I have made some, too.
We are talking less and less
And inside I'm cold and blue.

Each and every night I pray
That she will finally see
How much I want our friendship
back
And how much she means to me.

Whitney M. Baldwin, twelve

My Best Enemy

Examine the contents, not the bottle.

The Talmud

Once again, I was in a new school. So was a girl in my class named Paris. That's where the similarities ended.

I was tall, with a big, moony face. She was petite and skinny with a model's delicate features.

My thick, black hair had been recently cut short into a shag style. Her natural caramel blonde hair flowed to her waist and looked great when she flipped it around.

I was twelve and one of the oldest in the class. She was eleven and the youngest in the class.

I was awkward and shy. She wasn't.

I wore baggy overalls, sweatshirts and lime-green hiking boots. Paris wore rhinestone platform shoes, little twirly skirts and expensive, size-one designer jeans.

I couldn't stand her. I considered her my enemy. She liked me. She wanted to be friends.

One day, she invited me over and I said yes. I was too shocked to answer any other way. My family had moved six times in six years, and I had never managed to develop many friendships. No one had invited me over to play since I was young enough to actually play. But this girl who wore tinted lip-gloss and the latest fashions wanted me to go home with her after school.

She lived in a fun part of town that had two pizza places, an all-night bookstore, a movie theater and a park. As we walked from the school bus stop through her neighborhood, I tried to guess which house might be hers. Was it the white one with the perfect lawn or the brown-shingled three-story house with a silky golden retriever on the front porch?

Was I surprised when she led me into an apartment building, which smelled like frying food, chemical cleaning sprays and incense! She lived on the fourth floor in a two-room place with her mother, her stepfather, her two brothers and her sister.

When we got to the room she shared with her sister, she took out a big case of Barbies—which was my next surprise. I would have thought she'd outgrown them. I had never played with them. But we sat on the floor of a walk-in closet, laughing as we made up crazy stories about the Barbies. That's when we found out that we both wanted to be writers when we were older and we both had wild imaginations.

When we got bored making up stories, she took out a small case of make-up and taught me how to put on lipstick and blush. I still thought that I looked like a clown; my face just wasn't made for make-up. Unlike me, Paris looked about eighteen years old in make-up.

We spent that afternoon screaming with laughter. Our jaws ached from smiling so much. She showed me her wardrobe, which had mostly come from a designer clothing store down the block. The woman who owned it used her as a model sometimes for her newspaper ads and gave her clothes in exchange.

Paris had the whole neighborhood charmed. The bookstore owners lent her fashion magazines, the movie theater gave her free passes and the pizza place let her have free slices. Soon I was included in her magic world. We slept over at each other's houses, spent every free moment together. Sometimes Paris and I stayed up the entire night talking. We never ran out of things to discuss, whether we were making detailed lists of boys we liked or talking about the meaning of life.

She was too poor to have a telephone, so when I was forced to be apart from her, I would dial the number of the pay phone in the pizza place. If I was lucky, Paris would be nearby and answer it.

She was my first real friend since childhood, and she helped me get through the rough years of early adolescence. My dark hair grew out and I learned to love being tall. Eventually, I found a shade of lipstick that didn't make me look like something from *Scream II*.

Nothing bad happened in our relationship—except for growing older. We ended up going to different junior high schools and eventually drifted apart.

Since then I've had other wonderful friendships. But Paris taught me an amazing and very surprising thing about making friends: that your worst enemy can turn out to be your best friend.

Dakota Lane

Heaven Sent

*You will suffer and you will hurt. You will have
joy and you will have peace.*

Alison Cheek

Making the transition from middle school to high school
is always a tough one. Luckily, I had my five best friends,
Kylie, Lanie, Laura, Mindy and Angela, to help me through
it. We experienced our most important moments together
and shared everything, the good and the bad. Their friendship completed me. With their help, I went from being a
shy little girl to a confident and excited young woman. Life
without them was unimaginable, or so I thought.

The unexpected all began on a beautiful spring day
during my sophomore year. Life was perfect. It was a
Friday and the weekend was upon us. After my friends
and I made our plans, I said good-bye to each of them and
gave them all a great big hug. As always, I told them that
I loved them and we went on our own ways.

Laura and I decided to go to the mall and do some
shopping before we went out that night. As we returned
to her house, I noticed something very odd: both of her

parents were home and waiting outside. I knew right away how peculiar this was, since even Laura seemed surprised to see her father home so early. As we approached the door, Laura's father quietly uttered, "Reality is going to hit right now." My stomach sank and my heart began to pound quickly. *What was he about to tell us?*

Once I found out, I no longer wanted to know what he was trying to say. Seeking comfort, I looked into the eyes of Laura's mother but saw her eyes fill up with nothing but tears. As she tried to speak, she choked on her words. But slowly the words came. The five words that would forever destroy my life were, "There has been an accident."

Images of the people I loved raced through my mind as my heart began to beat faster. My first instinct was to retreat to denial. Nothing was wrong, nothing had happened and no one was hurt. This would all go away and things would be back to normal in the morning. Unfortunately, I couldn't run away from the truth. I sat on the edge of my seat in shock as I was told the news.

My best friends had been in the accident. Lanie and Mindy had walked away. Kylie, however, was in bad shape. I soon realized that no one was telling me what had happened to Angela. As I prepared to ask, I took a deep breath and swallowed hard. Deep down inside, I already knew what I didn't want to hear. I tried to ignore my instincts. After all, Angela couldn't be dead. She was only fifteen!

Then the news came and there was nowhere I could run to escape. Angela was dead. After hearing the news, all I could do was laugh. This had to be some kind of sick joke. My inner refusal to accept what I had been told prevented me from crying. I had no tears. I was in shock, utter shock. From the moment the accident had happened, each of our lives had been changed forever.

As I arrived at the hospital, the first person I saw was Lanie. Even though it truly was Lanie, this wasn't *my*

Lanie. The Lanie I knew was full of spunk. As I looked into her eyes, I thought I was looking into the eyes of a stranger. For the first time in our lives, she was out of my reach. I was devastated to see her in so much pain. She couldn't even speak to me.

As if that weren't hard enough, I was then told that before I could see Kylie, there were certain conditions that I had to agree to. I was to remain calm and tell her that everything was going to be okay. The hardest part, though, was being told that I couldn't cry, because this would upset her. I quickly agreed. I just wanted to see her.

I walked into the emergency room to find Kylie hooked up to many machines. She was screaming and crying. It was beyond difficult to pretend that all was well when all I could see was the hell that she was going through. My heart stopped. She was in agony and I could do nothing but watch. As I told her that I loved her, I felt my eyes well up with tears, so I turned and ran away.

Once I was outside of Kylie's room, I tried to regain my composure. However, I panicked once again when I found out that Angela's father was on his way over to the hospital to check on the other girls. My only instinct was to run, and that is exactly what I did. I ran as fast as I could to the other side of the hospital. I was not running away from him, but from the truth. I just couldn't bear facing him. I knew if I did, I would have to face the truth that Angela was gone forever. I wasn't ready for that truth. Somewhere deep down, I was still hoping that this was really an awful nightmare that I was going to wake up from any minute. Unfortunately, it wasn't.

That night all of my friends gathered at Laura's house. We consoled each other and reminisced about the times we had shared with Angela, times that we would have no more. At this point, I was still not allowing myself to grieve. If I did, it would mean that I believed it was true. I knew it was true but I could not accept it, so I didn't.

Later that week was the viewing. The once-vibrant young woman lay lifeless and cold. That was not my Angela; I did not know or recognize that person. What followed was the funeral. That was where the spirit of the Angela that I knew actually was.

It was a beautiful sight to see the community come together to express their love for her. The microphone was open to all of those who wanted to share their personal memories or their love for Angela. Seeing all the people that were there to remember her made me realize that Angela not only touched my life but the lives of everyone she came into contact with. She was my sunshine, and now without her my days were darker. How does a person live without the love, warmth and security of her best friend?

I didn't think my life could get any worse, but I was wrong. Without notice, I was told that my parents were getting a divorce. As soon as I heard the news, I automatically wanted to call Angela. After all, she was the one I always ran to when I needed someone to talk to or cheer me up. But she was gone.

All my friends were still hurting from the devastation of losing Angela, so I didn't think that I could burden them with my new crisis. I ended up feeling completely lost and abandoned. I bottled up all my thoughts, questions and frustrations inside of me. I thought that meant that I was strong. It took me some time before I realized that there was someone that would always be there for me no matter what happened: God. He always had a way of coming into my life with open arms when I had nowhere left to run. I soon learned that God has a mysterious way of working. This time, he placed a situation in my life path that enabled me to grow as an individual.

Unexpectedly, Brenda Hampton, the creator, writer and executive producer of *7th Heaven*, came to me and asked if

I would be willing to do an episode about "dealing with the death of a young friend." Up until this point, I had not let myself grieve over the loss of Angela. Simply put, I had been acting. I had put up this perfect façade that I was totally happy. When Brenda asked me if I was willing to do this episode, I suddenly realized that I needed to let out my emotions and fears if I ever wanted to get over my pain. As a result, I agreed to what Brenda proposed, and she developed "Nothing Endures but Change."

At first, I wasn't prepared for the emotional tidal wave that would be released. Filming that episode was both emotionally and physically exhausting. Emotions that I had ignored for so long were now being unleashed, and I did not know how I was going to deal with them. Luckily, this time around I felt comfortable enough to turn to my friends and family for the love, advice and security that only they could offer. I came to the realization that it was okay to hurt. Once the tears came, they didn't stop until weeks after. That was when I realized that even though Angela wasn't physically with us any longer, her spirit had never left my side.

One day, after visiting Angela's grave at the cemetery, I was listening to the radio. I noticed that the songs playing were those that I always associated with Angela and our friendship. Five of "our" songs played back to back. As I came over a hill, I saw a beautiful rainbow. I immediately got chills all over my body. I knew that this was a sign and it instantly caused me to smile. To all of my friends and me, rainbows had symbolized our friendship with Angela. There she was, as beautiful as ever, just reminding me that she was still by my side and had never truly left me. I cried, but this time out of happiness and joy. I knew then that I have an angel watching over me, now and forever, and her name is Angela.

Beverley Mitchell

Keeping in Touch

There is one thing better than making a new friend, and that is keeping an old one.

Elmer G. Leterman

Two years ago my family moved. The day that we left, my best friend and I cried together in my empty bedroom for hours. I was miserable and homesick during the five-hour car ride to my new house. Life was unbearable.

When we finally arrived at my new house, I ran to the phone to tell my best friend my address and phone number. We talked for a little while, but I had to hang up because the long-distance call was expensive.

On the first day of school, I called her to tell her how it went. Then, on Halloween, I sent her a letter and a picture of my new friends and me.

Finally, she wrote me a letter. It wasn't even a letter—just a bunch of pieces of paper saying, "Best friends forever."

When I finally got her e-mail address, I e-mailed her the longest letter I have ever written. I never received an e-mail back, and by the third e-mail letter with no response, my messages grew shorter and shorter. With each passing day, I got angrier and angrier. I never received a reply from her.

Mom said that I could always call my other friends, that I didn't need to always call her. Give up on my best friend? Give up on the person I had known all my life? The person that I had gone from diapers to Barbies to nail polish with, and who had been in the same class with me from the first through the fifth grade?

My first answer was automatically, "No way!" But after five more e-mail messages, three phone calls and two more letters, I started to consider what my mom had said. Every night for about a week, I stayed up in bed thinking, *Should I give up? Should I keep trying?*

The way I looked at it, if I'm her best friend, she'd take a minute to push a few buttons on the phone, or type a short "hello" on the computer, or scribble a few words on a piece of paper. To me, keeping in touch is part of being a friend and is important. To her, it really didn't seem to matter.

After two years of disappointment, I finally got a phone call from my best friend. She told me how sorry she was for not writing, and about how busy she had been. It was so unexpected, I forgot about everything that happened and how angry I had been at her. I forgave her. I guess keeping in touch just isn't her style, and it didn't mean she didn't care about me.

I came to realize that true friends never really lose their special connection. Even after two years, it felt like we had just talked yesterday. Now she and I write regularly—or at least she *tries* to, and *she tries hard.*

What more could a friend ask for?

Emily Burton, eleven

The Mysterious Book Bag

The homemade book bag was sprawled across my bed. It appeared to have taken over the entire room. I hovered in the doorway just staring at it, a little afraid to move toward it. I closed my eyes for a second, trying to imagine the large shoulder bag gone. I carefully visualized a nice, normal store-bought backpack in navy blue or black.

I opened my eyes again. It was still there. The large sack was the color of rust, and fuzzy, like a stuffed animal. I knew that my mom had spent all day happily sewing as she envisioned me proudly walking from class to class with it flung over my shoulder.

To make matters worse, I realized that the fabric was actually left over from a toy horse that my mom made for me when I was a baby. Now there was sentiment attached to it. I entered the room and picked up the gift. My mother had even quilted little running horses along each side. And, just to make certain that no one would be confused as to who owned this furry monstrosity, Mom had embroidered my name on one side.

If I had been eight and not twelve, I would have been thrilled. The book bag was huge, with numerous pockets. The thing would easily hold all of my school supplies, and it was sturdy, too. It would last, so I couldn't hope that it would soon fall apart, giving me the perfect excuse to be rid of it.

"Do you like it?" my mother asked.

"Yes," I said in a halting voice. "Thank you."

"Well, if you don't like it, you don't have to use it," Mom said sadly.

"Oh no, Mom, I love it," I lied, picking the bag up and rubbing the soft fabric against my face. The last thing I wanted to do was to hurt her feelings. "You used the same fabric from Flaming Star," I said with a smile, letting her know that I understood the connection to my childhood stuffed animal. "Thanks," I muttered again and hugged her.

After a while, I got up the nerve to load the new bag with notebooks, pens and other school supplies. *It is kind of cute,* I tried to convince myself.

The next day I was to start seventh grade at a new school, in a new state, in the middle of the school year. I was nervous and excited all rolled into one.

That first day at school I heard the whispers. "Have you seen the new girl? She's from California. Did you see that big furry bag?" Then there were giggles.

Because I started school in the middle of the year, all of the lockers had been assigned to other kids. There was no storage available for me, so I was forced to haul all my stuff around in the oversized fuzzy bag, making me seem suspicious.

I soon became known as "the weird girl with the huge, fluffy horse bag."

Wild stories flew back and forth about what I kept in the bag that never left my side. *Drugs?* some kids wondered. *Clothes? Is she homeless?*

There was nothing interesting in that bag, just my coat during cold weather, school books, papers and pens. Eventually, most students pretty much ignored me, but some of the kids teased me about the fuzzy horse bag. People grabbed at it, pretended to pat it like a dog and tried to toss their trash into it. My teachers didn't seem to notice, probably because I didn't ever complain or ask for help.

As the year progressed, I started to hate that bag. I blamed all my problems on it. I felt helpless and alone, miserable, and homesick for California and my old friends.

One day toward the end of the school year, my math teacher assigned each student a partner to work with on word problems. I was told to work with Debbie, a popular redheaded girl who was in several of my classes. She smiled and waved me over toward her desk, so I grabbed my notorious bag and quietly moved toward her. As I sat down, I realized that I had never spoken to her before.

"So, what's in the bag?" Debbie asked loudly with a grin. The students working at the table next to us turned to hear my answer.

"Um, just books and stuff," I stammered, caught totally off guard.

"Can I see?" she boldly asked.

Then she held out a hand for my bag. I was so shocked that I simply handed it over without a word.

By this time, numerous other kids were watching us.

"So, why do you have clothes in there sometimes?" Debbie asked.

"Just my coat or a sweater or whatever I wore to school." I replied.

"But why?" Debbie tilted her head with the question. "And, why on earth do you cart around *everything,* for *all* of your classes? Do they do that in California?"

"No, in California I had a locker!" Then I explained. "They were all out of lockers when I got here this year."

Then Debbie started to laugh—not at me, but at the situation. "You mean, you've just been carrying your stuff around all this time because the school didn't have enough lockers?"

I nodded.

"This happens every year. The school doesn't have enough lockers, so lots of us have to share." She started giggling again. So did I. "There's, what, a week left of school," Debbie said through spurts of laughter. "But, you can share with me if you want. That bag is kind of funky— very chic when you think about it. One of a kind."

Then Debbie stood up, still grinning. "Hey everyone. Guess what? Laura's bag is just full of school stuff!" she exclaimed. "No locker," she said with her hands up and shoulders scrunched, as if to say, "What was she supposed to do?"

"All right, Debbie, that's enough," the teacher said loudly. "I'm glad that's settled. Now get back to math!"

Debbie rolled her eyes and handed me a piece of paper with her locker combination scrawled on it. "Wish I'd asked you about that bag months ago," she whispered. Then she asked me something I never thought I'd hear. "Do you think your mom would make *me* one?" When I nodded, bewildered, she started laughing again. "I think we're gonna be friends," she declared, loudly enough for the whole class to hear.

And we still are.

Laura Andrade

A Friendship to Remember

For some, life lasts a short while, but the memories it holds last forever.

Laura Swenson

Her name was Emma. She was the new girl in school. I remember feeling very sorry for her because every student was staring, pointing and whispering about her. She was extremely small, very thin and, worst of all, she was a twelve-year-old girl who had no hair.

Emma ended up in my homeroom. She was introduced to everyone that first day and was then told to find an empty seat. Emma took a seat two rows away from me, one chair up. She lay her head down on her new desk, crossed her legs and put her hands over her face. She tried to conceal her embarrassment but everyone could sense it.

At lunch, Emma sat at a table alone. I think she was too frightened to approach anyone, while at the same time everyone was too frightened to approach her. About ten minutes into lunch, I decided to leave my table and walk over to her. I pulled out a chair and sat down. I said, "Hi, my name is Veneta. Do you mind if I sit with you?" Emma didn't answer, but nodded, never picking her head up or raising her eyes to see me. Trying to make her feel more comfortable, I began talking just like I had known her forever. I told her stories about our teachers, the principal, and some of my friends. By the end of the twenty minutes that we sat together, she was actually looking at me right in the eyes, but there was still no expression on her face. She simply looked at me with a blank stare.

When the bell rang and it was time to go to our next class, I stood up, told her it was nice to get to talk to her and went on my way. I felt terrible walking away, as I had been unable to get her to talk or even smile. My heart was aching for this girl because her pain was so obvious to me.

It wasn't until about three days later, when I was at my locker getting things ready for class that Emma finally said hi to me. "I just wanted to say thank you for talking to me the other day," she said. "I appreciate you trying to be nice to me." When she began to walk away, I gathered my things and chased her. From that day on, we were inseparable.

This girl just captured my heart. She was loving and caring, compassionate and honest, but most of all, she was lonely. We became best friends, and in doing so, I set my twelve-year-old self up for the most devastating thing I would ever experience. I found out that Emma had cancer and was not given a very good chance of beating her disease.

For five months, Emma and I were the best of friends. We were together at school every day and then together almost every night to study or just hang out—and, of course, every weekend. We talked, we laughed, we joked about boys and we fantasized about our futures. I wanted to be her friend forever but I knew that it was not to be the case. After five months of being best friends, Emma became very, very sick.

I spent all my free time with her. I would go to the hospital when she was there and sleep over at her house whenever she was home. I knew in my heart I had to make sure she understood that she had become my best friend in the whole world—the sister I never had.

I was at home one Sunday, sitting with my dad watching football. The phone rang and my mom answered it. I could hear her mumbling and then she hung up. She walked into the room, her eyes red and tears streaming down her face. I knew instantly what had happened.

"Is Emma all right?" I asked. Mom's inability to reply answered it all.

Emma had been rushed to the hospital. She had gotten a very high fever. The news was not good. Her cancer was not responding to any treatments—it was spreading. Emma was losing her battle to stay alive.

Three days later, Emma passed away at home, in bed. She was just twelve years old. I remember feeling numb, knowing that she had passed on, but not quite understanding the finality of it all. Over the next couple of weeks, I quickly learned the hardest lesson I have ever had to learn in life.

Not only did I have to learn to deal with death, mentally and emotionally, I had to learn to grieve. I hadn't yet been able to do that. Then one day, her mom came over and handed me a box. She said she had found it in Emma's things. There was a note on it, saying to give the box to me when she was no longer here. I took it up to my room, stared at it for an hour or more, and then finally got up the courage to open it.

Inside, I once again found my best friend.

Emma had put several pictures of her and me in the box, some of her favorite jewelry and, most important, a note to me. I began to sob but I managed to read it.

"I never thought I would ever know true friendship,"

she began. "I was always treated like an outsider, a circus freak. If anyone talked to me, it was usually to ask what was wrong with me or, even worse, to ask me if I was going to die.

"You are my very best friend in the whole world and I will never forget you. If you are reading this, I am in heaven. Please don't cry. I'm happy now, and I'm no longer sick or bald. I'm a beautiful, perfect angel.

"I'll watch over you every day of your life. I will be there for you during your first heartbreak and I'll watch with joy on your wedding day. You deserve the best, Veneta. Never change and never forget our friendship. I'm so grateful God allowed me to know you. I will be waiting to see you again. Love, Emma."

Reading that letter changed my life. Although she was the one who was sick and losing her life, she had taken the time to make sure I would be okay. She wanted to make sure I could cope with losing her.

Her death was the hardest thing I've ever had to experience. But I believe that God put our lives and our hearts together for a reason. We needed each other. Emma needed a friend, and I needed her strength and courage. Even to this day I thank God for Emma. I also still talk to Emma every day. I know she hears me and I know she looks out for me. Our friendship will never fade or die away. People may come and go, lives may change in an instant, but love and friendship will last forever.

Veneta Leonard

Friends at First Sight

Remember, the greatest gift is not found in a store nor under a tree, but in the hearts of true friends.

Cindy Lew

Bam! The car door closed as I ran to the gate. There was Jesse, waiting for me. He was the only kid who was tall enough to reach the lever on the gate at our daycare sitter's, Mrs. Rogers. He greeted me with a smile and we ran inside. After my mom signed me in, she called me back over to give me a kiss good-bye. I kissed her as usual and said, "See ya later, alligator!" She replied as usual, "After a while, crocodile!"

Jesse and I always wanted to play outside. I was about four or five when Jesse and I discovered how to dig perfect tunnels; we even planned to sneak away down the tunnel to my house and then to China.

One day, while starting one of our digs, we lifted up this old rock and found two scorpions. It was very frightening, so we ran straight inside screaming, "It's Scorpion Invaders! They just arrived!" All the other kids followed us in, and until the "invaders" were gone, we played inside.

Just before lunchtime, Jesse jumped up and down on Mrs. Rogers' couch—something that we were forbidden to do. He got in so much trouble! During his time out, I sat by him. I wasn't supposed to but I did anyway. Then, at lunchtime, as usual, I pulled the sticker off my apple and gave it to Jesse. It was a tradition to give the sticker to your friend, so I always gave mine to Jesse and he always gave his to me.

After lunch, we finally got to go outside, since Mrs. Rogers' husband killed the two scorpions. Jesse got on the swing and I pushed him back and forth until it was time for our naps.

After what seemed to be the longest naps ever, Jesse and I stayed inside and played a game that we had just made up. It was called Kitty Transporters. We were small enough to fit under an old chest-of-drawers where we pretended like we were in a time travel shuttle that was transporting us to our newest location. We were kitties following our instincts as to which way to go and when to get ready to fight. We played and played all through snack time and when everyone else left, Jesse and I went outside and played our game in the sandbox until my mom arrived to pick me up.

That was a typical day for us at Mrs. Rogers'. Somehow, Jesse and I always got along. We never got bored, because we used our imagination and we just loved playing together.

Flash forward: Jesse's in the seventh grade at the same school where I'm now in sixth grade. We usually don't get to see each other except in passing period or at lunch. I think I embarrass him a little by always saying hi and bye, but he never shows it.

As you can see, Jesse and I have always been friends. We went to the same baby-sitter every day since, well, forever. We know each other so well that I could tell you just about anything about him. For one thing, he's smart. He can build a whole computer in one day, so whenever I'm stuck on the computer I always call him for help and advice. Jesse loves jokes and he always has a joke that will cheer me up whenever I'm down. He's truly the most kind and generous friend anyone could ask for.

I thought it was really, really nice of him to show up at my twelfth birthday party this year. Except for Jesse, it was all girls, but he didn't seem to mind. Ever since I was three or four, I've always invited him and he's never missed one single birthday party of mine. He has always gotten me a Barbie *every* year. I love Barbies. I collect them still today, so he got me one this year. His face turned bright red when I opened his gift and said, "I got a Barbie!" After the party, I said, "Thank you. I can't believe you came!" He replied, "Hey, that's what friends are for." Then he grinned, gave me a hug and said, "Happy birthday!"

I know that some friends just come and go—but not Jesse. Even though he's a guy and I'm a girl and we're definitely growing up, we are friends to the core. Our friendship was meant to be from the first time we met.

Because of Jesse, I truly believe in friends at first sight!

Stephanie Caffall, twelve

Tears in the Bathroom Stall

The only real mistake is the one from which we learn nothing.

John Powell

As a sixth-grader, I began noticing how other kids were separating into cliques. There were the geeks, the jocks and the popular cool kids. I wasn't sure where I belonged. And I think that was the problem.

Our teacher had assigned "secret buddies" for the coming week. The purpose of this assignment was to do nice things for your buddy without letting them know who was doing it. We could leave encouraging notes on their desk or mysteriously leave a card in their backpack or book. Our teacher wrote each kid's name on a piece of paper and threw them into a bucket, then we each closed our eyes and drew the name of the classmate who we were to secretly befriend and support over the next five school days.

By the middle of the week, everyone, including me, had turned this assignment into a contest to see whose secret buddy could leave the best gift. Instead of encouraging notes, we left stationery sets on our buddy's desk. Instead of giving compliments, we were giving bubble gum, lollipops and even money. It seemed that everyone was getting cool presents from their buddy. Everyone except me, that is.

My buddy followed our teacher's directions without a fault. I received handmade cards, notes with nice thoughts and countless smiley-face pictures proclaiming that I was one of the nicest girls in the class. My buddy seemed to think highly of me from the notes that were left, but the lack of gifts made me wonder what was up with whoever had pulled my name.

On the last morning of our assignment, I walked into my classroom and noticed that there was a package on my desk. At last, my buddy had grasped the idea that everyone else had! I ripped open the tissue paper and just stared down at my desk. There sat a canister of perfumed powder. The girls sitting near me giggled and went off about the "old lady" gift I had received. And to make matters worse, the powder had already been opened. I felt my face turn red as I shoved it into my desk.

I tried to forget about the embarrassing gift, but when I was in the bathroom before recess, the same girls who had seen me open the powder started talking trash about my secret buddy for giving it to me. I quickly joined in. "How lame," I heard myself saying. "What could my buddy be thinking by giving me such a stupid gift? My grandmother wouldn't even want it."

The girls laughed at my remarks and filed out of the bathroom. I stayed to wash my hands and let the water run through my fingers as I thought about what I had just said. It wasn't normally like me to say mean things like that about someone.

As I turned off the water, I heard a creak. I turned around to see one of the bathroom stall doors open. A girl from my class took two steps out of the stall and looked up at me. There were tears streaming down her face. "I'm your secret buddy," she whispered to me. "I'm sorry about the gift." Then she ran out of the bathroom. Her sobs stayed with me long after the door had closed.

My secret buddy was a girl named Rochelle, a girl who came from a poor family. She and her siblings were targets at school for those who felt they were better just because their parents had money. Yet through all the teasing and harassment, Rochelle never had a bad word to say back to anyone. She just took the horrible treatment silently.

I was sick to my stomach as my cruel words ran through my mind. She had heard every single thing that had been said. And, once again, she silently took it in. How could I have been so mean?

It took me a few days, but I finally found the courage to face up to Rochelle and apologize. She told me that she had felt bad all week about not being able to leave any cool gifts for me. Her family could not afford it. So finally, her mother had given up the one thing that was a luxury to her so that Rochelle would have something to give. Her mother had assured her that the nice girl Rochelle had talked about would like the powder. Rochelle couldn't wait to get to school that morning and put it on my desk.

And I had ruined everything for her.

What could I say to Rochelle? How could she ever forgive me for making fun of her? Along with my apologies, I told her the truth. I admitted that I had only said those things to be cool, to try to fit in. I didn't know where I belonged, I explained.

Rochelle looked me in the eyes and said that she understood. She had been trying to fit in, too. "We aren't that different from each other, are we?" she smiled. Her simple words, spoken from her heart, found their way straight into mine.

Up until then, like everyone else, I had avoided the "Rochelles" of the world. But after that day, I gained respect and admiration for people like Rochelle—people who give from the heart.

Cheryl Kremer

The Cool Girls

I sat in my living room staring out of the bay window. I didn't want to wait outside for the school bus—no, that would seem too anxious. I had decided that I would wait until I could see it coming down the street, and then casually walk out the front door. After all, I was cool now. I was entering the fifth grade.

Much to my dismay, the sight of the bright yellow bus coming toward my house sent me into a knee-jerk reaction, and I found myself running into the driveway—running and tripping. My backpack went flying and I landed on my hands and knees. Luckily, there were no major scrapes and I was able to return to a standing position almost immediately. The only thing I felt was the intense rush of heat to my red cheeks.

As I climbed the bus steps, the driver asked if I was okay. "Uh . . . yeah," I quietly replied. "It's nothing." I quickly examined all the kids' faces for any type of reaction. Most seemed to be staring out the window. Maybe no one had seen my spill.

I slowly moved toward the back of the bus to find two girls staring at me. As I sat down in front of them, I heard one of them burst out into a full-blown laugh, while the other quietly chuckled. They were whispering—about me, I was sure. I crossed my hands on my lap and pretended not to care.

I felt them watching me, even though my back was to them. They were definitely older—maybe seventh-graders—I wasn't sure. I sat frozen in my seat, feeling like the dorkiest kid in the world, as tears formed in my eyes. This was not the impression I had been hoping to make, especially to the older kids. Then, much to my surprise, one of them tapped me on my shoulder and introduced herself.

"Hi, I'm Jessica!" she exclaimed. "Are you going into sixth?" In my mind, I quickly went from dork to super cool. Maybe they thought I was older. Wow! I shyly replied, "No, fifth," as I turned around and smiled. "Oh," the other girl giggled, "Fifth grade!"

I suddenly felt accepted. They knew how old I was, they had seen me fall—and yet they still wanted to talk to me. I had already made two friends and hadn't even arrived at school yet! I was already seeing in my mind how cool it would be, to be walking through the halls and saying hi to my new seventh-grade buddies.

As it turned out, I rarely saw them in school, but I was happy enough to just be bus pals. I sat in the same seat every day on the bus, just in front of them, and waited for them to talk to me. One day, they asked to see my lunch box. "Wow, it's really cool," they both commented as they took my pink-and-white-checkered box from my hands. I couldn't *believe* how much they liked me. They returned my lunch box and thanked me for letting them see it. "Oh, no problem," I giggled, filled with smiles both inside and out.

When I opened my box at lunch that afternoon, *my lunch was gone.* The empty box resembled my heart, as it sank to the pit of my stomach. I never even paused to think of another possibility. In one single moment, everything made such painful sense. They were never interested in me, they were not my friends, and this whole time I was some kind of joke to them. I felt like a fool—right back to the moment I tripped in my driveway. That was how they saw me; that's who I *really* was. Some little dorky fifth-grader thinking she was actually fitting in with the older kids.

I never cried. I never said a word. I didn't tell my teacher because I didn't want to get them in trouble. They already thought I was a dork. I didn't want to add "tattletale" to the list. I simply closed the box and sat in silence for the rest of the lunch period. I had no appetite anyway from the thought of having to face them on the bus that afternoon.

When I stepped onto the bus, I only saw Jessica sitting quietly alone in the back seat. I slipped into a seat in the front without making any eye contact with her. There was no sign of Jessica's partner in crime. I held my empty lunch box tightly against my legs and quickly got off the bus as it reached my house. When I got to my room, I finally burst into tears.

The next morning I vowed not to even look to the back seat, which of course I did anyway. It was only Jessica alone once again, not looking quite as cool and confident without her friend. As I sat once again in the front seat, I suddenly felt a presence behind me. "Hey," Jessica quietly muttered as she tapped me on the shoulder. I turned around and managed a slight smile. "Look," she proceeded, "I'm really sorry about the lunch thing." I wanted to just say it was okay, but I couldn't manage to speak. She went on to tell me that Cory had been getting in a lot of trouble lately and had gotten kicked out of school. Her parents were sending her to boarding school and she wouldn't be on the bus anymore. With that, Jessica handed me a brown paper bag filled with a freshly made lunch, as well as some cookies her mom had made. "I hope this makes up for it," she told me, and returned to her seat. So, Cory had been the troublemaker, because when she wasn't around, Jessica was really pretty nice.

Jessica and I sat in silence for the rest of the ride. When we arrived at school, I waited for her as she stepped off the bus. "Thanks for the lunch," I said. We smiled at each other, and then walked to our own classrooms.

Eventually, Jessica and I became real friends. Sometimes we hung out at each other's houses after school, and there was never a mention of Cory. We had a lot of fun together and the age difference seemed to disappear. I never even thought much about the lunch incident again. All I could think about was how Cory had gotten some free food but, in the process, lost two really nice people as friends.

Mel Caro

3

ON FAMILY

When monsters lurked beneath my bed,
And scary dreams ran through my head,
When thunder growled those sounds I dread,
There you were, my father.
When scuffed-up knees made me cry,
Soft hankies wiped my sad eyes dry,
Coaxing me each time I tried,
There you were, my mother.
Who held my hand when I was scared,
Ate candy that he should have shared,
The things I did because you dared!
There you were, my brother.
In times of trouble, times of need,
I feel such strength surrounding me,
Without whose love I can't succeed,
I love you all, my family.

Lisa-Dawn Bertolla

Hey, Remember When?

When I look back on my childhood I will always remember the bond and memories I have forged with my cousins. There are five of us, including my brother Jack, my cousins Marleigh, Weston and Michael, and myself that are particularly close. Every summer, since I was six or seven, I have spent time with them. Every summer, I bring home unforgettable memories that I know I will keep forever.

Each time I see my cousins, we play a game called, "Hey, remember when . . . ," and we remember all the crazy things we've done in the past.

"Hey, remember when Jack ordered room service at the Disneyland Hotel right when we were about to leave? Aunt Pam got so mad that Jack had to pay for it, and we didn't even get to eat the food!" Yeah, that was funny.

"Remember when Kyle lost at the game Spoons, and he had to sell plums on the street corner in a purple dress wearing a sign around his neck that said 'Plum Boy'? Yeah, and the police helicopter and a patrol car showed up because some lady reported a suspicious guy hanging around on the corner soliciting for money?"

"Remember when Jack spent the entire weekend in

Lake Tahoe trying to talk like Jim Carrey? No really, every-thing he said was straight out of a Jim Carrey movie."

"Remember when we were at The Good Guys, and Weston decided to test the video camera that showed up on the big screens in the store by putting the camera down his pants? That totally got the attention of every-one in the store!"

"Remember when. . . ?" And it goes on like this for hours.

One summer the five of us were with our Aunt Kathi and Nana (our grandmother) in Palm Springs. During the day it was 115 degrees outside and the pool heated up to more than 100 degrees. So when it got really hot, we went to the coolest place around: the air-conditioned mall.

One day at the mall we went into a shop that sold home furnishings. One section of the store had two huge racks of pillows. Michael decided it would be fun if we buried him under all those beautiful new pillows. So, of course, we did. In less than two minutes, all of the pillows were off of the shelves and on top of Michael and he was no longer visible. We were all laughing and enjoying our-selves when we spotted an older lady who worked at the store coming our way. Immediately, the four of us quickly walked away, laughing to ourselves as the saleswoman started placing the pillows back on the shelves. Suddenly, Michael, thinking it was us, jumped out from under the pillows yelling really loudly, "Raaaahhhh!"

The saleswoman jumped about three feet into the air and screamed so loudly that everyone in the store stopped and looked at her. Michael, realizing his mistake, started running. Before I knew it, he was behind us yelling, "Go, go, go!" We were off to the races. The five of us ran out into the mall as the lady and Aunt Kathi, who had realized that we were in some sort of trouble, started towards us. We ran several stores down and ducked into Millers Outpost and pretended to be shopping.

When Aunt Kathi caught us, we all had to go back into the store, pick the pillows off the ground and place them back on the shelves. Most importantly, we had to apologize to the lady, who was not very pleased with us, nor our aunt and Nana, who were supposed to be in charge of us. The "pillow incident," as we have come to call it, will always have its place in the "Hey, remember when?" game. I think we'll be playing that game when we're all old and sitting around in rocking chairs!

"Hey, remember when Michael had to go out in public in a one-piece woman's bathing suit? . . . or how about the time that . . .?"

Kyle Brown, sixteen

Gains and Losses

The mind can have tremendous control of the body; very few ailments can defeat focused energy and a determined spirit.

Katherine Lambert-Scronce

Most of us have experienced unforgettable moments in our lives. The moment that I will never forget happened in my family.

For the first fifteen years of my life, I was the only child in my family. I didn't have any siblings. Fortunately, I've always had my parents, who love and care about me a lot. They help solve any problem and they will do anything for me. What I'd never really thought about is that, some-day, one of them could no longer be there for me.

One day, I found out that my mother was pregnant, which was big news in my family. Everyone was excited and happy, especially me. I imagined that I would have a baby brother, and I thought about playing and having fun with him. He would have a cute face and look at me with his naive eyes, begging me to play with him. I was expect-ing that day to come soon. I kept asking my mother questions about what my brother was going to look like, what he would eat and when he was going to be born.

Finally one morning, my mother went into labor and she and my father went to the hospital, while I went to school. Of course, I thought everything would be fine. After all, women have babies every day. Thus, I was hoping to see my baby brother as soon as I got to the hospital.

After school, when I went to the hospital, my brother had already been born. But my mother was still inside the operating room, while my father waited anxiously outside. After waiting for a long time, the doctor came out and told us that after my mother had given birth to my brother, they had trouble stopping the bleeding. He told us not to worry; my mother would be fine. Then, he went back into the operating room. Seconds later, lots of doctors and nurses rushed inside. My father and I were growing more anxious by the minute. Waiting was very painful for us, because we had finally realized that anything could happen and all we could do was wait.

At 7 P.M., my mother came out of surgery. She lay on the bed with an oxygen mask and an IV. Her skin was ghastly pale, and her eyes were closed.

"Mom, Mom . . . ," I called to her, but she didn't react. The doctor told us that if my mother survived this night, she would be fine. Then the doctors sent my mother to the intensive-care unit.

Inside the room were many instruments for checking blood pressure, pulse rate and heart rate. Standing next to the bed, I tried to talk to my mother, whether she could hear me or not.

"You have to wake up, you have things that you have not done yet. . . . You have me, my father and your newborn son. You cannot just leave us . . . and you will be fine . . . trust me. . . ."

I was scared to death. At that moment, I felt that I would lose my mother forever—that she was never going to come back.

Many thoughts flashed through my mind. *What would life be like if the unthinkable happened—life without my mother?* I could only imagine that my life would be full of darkness, sadness and hopelessness. I would lose my closest relative, my dearest friend, and I would never again have the chance to enjoy the love of my mother. Remember, during these fifteen years, my mother was always around, watching over me, no matter what. I could not imagine how I was possibly going to survive without her.

Of course, I told myself that it would not happen, that she might leave me after thirty, forty, fifty or more years, but definitely not now, not yet. It was too early. I wasn't ready to let her go.

After I slowly came back to reality, I noticed that a flood of tears was running down my cheeks.

My mother survived that night. You can imagine my great relief when she woke up the next morning. I was so excited. I gave her a big hug as I cried tears of happiness.

My mother told me that she had actually heard the words that I had said to her when she was unconscious. Three times she had almost stopped breathing, but she told herself to stay alive, for us, her family.

Later, many nurses said my mother was incredibly lucky to survive because she had lost a lot of blood. Of course, I gave them the most glorious smile, which said it all.

Today, my brother is almost two years old. On the day of his birthday, I always remember this unforgettable event in my life. I remember that I'm a really lucky person, with great parents and a wonderful little brother.

Xiao Xi Zhang, seventeen

Forever Garrett

We shared so much laughter, shared so many tears.
We had a special friendship that grew stronger each year.
We were not siblings by birth but we knew from the start,
We were put together, to be siblings of the heart.

Megan Youpa, 13

I followed Garrett into the kitchen to find Mom. Garrett had been with our family for about a month, and even though I was only five and he was eight, we had been getting along pretty great. Like me, he had a lot of energy and liked to run and play ball. Up until Garrett came to live with us I had played with three boys who lived on our street that were around my age. They liked Garrett right away, and the five of us had been playing together every day. Now, Garrett and I had argued and he was mad at me.

"I want to go back! I don't want to be here anymore," Garrett announced to Mom.

Garrett's face was set with determination and his eyes were shiny with unshed tears. I looked at Garrett and my face crumpled. I started to cry.

"I hurt him, Mommy, I hurt him. I didn't mean to!" I liked Garrett, and I didn't want him to go back to the adoption agency where he had lived before he came to us.

"You two wait until your father comes home tonight," Mom said as she cleaned both of our faces. Then she made me blow my nose as she said, "He'll have something to say about this."

When my dad got home that night, he sat us down and said that when he and my mom married they had a dream. They wanted to have a big family with both biological children and adopted children. He and Mom had been involved in the civil rights movement and wanted to adopt kids of mixed racial background because they knew how hard it was for these kids to get adopted. He told me that we were lucky to have Martin, my little brother who was a baby, and Garrett come to us.

Then Dad explained to Garrett that sometimes in families there are arguments and disagreements, but that didn't mean that we didn't care about each other. I knew all about that—I had had plenty of disagreements with my sisters and we always got over it. Dad said that Garrett belonged with us now and that was the way it was going to be; we were a family and families stick together forever.

I don't know who felt better after Dad's lecture, Garrett or me, but I do know that I really can't remember having another bad argument with Garrett after that day.

When I was in the third grade, our family moved from Wichita Falls to San Antonio. When I was younger, we had moved a lot because of my dad's job in the Air Force. In fact, my first words were in Italian because we lived in Italy when I learned to talk. But this was the first time that we had moved since Garrett and Martin had become a part of the family.

I didn't like moving. I was pretty shy anyway, and trying to make new friends wasn't the easiest thing for me. There was one exception: when I got on the playing field, whatever it was—soccer, football or volleyball—I felt like I was at my best and I was myself, 100 percent. On the playing field I could make friends. Garrett and I had that in common. We both loved sports.

I used to watch him play soccer and baseball and be amazed at how well he could play and how fast he could run. Not only was he fast, but he was also so competitive that what he lacked because of his size he made up for with his speed and aggressive actions.

Garrett would take me to play ball with the other kids, and when he got to pick his team, he always picked me first. I was his secret weapon. He liked to see the surprised looks on the faces of the boys on the team when I ran circles around them. Even though I was younger than most of the kids and I was a girl, I was a better player. With both Garrett and me on the same team, we couldn't lose.

Pretty soon, our whole family felt settled in our new home and started to love living in San Antonio. We lived right on the base and had tons of freedom to come and go without my mom or dad having to worry about us.

When we were finally all perfectly happy in San Antonio, we moved again. I was in the sixth grade, and for me it was the hardest move I had ever experienced. I had to leave behind the friends I had made and start all over again. Although our move was back to Wichita Falls, I didn't remember very much about living there before and missed my life in San Antonio. I told myself that the moving didn't matter, because my true home was the playing field. I threw myself into every sport that was offered, and I started to feel better.

We had been back in Wichita Falls for about two and a half years, and I was in the eighth grade, when we found out something terrible about Garrett. It was the beginning of his fight for life.

Garrett had chosen to attend a small Catholic high

school instead of the larger public school, and he went out for football. During one of the first games, Garrett was tackled and had a hard time getting back up again. One of the dads attending the game was a doctor, and he went over to take a look at Garrett to see if he could help. He noticed that my brother had several large bruises on his back. He knew these bruises were not normal, and the doctor told my parents that Garrett shouldn't play again until he was checked out.

When my parents took Garrett to the doctors they did several tests on him to find out what the problem was. He was eventually diagnosed with aplastic anemia, a disease that happens when a person's bone marrow is either destroyed or not able to function correctly. People with aplastic anemia can bleed to death from internal hemorrhaging. The doctors told my mom and dad that all they could do for Garrett was to put him on steroids, and that might help. Then, they told Garrett that he couldn't play contact sports anymore at all.

I was shocked. My brother, Garrett, not play sports? That was impossible. But it was true. For months, all he could do was watch. I felt horrible for him and couldn't even imagine how I would feel if the doctors had told me the same thing. I think I even felt a little guilty that I could still do everything that we had once done together, and he couldn't.

Then, to the amazement of us all, Garrett went into remission. He was back to his old self, and the doctors gave him the go-ahead to play ball again. Garrett went out for baseball and I was so glad to see him on the field again. We all were. Life became normal again.

Garrett was fine for several years until he had a relapse when I was eighteen. During the next six years he moved to California to live with our grandmother and to go to college. While on a trip home to Texas to visit our mom, he met the woman who was to become his wife. They had a son, Dillon. Garrett also spent those years fighting for his life. He had to have several series of very painful treatments, but he never gave up. During that time, whenever I would think that I had it rough during training, I would remember what Garrett was going through. I thought if Garrett could go through what he was experiencing, I could tough it out, too. His determination gave me the strength to excel during my games. Garrett was able to come to Atlanta in 1996 and see me play in the Olympics where we won the Gold Medal.

In February 1997, the doctors attempted a bone marrow transplant on Garrett. The transplant itself was successful, but Garrett had many complications. In April 1997, my brother Garrett died at the age of twenty-eight.

In honor of my brother, Garrett, I started a foundation. Once a year, the foundation stages the Garrett Game, an all-star soccer game that raises money for bone marrow research. In 1999, during the half-time celebration, we brought together bone marrow recipients with their donors. It was the first time any of them had met each other and everyone was crying and laughing. It was one of the most rewarding experiences of my whole life and one of my best memories.

Although Garrett didn't live to see us play the World Cup in 1999, I felt his spirit with me every step of the way. I know that he is with me during all of my games, encouraging me to do my best. In my heart, my brother will always live on. In my mind, I can still see him playing— running hard, with that look of determination on his face. With him as my example, I have been inspired to never give up, to always play to win, to work hard with my teammates and to have my heart in the game. Garrett was one of the best athletes that I have ever known, but he was much more. He was my hero, my friend, my inspiration and my brother . . . forever.

Mia Hamm

Supper David

David is the baby. Ginny is the oldest, then Johnny, and then me. Sometimes, we have to help watch David. He plays quietly for Ginny and Johnny but not for me, even when I try to get him to watch cartoons. He will sit still for a little while, but then he'll drag out a book and ask me to read it to him.

David always smells like mustard. His favorite sandwich is mustard on plain hard bread. The smell makes it hard for me to concentrate on reading a book to him. And David sucks his thumb. His thumb is in his mouth for so long that it stays wrinkled, shriveled and wet all the time. It sticks to the paper when he tries to help me turn the pages of a book. When I can't read the words, I make up stories to match the pictures. David doesn't know because he is too little to read.

David loves costumes—he will wear anything. Ginny and Johnny dressed him up in Ginny's fancy green flower-girl dress. They put a yellow dust mop on his head to make him look like a princess. David became "Davaleena" as he twirled around the kitchen and sang in a squeaky voice.

My mother made a costume for David out of a pair of

blue long underwear, a blue undershirt, a red dishtowel and red underpants. With his arms straight out in front and the dishtowel flapping behind, David becomes Superman. I made a sign for his chest that reads "Supper David." Johnny told me that I spelled "super" wrong, but I don't care. David can't spell either.

David never keeps his clothes on. He runs around the house naked. My mother says that David is going through a stage and that children have to learn how to take their clothes off before they can learn how to put their clothes back on. I don't remember that I learned to get dressed that way.

David likes to show off. In the middle of one of my parents' dinner parties, David took off his clothes and ran out the back door. When we caught up with his naked little self, David was busy jumping up and down on top of the car, waving good-bye to the company. My father laughed so hard that he snorted and tears streamed down his face. When the grown-ups were done laughing they went inside. I stayed outside to watch David.

My mom yelled, "Grandma's on the phone!"

"Vroom, vrroom!" said David.

"Mo-om! David is jumping up and down on the front seat of the car!"

"Barbara, please! Not now! Yes, Grandma, the children eat their vegetables."

"Honk, honk," said David.

"Mom, David is pretending to honk the horn in the car."

"Barbara, I've told you that I'm talking to Grandma. I can't talk to you right now. Yes, Grandma, the children are always in bed by eight."

"Wrr, wrr," said David.

"Mom, David is turning the steering wheel in the car!"

"Barbara! Yes, Grandma, the children are always polite."

"Ert, ert," said David.

"Mom, David is moving the handles next to the steering wheel!"

"BARBARA! Yes, Grandma, the children are healthy. Thank you."

Then I noticed that our car was moving. David was backing the car down the hill of our driveway!

"MO-OM, DAVID IS DRIVING THE CAR!"

I have never seen my mother run so quickly. She leaned into the car as it was moving down the hill—picking up speed as it went—pulled David out through the car window, smacked his bottom, and then hugged him tightly. The car hit a tree and stopped half way down the hill. They both started to cry. So did I.

My mother turned toward me, and gave me a hug, too. We all stood like that for awhile, and I thought how much I really loved David even though he is a pain sometimes, and how I would have missed him if anything had happened to him. I made up my mind that Mom was a hero.

I decided to go to my room and pull out my construction paper and crayons. Then I made another sign. It said, "Supper Mom." Somehow, I didn't think my mother would care if I didn't spell it right.

Barbara Lage

I Flushed It

It was a hot day in Florida. The school year had just ended and it was time for summer vacation. We had just gotten a little black dog who we named One-Eyed. We chose that name because he could only see out of one eye.

Everybody wanted to do something for the dog: feed him, teach him tricks and take long walks with him. Everybody was so happy to have this active, playful, shaggy, sable-coated new addition to our family. Everybody, that is, except my mom and me.

All my mom saw when she looked at the dog was someone else to clean up after. Shedding, messy, muddy, he pounced all over the house. All Mom seemed to care about was getting the house cleaned. My mom began to put Clorox in the tub. There was no messing with Mom when she started cleaning, so I decided to move out of the way. Actually, getting out of the way is a move I'd been practicing for a long time.

Being the youngest in my family has had its advantages, of course. I won't deny that. More than a few times I was spoiled or everyone was convinced that I was the cutest. It wasn't all bad to get this attention.

But being the youngest also came with its fair share of

troubles. I was often told what I couldn't do and why. I realize that I practiced getting out of the way because most of the time I was being *pushed* out of the way. "You're too young!" "You're too little!" "You'll mess this up!" they'd often say.

I also knew that my family loved me. They always tried to protect me, help me and take care of me, but I couldn't wait to show them I could do things by myself.

Every time I asked my brother or my sister if I could pet One-Eyed, they would shout, "No!" or tell me that I had germs. Once, they even convinced me that I had so many germs, if I touched One-Eyed he would die! I really believed them and was scared that something terrible would happen to the dog. Once I even confessed to my mom that I touched the dog when no one noticed. At first, my mom seemed very confused about what I was telling her, but then she realized that they were playing a joke on me to keep me away from the dog. My mom scolded my brother and sister, "You better stop teasing your little brother!" Little brother! That's exactly what I was. That really got my blood boiling. I was so mad, I wanted to break something!

I wasn't going to let them make me move out of their way this time! I took one look at the dog and decided, "I'll show them what a little kid can do!" I took the dog into the bathroom. "I'm going to give you a bath!" I said. One-Eyed looked at me strangely; he obviously didn't understand what I was saying. I looked at the sink. *Too small*, I thought. I looked at the tub. "It stinks like Clorox." Then I saw it. The perfect place for a dog bath—the toilet!

I took my sister's shampoo and poured it into the toilet. Then I put the dog in. I was scrubbing all the dirt off the dog with our towels. The finishing touch was to pull down the lever, which I did. But the sound of the toilet made the dog panic like crazy! He tried to escape, but the shampoo was too slippery. While the water was going down, One-Eyed's legs were going down with it. I was scared, and I didn't want One-Eyed to get hurt. I didn't want to get into trouble or for anyone to find out. I went running down to the garage.

My mom was standing there and laughing, as if she was expecting me. I didn't know what to say. I tried to catch my breath. Then I told her what just happened. I thought she would punish me. I didn't expect my mom would be . . . laughing!

As it turns out, I later discovered that my mom knew what was happening all along. She always seemed to be a pretty good spy, I guess.

Oh, and if you're wondering, One-Eyed was fine: but he did stay away from me for a while. Even though we never actually had a conversation about my being the youngest, I think Mom understood what I was trying to do. I was trying to make my own place in our family . . . trying, maybe sometimes in a weird way, to declare my independence. Flushing the dog down the toilet might not sound like a Declaration of Independence, but for a six-year-old, well, it was my best shot!

Pier Novelli, twelve

This Old Chair

The meaning of things lies not in the things themselves, but in our attitude towards them.

Antoine de Saint-Exupery

"Mom! I'm home!" John slammed the door and dropped his books on a nearby chair. "Something smells good." With his nose in the air, he followed the sweet aroma into the kitchen.

"Hi, John, home already?" His mom turned around. She had just placed a sheet of fresh-baked cookies on the counter near the open window.

John reached for a cookie and looked outside. Shafts of sunlight slanted through the clouds, tempting the flowers to bloom. And a robin sang a bubbly song. It was the kind of day that made John feel warm inside. Pop-Pop, John's grandpa, who lived with them since Grandma had died, came shuffling through the door. With his face to the floor as if looking for something he mumbled, "When the robin sings . . ." He paused trying to remember what he had started to say.

"Spring is here," John's mom finished the sentence.

"And you know what that means."

"Sure," John volunteered. "Our annual fishing trip is coming up."

Amused, Pop-Pop winked at John while heading straight for the cookies.

"I was thinking more of our annual spring cleaning," John's mom suggested. "Tomorrow, John, you have no school and I can use some help, okay?"

"Okay, okay," John agreed reluctantly.

The next day John and his mom cleaned the house. They cleaned upstairs, downstairs, inside, outside, until everything was spotless. Exhausted, they sank into the couch. Wearily pointing to Pop-Pop's chair, John's mom exclaimed, "Oh my! That old chair has got to go. We'll buy Pop-Pop a new one."

It was true, John had to agree. The chair was unsightly. It was faded and worn and in some places even torn.

"John, come and help me." John's mom sprang to her feet. "We'll take the chair to the curb. Tomorrow the garbage truck is picking up on our block."

As they attempted to move the chair, Pop-Pop worked his way through the door. Seeing what was happening, he quickly blocked their way. "Oh, no!" he protested. "You can't take my chair."

"It's old. . . . It's worn. . . ." John's mom argued, a slight edge to her voice.

"No," Pop-Pop persisted, trying to push his chair back into place.

"But Pop, we'll buy you a new one," John's mom tried to persuade the old man.

"I don't want a new one," Pop-Pop's voice trembled.

"I give up." John's mom let go of the chair. "We'll discuss it tonight when Matt gets home." Matt, John's dad, was still at work. With a sigh of relief, the old man sank into his chair and closed his eyes.

"Pop-Pop, why won't you let us get rid of the chair?" John asked when his mother left the room. "It's so old."

"You don't understand, John." Pop-Pop shook his head from side to side and after a long pause he said, "I sat in this chair, with your grandma right here, when I asked her to marry me. It was so long ago, but when I sit in this chair and close my eyes I feel she is near." The old man tenderly stroked the arm of the chair.

It's amazing, John thought, *how Pop-Pop can remember things from the past. In the present, he forgets almost everything.* John sat down on the floor by Pop-Pop's feet and listened as the old man went on.

"And the night your father was born, I sat in this chair. I was nervous. I was scared when they placed the tiny babe into my arms, yet I was never happier." A smile now flashed across his old face.

"I think I'm beginning to understand," John said thoughtfully.

"Many years later," Pop-Pop's voice broke and he paused a moment before he continued, "I sat in this chair when the doctor called and told me that your grandma was ill. I was lost without her but the chair gave me comfort and warmth." The old man's sadness seemed to grow as he recalled that fateful day.

"I'm sorry, Pop-Pop." John looked at his grandfather and said, "I do see now. This is not just any old chair. This chair is more like a friend."

"Yes, we've gone through a lot together." Pop-Pop fumbled for his handkerchief, and trumpeted into it.

That night, however, when John and Pop-Pop were asleep, John's mom and dad carried the chair out to the curb. It was a starless night. Spring had retreated and snow fell silently from the black sky and covered Pop-Pop's chair with a blanket of white.

The next morning, when John came downstairs,

Pop-Pop stood by the window and looked outside. A tear rolled down his hollow cheek. John followed the old man's gaze and froze. Snow-covered, the chair stood at the curb out on the street. The clamor of the garbage truck pulling up to the house shocked John into action. He ran outside. "Wait! Don't take that chair," he shouted, flailing both arms in the air as he rushed to stop the men from hauling the chair away. Then he ran back inside and faced his mom. "Look at Pop-Pop, Mom. You can't throw out his chair." John swallowed hard before going on. "This is not just a chair. This chair has been with Pop-Pop for a very long time. This chair is like a friend."

John's mom turned and looked at the old man. Slowly she walked towards him. With her middle and ring finger, she wiped away a tear. And then she took the old man's face into both her hands and said, "I'm sorry, Pop-Pop. I guess . . . I just didn't realize how much the chair meant to you. John and I will bring your chair back inside."

They brushed off the snow with their hands and heaved the chair back inside. They placed it next to the fireplace so it could dry. John's mom stepped back then, and as if seeing the chair for the very first time she mused, "Mm, I guess it does give the room a certain touch of character."

And John and Pop-Pop wholeheartedly agreed that the living room had been rather dull without this old chair.

Christa Holder Ocker

Cookin' in Brooke's Kitchen

Let us not be content to wait and see what will happen, but give us the determination to make the right things happen.

Peter Marshall

When I was six years old my five-year-old cousin, Juliana, got sick. My brother and I were in the family room watching television when my mom came in to tell us the bad news. I wasn't really sure what "cancer" meant, but I could tell it wasn't a good thing. My parents' faces were full of worry and tears, and that was enough to make me cry, too.

I asked, "Mom, what's the matter with Juliana? What *is* cancer?" My mom told us that Juliana had been diagnosed with ALL leukemia, a cancer of the blood and bone. My brother and I were so frightened, we really didn't even know what to think.

When we went to see Juliana in the hospital, she was lying in bed, and she had all these tubes and things hooked to her. It was confusing and scary.

As her treatments continued, Juliana seemed to be getting sicker and sicker. Every time I visited her, she looked different. The medication she took caused her to gain a lot of weight, and she lost all of her long, beautiful hair. I couldn't understand what the doctors were doing to her—it seemed like they were making her feel worse—not better.

Seeing my cousin in so much pain made me feel like my own heart was aching. Something needed to be done. I knew I wanted to help her get better faster, but at six years old, I wasn't sure how I could make a difference—I just knew I had to do something to help my cousin.

One night after we visited Juliana, all the way home I couldn't stop thinking about her. A hospital can be a very scary, cold place. I imagined how alone Juliana must have felt lying there during the night.

When we got home, I sat down at our kitchen table. I always liked writing stories and drawing pictures, and I started working at it like I had done so many other nights. But this night was different—I was thinking about Juliana. I thought, *What if I can sell my drawings? Then I can give the money to Juliana's doctors to help her get well faster and out of that hospital.*

When I told my parents, they thought it was a wonderful idea—but then we came up with an even better one. We would make a cookbook. I really liked cooking and baking plus writing and drawing—a cookbook had all these things combined.

The very next day, I asked all of our family and friends to send me their favorite recipes. To my surprise, everyone jumped at the chance to help. Mom helped to put everything together. Grandma typed recipes while I drew pictures that went into different sections of the cookbook. My idea for a small cookbook quickly grew to over one hundred pages.

The local skating club paid for the first printing. We sold almost 300 books in our first week. I couldn't believe the response. I felt really good! I have never felt anything like it before.

Now the cookbook, which is called, *Cookin' in Brooke's Kitchen,* is in its fourth printing and, because of many requests, I am starting on a second cookbook. My wish to help my cousin has ended up helping lots of people. The money from the cookbook has all been donated to the Leukemia Research Fund of Canada. In fact, enough money has been raised to fund two research fellowships. I have been lucky enough to meet many leukemia survivors, and lots of them have shared their stories with me. Hearing their stories made me feel important and like I really have been able to make a difference.

Juliana recently turned eight and she is doing great! I often think back to the times we sat in the hospital making miles of paper chains to pass the time. We must have decorated most of her hospital wing! The coolest thing is that she says I am her best friend and favorite cousin.

Now that my cousin Juliana is healed, I am too. The heartache I felt was a part of the love I have for my family. I'm glad that not only was I able to help heal the pain within my own family, but also to help with what happens to other families, too. I guess life is all about mixing up the right ingredients—it takes equal parts of love and action to make the world a better place.

Brooke Harrison, nine
As told by Eryc Stevens

[EDITORS' NOTE: *To find out more about leukemia log on to* www.leukemia.ca *or* www.leukemia.org.]

Paybacks

Revenge is often like biting a dog because the dog bit you.

Austin O'Malley

I learned the danger of revenge and letting a "payback" escalate out of control the day I woke up with a long, curled black mustache on my upper lip. My sister had ever-so-carefully drawn it with a permanent marker as I slept!

It all began when I was eleven, the summer before I started seventh grade. My family had moved across state and since my boyfriend, David, and all of my childhood friends were in another town, I was miserable and dreading the start of a new school year. My sister, Rose, who is two years older, was bored and angry. And so, that summer we shared a room and a lot of pent-up frustration toward our parents and our situation. I guess feeling so powerless about an unwanted move made us feel a need to reclaim our power—any way that we could.

Our emotions led us to play crazy "practical jokes" on each other, which then spiraled into getting even, or paybacks, as we called it. It was my sister who really started it all.

I had met our neighbors, Randy and Britt, who were close to my age and a lot of fun. One night, when it was time to go in due to our curfew, I stayed out talking to my friends after Rose went in the house. When I finally went in, I quietly crept upstairs without turning on any lights. My sister had anticipated my every move and had piled chairs in the entry to our room. Of course, I came crashing into them and had to bite my lip to keep from yelling when I smacked my knees!

My surprise and anger turned into a plan to do a payback the next night. So at bedtime, I turned off the lights when my sister went to brush her teeth and took out a hidden bottle of airplane glue, which I poured onto the middle of her pillow. I had a vision of her waking up with the pillow all stuck to her head. But my plan was destroyed when she came in and smelled the glue.

"What is on my pillow?" she asked with wide eyes as she turned on the light.

"I don't know," I said innocently. Then I started to laugh so hard that I couldn't breathe.

"Mel Ann, you are so stupid!" she said with controlled anger in her voice. "So now if you don't want me to tell Mom and Dad that you ruined my pillowcase, you'll go make me a sandwich."

"Fine," I answered with resignation. I didn't feel like getting grounded, so I quietly went downstairs to the kitchen without waking my parents. But once I got there, more thoughts of revenge got the better of me, and I mischievously added hot sauce to Rose's sandwich. Rose got a hot mouthful in the first bite, so she yelled, "That's *it!* Now I'm telling on you!"

"No, no!" I begged her.

"Okay, then you eat it!" she demanded. So, I took a bite

and instantly my mouth was on fire! I quickly and quietly
went through the upstairs hallway to the bathroom for a
glass of water.

When I returned, Rose said, "Okay, if you eat one more
bite, we're even."

"All right, give it here," I said with a growing frustration
about the mess I had created.

But this time when I took a bite, I gagged! I ran out of
the room and back to the bathroom. Rose had put cold
cream in the sandwich! That was it. I hit her really hard
with a pillow and started chasing her around the room
trying to whack her again. Finally, our yelling woke up
our parents, who were not pleased about being awakened
from a sound sleep late at night by ridiculous stunts—
especially the night before the first day of school. We tried
to explain, but in the end, my mom just sternly said, "I
don't think this is funny. Now go to bed! And . . . you're
both *grounded!*"

As she walked out of the room, Rose mumbled, "This is
your fault! You got us grounded!"

"My fault? You started it with those stupid chairs!" I
replied with anger.

Finally I went to bed and knew I'd think of an even
better payback the next day. But little did I know what
startling surprise the next morning would bring me.
When I woke up, I went to the bathroom. As I walked by
the mirror, I suddenly stopped to stare at my reflection.
My sister had taken a black marker and drawn a long
mustache on me that curled up onto my cheeks.

"Mom!" I yelled and ran to show my mother.

But my tired and grumpy mother was in no mood for
more pranks. So, she simply grounded my sister (again)
and told me to "go to school." I was horrified! I scrubbed
my face until only a little marker still showed, but then
the hard rubbing made raised, red welts in place of the

marker! I showed up at school looking totally ridiculous and realizing that paybacks never end; they only escalate into bigger messes.

Even if you think you've pulled off the greatest joke on someone, like your sister being glued to her pillow, you've only invited trouble to find you next—like a big, black mustache.

Mel Ann Coley

A Life's Moment

*Consider, when you are enraged at anyone,
what you would probably think if he should die
during the dispute.*

William Shenstone

One cold morning, I was getting ready for school. Our mom would be late if she didn't leave for work soon and she and my sister, Kameron, were fighting over something that had happened the night before. Mom left for work in a bad mood because of the fight they had, and my sister was really upset about what had just taken place. She came upstairs and told my brother, Shawn, and me to get our coats because it was time to leave.

Shawn and I hurried and got in Kam's car so we wouldn't be late for school. I asked my sister, "Are you okay? What happened between you and Mom this morning?" My sister looked at me with the glare that I often get from her when she is frustrated about something, and said, "I don't want to talk about it. We just have a disagreement over something and it's just confusing to me right now."

I looked at Shawn and he looked at me, and I could tell from the look that Shawn gave me that he was trying to tell me, "Don't ask about it—just keep quiet." Kam backed out of the driveway and we headed up the street. We were going pretty slowly, and Kam was watching out for other cars. Then she started to talk to me about what had happened with her and Mom.

"We had a fight, and it's nothing bad; but we both just really believe strongly in our own opinions. I really hate that, because we get into fights a lot because of it." As my sister was talking to me we had gotten to the end of our street.

Then, all of a sudden, a car that was coming from the opposite direction, going 90 miles an hour, rammed into ours. Our car spun out of control and hit the opposite curb. Kam and I were screaming. After our car finally stopped, we all got out of the car to look at the damage. I kept asking myself, *Is this real? Did this just really happen?*

My sister was in tears because she had just been in a car accident a month before and had to have back surgery. She called 911, and then she called our mom. Everything was a mess. It turns out that the guy who hit us was only eighteen and he had been racing some of his friends. Kam's car was in really bad shape, and she was in a lot of pain.

My sister talked on the phone to our mom for a long time, crying and telling her that she was sorry, that we could have all been killed and she wouldn't have been able to say good-bye. Kam could have died in that accident and it would have been so sad because she and our mom had fought right before it happened.

I could have lost Kam that day, and now I tell my family every day that I love them all. It just goes to show you that you never know when you could be gone. You need to appreciate the time you have with your loved ones. Life isn't promised to anyone, and it could be here one minute and gone the next.

Jordan Mitchell, thirteen

The Great Fish Story

Great things are only possible with outrageous requests.

Thea Alexander

One summer afternoon, my grandpa and I were out in his boat fishing, when I ran out of line on my fishing pole. Grandpa felt sorry for me, so he handed me his best, luckiest fishing pole to use.

On my second cast, the pole slipped out of my hands and went flying into the lake. I tried to grab it before it sank into the dark water, but I was too late. I jumped into the water after it, but it went down, down, down.

I climbed back into the boat feeling totally defeated. Then Grandpa came up with a plan to try to snag the line with our other two poles, by casting them down to grab the sunken line with one of the hooks. We tried about five times, but we had no luck. I felt so bad. It was Grandpa's favorite pole, and now it was lost forever.

Grandpa, not willing to give up yet, said, "Okay, Max, this will be our last time." Just then, my grandma, who had died two months earlier, popped into my mind. I thought, *Maybe Grandma can help.* So I prayed, *Grandma, please help Grandpa and me find his fishing pole,* over and over while I watched Grandpa hook his special silver lure onto the line.

When he was done fixing the lure into place, he threw it into the lake and dragged it around on the bottom. I kept praying to Grandma as I watched the line circle around the lake. When Grandpa reeled the line in, he had caught the sunken line in the middle! He pulled and pulled on one end of the line and then, out of the depths of the lake came his favorite fishing pole! I couldn't believe it! As he pulled, he noticed a tug and a strain on the line. It took some strength to bring it in. Suddenly, we heard a splash and there, on the end of the line was a beautiful fourteen-inch bass!

Grandpa and I laughed our heads off, while I thanked Grandma over and over in my head. I decided to tell Grandpa how I had been praying to Grandma as he searched for the pole. "Yep," he said, "I bet she did do this for us. That would be *just* like her."

When we told people what had happened, they said that it was "*the* fish story of all fish stories."

Two weeks after that incredible fishing trip, my grandpa died. I lost my amazing and wonderful grandma and grandpa within three months. It was so hard for my family to give them up.

Now I often ask both of them to help me with lots of different things. And you know what? After that amazing moment out on the lake, I know that they haven't really left me, and they *definitely* hear me.

Max Alexander, ten

Just the Two of Us

How rare and wonderful is that flash of a moment when we realize we have discovered a friend.

William E. Rothschild

Sometime, in your lifetime, you may be lucky enough to come across a person who knows exactly how you feel and is always there for you. Someone who loves you for who you are and doesn't judge you. Someone who believes in you and urges you to listen to your heart, no matter what anyone else thinks. This person helps you through your hardest days and assures you that tomorrow is always another day, a fresh beginning.

I didn't have anyone like this, until a stranger moved into my house, and became my sister.

When I was seven years old, my mom died, and my life changed forever. My dad became a widower and our family was left without a mother. Then, about two years ago, when I was twelve, my father remarried. My stepmother, Shelly, moved from New York to our small house in Missouri. She also brought along her daughter, an energetic and lively eleven-year-old named Ariele. With her beautiful blue eyes and winning smile, Ariele was always the center of attention. I never thought that I could bring myself to love her as a sister, because we didn't know each other at all.

It's amazing how opposite we are. I am a perfectionist and a neat freak. I say what I think people want to hear, and I hide what I'm really feeling. Ariele is so full of life, she lights up the room. She's extremely funny and cheerful, celebrating every moment of life. She always manages to crack my frown, figure out my problems and decode my weird moods. I hate to admit it, but even though I am one year older, she knows more about what really matters than I could ever hope to. There was one experience where I really found out how important it is to take each day as a blessing, and how to make the best of it.

Only a year and a half after Ariele came to live with us, my father accepted a new job as head of a private school. The benefits were great, but the only problem was that we would be forced to move across the country to Boston. I was going to have to leave all the people that I had grown to love and care about. I felt helpless. My life was a roller-coaster ride of mixed emotions, and I was stuck aboard, unable to make decisions or get off. But the one person who really helped me through my pain was my stepsister, Ariele. She had the best attitude from the start. She had just left her life in New York and moved when our parents got married. And although she had grown to love her new home, she realized that Boston was good for the family.

A few months later, after selling our home and packing up, we drove with our parents from St. Louis to New Hampshire, where both of us would attend camp. We had to leave for the summer, knowing we wouldn't be back for a long time. But the ride across the country was one of the most memorable few days. We were on the road in a stuffed minivan, filled with luggage and food, but Ariele and I loved it.

Because the car ride was so long, our parents went out of their way to stop at places to show us some of the country. At Niagara Falls, after observing the magnificent display, we decided to get even closer to the edge and climb to the point where people get soaked by the freezing waters. As Ariele and I neared this breathtaking waterfall, and as I watched my sister laugh with joy and shriek from exhilaration, I saw everything in a new light. I hadn't been living each day fully with the excitement or joy that Ariele demonstrated to me.

With soaked jeans and high spirits, we climbed even higher, so that the foggy mist blinded us, and we huddled together to keep ourselves warm. Her shaking arms hugged me, and she told me that she loved me. Then she stood before the mighty waterfall, eyes closed, and arms spread out wide, to let the water soak her . . . giggling as dripping strands of hair tickled her face. She looked so beautiful. There was something so magical about that moment that it will always remain in my memory.

As I looked at her, I thought of how drastically my view changed when Ariele came into my life, and I remembered all the things she urged me to try. There were so many times she made me feel like a little kid, just having fun like the time in a park a few months ago. We went on a walk and passed by a large, sloppy puddle of mud created from the rain the day before. She started playing in it, covering her hands and legs with the mud, and urged me to do the same. I hesitated, because there were so many people around, but then I thought, *Who cares?* So, together, we slipped and slid in that mud and had the best time.

I thought of the many times we've been at the mall, and I've seen something I have really liked but didn't want to spend my money for it. Her mouth will turn up in a mischievous grin, and she will say, "You only live once!" Then I end up buying the shirt or CD that I wanted so badly. And during these moments, I can't help realizing how much I owe her for giving me another shot at life, another chance.

Before Ariele moved in, I was so scared of risking things and too shy to express myself as I wanted to. I was reluctant to step out of my preteen mind and enjoy those little pleasures. Even though she may not be aware of it, she has taught me that the person who risks nothing, will gain nothing. Pain and disappointment may be avoided, but one will simply never grow or learn. Without risks, one misses out on the incredible opportunities and experiences that make life worth living.

I owe everything to her. She is my better half and my best friend in the world.

So whenever we fight about our shared room, boys or simply how we've been acting toward each other, I remember all the times we've spent together and realize that no matter how hard and impossible it seems at times, we always find a way to work it out. And through all of our family ups and downs, we'll be in it and stay in it— together. Two sisters who bring out the very best in each other, every single day . . . and in every possible way.

Miriam Bard, fourteen

The Gift

One day a handsome black tomcat appeared at our back door. His coat had a white bib and four snowy paws, making him look like he was wearing a tuxedo. His tail was as crooked as a corkscrew.

My four-year-old brother Daniel and I had never had a pet. We both instantly fell in love with the gentle black and white cat. All that first afternoon, the three of us played together. When it got dark, we begged our parents to let our new friend come inside so we could feed him. Mom shook her head. "It might confuse him," she explained. "This cat looks too healthy to be a stray. He must have a home already."

But the next morning, the tuxedo cat was still there. He waited patiently by the front door like a butler at a mansion. "Yea!" said Daniel. "He wants to be our cat!"

It did seem like he was telling us something. He stuck around all day, playing with Daniel and me outside. When we went into the house, he jumped up on the barbecue and watched us through the window. The last thing I saw that night were his green eyes, staring in at me.

The next day, our parents warned us that we needed to try our best to find his owners. My mom helped me make a flyer that said "Found: black and white cat with crooked tail" with our phone number on it. I drew a picture of the cat on each one and we hung them around the neighborhood.

The second day, I named him Alley, as in "alley cat." The third day, our dad and mom let us put some food out for him. The fourth day, our parents broke down and we got to bring him inside.

Alley let me carry him like a baby, from room to room. Daniel built LEGO castles all around him. He followed us all around the house and at bedtime he jumped on each of our beds while we got tucked in, as if he was saying good night to us.

Alley was a dream pet.

Our family woke up from the dream about two weeks after we adopted him. That was the day a big, tattooed man appeared at our door holding one of our "Found Cat" flyers. Before anyone could say anything, Alley strolled over to the man and rubbed on his leg. It was obvious that they knew each other.

"My name's Mark Johnson," he announced, casually picking Alley up. "I see you've met my only roommate, Dewey. He kinda wanders when I'm out of town. Can I offer you good people a reward for watching him?"

"No," Dad said with a sigh. "It was a pleasure to have him as our guest." The rest of us were completely silent. At the door, Mr. Johnson turned back and faced us kids. That's when he must have seen the tears in my eyes. "Wow. I'm sorry," he said. "I didn't realize you kids had gotten so attached. Hey, I only live a few blocks away. If you two would ever like to visit old Dewey . . ."

"His name's not Dewey!" Daniel yelled at the top of his lungs. "It's Alley!" He ran sobbing to his room.

Mr. Johnson's eyes widened. The full meaning of his visit had sunk in at last. He slipped out awkwardly. Over his shoulder was slung Alley. Alley's unreadable green eyes looked back at me all the way down the walk.

For days, I found myself staring out of the window at the barbecue as if Alley might suddenly rematerialize there. Daniel went through spells of bursting into tears. Our parents tried to console us by keeping our family schedule full and entertaining. They even talked about going to the pound to pick out another pet.

Then one day, I heard Daniel yell, "He's back!" We all hurried into the family room. Sure enough, Alley was there by the door nuzzling Daniel, his crooked tail lashing Daniel's legs.

He had found his way home.

My heart was jumping with joy. Then Dad said, "Daniel. Sarah. He can't stay. He's not ours, remember?"

Daniel and I both looked at him like he was crazy. "But Dad . . ." Daniel began.

"Do we have to tell that Mr. Johnson guy?" I asked, looking into my dad's eyes.

Dad nodded his head. Even though I could tell it made him sad to do it, he looked up the name and left a message on Mr. Johnson's machine. "Your cat is here again," Dad said. "Would you please stop by and pick him up?"

I felt like this would be the last time we would ever see Alley. I figured Mr. Johnson would lock him up in his house. For the rest of the day we played with him; making cat fortresses out of cardboard boxes, dangling strings around corners, petting him and feeding him treats. Alley went along with it all, just like he expected that kind of treatment and wanted nothing less.

When Mr. Johnson arrived at 8:00, I had made a decision. I waited in the hall behind Daniel and our dad, holding Alley in my arms. As soon as Dad opened the door, I said to Mr. Johnson, "I think he wants to live with us."

"Sarah . . ." Dad began.

But Mr. Johnson nodded at me, letting me know it was all right. Then he squatted down, so that he would be at the same level as Daniel and me.

"You know, Sarah, I think you're right. He seems to have made a decision. I think he must like kids," he said with a wink. He set down a small cardboard box. "I didn't come to take him. I just came by to bring you these." Inside was a bowl and several cans of cat food.

"You're letting us have him?" I asked, stunned. "Like a gift?"

"Well, kind of," he said with a shrug. A tattoo-scrawled arm darted out as he petted Alley. "Bye, Dewey. I'll miss you. But I have a feeling you'll be in good hands."

And, just like that, Mr. Johnson was gone. None of us ever saw him again.

From then on, the tuxedo cat was ours. In no time at all, he became a respected member of our family. He was a fierce hunter, yet he remained extremely gentle with us. Whatever room the family was in, Alley was there. Whenever Daniel and I were ready for bed, Alley popped in to say goodnight.

Sometimes I wonder what made our cat decide to stop being Dewey and want to become Alley. We will never really know, but it gave us all an example of what giving is all about. Because the truth of the matter was that Mr. Johnson hadn't given his pet away.

Alley had given himself to us.

Sarah Strickland
As told by Craig Strickland

4

ON LOVE

True treasure is not found in pirate ships,
in chests of silver and gold.
True treasure isn't ruby rings
and jewels from long ago.
You don't need to use a treasure map
and find chests beneath the sea.
True treasure is simply the love
and joy found in you and me.

Leigha Dickens, eleven

Bobby Lee

Love and kindness are never wasted. They always make a difference. They bless the one who receives them, and they bless you, the giver.

Barbara De Angelis

I walked home with my little brother every day the same way, past an oil refinery. Mom always told us to walk together and never to talk to strangers. One day, that walk home changed forever. As my brother and I passed the oil refinery, I heard an old man's voice.

"Hey there, children."

I turned and saw a very old man standing there with a sweet smile on his face.

"Hi," I answered, still keeping my distance.

"Would you like a soda pop? I know you walk by here every day. I don't mean you any harm."

I was already hot from walking and carrying my heavy backpack, but I knew what my mother would do once my little brother ratted on me for talking to strangers.

"No thanks. I'm not allowed to talk to strangers," I replied.

"Oh, I understand. And your mama's right. My name's

Bobby. Now run along," he said as he disappeared behind the gate of the refinery.

What a strange man, I thought. But I also felt bad, thinking I may have insulted him by calling him a stranger.

I went home and reported to my mom what had happened. My mother told me that I was right not to talk to strangers, so I tried avoiding this stranger for the following few days, but it was impossible. Other streets were not as safe to walk on, and every time we passed the refinery, a familiar voice would say, "Hello there, children."

Then one day, my family was taking a walk around the neighborhood. We were just about to pass the refinery when I noticed the gate was ajar. I remember silently praying that Bobby would appear and prove once and for all that he was a "good" stranger. And there he was.

He smiled as he approached my mother, "Well, you must be Little Miss Pretty's mama! And you must be her daddy! It is so nice to meet you."

The genuine smile and surprise on my parents' faces were all I needed to see. They spoke for a few minutes and then, walking home, my parents said it would be safe for us to visit Bobby after school.

My brother and I would stop to visit Bobby after school every day after that. He would invite us into his tiny office to talk about my schoolwork, my friends and sports.

It wasn't long before I started getting a few friends to walk home with me just to meet Bobby. Before long, a group of about fourteen kids went daily to visit Bobby and receive our sodas and gum. Thinking back, I now realize that Bobby bought all those treats just for us . . . and there were a lot of us to treat!

We visited Bobby every day after school for about three years! My mother finally decided it was time to do something nice for Bobby. So, with some thought and a lot of effort, she arranged for a plaque-giving ceremony to be held at the refinery on Father's Day. All of the children who visited Bobby, and even some of their parents, were invited. And you know what? Most of them came.

On the plaque, my mother had engraved "To the Neighborhood Grandfather," and all of our names were engraved below that. I remember that Bobby cried when he received it. I don't think he'd ever been surrounded with so much adoration in his long life.

The following holiday, my mother gave Bobby an enlarged photograph of the "Neighborhood Grandfather ceremony" with all of us kids standing around him.

One cold afternoon in February, we stopped by as usual, only to be told that Bobby had died. I remember crying for days after hearing the news. He really had been like another grandfather to me.

My mother went with two other mothers to the funeral service. There, right on the coffin, were three items: the American flag folded into a triangle shape (as is customary for war veterans), the plaque we gave him and the photograph of that memorable Father's Day ceremony with all of us kids standing around him. Bobby had no children. I guess *we* were his children.

To this day I think about him—an old man with no responsibilities to family, taking in a group of "strange" little kids who ended up meaning so much to him. I know now there was a reason why I met Bobby and why a group of us went to see him every day. He was able to die knowing that somebody loved him.

Daphne M. Orenshein

Love Lives On

Whatever happens inside of you that makes you fall in love with horses happened to me. I devoured every horse book I could get my hands on, checking them out of our library again and again. *Man O' War*, the true story about the greatest thoroughbred racehorse of all time, was my favorite. I must have read that book ten times. I pictured myself owning the huge red horse, loving him with all my heart, but knowing I could never ride him because he was a champion racehorse, not a pet.

I asked my parents if I could take riding lessons and they agreed. I learned to ride well, made many friends at the stable, and my love of horses and the sport of riding grew.

After a year of lessons, I decided that what I wanted more than anything on Earth was a horse of my own. I asked my parents, and they agreed—*if* I earned half of the money to buy the horse. I worked all summer and saved one hundred dollars, a fortune in those days. At last, my dad said, "Find your horse, girl!"

Two hundred dollars wasn't much to buy a horse, and the one I had my eye on was going for five hundred dollars. "A deal is a deal," said my dad, so I could only watch as the beautiful black mare was sold to someone else. Disappointed, but still determined, I was introduced to a woman who told me that she had a horse she would sell me for two hundred dollars, but she doubted that I would want him, explaining that she had rescued him from an abusive owner and that he hadn't been ridden in years.

As we walked to the back of the stables, I was so excited that my heart was pounding. The woman explained that she thought I was a good horsewoman and that when she heard that I was looking for a horse—on a limited budget, no less—she had thought that perhaps it was time for this horse to come back to the world.

We walked up to the stall and she opened the door, cautioning me "not to expect too much." I was trembling with excitement as the sunlight spilled into the stall. There he was, an old giant of a thoroughbred, with gray sprinkled through his shiny, flame-colored coat. He turned and looked cautiously at us, and as I stepped into the stall he flattened his ears and bared his teeth. The woman explained that he had been beaten and had a mistrust of strangers, but that he wasn't mean, just afraid.

"What's his name?" I asked.

"We call him Rusty," she said.

"Rusty," I called gently, and his ears came up at the sound of his name. The woman handed me a carrot, and I held it out to him. He stepped forward slowly, but before he took the treat, he turned his head slightly and looked into my eyes. We held the gaze for just a moment, and then he took it from my hand.

When he was done munching his carrot, we led him out into the sunlight. What I saw was the most beautiful horse I had ever laid my eyes on. What most others saw was a twenty-year-old, swaybacked horse, sporting a potbelly.

"I'll take him!" I cried, startling him so that he jerked his head back and snorted all over me. I laughed and reached up to pet the long, white blaze that ran down the front of his nose, and he lowered his head and begged for more.

That summer we were inseparable, and I spent all my free time riding him. He grew strong and energetic for his age. I often saw the woman who had sold him to me, and she would tell me how good he looked.

That fall, we moved Rusty to a small stable near our home, so I could ride him as often as possible during the school year. I began getting involved in the world of competitive horse showing. Rusty thrived on all the attention and competition, and even though he usually was twice the age of the other horses, the judges loved him, and we took home many blue ribbons during the next two years.

But one morning, as I arrived at the stables to go riding, something was different. Instead of standing, ears pricked forward and bellowing a hello, Rusty was still laying down in his stall when I walked up. He rose when he saw me, nickering softly, and I figured maybe it was just his age getting to him. After all, he was twenty-two years old. We rode quietly that day, stopping for lunch to share the same sandwich and chips. How he loved potato chips! But he was not hungry, and when I told my dad about it, he decided to call the vet.

The vet came to see him, and what he said was a shock to us. He believed that Rusty had cancer, and he referred us to a specialist for further tests. My parents and I had talked about the situation, and we decided that due to his advanced age, if the specialist told us that he was suffering, that we would elect to have him humanely put to sleep. I understood this on one level; on my heart level I was crushed.

That morning we loaded Rusty into the trailer and I waved good-bye to him, pretty sure it was for the last time. My parents had thought it would be best if I didn't go with Rusty to the vet. I had spent the entire night before with him, crying and laughing, remembering all the things we'd done together and the lessons we'd learned. I'd thanked him for being there for me during a tough time in my life when I didn't think anybody cared, but I knew he did. Unconditional love, that's what he had given me.

Later that day, I was lying on my bed at home, all cried out, when my dad came in. He told me, "There is a guy out front who wants to see you." I was fifteen years old, and I figured it was just one of my school friends coming by to talk. I asked my dad to explain that I couldn't come out now, but he said, "Honey, you'll want to see this boy."

I rose up from my bed and looked out the window. There, backed up into our driveway, was the horse trailer, and inside was Rusty! I tore outside and jumped up next to him, hugging his neck and crying with happiness. He stood quietly and took in my love, and when I stepped back, he turned his head and looked into my eyes, as he had done years before, and winked.

Rusty stayed with me for another happy year before the cancer took him. By then, we were a little more prepared.

All these years later, I still miss him. But, even though he isn't here physically, I realize that love lives on, and that Rusty will live in my heart forever.

Laurie Hartman

Dusty, the Wonder Dog

When I was a kid, my godparents, Uncle Nell and Aunt Frances, brought me a four-month-old puppy. She was half German shepherd, half collie. As her pink tongue tickled my face with wet licks, it was love at first hug.

My family named the puppy Dusty. Although I wanted to lay sole claim to her affections, in a family of seven kids, no one lays permanent claim to the family pet.

Dusty was *our* dog, not *my* dog. We soon realized that she had the patience of Buddha. My baby sister often transformed Dusty's warm fur into a nap-time pillow— falling asleep on the rug. Like a protective mother, Dusty waited—without moving—until my sister woke.

Dusty doubled as a school crossing guard, too. Monday through Friday she'd walk us kids two blocks to St. Patrick's Parochial, looking both ways to check for traffic before allowing us to cross the street. We'd wave good-bye as we entered the door, knowing Dusty would be waiting at the school door to claim us at the close of the school day.

Of all the contributions Dusty made to our family, one incident stands out far and above all others.

Late one night, Dusty rushed to my parents' bedroom.

She barked and barked. When she got no response, Dusty raced upstairs to my bedroom and my brothers' bedroom and barked again and again. When she failed to fully wake us, she flew back down the steps and returned to my parents' room. Finally, she got Mom's attention.

"What are you doing, Dusty?" Mom snapped, still halfway in dreamland. Dusty persisted. Finally my mother gave in. "Okay, what is it?"

Dusty whined and rushed out of Mom's room. Thinking the dog needed to be let out to relieve herself, my mother followed Dusty to the front door.

When Mom opened the door to let her out, Dusty tore across the street, not stopping to do her business as my mother had assumed. Then she discovered what Dusty already knew. The house across the street—where my best friend, Marianne, and her family lived—was on fire. All of Dusty's middle-of-the-night craziness had served a purpose: she'd been trying to call for help.

My mother alerted the fire department immediately. Soon, the firemen in their trucks roared up the street, squelching the blaze and saving my best friend's family from harm and their house from total ruin.

My mother refused to take credit. "It was Dusty," she told the firefighters. "She saved them. Not me."

I put my arms around my dog's neck and kissed her square on the tip of her wet nose. "Thank you for saving Marianne," I whispered into Dusty's tan and black ear. "You're the bravest dog I've ever known."

Dusty wagged her tail and licked my face. That old familiar rush of puppy love overtook me. I smiled and promised to let her sleep in my bed for the rest of her life.

Mary Saracino

The Teacher Who Cared

A teacher affects eternity; no one can tell where his influence stops.

Henry Adams

Mrs. Barrow, room 501, room 501, I repeated to myself as I scanned the hallways looking for the room number. It was my first day of fifth grade and I was really scared.

I came to the end of the hall and found an open door. Stepping into the room, I suddenly felt out of place. I tried to act normal, but Mrs. Barrow saw right through me.

"Good morning, Courtni. You may pick your seat."

I glanced about the room and took an empty seat near a girl named Wendy Barber. As the year slowly progressed, Wendy and I became good friends. I felt no closeness to Mrs. Barrow, though. I saw her as "just another teacher."

Mrs. Barrow had us write a paper on what we wanted to be when we grew up. Some kids asked why. She explained that when her former students graduated, she liked them to come back and share their fifth-grade dreams together, as a memento of their childhood. I decided right then and there that I liked Mrs. Barrow.

Then, my grandmother, who lived with us, was diagnosed with pancreatic cancer. About a month later, Grandma slipped into a coma and died. Losing her was unbearable for me. I missed some school because I was so sad.

At the funeral, I was sitting there feeling sorry for myself when I looked up and saw Mrs. Barrow standing there. She sat down next to me and held my hand. She comforted me by reminding me that now Grandma had no more pain or suffering. It had never occurred to me that it was better for my grandma this way. All I thought about was how sad it was for me.

After the funeral, we went to my aunt's house to see the flowers that had been sent. My mom handed me a pretty ivy plant in a pink pot. The attached card read:

> Courtni,
>   I'm sorry about your grandmother. Never forget, I love you. You are like one of my children.
> With love,
> Mrs. Barrow

I wanted to cry. I took the plant home, watered it and put it in my grandma's old room. I am in eighth grade now and I *still* have that plant. I never thought a teacher could care that much about her students: now I know.

I say this with all my heart: Anyone who is lucky enough to have a teacher like Mrs. Barrow in their life, even for a short while, is privileged beyond words. She may not know it, but she means more to me than she'll *ever* know. I can only hope this gives her inspiration and repays to her a tiny portion of what she has done for me.

To Mrs. Barrow—I love you very much. You're much more than a teacher—you are like a mother to me.

Courtni Calhoun, thirteen

The Act of Love

I hate pulling weeds! I thought. *It's hot. It's sticky. And it's Saturday!*

Still, I made sure to pull every stinking weed out of that flower garden. My dad was Mr. Perfecto Lawnman. He could detect a single weed a mile away. And if he spotted so much as one little clover, I'd be back pulling weeds for the rest of the day.

"Dad, I'm done," I shouted from the garden, feeling sure that I had done a good job.

Dad stormed out of the house. "Don't be yelling outside, Kathy," he grumbled. "Use those two feet of yours and come get me."

Suddenly, a sick feeling came over me. It was the kind of feeling I had when my dad was going to find that one stinking little clover.

"Geez," Dad said, waving an irritated finger, "you missed a spot."

I sighed, went to the spot and pulled the weeds. Afterward, I looked back at Dad, still standing there with a scowl on his face.

"Okay," he said, turning away, "I guess you're done."

As Dad walked back to the house, I wondered if I'd ever

done anything good enough or right enough for him. Sometimes, I wondered if he even liked me.

Like the night I had taken out the trash without being told. That was a big deal for me. But Dad didn't see it that way. He was mad because I didn't put the trash can lid on tightly enough to keep our dog out.

Well, I'm sorry, I thought, *but I can't help it if Sugar's a trash picker.*

The other day, when I was in a rush to get to school, Dad stopped me at the door. In his hand was a topless tube of toothpaste, the same one that I'd used just moments before.

"Where's the cap to the toothpaste?" he asked, his eyebrows bunching in the middle. "And how many times do I have to tell you? Squeeze from the bottom!" *At least I brushed my teeth,* I thought.

Just then, a sloppy, wet tongue washed over my face, breaking me from my thoughts.

"Sugar!" I said, hugging her tightly. "Where did you come from?"

Sugar looked at me, her big sloppy tongue hanging to the side. I smiled.

"At least you like me." Then standing up, I brushed the dirt from my knees and headed for the house.

Two weeks later, on the morning of another weed picking weekend, I was sick. I was sweaty and feverish and I ached all over.

"Let's go," Dad said, lifting me from the bed. "You need to see a doctor."

"Please, no," I said, in a shallow, sickly voice, "I'd rather pull weeds."

He took me anyway, and the doctor said I had pneumonia. The only nice thing about it was that I didn't have to pull weeds. I didn't have to take out the trash. And since I had to stay in bed, I didn't have to brush my teeth.

If having pneumonia was ever good, it was good then. And as I rested, Sugar stayed with me, lying down beside my bed. She liked me.

That night a noise woke me from my sleep. I opened my eyes just a sliver, and I saw a tall, slender form. Enough moonlight shined through my window so that I could see it was my dad. But why was he there? I didn't say, "Hi, Dad," or anything like that, I don't know why. He came up to me and put his hand against my forehead. When he took his hand away, I saw him lay something on my nightstand. He looked at me again, then left.

When he was gone, I reached over to the nightstand and picked up a necklace. It wasn't like any I'd ever seen before. Dangling from a golden chain was a puppy in a basket, and the puppy looked just like Sugar. With shaking hands, I held that necklace to my heart and cried. My dad, who never gave hugs and never said, "I love you . . ." had just said it all.

Kathy Kemmer Pyron

Cry When You Are Sad

*Never apologize for showing feelings. Remember
that when you do, you apologize for the truth.*
Benjamin Disraeli

On a sunny Monday in April, I had two loving grandmothers near me, but when Tuesday came, only one was
left. One of my grandmothers who was dear to me, had
died. I had a feeling that this awful day was going to come
soon, but now that it was here, all I wanted to do was cry.
But I wasn't brave enough to shed a tear, for I was always
taught that boys should never cry.

Later, as the time came for the funeral activities, I had
the hardest time keeping my sadness inside.

My relatives soon arrived from all over the country. I
really had to hold back my tears now that my relatives
were here, because I did not want to look like a crybaby in
front of them. I figured out that my parents, my sister and
myself were the only ones that had lived in the same
town as my grandma. That explained why her death was
hitting me the hardest, while my cousins seemed as
though they were here just to get away from home. They

really hadn't known her like I had.

Soon, all of my relatives gathered at the funeral home, waiting for the viewing to begin. What I thought was going to be the easiest part of my grieving turned into the hardest.

The moment I walked into the room where my grandma was laying in a coffin, my heart dropped. This was going to be the last time that I would ever see her. At first I was afraid to proceed with the rest of my family up to her coffin, but then I realized that I would have to sooner or later. I grabbed hold of my mother's hand and kept my mind on remembering not to cry.

When I came up to the kneeler, in front of where she was laying, my mother made me do something that almost brought me to tears. She told me to touch Grandma's hand, for that was going to be the last time that I would get a chance to touch her. I reached over to her hand very slowly, afraid of what she might feel like. When my hand touched hers, I was relieved for a moment. She felt the same way she always had, except a little cooler than usual.

When I looked up at my mom, she began crying uncontrollably. I knew this was the time that I really had to be strong. I reached my arms around her and slowly walked with her back to our seats.

During the next few hours, I met many different people. All of them were telling me that they were sorry about my grandma passing away. I just smiled and reminded myself not to cry, because I had so often been told, "Boys should be strong and not cry." I kept reminding myself that soon this night would be over, but the next day would be the actual funeral . . . the last good-bye.

My mother woke me early the next morning, making sure that I looked my best. I promised myself when I was getting dressed that I would hold back my tears no matter what. I had to be strong and help my grieving parents.

When we arrived at the church, we all waited as they took my grandma's coffin out of the big black hearse. We had to follow it in so everyone knew that we were family. Once inside, we took our seats. My family sat in the very front because we were the closest to my grandma. I was surprised to see that even before the service began, my parents were crying. I was trying to hold back my tears, but as the priest began talking about my grandma, it seemed as though not crying was going to be an impossible task.

About halfway through the mass, he began telling the people about how much my grandma was loved by her family and friends. He then mentioned how every night I stayed with her while my parents were working. That reminded me of all of the good times we had together throughout my life. In the summer, we would glide on her swing. In the winter, we would always ride sleds down the big hill behind her house. There were so many good times that went through my mind that I almost forgot where I was. I began to realize that those good times were gone forever. At this exact thought, I began to cry uncontrollably. I didn't care anymore about what other people thought of me. It was something that I just had to do. I could not hold back my sadness anymore.

When my father noticed me sobbing, he leaned me up next to him and we cried together. My father, my mother, my sister and I sat next to each other, crying as if the world was going to end. At this point I promised to myself that if I ever had a son, I would tell him: "Real boys show emotions. Cry when you are sad, and smile when you are happy." This was the last time I would say good-bye to my grandmother, but I was a better person for letting my tears show everyone just how much I loved her.

Jonathan Piccirillo, fifteen

Only Love Lasts Forever

Yesterday, after telling my brother, Rhys, and me to stop playing like wild animals in the house for what she said was the thousandth time, Mom went to take a bath. That's when it happened. We were playing around, bopping each other with pillows, when one slipped from my brother's grasp and smashed the glass dome on the coffee table, shattering it into a zillion pieces!

With her supersonic hearing, my mom heard the tremendous crash and then the sound of glass hitting the tile. Wasting no time, she came flying into the room to find out what had happened. I was sure my brother and I were dead meat and she was going to start yelling at us, but instead she just knelt by the pieces and began to cry.

This made Rhys and me feel pretty awful. We went over and put our arms around her, and she explained to us why she was so upset. Under the shattered glass dome was a white porcelain rose. Dad had given it to her on their first wedding anniversary. He had said that if he ever forgot to bring flowers for an anniversary in the future, Mom was to look at that one. It was like their love—it would last a lifetime.

Now it lay chipped on the floor, one petal gone. We

began crying, too, and offered to glue it for her. She said that wouldn't really fix it. Now that it had been broken, the value of the "limited edition" had lessened. We got our piggy banks out to pay for it, but Mom replied that to her the rose represented Dad's love and could never truly be restored.

As Mom slowly began to pick up the mess, we tried everything we could think of to cheer her up, but even our best funny faces didn't work. Mom just looked away. Rhys and I were even really nice to each other, which always makes her eyes twinkle, but she didn't seem to notice. The tears kept coming down her cheeks as she cleaned up the mess.

After everything was picked up and Mom was on her way back to the bath, I stopped her in the hall and said I had something important to tell her. She tried to go around me, replying "Not now," but I wouldn't let her by. I told her, "I want to say something very important; it's a rule of God."

I put both hands on her shoulders and told her, "All things can be broken, Mom; everything breaks sometime. The only thing that isn't like that is love. It's the only thing that can never be broken."

Mom hugged me very tightly then and finally smiled. She said that I was pretty wise and understood some things that even much older people didn't!

After dinner that night, we had a family meeting. We discussed mistakes and the importance of learning from them. Mom glued the petal back onto the rose. The tiny petal now had a thin, almost invisible line of glue. Then Mom softly said, "Even though other people have 'limited edition' roses, mine is truly unique. Its tiny flaw reminds me of something more important: the realization that only love lasts forever."

Denise and Rett Ackart

The Reason for Living

Love cures people—both the ones who give it and the ones who receive it.

Karl Menninger

I'm only twelve years old, but I know sadness and the fear of death very well. My grandfather has been smoking since he was a young teenager, and now he has a terrible disease called emphysema that ruins the respiratory system.

Ever since my grandmother died, my grandfather has been depressed—mad at the world. He is a very ornery man and has said some hurtful things to nice people. But when he is around me, it's like a whole soft side of him becomes exposed.

Recently, my grandfather got very sick. He underwent surgery on his throat and had to use a machine called a respirator to help him breathe. The doctors thought that his days were numbered, but miraculously he recovered. He was taken off the respirator, but still he couldn't talk. It strained his voice badly to make the slightest noise.

While my grandfather was in the hospital, my mother

and I flew to Pittsburgh to be with him. We were very fearful we wouldn't see him again.

When we reached my grandfather's hospital room, I was shocked by his condition. He looked so sickly. He was hardly able to even grunt. Somehow though, he managed to mumble, "I . . . you."

"You what, Grandpa?" I whispered. He didn't have the energy to answer me. He had exhausted all his strength with those two syllables, "I . . . you."

The next morning my mother and I had to leave. I kept wondering just what it was he had tried so desperately to tell me. It wasn't until I was back home in Georgia that I learned what he had tried to say.

A week after we returned home, my family received a phone call from one of the nurses in the hospital. She told us that my grandfather had said, "Call my granddaughter and tell her 'love.'" At first I was a little confused, thinking *why he would just say, "love." Why not, "I love you?"* Then it hit me. The day we were in the hospital he had been trying to say, "I love you." I was really touched. I felt as if I was going to cry, and I did.

After many painful weeks, my grandfather was finally able to talk. I called him every night. Normally he had to stop after about five minutes because he was too weak. No matter what, though, every time we hung up he would say, "I love you" and "I'd do anything for you." These, along with his moving words, "You're the only reason I live," are the best compliments I have ever received.

My grandfather is still very ill and I know our time is limited. I feel very honored that he has shared his feelings with me. I have learned a lot from this experience. But the most important thing I've learned is that a simple "I love you" is really not simple. It's a reason for living.

Lauren Elizabeth Holden, thirteen

5

ON CRUSHES

I've never felt this way before
It's all brand new to me
My head is spinning, I can't breathe
You are all I see.

I long for you to notice me
I wish you'd ask me out
So this is what first love is like,
And what a crush is all about.

Amanda Beatty, twelve

Tasting the Moment

When I was twelve, I wanted to have a summer romance more than anything I had ever wanted before—more than being able to drive a car and more than having big boobs—I wanted to fall in love.

I had no idea what falling in love meant though. I thought that a romance would make me feel different—older and experienced. My friends all had experience with boys. They knew how it felt to have someone else's hand squeezing their hand or to have somebody smile at them for no apparent reason. I was starting to feel certain I never would. And then I met Erik.

Every summer my parents and I would go on vacation to the same RV campground. The campground was a haven for potential summer romances. My friends and I would check out all the new campers, hoping there might be some new love interest. We would talk about romance and imagine what we would do when we did have a boyfriend.

"I'd sit with him at the campfire," Trish would say.

"We'd go for walks, holding hands," Kelly said.

And I never said anything. I didn't know what I would do if I met a boy I liked. I never had much to say to boys. I couldn't remember the punch lines to jokes and didn't know what kind of questions to ask to get a conversation started. Whenever I did meet a new boy, I'd stammer and mumble, tripping over my tongue as often as I tripped over my own feet.

Then that summer, three baseball teams with twenty fifteen-year-old boys on each team camped at our park.

Everyone was in heaven!

Everyone . . . except my father.

"You are to be inside at ten o'clock tonight," he said. In all those previous years, I never had a curfew at the campground. Neither had my brother. Except this time. My brother was still allowed out and I, like Rapunzel, was locked in my tower while the rest of the world (my friends) were being swept off their feet. Unlike Rapunzel however, I knew what I was missing. They were all going to have another romance while I, once again, was not.

"Oh Andrea," Kelly had said the next morning. "It was so amazing! The guys on this team are so cute!"

My stomach crashed to the floor as she listed off their names. *Taylor, Matt, Anton, Erik* . . . I had missed it again.

"And we're going to their game this afternoon!"

I was allowed to go to the game. The game itself wasn't great—they weren't the best players and they weren't even playing on a very good ball field. It was out in the country and it didn't have any bleachers. We had to sit under this old, wooden canopy that had a few picnic tables. It was sunny and hot and we were dying of thirst, but I LOVED it.

My friends pointed out each of the players that they had met the night before. We were sitting pretty far away, so it was hard to tell what they looked like, but I felt that this was what having a romance was all about—going to watch your guy play baseball and cheering him on.

"And that's Erik," Kelly pointed out this guy who was kind of skinny with a few loose curls that stuck out from underneath his baseball cap. He looked over at us girls, waved and smiled. My stomach was flopping around like a fish on dry land.

They lost their game and the tournament. We spent the rest of the day swimming and hanging out on the beach. Erik and I went for a walk on a road just outside our campground. He held my hand as soon as we were outside of the park. I hadn't thought about what a guy's hand would feel like holding mine.

It was fun walking with him, holding hands. We walked along a dirt road leading to a hill through a grove of poplar trees. In the midst of the trees, at the top of a hill, was a giant rock. We sat there for a few minutes, still holding hands. He kept smiling. His teeth were so white they were glowing in the early darkness. I could smell him— sort of a mixture of bug repellent and lake water. He slowly leaned his head closer to mine.

This has to be what falling in love feels like, I thought. I was so totally nervous that my stomach was doing flip-flops.

His face was just inches away and then his lips pressed against mine. His lips opened just a little and I followed his lead, opening my own lips just a little. As I did, I felt this odd little gurgle creeping up in my throat. The next thing I knew, I let out this tremendous burp right into his mouth!

Mortified, I excused myself and looked away. I wanted to run away but he was still holding my hand.

Then, weirdly enough, he laughed. Then I laughed too, and the "romance" of my first kiss was over. We walked back to the campfire holding hands.

Finally tasting a kiss didn't change me, make me feel older or more self-confident around boys. But I discovered that sometimes people like Erik come into your life and can help make an embarrassing moment a little easier.

Andrea Adair

Clueless

A person wrapped up in himself makes a small package.

Harry Emerson Fosdick

I fell in love with him because he was the most popular guy in school.

He was the new boy in town, and he and his brothers had become the rage of the whole school. Not only were they all the most handsome hunks we'd ever set our eyes on, they were also musicians. And Peter—he was the lead singer. How cool is that!

I was at home, sick, when he joined our school. My friends would call me up and rave about this great new guy that I just *had* to see. My curiosity rose even higher when they told me stories of how he'd play the guitar in class, never have any homework done and didn't care about anyone or anything. When his trips to the principal's office had beaten the school record, I was intrigued. This was one guy I just had to meet.

I had gotten sick at the beginning of the school year, so when I came back to school fifteen days later, all the seats in our class had already been assigned—except to Peter and me. Our teacher set up two chairs and a table on the side of the class—a temporary arrangement until she could fit us in.

Our first day was a complete disaster. Not only was he stubborn, selfish and immature, but he made it a point to argue with me about everything.

"What's the circumference of a circle?"

"It's not *that!*"

"World War II started in 1939, right?"

"Yeah, if history textbooks are all correct."

"What's the capital of Finland?"

"Why? You planning on going there?"

Soon, we were in each other's faces all day long. I swear, if it hadn't been for his hazel eyes, I'd have killed him. Finally, one day our teacher warned us that we better start getting along or she'd make us sit together through the entire semester. Not wanting to spend a moment with him longer than was necessary, I decided to give it a try.

Being nice to him wasn't as hard as I had imagined. It was *impossible!* His atrocious attitude, sarcastic comments and blatant disrespect for everyone around him was more than I could take. But once he'd start to sing, you'd forget everything in the room. The only thing you'd hear was his voice, the only thing you'd see—his eyes.

With each passing day, we became closer. His atrocious attitude now seemed pretty cool, and the sarcastic comments were kind of funny. It was hard not to like him after getting to know him. Then I went a step ahead and fell utterly head-over-heels in love with him. Little did I know a spark had hit both sides.

A common friend, who'd noticed the change of attitude, decided to play Cupid. So, he asked Peter out for me, without asking me! Then asked me out on behalf of Peter, without asking him! We ended up going out and laughing over what had happened!

A week later, we were officially a couple. I felt so lucky to be with the guy all the girls were literally drooling over. He was charming. He was funny. Best of all, he was popular. I could feel other girls' eyes piercing into my skin as I sat with him and laughed at the latest escapade in his life.

Popularity has its consequences, though. About a week after we'd started going out, I discovered a secret. He'd been going out with another girl, too. And another. He was leading us all along the same sweet path, with none of us having the slightest clue of what was going on. As soon as I found out, I decided to dump him. I wasn't about to take any of this.

The so-called relationship ended in the drain. With so many girls running around trying to impress him, he found it very convenient to play with each one's emotions.

For him, it was a popularity game. The one with the most girlfriends wins. Me, I don't work like that. I wanted exclusivity. In the end, we finished where we had started—detesting each other's guts.

I fell in love with him because he was the most popular guy in school. I fell out of love for pretty much the same reason.

Mridu Khullar

Teasing Tami

I didn't have the best self-image in junior high, and there were two things that I fell back on in order to be accepted: athletics and humor. I've always been a decent athlete and I have always been able to make people laugh. Unfortunately, sometimes the laughter came at someone else's expense. At the time I didn't fully realize what I was doing to other people around me, especially Tami.

When I found out that she had a crush on me, I did everything possible to get her to stop liking me. While some of the boys in my class were starting to be interested in girls, I just wasn't there yet—in fact, the whole thing kind of freaked me out. Instead of trying to let her know that I wasn't ready for a relationship with a girl yet, I went out of my way to make things miserable for her. I wrote stupid songs about her that made my friends laugh whenever they saw her, and loudly told crazy stories about having to save the world from "Tami, the Evil Villain."

Everything all changed about halfway through the year though, when Mr. Greer, my favorite P.E. teacher, stopped me in the hall one day.

"Hey, Michael, you got a second?"

"Sure, Mr. Greer!" I said. Everybody loved Mr. Greer, and I looked up to him like a father.

"Michael, I heard a rumor that you've been teasing Tami and making her life miserable." He paused and looked me straight in the eye. It seemed like an eternity before he continued. "Do you know what I told him? I told him it couldn't possibly be true. The Michael Powers that I know would never treat another person like that—especially a young lady."

I gulped, but said nothing.

He gently put his hand on my shoulder and said, "I just thought you should know that." Then he turned and walked away without a backward glance, leaving me to my thoughts.

That very day I stopped picking on Tami.

I knew that the rumor was true and that I had let Mr. Greer down with my actions. More important, though, it made me realize how badly I must have hurt Tami for Mr. Greer to want to talk to me about it. He not only made me realize the seriousness of my actions, but he did it in a way that helped me to save some of my pride. My respect for him grew even stronger after that.

Even though I did stop teasing her, I never was brave enough to apologize to Tami for being so mean to her. She moved away the next year, and I never saw her again.

Just because I didn't know how to deal with Tami liking me, I still should have known better than to handle it the way I did. I think I actually did know better, but it took my favorite teacher's gentle guidance to help me change my ways.

Michael T. Powers

The Note

Kind words do not cost much. Yet they accomplish much.

Blaise Pascal

When I was in the fifth grade, I fell in love—real love—for the very first time. It only took about a week into the school year for it to happen, and I was completely, head-over-heels crushing on Mike Daniels. No one ever called him just Mike; it was always one word—Mike Daniels. Blond hair that stuck up in every direction and blue eyes that crinkled in the corners when he laughed—visions of Mike Daniels occupied my every dream.

To say I wasn't the most popular or prettiest girl in our class would be an understatement. In fact, I think I must have been the original geek. I was so skinny that I still had to wear days-of-the-week panties and dorky undershirts when most of my friends were starting to wear bras and more grown-up undergarments. My mom made me wear brown orthopedic lace-up shoes to school every day, because I had a foot that turned in and my parents wanted to "correct it before it was too late." Right smack dab in the middle of my two front teeth was this giant space that even gum surgery the year before hadn't fixed, and the two teeth on either side of my front teeth overlapped, making me look like I had fangs. Add a pair of thick glasses, thin baby-fine hair (with a home permanent from my mom—help!), knobby skinned-up knees and elbows—and what do you get? A kid that only a parent could love.

I wouldn't—couldn't—tell my friends that I was in love with Mike Daniels. It was my secret to write about in my journal. In my dreams, Mike Daniels would all of a sudden grasp what a beautiful soul was hiding inside of my gawky body and realize that he loved me for who I *really* was. I spent hours writing poetry for him and stories about him, until one day I got up the nerve to actually write to him about how I felt.

Our teacher, Miss Finkelor, was really awesome about most things, but the one thing she was majorly serious about was not writing notes to each other during class. Everyone did it anyway. Except me. My only shot at self-esteem was being teacher's pet, and I excelled at it. I loved it so much it didn't even bother me when kids teased me about being the teacher's favorite.

It was a huge decision for me to go against the one thing that Miss Finkelor detested—note passing. But I knew that there was no other way to tell Mike Daniels about how I felt—and I also knew that if I never told him, I was going to burst . . . or maybe even freak out. I vowed to do it on Monday morning.

So, first thing Monday morning, in my very best printing, I wrote, "I love you." That was it. Nothing else—no flowers, no poetry—just, "I love you." I passed it to Dianne, who sat between me and Mike Daniels, and whispered, "Give this to Mike Daniels," trying to look really casual, like it was a request to borrow a book from him or some-thing. I held my breath as I watched him open and read it—then read it again. Then he folded it up and put it into his pocket. *Oh my God, what have I done? What if he shows it to his buds at recess? They'll all laugh their heads off. I'm a fool. An idiot. Why did I tell him?* I felt like I was going to throw up.

I was so involved in feeling like I was going to hurl, that I didn't even feel Dianne punching me in the arm. Then she shoved a note in my hand. Slowly, I opened it. It was my own note. *Great, he thought it was so stupid that he sent it back to me,* I thought. Then it dawned on me—he had writ-ten something on the back of it. "I like you, too. I'm glad we're friends."

I didn't know whether to laugh or cry. I was so relieved that he didn't trash me—that could have easily hap-pened if Mike Daniels hadn't been a really nice guy. With that one little gesture of kindness, Mike Daniels made me feel special—and, not only that, but I felt that somehow, he *had* seen the real me hidden in the body of a fifth-grade geek.

I kept that note for years—all the way through the eighth grade. Whenever I felt bad about myself, I would reread Mike Daniels' note and remember that act of kind-ness. It didn't matter to me what inspired him—if it was pity, or the recognition of things to come—that note gave me strength to go through the challenges of the tough years that followed fifth grade.

Patty Hansen

Not My Boyfriend

That's the penalty we have to pay for our acts of foolishness—someone else always suffers for them.

Alfred Sutro

"Jason likes you," Kellie said, as she sat down next to me on the bus. "He wants to know if you'll go out with him."

"Jason?" I said, surprised. After all, I knew who he was since we rode the same bus to and from school, but I didn't really know him. He was in seventh grade—a year younger than me—and we had never even talked to each other. I had certainly never thought of him as a boyfriend or anything.

"I'll have to think about it," I said. I really couldn't imagine being his girlfriend. But, on the other hand, some of my friends had boyfriends and others had guys who liked them. I wanted one, too.

When the bus reached my stop, I practically danced down the street to my house. "You must have had a good day," my mother smiled when she saw me.

"I did!" I said. "Jason likes me! He wants to be my boyfriend!"

After explaining to my mother who Jason was and reassuring her that, no, I wasn't too young to have a boyfriend, I decided to say yes to Jason. *It will be the most romantic day of my life,* I said to myself.

The next morning, I spent extra time on my hair and put on my favorite perfume. Kellie and Jason were both already in their seats when I got on the bus.

"Well?" Kellie asked, leaning over the back of her seat. I wondered why she, another seventh-grader I knew only as someone on my bus, suddenly had such an interest in my love life.

"Yeah, I guess I'll go out with him," I responded, trying not to sound too excited.

She got up and headed to the back of the bus, where Jason sat with some other seventh-grade guys. "She said yes," she told him. Suddenly, the bus erupted with chants of, "Whooooo . . . Carol and Jason." I didn't pay any attention. *I have a boyfriend,* I thought to myself all the way to school. *I'm going out with someone!*

Before going into school, I stood talking to some of my friends. Of course, the topic of conversation was my new boyfriend. Every few minutes, I glanced over at Jason who was talking to his friends at the other end of the sidewalk.

I wasn't sure if I should go over and talk to him. I wanted to, but the only thing I could think of to say was "So, you're my boyfriend," and since I didn't want to sound stupid, I stayed put.

Finally, I saw him walking over. He was looking right at me, so I broke from my friends and smiled at him. He didn't smile back, though. Instead, he stopped and said, "I don't want to go out with you."

"You don't?" I choked out, trying to catch my breath.

"No," he replied. "Kellie was bugging me yesterday. She

kept asking me who I like, so when she asked if I liked you, I said yes just to shut her up. Sorry if you thought I was serious."

Then the bell rang and everyone headed inside. I felt as if someone had punched me in the stomach. All the guys snickered as they walked by me and I wanted to just crawl into a hole—to go home, get into bed and never leave my room again. I walked slowly into my classroom, wondering why the day that was supposed to be the most romantic of my life had turned into the most humiliating.

I couldn't concentrate all day, and I stared into space through most of my classes, but none of my teachers seemed to mind. The story had gotten around, so they probably all knew what was wrong.

When I got home I slammed the door of my room and cried for hours, not because that particular guy didn't want to go out with me, but because I felt so stupid to have created an entire romance with Jason based on a conversation with Kellie. When I realized that I wasn't upset about Jason not being my boyfriend, I stopped crying.

In the six months that remained until I graduated from eighth grade and moved on to high school, I never talked to Jason again. In fact, if we hadn't been on the same bus, I probably would have forgotten all about him. I'm glad I didn't, though. The next year, a girl I knew slightly told me that she knew a guy who liked me.

"If he likes me, he'll have to tell me himself," I replied.

And he did.

Carol Miller

Without the Kisses

There is never a better measure of what a person is than what he does when he is absolutely free to choose.

William M. Bulger

In the eighth grade, all I wanted was to be alone with my first boyfriend, Mark. His family had just moved to our town and I barely knew him, but he had a nice smile, and my friend Victoria thought he was cute, too. The second week after he started at our school, he asked me to go out, and I said yes.

Mark and I didn't talk much, but he gave me his navy blue and white jacket to wear and waited for me at my locker each day after sixth period drama class.

Over the next few weeks, we went to each other's house a few times, but our parents would never leave us alone. At Mark's house, we made popcorn and watched family movies with his mom and dad. His mom called our movie nights "double dates," which made Mark blush and then roll his eyes when she wasn't looking. My parents were just as paranoid, and even more embarrassing. My dad was so weird about me going with a guy that he had a mental block against Mark's name. My mother was so sure we shouldn't be alone together that she once decided to rearrange the kitchen cabinets at nine o'clock on a Saturday night, just so she could keep an eye on us in the adjacent family room.

It seemed like my older brother, Dirk, was always allowed to be alone with his girlfriend, Maggie. I could only imagine what they were doing and I thought, *If Dirk gets to be alone with his girlfriend then I should get to be alone with Mark.*

At Mark's locker the next day, I told him what I had been thinking about, and his brown eyes bulged from his head. He told me he would come up with a plan to get us alone that weekend. The rest of the week seemed like a month. I kept imagining how his lips would feel when they touched mine. I had watched actors kiss on TV practically every day, but wished I had paid better attention to how they did it. I worried that my lips would get dry, that my braces would cut him and that my tongue wouldn't know what to do. The more I thought about it, the more the whole thing grossed me out. But my friends Victoria and Shauna had both been kissing boys since the seventh grade, and I felt like a prude around them. It was all they ever talked about, it seemed. I figured I should just get it over with once and for all.

That Saturday, Mark told his parents we were going for "an evening stroll" to feed the ducks at the lake a block from his house. In preparation for the big night, I took forever to curl my long hair, but I didn't use a lot of hair spray just in case he wanted to run his fingers through my hair. I wasn't sure why he'd do that, but people were always doing that in the movies.

The sun had just set when we made our way down his street, pretend-balancing on the center white line in the road. Three houses down from Mark's on the corner sat a pitch dark, vacant house under construction. That house was at the center of his plan, which I thought was brilliant until we got there and saw how creepy it was. Mark quietly led me through the side gate and across a pile of dirt that must have been part of the construction. I could feel dirt slipping into my sandals, grinding between my heel and sandal as we made our way to the back of the empty house. Mark yanked the chrome handle on the sliding glass door and pulled it open easily. I looked down to swat a mosquito dining on my leg and saw my heartbeat through my shirt.

Inside, the music from a single cricket echoed around us, making the house seem bigger than it looked from the street. At first I wanted to go back to his house, but then Mark gently placed his hand on my shoulder and led me to a spot near the fireplace. Mark pulled two cement blocks across the floor, making a screeching noise so loud I could still hear it after it stopped. He placed the two blocks next to the fireplace and we sat. And sat. The amber light from the neighbor's back porch placed a halo around Mark's eager yet fearful face. He raised his eyebrows higher each time he looked over at me. I fidgeted with my pink and green friendship bracelet and tried to push the sand out of my sandals with my toes. Mark tapped out a drumbeat on his knee, but I could barely hear it because the cricket was so loud. It sounded like the cricket was sitting on my lap.

How long are we going to just sit here? I thought. It seemed like forever until finally, Mark spoke. I nearly jumped when he turned toward me. He made such a quick move on the cement block that it sounded like he ripped a hole in his shorts. Then he looked deep into my eyes and whispered, "Is Mr. Bergman hard for Algebra One?"

"Uh," I looked down at my hands and realized that I'd tied a knot in the end of my friendship bracelet. "He's hard, but he warns us about pop quizzes."

It turned out, he liked Mrs. Fir for English but thought Mr. Wright was an idiot with his horn-rimmed glasses and bad jokes. That started a long conversation about all of our teachers and their crazy quirks, and by the time we left that empty house, we were laughing so hard that we couldn't hear the cricket anymore. I must have licked my lips a thousand times that night, thinking, *At any moment, he'll kiss me.* But after all the anticipation, I'm glad he didn't. Even with all the pressure from our friends at school, we managed to skip the kissing and just get to know one another. At least for that night.

When it came down to it, we were too young for soap opera love scenes or swollen lips from kissing with braces on our teeth. That night, as we walked back to his house holding hands, I wondered if it was my hand or his that was so warm.

Jennifer O'Neil

6

ON DEATH
AND DYING

She'll stay with you
  As long as the wind blows
  She'll always be in your heart
  She didn't leave you all alone
  She has eternal life
  Her spirit is always within you
  And if the sun shines in the sky
  And rain should fill the air
  And a rainbow lights up your day
  Know that she is there.

Karli McKinnon, ten

April Morning

The date was April 19, 1995. I was getting ready for school like I usually did, and my mother, Diana, was getting ready for work. She worked at the federal building in Oklahoma City.

As I left for school, I told my mom good-bye. I told her that I loved her and that I would see her after school. Little did I know that I wouldn't be seeing her after school, and that my life would soon be changed.

Around 1:30, a call came over the intercom, asking for me to come to the office to be checked out from school. I thought, *Cool, it must be my mom.* She would always surprise me like that and take me somewhere.

When I got to the office, instead of my mom, it was my grandpa and my aunt. They were both crying and had confused and worried looks on their faces. I didn't have time to ask what was wrong. They grabbed me and we drove in a hurry to my house.

When I went in, my whole family was sitting around, crying and watching the news. I didn't see my mom there. My eyes glanced at the TV and I saw the building where my mom worked. Most of the building had been blown up. People were coming out bleeding. I knew from that moment on, there was a chance my mom wouldn't be coming home. So I fell to my knees and began to pray. The only thing that was going through my mind was, *How could God let me down like this?*

We all stayed at my house and waited to see if maybe they would find her alive. Hours went by and nothing happened. During that time I saw my mom's friends coming out on stretchers. They were lifeless. I began to feel hatred toward whoever did this and cried even more. I felt useless. I couldn't do anything. But my family was there and they helped me.

Days went by with no answer. I was in shock. All I wanted was my mom to come home and tell me that everything would be okay, but that wish never came true.

One Wednesday morning, two and a half weeks after the bombing, the crying of my aunt and grandma woke me up. I got out of bed to see if they were okay. They told me that my mom had been found.

I was so happy I couldn't believe it. God had answered my prayers! I asked when she was coming home. They said she wouldn't be coming home. I was a little confused. Then they told me that she didn't survive the bomb. Mom worked on the seventh floor of the building. She was found on the second floor. I began to cry, and I thought, *How could God let this happen?*

My mother was the number one thing in my life, and now she is the number one thing in my heart. She did come home on the day of the bombing, not to our home but to her home in the sky. Now I feel that my mom is just waiting for the day when I come home. In the meantime, I will try to make her proud of me and always remember how special she was. Those thoughts and beliefs are what help me get through every day of my life.

Justin Day, fifteen

Ryan's Story

The most daring, courageous and patient person I have ever known was my cousin. Ever since I can remember, my cousin, Ryan, and I seemed to have a special bond. I have two special memories of Ryan when we were very young.

The first one happened on a hot summer day, at Disneyland in California. I can still hear the laughter and voices from people around us. I remember looking up when Ryan pointed toward the sky. My Mickey Mouse balloon and his were tangled up together.

The second memory I have is when Ryan and I were playing with little cars in our grandparents' family room. He had a green car and I had a brown one. I smashed my car into his and broke it. I didn't mean to, and I felt bad. Looking back, I now realize how important and special memories are.

Then my Uncle Rick, Ryan's dad, moved his family to Pocatello, Idaho. I didn't get to play with Ryan anymore, but we kept in touch by phone.

It had been some years since I had heard from them, until one particular evening. Ryan was seven and I was six at the time. After my Uncle Rick and my mom had talked, my mom hung up the phone. That's when she told me that Ryan was sick.

Ryan had leukemia. It was in his bloodstream and eventually it went into his bone marrow. Can you imagine? A seven-year-old! I don't know how he had the courage to live, each day knowing that he was dying of cancer.

After that, we kept in touch a lot over the phone. Finally, when he was eleven, they came to California to visit us for two weeks. Ryan was able to come because he had wished for this, and the Make-A-Wish Foundation was paying for it. This special foundation tries to make terminally ill children's wishes come true. Ryan wanted to go to all of the nearby theme parks like Disneyland, Universal Studios and Sea World.

One day during this visit, Ryan and I went in-line skating together. We sat down on the curb, and we talked about when we had been little together. He told me his memories of us and I told him of mine. He remembered the balloons at Disneyland. It meant a lot to both of us that we remembered the same things.

Eventually, the two weeks came to an end, and Ryan and his family went back to Idaho. We kept in touch throughout the next year. When Ryan was twelve, he needed a bone marrow transplant, but the odds were against him. The chances of finding a matching donor were one in ten million people, so Ryan had to have an experimental transplant. It had been tried only once before, and the man had died. The doctors took Ryan's father's bone marrow and gave it to Ryan. Ryan lived through it.

About a month before he had this transplant, I talked to him on the phone. I felt embarrassed to tell him that I loved him, but I told him anyway, right before I hung up. Finally, Ryan died. He had so much medicine, and so many chemicals in his body, that his lungs couldn't help him breathe anymore, and they collapsed.

I was sad when he died, yet I felt peaceful about it. I was so glad that I had worked up the courage to tell him that

I loved him. Now I'll never be ashamed to tell someone that I love them before it's too late.

Although I miss him, I think it's better that he isn't suffering anymore. Now Ryan walks with God in heaven.

Kelli Frusher, fourteen

My Life

Sometimes life can be a pain
When your life stays the same
I've had cancer not once but twice
And it isn't very nice.

I hate cancer really a lot
It ties my life up in a knot
Sometimes I think the doctors lie
At times I think I'm going to die.

Before I end up in a coffin
I'll do my fun things soon and often
I had my transplant—it wasn't fun
It's hard to believe that I'm finally done.

Sometimes I wish I could roll over and die
Now I think I'm going to cry
When you're there you have to roll with the punches
Especially when it comes to their nasty lunches.

When I went to receive what my dad had to give
I was the second to do it, but the first to live
It was hard for us all—it could make you hysterical
But if you think about it . . . I'm a living miracle.

Ryan Alexander

[EDITORS' NOTE: *Ryan was twelve when he died on November 9, 1994.*]

I'll Never Forget Him

His name was Matthew. I always called him Matt. He had white-blonde hair and blue eyes. He always had to do everything that annoyed me, but I guess that's what little brothers are for. Inside I still loved him. He was only four when he died of meningitis.

It was a beautiful winter day. I woke up, got ready for school and went to the bus stop. When I stepped on the bus that morning my brother, Matthew, was outside riding his bike. That's what he did every morning.

After a normal day of third grade, I rode the bus home looking forward to playing with my friend, Jessica. Two years ago she had moved next door to us with her parents, her little brother, T. J., and her sister, Brittany. They were all attached to Matt, like they had known him forever. When I got home I went straight to Jessica's house.

At three o'clock that afternoon, my grandmother, who I call Nana, and my other grandmother, who I call Grandma, took Matthew to the doctor. My grandfather said that Matthew was complaining about not being able to move his head or neck.

The doctor examined Matthew and diagnosed him with the flu. My grandmothers were told to give him something for his fever and that he would be fine in the morning.

When they came home from the doctor's office, they put Matthew in my room. I remember getting a sleeping bag and finding a cozy spot in front of our fireplace. I don't know all of the events that took place that night, but my Nana told me what she recalled. She said that Matthew woke up and had to use the bathroom. By then he was so weak he couldn't even walk on his own. His eyelids were stuck together, and he had little purple splotches on his face and arms. He had to be carried to the bathroom.

I woke up later and heard the ambulance driver in our kitchen. He was saying that he wouldn't take my brother to the hospital in the ambulance because "it's only the flu." Since the ambulance driver wouldn't take him, my Nana and Grandma got ready and drove him themselves. When they were about halfway there, Matthew started to hallucinate. He said, "Sissy, my feet are burning." By the time they were at the hospital and the doctors diagnosed him, it was too late. They couldn't do any more for him.

My mom and dad woke me up at about 6:30 the next morning. I knew there was something wrong. It sounded like they were crying. Maybe they were. But when they told me what had happened, I wasn't sure if I was awake or still dreaming. I remember not crying, but inside I felt like it. Later that day, a lot of people we knew came to our house. They all asked if they could do anything for us. But they couldn't bring Matthew back.

Over the next few days, I tried not to think about what happened. I knew my brother was in heaven, but I wanted him back. A few of my teachers took off from work to come to his funeral. For awhile, I couldn't concentrate at school, but eventually things got back to normal—as normal as they will ever be without Matthew.

A few years later, at a youth rally, we were asked to write advice on a piece of paper and throw it back into the air. I wrote, "It helps to cry when you lose someone." And today, I *know* it's true.

Megan Weaver, twelve

An Angel in Disguise

Love is the only force capable of transforming an enemy into a friend.

Dr. Martin Luther King Jr.

When I first met Damon, he was working on a fence that divided our property. My mom and I were in the field across from him. He seemed like a nice enough guy once we were acquainted, but since his kindness was being directed toward my mother, in my mind he became the devil in farmer's clothing.

I had just turned ten and the only man I had ever been around a lot was my father. So when Damon and my mom began to see more of each other, I didn't know how to handle it. My dad had not been a great example of the male species, so Damon didn't have a chance in my heart. To put it bluntly, I hated the man.

The only reason I could figure why Damon kept hanging around was so he could hurt our family and cause us all a lot of pain. Now I couldn't let that happen, could I?

For about six months, Damon tried every way imaginable to win my approval. He bought me things and was always taking my side in everything, no matter if I was right or not. He let me get away with everything. So, of course, I kept up my attitude even more. I was seeing this grown man begging for me to like him or at least accept him. So for just as long as he tried to win me over, I shot down every single attempt with a harsh word or a hatred-filled look. Sometimes I would do both.

But he never quit. Every time I hurt him, he just kept right on trying. Eventually it began to work and finally Damon and I became friends.

Surprising as it may seem, that crazy old man and I had a lot in common. He understood me more than I thought anyone could. Damon was a lot of fun to be around, and my friends and I loved going places with him. He liked to do all the things we did.

I remember him saying once, "I would rather you kids be with me having fun than be out on the streets getting into real trouble." He loved kids and he wanted all of my friends and me to be safe. He wanted to provide a place for us to call home.

Damon had two daughters. Mom had Nichole, Josh and me. All of our friends became part of the family. Whether we were working or eating dinner together, we always had fun and always found something to laugh about.

Although we didn't always get along, those times are nothing compared to the really good memories I have of Damon. For five years of my life, he was always there. Damon became the father I had never had. We had an unspoken bond between us that made us inseparable. I liked working with him and watching him work.

Right before my sixth-grade summer, Damon and I bought two bottle-fed bull calves. I called one Floppy, because of his ears, and the other Doofus (Doofus was named after Damon). We had fun with them because it was something we could do together. We built a pen in the barn for them and took turns feeding them about five to ten times a day. Usually Damon was the one taking turns.

He knew how I longed for a horse and, although he wasn't quite "cowboy" material, he made sure that I got one.

Damon not only gave me material things, he also taught me a lot of things about life and how to live it. When I met Damon, I was going through tough times. I had just realized that my daddy wasn't the saint I had thought he was, and like I said, the male species wasn't on my list of things to like. I lived in an unhappy world, and Damon was the only one who was able to get the walls around my heart to fall. I had always kept my emotions bundled up inside, and he showed me that talking was a good thing. I was finally happy with myself and my life, thanks to him.

One day out of the blue, Damon had a cerebral aneurysm. Earlier in the year my Papa Troy had had an aneurysm and had died the first night. So, regardless of what anyone told me, I was thinking the worst. But Damon survived the first night and the next night, too, and we all became hopeful. He was in a room in the ICU wing of the medical center.

After the aneurysm, he also had a few strokes and because of them he could not speak. I did not like going to see him because Damon was not "Damon" without his voice. He also looked so weak and helpless, and it hurt me dearly to go see him. I always got a knot in my stomach when I went to the hospital. But I went with hopes that he would respond to me.

Each time I went, though, I could not make myself talk to him. Damon was in ICU for about two or three weeks, and for a while he seemed to be getting better.

Then we found out that Damon's insurance would not pay for the type of care he was getting. He would have to be moved out of the hospital. In July, we moved Damon to a rehabilitation hospital in a nearby town. It was the closest thing we could get to home.

After Damon was moved, I only went to see him three times. I hated seeing him in that environment. Around the middle of November, Damon developed some kind of disease in his bloodstream and his health began to gradually decline.

In December, I went to see Damon because my mom said he was a lot worse and that he might like to see me.

When we went into the room, Mom explained to me that if I was going to hold his hand or touch him in any way I had to have gloves on because he was really sick. I was standing beside him watching him struggle for every breath, watching him suffer, and I couldn't do anything to help him. I broke down. I had been holding it in for so long I just couldn't do it anymore.

That night at home I went to bed with a heavy heart. I prayed that Damon would quit suffering regardless of the cost to me. I prayed that I could see him one more time. But I didn't want to see the man lying in that hospital bed. It wasn't Damon. I wanted to see the Damon that I remembered: the one that I hadn't seen in almost seven months. After I had prayed, I was afraid to go to sleep. I was afraid that if I dreamed about him, which I often did, I would wake up to find him gone.

But I didn't dream about him again until Tuesday, December 22. That night I woke up around eleven o'clock to my mother's crying. At that moment, I knew. My brother came and told me, and I went and sat with Mom for a while. But I went back to sleep shortly and I slept soundly the rest of the night.

In the dream I had that night, I saw Damon on his

tractor. He was smiling and I knew it was him. I also realized that he was free from any pain.

On the day of the funeral, I was a wreck. I finally realized it was over. I was going to miss him so much, but then again, I had been missing him for seven whole months.

It is now just over a month since we laid him to rest. As I write this, I still get a little teary-eyed. Damon was the greatest man I have ever met but I never told him. I never even told him that I loved him. I always thought that there would be time for that later.

Now, in everything I see, I am reminded of him. I miss the sound of the tractor and the smell he had when he came in after a long day of work. I even miss the annoying way he laughed. I just wish that one more time Nichole and I would be able to laugh with him.

Life is such a precious thing. Every day is taken for granted. There is a song called "One Day Left to Live," and I think everyone should live by it. It says to live your life like you have one day left to live. Don't live for the future and don't live for the past. Live for right now. Because right now is the only time that matters.

Megan Jennings, fifteen

My Little Superman

I babysat a little boy several months ago,
When I'd say, "It's bedtime," he always pleaded, *"No!"*
I still remember everything we did so well,
I'd let him stay up late then whisper, "I won't tell!"

We usually made cookies, or at least we'd try,
They would burn, and we'd laugh 'til we'd cry!
Movies, popcorn, pillow fights and Nintendo,
Beanie Babies were another favorite, from the 'Ty' Co.

His role model was Superman, how he loved him, too!
No one could've known what this boy would do.
He always brought joy into so many lives.
Why? Oh, why would he have to die?

He loved to play baseball, and sing in the choir,
But he had to give them up because his muscles would tire.
Still, he kept on smiling, through the pain, of course,
Even when he took a turn for the worse.

After treatments failed and several weeks went by
Home at last, he came . . . perhaps to die.
Family and friends brought a lot of gifts
And then one day my sister and I went over for a visit.

We watched one of his favorite movies, called *Child's Play*.
The last time that I saw him was on that day.
Imagine yourself at ten years old meeting your fate.
His whole family was with him on this sad date.

They all hugged him and said not to be scared
They told stories and memories that they all had once
    shared
He is an angel now, in a much better place
And I doubt that anybody will ever forget his smiling face.

Now he is home, and at peace once more
How I wish that I could come once again to his door
I will not forget him, I don't think I ever can
He was a real-life hero . . . my little Superman.

KeriAnne McCaffrey, fourteen

Grandma's Cloud Game

I worked hard picking that bouquet of dandelions from the field in back of Grandma's house. When I presented my gift to Grandma she smiled and hugged me.

"Oh, child," she'd said, "you warm the cockles of my heart."

"You have cockles in your heart, Grandma?"

She laughed. The best part of Grandma was her laugh. It wasn't exactly the sound so much as the way it filled her whole face, and the way her belly made her white apron wiggle.

Grandma placed the dandelions in a glass jar filled with water. They stayed on her kitchen windowsill until every last one of them was as brown as the wood it was sitting on.

Grandma smelled like vanilla and coffee. I remember the first time we made cookies from scratch. I thought one of the cups of stuff she put into the bowl was "scratch." She explained, "There are two kinds of cookies; store bought and scratch."

She had a secret recipe and it was magical because it didn't matter if we put raisins or nuts or even chocolate chips in the batter, the cookies always tasted like heaven.

Grandma gave me her secret scratch recipe and I keep it in my wooden treasure box under my bed.

I also have a four-leaf clover in my box. Grandma taped it to a piece of cardboard for me. We spent two hours crawling around on our hands and knees in her backyard looking for that four-leaf clover. We held hands and danced in a circle when I finally found one.

I loved spending the night with Grandma. She taught me how to play Rummy. I always added up the points because she said I was such a good counter.

The smell of coffee was usually what woke me up in the morning. Breakfast always tasted great. Breakfast started with a big kiss on my forehead followed by orange juice. Sometimes we had eggs, but Grandma knew pancakes were my favorite. She always made more pancakes than we could eat. We crumbled the leftovers and scattered them in the backyard for the birds. I think the birds came from miles around to visit her backyard when I spent the night.

Grandma had what she called a "bottomless" candy dish. We could eat candy in the afternoon and after dinner in the evening. The next morning the candy dish was full again. It always held my favorite kind—white buttery mints. Grandma taught me to hold them on my tongue and feel them magically melt. We held contests to see who could keep their mint on their tongue the longest. Most of the time Grandma won that game.

Grandma's porch swing was my favorite place in the whole world. She sat on one side. I sat beside her and leaned against her, my feet and legs taking up the rest of the swing. I could smell Grandma's cookies in her cotton apron and coffee on her breath as she hugged her arms around me. We found pictures in the clouds as Grandma gave the swing a nudge once in a while with her foot.

Mostly, we talked. We talked about the neighbor's good

corn crop. We talked about Dad's job and Mom's charity work. I told her my most important secrets and she crossed her heart she would never tell.

"Someday," she told me, "when I'm living with the angels, you look up into those clouds and say hi to your old grandma, okay?"

"Okay, Grandma, I will." I never worried about that day because I knew it would never come.

That was two months ago. Mom and Dad are in the house now packing Grandma's belongings. I am sitting on Grandma's porch swing, giving it an occasional push with my foot. The backyard is quiet. There is no laughter. I don't know if I will ever laugh again.

Grandma is here. I feel her presence everywhere. Her kitchen still smells like vanilla and cinnamon and coffee. Maybe she's just playing our game of hide-and-seek and she's out of sight just beyond that old lilac bush she loved so much. I know better, but I sure wish that was true.

A white, fluffy cloud moves across the sky, directly overhead. I look up, remembering our "pictures in the cloud" game. The wind shuffles the cloud as I watch. I see Grandma! There she is, sure as the world! Her wings are spread wide and her white dress is falling in folds around her feet. She has a happy smile on her face!

"Hi, Grandma," I call out, "I love you!" I knew she was there! She just doesn't need this old house and all the stuff in it anymore. I see her gently wave. Smiling, I spread out on the porch swing to watch her as she floats across the sky.

Nadine Rogers

Mr. Oberley's Star

I was nine years old the last summer that we lived next to Mr. Oberley. By then, he was retired and living alone—if you could call sharing a house with about twenty-five cats living alone. Early in the morning, I often heard shouts from his porch.

"Where did you come from?" His voice shattered the morning quiet. "Go away, Kitty! The hotel is booked!"

I smiled, knowing it was another stray. Mr. Oberley grumbled and complained, but never once did he turn away a needy cat. Their happy mewing often drifted out his open windows. Mom and Dad called it "The Cat Chorus."

Mom told me Mr. Oberley used to be a veterinarian. Once, just for fun, he wrote a cookbook for cats. But now he spent his days in the garden, among the daffodils, his arthritic back as stiff as a board. He joked that he was too old to be good for anything but conducting The Cat Chorus.

Sometimes my parents would let me stay up late. One night Mr. Oberley and I sat together, watching the night unfold. We breathed in the sweet perfume of lilacs as lightning bugs flickered like stardust strewn across the

lawn. A parade of cats trampled over my stomach before
scurrying into the purple dusk.

As the first star appeared, Mr. Oberley squinted into
the sky.

"Life is so much larger than we can imagine," he said.
He chuckled softly, rustling my hair. "Usually we think
it's our problems that are so vast. Look, Cindy, sweetheart, look over there." He pointed to the largest and
brightest star.

"One of these days, I'm going to climb that star and
make it my swing," he said. "I'll ride it across the whole
wide galaxy and see everything there is to see."

My first worry was, "But what if you fall?"

"I won't fall," he told me. "And just think, from the van-
tage point of my star I'll be able to watch you grow up. I'll
even be able to hear the cats sing."

I thought long and hard about that. The following day,
I told Mr. Oberley, in a most somber voice, that I did not
want him to go off chasing stars.

"I'll miss you too much," I said. "And what about The
Cat Chorus? The cats only sing when you're here."

It was true. Last year, when Mr. Oberley visited his sister, the cats had refused to sing at all. I bribed them with
their favorite shrimp-flavored treats, but they didn't give
one lousy meow . . . not until Mr. Oberley came back.

"I don't know," he said, tiredly. "Having a star to ride
sounds pretty good when you have a body as old as
mine."

Later that summer, Mr. Oberley became ill. His niece,
Sarah, came to take care of him. The long, hot days passed
slowly as I waited for him to get well again.

One day Mom and I brought him some chicken soup. I
was shocked to see how thin he had become. He was
almost too weak to lift his spoon. The worried cats sere-
naded him tirelessly, day and night.

The daffodils and lilac blossoms had wilted, but the roses were in full bloom the day Sarah knocked on our door.

"How is Mr. Oberley?" I asked right away.

His niece took a long, slow breath. "He told me to give you a message," she said finally. "He said you would know what it means."

"He found his star, didn't he?" I said, watching her eyes fill with tears. "Mr. Oberley went to ride on that great big old star."

Sarah nodded yes.

"And the cats?" I asked. "Who will take care of them?"

"I will," said Sarah. She planned to move into Mr. Oberley's house with her husband and young daughter, who was my age.

"Now you'll have a friend," she said.

"But Mr. Oberley is my friend," I insisted.

"Forever and always," said Sarah, wiping her eyes.

After Mr. Oberley's death, his cats refused to sing—except at night, after the first star lit the sky. And when that great big old star appeared, they sang until their hearts nearly burst. I knew then that it had to be true: Mr. Oberley was up on his star, just as he'd wanted.

Cynthia Ross Cravit

She Is Now My Sun

In the final analysis, the question of why bad things happen to good people transmutes itself into some very different questions, no longer asking why something happened, but asking how we will respond, what we intend to do now that it happened.

Rabbi Harold S. Kushner

To me, life is a gift no matter what shape or form.

One Thursday in April, I was awakened by the noise of my parents talking and making breakfast upstairs. My older brother and sister were upstairs running around trying to put their things together for school. I put on the new skirt I'd bought over the weekend while thinking about how I was going to make my day perfect. I ate breakfast with my family. Then my mom offered to walk me to school instead of my dad driving me. She said she wanted to walk for exercise, so I thought it would be fine. My dad said that he wanted to take me—that he had a weird feeling. But my mom and I both agreed to walk.

As we were walking down the hill to my school, we

were talking about how the body is like a chocolate-making machine—when you put the wrong ingredients in, like alcohol or drugs, the chocolate will come out wrong. Weird, how you remember certain stuff, like I did that conversation.

Holding hands, we crossed the crosswalk to get to my school, and that's when it happened.

A car came really fast, and my mom tried to push me out of the way, but I had already run to the sidewalk. When I turned around, I saw my mom flying through the air, her hands crossed and her eyes shut. For me, everything was in slow motion. Mom landed on her head, and it started to bleed. I screamed uncontrollably while some people called my dad and the police. Soon, I saw my dad come rushing down the street in his car with the most scared look on his face. He and I followed the ambulance to the hospital.

While we waited in the waiting room, I remember feeling like this can't be happening to me. I also felt that my mom's pain was happening because of me. If she hadn't walked me to school that day, none of this would have happened. When the nurse finally came to get us, I was scared of what I was going to see, but I ran and hugged my mother. I started to feel dizzy, so the nurse told me to sit down.

Later that day, we went to pick up my sister and then my brother. When we told my sister the horrible news, she started to scream and cry. When we told my brother, he just stayed silent. We all went to visit my mom at the hospital that night, and the next day at school, everyone made her cards.

A few days later, Mom was much better, it seemed. They let her come home, and when I got home from school, I saw my mom up and about trying to clean the house. I was so shocked! I dropped all my stuff and ran to give her a huge hug. (Oh, how I wish I could do that now!)

A few months passed, and she became healthy again. My family and I cherished her much more then we had before. That summer we went to Disneyland. She was so excited that she would walk ahead of us like she was a little girl again. I loved those times.

Then on a dark day in October, she came down with this mysterious illness. She had a fever and pains in her face. Then she would need blankets because she was cold. Thinking that the pain in her face was because of her teeth, she had a root canal done. A few months later, her vision started to get blurry, and she couldn't taste her food very well. I got scared from not knowing what was happening to my mom. I just knew I wanted her back the way she had been before, when she was healthy

Soon, my mom started to lose her balance when she walked, but she still tried so hard to walk across the hall to kiss my sister and me good night. Then, finally, she couldn't even swallow or balance her head on her neck. She would stay in her bed all day in so much pain. I know she was scared. She tried so hard not to let us know, so we wouldn't get depressed!

Then in late March, I had a sleepover for my birthday with a few friends. The next morning, my mom left my house early in an ambulance to go to the hospital. I didn't realize that that was going to be her last day in our home. I wish I'd known that, so I could have spent more time with her. But I'd go visit her in the hospital about every day. When I would leave I'd say, "I love you, Mom. When you get home, I promise we'll go to Hawaii together."

The doctors took all these tests, biopsies and scans, but they couldn't find anything wrong with her. She had so many surgeries and biopsies and X rays, but they still couldn't find *anything*. Soon she lost her ability to speak, but before she did, she told us that she felt that her mysterious illness was a result of the head injury that she had from being hit by the car. We were so frustrated because we could get no medical proof of what was making her sick so that they could treat her.

Then one day, Mom just stopped breathing, and they decided to put a tube in her throat so a machine could help her breathe. A few months went by with her in constant pain because of the irritating tube in her throat.

Every night I would go to sleep thinking of how lonely she was in her hospital room, and I'd be scared of what tomorrow would bring. Sometimes, when I was visiting her, I would just stare into her eyes, and I'd get this amazing feeling of comfort. I'd feel like no one could hurt her or me.

Whenever we'd leave the hospital room, I'd get to see that half smile that took up all her energy, and I'd hold on to it like never before. In those eight months of her being in that hospital bed, all I thought about was her: at school, at home, at night, at the hospital. All I wanted was my mom back. Nothing in the world could heal my heart—she was the only one who could. She was the biggest thing that was in my life and I wanted to help her so badly!

She was my best friend.

She was my hero.

She was my one and only mom.

When I was a little girl, I remember hearing about my friend losing her mom, and I thought to myself, *Nothing like that could ever happen to me.* Now I look at the world so much differently!

After many visits filled with tears and sadness, the day came that the doctors began losing hope. Finally, my dad had to make the biggest decision of our lives. The doctors wanted to take out the tube to see if Mom could breathe without the machine's help. My dad thought of what she would have wanted and made the difficult decision to let nature take its course. So, he told the doctors to take it out. We all had hope in our hearts that she would learn how to breathe on her own and come back home.

The day the doctors took the machine off, we went to visit her. She was so much happier because she was finally a bit more comfortable after so many months of having that thing taped to her neck. Still, that visit was different. Deep inside, we all knew what was going to happen. This visit was full of tears from both her and us. When it was my turn to go to her, I held her hand and kissed it softly and caringly. I looked hard at her, for I knew that it might be the last time that I could. I looked at her cheeks because that is where I would always kiss her before I went to bed. I looked at her lips, and I remembered all the those times when I got hurt and only her soft loving kiss would make me better. Then I looked into her eyes and got that feeling of comfort. I put my arms around her, and she tried to do the same, but her body wouldn't let her. I kissed her once more and went to the corner of the room where I could think of all our times together.

Then the time came when we had to say good-bye. I didn't want to believe it, but I knew what was going to happen. As we said our last good-byes, I saw that smile—the smile that could bring out the sun no matter how cloudy it is. And that's exactly what it did for me. I will remember that smile for my lifetime, for my spirit's existence—for eternity.

As we left her hospital room, I turned around and saw her lying there looking so peaceful, her arms to her side and a fading smile on her face. I blew her one last kiss, then turned around.

That same night, clouds flew into my heart and a thunderbolt burned a hole inside of me. She is now a part of the sunset. She is now a streak in the rainbow. She is one with the ocean. She is now my sun that cleared away the clouds.

As much as I want to feel sorry for myself and not let my life move on and to always feel the pain she had to go through, I know that she would say to me, "Life is a gift, Amber, no matter what shape or form. Live it like it's your last day. Live it to the fullest, and take *nothing* for granted!"

Those words lead me every day. Those words are why I am still here. I want to cherish my gift of life for my mom. Every breath I breathe is for her. Every step I take is for her. Every smile I smile is for her. I dedicate my every day to her.

And now, no matter what happens, I will remember that smile of hers, and I will smile in honor of her, knowing we both can take the clouds away and fill the world up with sunshine!

Amber Kury, eleven

The Baseball Spirit

Well, baseball was my whole life. Nothing's ever been as fun as baseball.

Mickey Mantle

It was summer, and my parents sent me to spend time with my grandpa for my thirteenth birthday. He had been diagnosed with cancer the Christmas before. I was in this strange rebellious stage, and I decided to bring my skateboard and skates and not spend much time with him. I knew some kids down the street, and I was going to hang out with them. I was a major baseball fan (I strongly favored the Cardinals), so when I was packing, I slipped my baseball glove in my backpack, too, thinking I could maybe play a little catch. I had planned everything.

Don't get me wrong, I wasn't trying to be mean or anything; I loved my grandparents, and it would be great to see my grandpa. I just wasn't planning on hanging out with him; but then, I never thought the spirit of baseball could bring two people together the way that it did that summer.

I was on the computer at my grandparent's house when Grandpa asked me if I wanted to play catch.

"Sure," I said, reluctantly.

We went outside to play catch, and at first I didn't think much of it, but with every throw, I realized that I was feeling more and more connected to him. I felt like I could have played catch with my grandpa forever. Later that night, he showed me his Mark McGwire first-baseman's mitt and his Mickey Mantle bat. I thought those were the coolest things in the world.

On August 13, we went to a St. Louis Cardinals' game at Busch Stadium. While I was watching *my* heroes, like Fernando Vina, Albert Pujols, Jim Edmonds and Mark McGwire, my grandpa was telling me all about *his* childhood heroes. Through that whole game, I felt even more connected to him.

Toward the end of my time in Illinois, I found Grandpa's book about Mark McGwire's historic 1998 season. He caught me looking at it so much that he decided I could keep it, and he signed it to me:

To: Caleb Mathewson
From: Maynard Mathewson "MATTY"
Remember the summer of 2001
Grandpa

I didn't think much of the autograph then, but later, I treasured it more than anything.

That night I had to get ready to go home, and we decided to go outside and play catch for what turned out to be one last time. My grandpa and I laughed and talked while I did my best imitation of the top Major League pitchers, not knowing how much I would treasure this moment later in life.

I came back to Illinois the next summer with my family to see him. My grandpa was confined to his bed and barely able to walk. The cancer had spread to every bone in his body.

The very last time I saw him was the last night I was there. I was in his room watching a Cardinals game on television with him. He struggled to sit up and said, "If anything happens to me, I want you to have my Mark McGwire first-baseman's mitt and my Mickey Mantle bat." It meant so much to me, I can't explain it. I could barely hold back my tears.

Two days later, his lungs filled up with fluid and on August 13, 2002, Maynard Mathewson died at 1:00 A.M., *exactly one year to the day* of attending that Cardinals game with me, which was still so fresh in my memory.

When I went to his funeral, on his casket there were two baseball caps. One was a Yankees cap and the other was the same St. Louis Cardinals cap that he wore to the Cardinals game that we attended together.

Because of my grandpa and the love for the game that we shared, I know that I'll always have the baseball spirit in me. The bat, the glove and the book that he gave me are always with me to remind me that my grandpa, Maynard Mathewson, and I will forever be connected by the spirit of baseball and the summer we spent together.

Caleb Mathewson, fourteen

Forever in My Heart

The only cure for grief is action.

George Henry Lewis

When my brother Nathan was only five months old, he was diagnosed with an extremely rare kidney disease called Denys-Drash Syndrome. At about the age of one, my brother's kidneys weren't good anymore and he was going to need a new one. He went on home dialysis, and then my dad ended up giving my brother one of his kidneys. Children who have organ transplants need to take medicine to keep their bodies from rejecting the new organ, and this medicine also weakens their immune systems. So, Nathan had a lot of trouble fighting off infections after the organ transplant and was often sick.

When Nathan was two-and-a-half years old, he caught pneumonia and was in the hospital. Finally, he was able to come home, but, two nights later, he died. Even though I was devastated, I knew that our family could make it through and everything would all be okay if we just stuck together.

About six months after Nathan died, his third birthday

came around, July 24. My birthday is a couple of days later, on July 29. Usually my family celebrated our birthdays together, but that year I really didn't feel like celebrating mine without him. So, we decided to go ahead and celebrate both of our birthdays and give the gifts that we would have given to Nathan to other kids.

That was Nathan's first toy drive. We gave all the toys to the children at the Cardinal Glennon Children's Hospital in St. Louis, where Nathan had stayed when he was in and out of the hospital. The following year, during the now-annual Nathan Weilbacher Toy Drive, I was able to donate $3,000 and over nine hundred new toys to the children at Cardinal Glennon. The toy drive that I started to honor my brother's memory gets bigger and better each year.

I once heard a saying that some lives go on forever in the hearts and the lives of the people they touch, and I know that this is true with my brother Nathan. I still miss him very much. I will always miss him. He touched my family and my life in so many ways. Recently, he sent me a healthy little brother that we named Nicholas Nathan. I know that my new little brother is a gift from Nathan, because I can see it every time I look into his eyes.

I want to thank Nathan for everything he has taught me and given to me, and I want him to know I love him. I realize that where he is now there is no more suffering and that he is at peace. Nathan, I will always remember you and I will always love you. You will forever be my little angel!

Lauren Ashley Weilbacher, thirteen

Guardian Angel

My dad's side of the family always meets on Christmas Eve to exchange gifts. My Uncle Terry and my Aunt Vikki and their kids, Colin, Maggie, Nolan, Ian and Jenal would come to celebrate Christmas at my dad's house. The December of 1995 was the last time I ever saw my cousin Colin.

I was staying with my dad for the weekend, about a week after Christmas. I was watching television in the bedroom, when he told me to come into the living room and asked me to sit down on the couch. Then he explained to me that my cousin Colin had died.

Colin had been at a friend's house and decided to go home. He called Jenal, his older sister, telling her that he was on his way. Colin never arrived, so on his way home from work Uncle Terry went looking for him and found Colin lying in the snow.

Uncle Terry called my Aunt Vikki, and they rushed Colin to the hospital. The doctors told them that Colin had had a stroke, and they put him on a life support machine. He would be able to live, but he would be a vegetable. My Uncle Terry held Colin in his arms while he and my Aunt Vikki made the hardest decision of their lives: to keep him on the machines or not. They felt Colin shouldn't live that way and decided to let him go. Colin Timothy O'Brien died on December 27, 1995, in Memorial Hospital. He was only eight years old.

I took it pretty hard. Colin and I were about the same age, and our birthdays were only three weeks apart. His viewing, when you go see the person in the casket, was about three or four days after his death. It was extremely sad. Everyone was crying. I still remember seeing him, lying there, so lifeless and peaceful. At his funeral, Father Cam, the priest at Corpus Christi where Colin went to school, said a few words and we all put flowers on top of his casket.

Afterwards, Uncle Terry and Aunt Vikki threw a huge memorial service for Colin at the Corpus Christi school gym. Uncle Terry said a few words, and I asked him if he missed Colin. His reply was, "Yes, I do. A lot." I remember thinking to myself, *so do I . . . a lot.*

After awhile, I couldn't take the fact that Colin was really gone. I couldn't seem to get it out of my mind. So, my mom and dad sent me to a place called hospice. It's a place where they help kids like me deal with the fact of death. I counseled with a lady named Michelle every Wednesday for about a month. We played with things like dolls and Play-Doh while I acted out how I felt about death and my other feelings. Michelle was very nice to me.

I also met with a group of other kids who had lost a family member or friend. We each made a book, which included a letter that we wrote to the loved one, a picture of us with our loved one and other things. The other kids were nice, and I made friends with one girl named Nicole, who had lost her grandma.

Later, I went to camp Evergreen, which was just like a regular camp, only we met in groups to talk about our loved ones, and death. Each camper has a counselor, or a "buddy," that they do almost everything with. My buddy was named Rebecca. On the first day, we all made a necklace with our name on the front and our buddy's name on the back.

I learned a lot from hospice. I understood that Colin was in a better place now and that he was happy. I still miss him every once in a while, and I get a little teary-eyed. But, life goes on. I turned thirteen this year, and I visited Colin's grave. I cried hard because he only got to live eight years of his life. He will never graduate from high school, get married or have kids.

I try to visit Colin's grave whenever I need to talk. I tell him what's going on with me, my friends, school, family, and even boyfriends. It makes me feel better. I believe that Colin is my guardian angel. Doesn't everyone need one?

Colleen O'Brien, thirteen

Dapples

When I first saw her, I knew we were perfect for each other.

And we were.

I had loved horses since I was six and having one changed my life. When I received her as a Christmas gift, I couldn't have been happier. Though she had been neglected and abused her whole life, over the next nine months, she gained trust with me. She soon followed me without my having to lead her, and we became the best of friends. I loved her.

Then, one day, I was riding her in the round pen when she suddenly bucked about four times. Birgit and Arnold, the people we boarded her with, thought that she was too high-strung for me. I cried as Birgit told me that there was a woman who was interested in buying her and would take care of her. The only words I could choke out were, "I don't want to sell her." The words they said after that were a blur because I was so upset I couldn't concentrate on what they were telling me. As I dismounted, I hugged her sweaty neck and cried. I'll never forget what Arnold told me next.

"She ain't goin' nowhere."

He said it to assure me they wouldn't sell her without my permission. Dapples nudged me apologetically. I left the round pen still crying. Over the next few weeks, she still bucked every time I rode her. However, I knew she wasn't trying to get me off intentionally, but she was bucking for some other reason I didn't know about. It made me sick inside that everyone was jumping to conclusions without considering what was going on with Dapples. My own mom even tried to talk me into selling her. I knew my mom was only concerned about my safety, and I also knew she didn't want to sell her any more than I did. My simple answer was always, "No." I would leave the room angry and upset all at once.

Then the unexpected happened. One morning at 5:00, I woke up to my mom talking on the phone to her work. All I can remember her saying is . . .

"Yes, I have a sick child." But I wasn't sick. *Who in my family was so sick that Mom would miss work for the day?*

Mom came into my room and gently shook me to wake me up. "I just got a call from Birgit," Mom said. "She said Dapples just doesn't seem like herself."

I panicked. Colic was the only thing I could think of. It was a horrible stomach sickness that can kill a horse within hours. There are lots of ways it can be caused, but not so many ways to make it go away. If the horse gets cramps, he wants to roll over on the ground to ease the pain. However, in the process, his intestines get twisted up, preventing his body from moving waste through correctly. This kills him if a vet cannot perform surgery and be successful in "untwisting" his gut. Also, if the horse eats dirt along with eating grass or hay, a stone will build up in his stomach and literally block his bowels.

When my sister, mom and I arrived at Birgit's house about an hour later, all I can remember is walking Dapples around in the arena for the next nine hours, trying to help move things through. We left that night exhausted and confused.

The next morning, my mom and I went out there, knowing that if there was no manure in her stall, we had to call the vet out for his last visit to her. I ran to her stall. I screamed as I saw the clean stall with Dapples lying in the corner. I picked up her head. She knew her time was near.

I didn't know what to do. How could I help her? She lay there in the wet dirt with her head in my lap. Her eyes were closed and her stomach was bloated. Two of her friends whinnied from other stalls close to hers. They knew her time was coming soon, too. My beautiful Arabian angel was suffering from colic, and no one could help her. When I looked into her eyes, the spunky Dapples I once knew was gone. All that was left was a helpless little mare, struggling to breathe. I stroked her beautiful face and as much as it killed me inside, I talked to her.

"Don't worry, Dap, you'll never be in a stall again. No more gates. No more saddle. You'll be a free Pegasus. Free to roam the skies. You'll forever live in peace. It'll be okay, Dapples. I'll be okay. I'll be fine. Just think about your wings. Think about your wings." I repeated myself many times. Not just for her, but for my own comfort. I must have told her I loved her a zillion times. I could hardly speak, because my throat felt as though it had closed in. I promised her that she would live in a big green pasture with no fences. I also told her that I would watch for a new star that night—a big, bright star.

While I told her this, she seemed to calm down a bit. I took her out in the arena and prayed for a miracle. She lay in the dirt, and I sat next to her, holding her head. About thirty minutes later the vet arrived, and it was time for Dapples to stop suffering. The vet took the lead rope and said it would be best if I didn't see this. I kissed her on the mane. I could smell the wet dirt in her tangled hair. It was sprinkling outside. Perfect weather for the worst day. "I love you, Dapples," I said before running to the barn.

About two minutes later, I heard her crash to the ground. My mom and I covered her with a blue tarp and then cried together until a truck that hauls away dead animals arrived. I couldn't watch. I sat on a bench at the front of the house.

Soon I saw that horrible truck of death drive away with poor Dapples in the back. The man drove away as though she was worth nothing. I buried my face in my mom's arms and just cried my heart out.

I'll never forget that awful day. I remember telling my mom on the way there to turn off the radio. I didn't want to remember the song that played, because I knew I would hate it for the rest of my life. I still sit in my room and cry sometimes because I know I could have proven to everyone that just because she bucked didn't make her a criminal. It's just like people. Everyone has a chance to be as good as they want to be. It all depends on what goes on in their minds and hearts. I will never know how well Dapples would have done if she would have survived. I am forced to wonder the rest of my life.

She left me before I was ready, but in the short time I owned her, she showed me how strong friendship can be. It can survive anything, even if everyone else is against it.

She also taught me how to trust, to love and to have faith in others. I had faith in her when no one else did. And that is something I'll never regret, or forget.

Nicole Buckner, twelve

7

ON ATTITUDE
AND
PERSPECTIVE

*Each morning when I open my eyes I say to
myself: "I, not events, have the power to
make me happy or unhappy today. I can
choose which it shall be. Yesterday is dead,
tomorrow hasn't arrived yet. I have just
one day, today, and I'm going to be happy
in it."*

Groucho Marx

Big at Heart

Every man stamps his value on himself. . . .
Man is made great or small by his own will.

J. C. F. von Schiller

My best friend's exceptionally small. We're in the fifth grade, but Larry's as short as a first-grader. Although his body's small, Larry's big at heart. He has a sharp mind, too. All the kids who know Larry like him a lot.

Sometimes he gets his share of teasing, but Larry knows how to handle it. When some smart-mouth calls him Dopey, Sleepy or Bashful, Larry just laughs and starts humming, "Hi, Ho!"

Larry loves sports, but he can't play some, like football. One tackle and he would be wiped out. But one sport seems to be made for Larry—baseball. He's our star player. The legs that are too short for track and hurdles can pump up and down, carrying him around those bases faster than you can see. He can slide to safety under a baseman before he's noticed. And when he's in the field, he catches and throws that ball like the biggest of us.

I remember when he first came to try out for our Little

League team. The coach took one look and shook his head.

"No, I'm sorry, but we need big, strong players. Tell you what—we could use a batboy!"

Larry just grinned and said, "Give me a chance to try out. If you still think I'm a weak player, I'll be the best batboy you ever had!"

The coach looked at him with respect, handed him a bat, and said, "Okay, it's a deal."

Well, obviously no pitcher could aim the ball inside Larry's ten-inch strike zone! He would be a sure walk to first base every time, and the coach knew how to take advantage of that. And when he saw how fast Larry's legs could travel and how well he handled the ball, he bent over, patted Larry on the back, and said, "I'm proud to have you on the team."

We had a winning season, and yesterday was our final game. We were tied with the Comets for the championship. Their pitcher, Matt Crenshaw, was a mean kid who never liked Larry—probably because he could never strike him out.

Somehow we held the Comets through the top of the ninth inning, and we were tied when it was our turn at bat. As Matt passed our bench on the way to the pitcher's mound, he snarled at Larry, "Why don't you go back to Snow White where you belong?"

I heard him and jumped up, ready to give Matt a punch, when Larry stepped between us. "Cut it out!" he yelled, pushing me away from Matt. "I can fight for myself."

Matt looked as if he was going to clobber Larry, but my friend held out his hand and said, "Let's play baseball, okay? I know you want your team to win and it must be tough to pitch to a shrimp like me."

"Chicken, you mean. You won't even swing at the ball!" Then he stamped off to the mound as Larry slowly dropped his outstretched hand.

We had two outs when it was Larry's turn at bat. The bases weren't loaded, but the coach told Larry to wait for a walk, as usual. Larry held his ground for three balls. One more and he would walk to first.

Then, for some reason—maybe because Matt had called him "chicken"—Larry reached out for the next pitch. It wasn't anywhere near his strike zone, but he swung the bat up and around. He connected. We heard a loud crack and saw the ball sail over all the outfielders. They had to chase after it, and Larry's legs started churning. Like locomotive wheels, they went faster and faster, rounding second and third and heading for home. The Comets finally retrieved the ball and passed it to the catcher. Larry slid safely under him as he caught it.

We had our winning run, the game was over, and we were the champs. After we were presented with our winner's trophy, we gave it to Larry and took turns putting him on our shoulders and marching around the field.

I was carrying him when we passed Matt. "Put me down for a minute," Larry said. He walked over to Matt with his hand extended again for the handshake Matt had refused earlier.

"It was a good game," Larry said, "and you came close to winning it. . . ."

Matt looked at Larry for what seemed like a long time, but finally Matt took Larry's hand and shook it.

"You may be a shrimp," he said, "but you're no chicken. You deserved to win."

Then Larry and I ran back to the rest of our team. We were all going to the pizza place for a victory celebration. I sure was proud to have Larry as a friend. Like I said, he's big in the ways that really count.

Mark Schulle
As told by Bunny Schulle

The Best Christmas I Never Had

To gain that which is worth having, it may be necessary to lose everything.

Bernadette Devlin

My sister, Yvonne, was fourteen the year our home and everything in it was destroyed. I was seventeen. Our home was heated by a wood-burning stove, and every fall, my family and I would mark dead trees, cut them down, haul the wood and stack it in the basement. The week before Christmas, the basement was half full of dry wood.

Yvonne and I were home from school, and she did as either of us had done a thousand times before: checked the furnace, tossed a few more logs on the fire and slammed the door shut.

At the time, I was upstairs sulking. I had a sink full of dishes to wash, homework to tackle and my grandfather, after a lonely day at home, wouldn't leave me alone. Stomping around the kitchen, listening to him chatter, I thought about how I couldn't wait to get out of this house, this town. *Lightning could strike this very spot and I wouldn't care.* Or so I thought.

The house seemed a little smoky, but that wasn't unusual. It often became that way after the furnace had a few new logs to chew up. I simply waved the smoke away and kept doing dishes and daydreaming of getting away from my family. My sister's cats were no help; they were as starved for affection as Grandpa, and kept twining around my ankles.

My sister wandered in and said, "Don't you think it's a little too smoky in here?"

I shrugged sullenly and kept washing dishes. But after another minute, we knew something was wrong. The smoke was much too thick. My sister and I looked at each other, then at our grandfather. He was the adult, but he lived with us because he couldn't take care of himself. If there were decisions to be made, my sister and I—high school students—would make them. The thought was daunting, to say the least.

Without a word to each other, we went outside and opened the garage door (foolish in retrospect) and stared in disbelief as smoke and flames boiled out.

We had no time for tears or hysterics. That would come later. Instead, we both turned and ran up the hill. My sister shot through the kitchen door and raced for Grandpa's coat while I searched frantically for my keys. "There's a fire, Grandpa," I said abruptly. *Where in the world had I put my purse?* "We have to get out."

"Oh. Okay," he agreed. Amiable as a child, Grandpa stood still while my sister jerked him into his coat. She made sure he was warm and tightly bundled, forced warm slippers on his feet and hustled him out the door. I was so busy wondering where my keys were and trying the phone, which was dead, I never noticed that in her great care to make sure our grandfather was protected from the elements, she had neglected her own coat and boots.

I glanced out the window, blinking from the smoke.

December in Minnesota was no joke . . . and no place for two teenagers and an old man to await help. If I could find my keys, I could get back down to the garage and probably, if the flames hadn't spread that far, back the van out of the garage. We could wait for help in relative comfort, and at least my mom's van could be saved.

Memory flashed; I had tossed my purse in my room when I'd come home. My room was at the end of a long hallway, far from the kitchen. Daughter and granddaughter of professional firefighters, I should have known better. But things were happening so quickly—my little sister and my grandfather were standing in the snow, shivering—I had to get the van. So I started for my room, the worst decision I've ever made.

The smoke was gag-inducing, a thick gray-black. It smelled like a thousand campfires and I tried not to think about what was being destroyed: my family's pictures, their clothes, furniture. I'd gone three steps and couldn't see, couldn't hear, couldn't breathe. *How was I going to make it all the way to my room?*

I wasn't, of course. I instantly knew two things: if I went down that hallway, I would die. Number two, what was I still doing in this inferno? Ten-year-olds were taught better. My sister was probably terrified, and in another moment, she'd come after me. How stupid could I be?

I stumbled back to the kitchen, took one last glance around my home, then went out into the snow.

Yvonne was sobbing, watching our house burn to the foundation. Grandpa was patting her absently. "That's what insurance is for," he said. A veteran of the New York City Fire Department, I couldn't imagine how many house fires he had fought. For the first time, I could see him as a real person and not my aged, feeble grandfather who took up entirely too much of my time with his endless pleas for me to sit down and talk to him.

"I'm going to the neighbors' to call for help," Yvonne said abruptly. She was wearing a sweater, jeans and slippers. I was in sweat pants, a T-shirt and socks. The closest neighbor was down the length of our driveway and across the highway, about a mile.

"Okay," I said. "Be careful crossing the . . ." But she was gone, already running through the snow and down the driveway.

Then I remembered Yvonne's three cats, which were, I guessed, trapped in the house. *When she remembered them*, I thought, *she would go right out of her mind*.

It seemed she was only gone for a moment before I saw her puffing up the driveway. "I called," she gasped, "they're on their way."

"You should have stayed with the neighbors and gotten warm," I said, mad at myself because I hadn't told her to stay put.

She gave me a look. "I couldn't leave you out here in the cold."

"Actually, I'm not that . . . ," I began, when suddenly Yvonne clapped her hands to her face and screamed.

"Oh my God, the cats!" she shrieked, then burst into hoarse sobs.

"It's okay, Yvonne, it's okay, I saw them get out," I said frantically, reaching for her. I could tell she didn't believe me, but she didn't say anything more, just wept steadily and ignored my fervent assurances—my lies.

As it swiftly grew dark, our burning house lit up the sky. It was as beautiful as it was awful. And the smell . . . to this day, whenever someone lights a fire in a fireplace, I have to leave the room briefly. A lot of people find fireplaces soothing, but to me the smell of burning wood brings back the sense of desolation and the sound of my sister's sobs.

We could hear sirens in the distance and moved out of the way as two fire trucks and the sheriff pulled in. The sheriff screeched to a halt and beckoned to us. In another minute he was talking to my grandfather while Yvonne and I sat in the back of the police car, getting warm.

After a long moment, Yvonne sighed. "I just finished my Christmas shopping yesterday."

I snorted . . . and the snort became a giggle, and the giggle bloomed into a laugh. That got my sister going, and we laughed until we cried and then laughed some more.

"I got you the CD you wanted," I told her.

"Really?" she said. "I bought you a new Walkman."

We listed all the things we had bought for friends and family that were now burning to cinders. Instead of being depressing, it was probably the highlight of the evening. The sheriff interrupted our spiritual gift-giving to open the door and say, "Your parents are here."

We scrambled out and raced down the driveway. If I live to be one thousand, I'll never forget my mother's face at that moment: bloodless and terrified. She saw us and opened her arms. We hurled ourselves at her, though we were both considerably taller than she was and nearly toppled her back into the snow. Dad looked us over, satisfied too that we weren't hurt, and some of the tension went out of his shoulders. "What are you crying about?" he asked, pretending annoyance. "We've got insurance. And now we'll get a new house for Christmas."

"Dad . . . for Christmas . . . I got you those fishing lures you wanted but . . ."

He grinned. "That reminds me. I picked up your presents on the way home." He stepped to the truck and pulled out two garment bags. Inside were the gorgeous jackets Yvonne and I had been longing for since we'd fallen in love with them at the mall.

We shrugged into them, ankle-deep in snow, while the house crackled and burned in front of us. It was a strange way to receive a Christmas present, but neither of us were complaining.

"We'll have to come back here tomorrow," Dad said. "It's going to be depressing and stinky and muddy and frozen and disgusting and sad. Most of our stuff will be destroyed. But they're only things. They can't love you back. The important thing is that we're all okay. The house could burn down a thousand times and I wouldn't care, as long as you guys were all right."

He looked at us again and walked away, head down, hands in his pockets. Mom told us later he had driven ninety miles an hour once he'd seen the smoke, that they both gripped the other's hand while he raced to the house. Not knowing if we were out safe was the worst moment of her life.

Later we found out the pipe leading from the furnace to the wall had collapsed, spilling flaming coals all over our basement. If it had happened at 2:00 A.M., we all would have died of smoke inhalation. In less than half an hour, our house transformed from a safe haven to a death trap. Asleep, we would have had no chance.

We lived in a motel for more than a month, and we spent Christmas Day in my grandmother's crowded apartment eating take-out because she was too tired to cook. For Christmas, Yvonne and I got our jackets and nothing else. My parents got nothing except the headache of dealing with insurance companies. All the wonderful things my family had bought for me had been destroyed in less time than it takes to do a sink full of dishes. But through it all I had gained long-overdue appreciation for my family. We were together. That was really all that mattered.

I'll always remember it as the best Christmas I never had.

MaryJanice Davidson

The Hidden Treasure

Old Man Donovan was a mean man who hated children. He threw rocks at them and even shot at them with a shotgun. At least that's what we had heard.

His small farm bordered our neighborhood where my younger sister, Leigh Ann, and I lived when we were growing up. His farm was long, narrow and quaint. It held two treasures. One was his beautiful fruit.

There were many varieties of fruit: pears, apples and lots more I just can't think of. The fruit naturally drew the children to his land. It made them into thieves. But my sister and I didn't dare to take his fruit because of the horrible rumors we had heard about Old Man Donovan.

One summer day, we were playing in a nearby field. It was time to head back home. My sister and I were feeling very daring that day. There was a short cut to our house that went through the Donovan farm. We thought he wouldn't be able to see us run across his property around the luscious fruit trees. We were almost through the farm when we heard, "Hey, girls!" in a gruff, low voice. We stopped dead in our tracks! There we were, face to face, with Old Man Donovan. Our knees were shaking. We had visions of rocks pounding our bodies and bullets piercing our hearts.

"Come here," he said, reaching up to one of his apple trees. Still shaking, we went over to him. He held out several ripe, juicy, red apples. "Take these home," he commanded. We took the apples with surprised hearts and ran all the way home. Of course, Leigh Ann and I ate the apples.

As time went on, we often went through Old Man Donovan's farm, and he kept on giving us more luscious fruit. One day, we stopped by to see him when he was on his front porch. We talked to him for hours. While he was talking, we realized that we had found the other hidden treasure: the sweet, kind heart hidden behind his gruff voice. Soon, he was one of our favorite people to talk to. Unfortunately, his family never seemed to enjoy our company. They never smiled or welcomed us in.

Every summer, we would visit Mr. Donovan and talk to him. He told us all kinds of stories we loved to hear. But one summer, we heard that he was sick. When we found out that he had come home from the hospital, we visited him right away. His voice box had been removed. When he placed his fingers on his throat, his voice came out as a whisper. We couldn't understand him, but through his eyes we could tell what he meant.

The next winter, word got around that Old Man Donovan had died. Leigh Ann and I were heartbroken and decided to go to the funeral. We were scared because we didn't know if the family would welcome us.

When we got to the funeral, the family kindly greeted us and said they were so glad we had come. We all wept mournfully, but our wonderful memories of Old Man Donovan comforted us.

During those summers with Mr. Donovan, my sister and I learned not to judge a heart until you know it. One may just find a hidden treasure.

Debbie King
As told by Ashley King, eleven

The Snow Angel

Love the moment, and the energy of that moment will spread beyond all boundaries.

Corita Kent

Ever since I was little, my favorite season was winter. I loved to play in the snow and enjoy the hot chocolate.

Unfortunately, winter never gave me the special gift of snow on my birthday. The snow disappeared before my birthday and started after it.

I would ask my grandmother why it didn't snow on my birthday. She would laugh and tell me I asked too many questions. But one day, she promised that she would make it snow when I was enjoying life to the fullest. I thanked her and asked for snow on my next birthday.

That year, before my birthday, my grandmother died. I was at an emotional loss, but angry because she had promised me to make it snow. The day of my sixth birthday, I woke up and ran to my window, hoping to see just one snowflake.

Unfortunately, there was no snow. I cried and cried all day because my grandmother had let me down.

Before my birthday every year, I would pray for snow but it never came. I felt mad at my grandmother; she had broken a promise.

By my sixteenth birthday, I had lost all hope of getting my snow, even though I still wished for it. During my party, I had the best time ever! I enjoyed the company of my friends and family, and I was truly happy.

I was outside with a friend when she asked me if I was having a good time. I told her I was having the best time ever! I was enjoying life to the fullest. Then I saw the white snow falling all around. I became like a little child on Christmas morning as I ran around screaming and laughing. I was so excited that my friends looked at me as if I were crazy, and I think I was. They asked me if I had ever seen snow before, and I laughed and said that I had, but that this was special snow. They all laughed at me, but I didn't care.

When I got home, my grandpa told me he had a gift for me. I was confused because he had already given me my gift. He gave me a small white box that had snowflake wrapping on it. The box looked old, and it was turning a little yellow. I asked him what it was and he told me to stop asking so many questions and just open it. I did, and nestled in white paper was a crystal snowflake with a card that said, "Happy Birthday."

I asked my grandfather how this could be. He told me that it was my grandmother's final wish to give me this on my "sweet sixteenth." I cried and hugged him, although he didn't understand. I said a silent prayer to my smiling grandmother angel who I was certain was, and always had been, watching over me.

Christine Fishlinger, sixteen

You'll Be Good for Him

I heard the rhythmic clatter of metal crutches coming down the hallway. I looked up to see ten-year-old Brian smiling at me in the doorway, his blond hair tousled. Every day, Brian arrived at school cheerful and ready to work.

Brian had a great sense of humor and loved his own jokes. He was my first "handicapped" student. Everyone who worked with Brian told me, "You'll be good for him."

Brian worked with the adaptive physical education teacher and swam three mornings a week. He kept a busy school-day schedule. Everything he did required more effort than it did for the other students.

One day, Brian agreed to talk to the class about his handicap. The students liked Brian and wondered what he did after school. He told them that he watched a lot of TV, or played with his dog. Brian felt proud to be a Cub Scout and enjoyed being a member.

The students then asked him why he used different paper and a special magnifying lens and lamp when he read. Brian explained that he had a tracking problem, and that he could see better out of one eye than the other. "I'm going to have another eye operation," he said casually. "I'm used to it. I've already had six operations." He laughed nervously, adjusting his thick-lens glasses. Brian had already had two hip surgeries, two ankle surgeries and two eye surgeries.

Brian explained how he'd been trained to fall when he lost his balance, so that he wouldn't hurt himself. I felt badly when he fell, but he didn't fuss. I admired his fortitude.

He said he often felt left out, then somebody asked if people ever made fun of him. He replied that he'd been called every name you could think of, but that he usually tried to ignore it.

I asked Brian if he ever became discouraged.

"Well, to tell you the truth," he said, "I do. Sometimes I get really mad if I can't do something. Sometimes I even cry."

At this point I ended the discussion. I felt the important questions had been answered. The students applauded.

"Can you walk at all without your crutches?" one of the boys shouted.

"Yeah," he said shyly.

"Would you like to walk for us?" I asked him gently.

"Yeah! Come on, Brian. You can do it!" several students shouted.

"Well—I guess," he answered reluctantly.

Brian removed his crutches and balanced himself. He proceeded to walk awkwardly across the room. "I look like a drunk," he muttered. It wasn't smooth, but Brian walked on his own. Everyone clapped and shouted.

"That's great, Brian!" I placed my hand on his shoulder.

Brian laughed nervously while I had to hold back tears. His honesty and courage touched me. I then realized that maybe I wasn't as good for Brian as he was good for me—for all of us.

Eugene Gagliano

Scott

It was time for the ice cream social fund-raiser that my small youth group had awaited for many months. The group consisted of five boys; one of them was Scott.

Scott always had a positive attitude. He looked on the bright side of things and never criticized anyone. But Scott was different from the rest of us. He was disabled. Oftentimes, he was unable to participate in activities. No one ever made fun of him to his face, but at times, people would snicker or stare in his presence. But Scott never worried; he just kept his head up high and ignored them.

Finally, the night of the ice cream social came. We rushed to the church basement and waited with scoopers in hand for the guests to arrive. One by one, people filed in, all hoping to get a nice, creamy glob of ice cream. But what they ended up getting was a hard, frozen mass. We waited for awhile for the ice cream to thaw, and eventually it did.

Once the ice cream thawed, we had another problem. It had melted into three pools of vanilla, chocolate and strawberry. But we persisted in serving it. We all had our chance to serve, except for Scott. So, being as kind as possible, we gave Scott a chance to scoop and serve.

As soon as Scott gripped the scooper, our ice cream troubles turned into the World's Greatest Ice Cream Massacre. Milky ice cream was flung in every direction. Scott wouldn't stop. He kept scooping and scooping and scooping. Then, suddenly, in the thick of the chaos, Scott stopped. We looked at Scott. Scott looked at us. And that's when I realized why he had stopped.

Scott was looking at a small, cute girl who entered the basement. Scott stated, "That's m-m-my friend." Our jaws fell open. The most beautiful girl we had seen all night was Scott's friend.

We pushed Scott out of the way, hoping that we could get to serve her. But Scott just looked at us and said, "I-I-I want to scoop the ice cream for her." We backed off.

The girl slowly approached him. Scott stood poised, ready to scoop again. The girl said, "Hi, Scott."

"H-h-hi," stuttered Scott.

She began to make conversation with him by saying, "Look. I got my new braces today." She looked up and gave a wide, bright smile to show off her gleaming braces.

"Th-th-they're neat," responded Scott. The two carried on a short conversation then the girl sat down.

That night I realized that somebody had overlooked Scott's problems and had seen him as a friendly, normal human being.

I realized something else, too. It was time for all of us to see Scott the same way.

David Ferino, twelve

Adam's Apples

After all, there is but one race—humanity.

George Moore

One afternoon, my son came home from school with a puzzled look on his face. After asking him what was on his mind he said, "Are all people the same even if their skin color is different?"

I thought for a moment, then I said, "I'll explain, if you can just wait until we make a quick stop at the grocery store. I have something interesting to show you."

At the grocery store, I told him that we needed to buy apples. We went to the produce section where we bought some red apples, green apples and yellow apples.

At home, while we were putting all the groceries away, I told Adam, "It's time to answer your question." I put one of each type of apple on the countertop: first a red apple, followed by a green apple and then a yellow apple. Then I looked at Adam, who was sitting on the other side of the counter.

"Adam, people are just like apples. They come in all different colors, shapes and sizes. See, some of the apples have been bumped around and are bruised. On the out-side, they may not even look as delicious as the others." As I was talking, Adam was examining each one carefully.

Then, I took each of the apples and peeled them, plac-ing them back on the countertop, but in a different place.

"Okay, Adam, tell me which one is the red apple, the green apple and the yellow apple."

He said, "I can't tell. They all look the same now."

"Take a bite of each one. See if that helps you figure out which one is which."

He took big bites, and then a huge smile came across his face. "People are just like apples! They are all different, but once you take off the outside, they're pretty much the same on the inside."

"Right," I agreed. "Just like how everyone has their own personality but are still basically the same."

He totally got it. I didn't need to say or do anything else.

Now, when I bite into an apple, it tastes a little sweeter than before. What perfect food for thought.

Kim Aaron

Who Said There's No Crying in Softball?

Character building begins in our infancy and continues until death.

Eleanor Roosevelt

Our team was playing softball against a team that we were tied with for third place. I was toughing out the position of catcher, and we were winning. However, my knees started to not feel so tough. In the bottom of the second inning they had started to hurt.

I've had bad tendonitis in my knees, and I just couldn't take any more abuse to them that day. So I limped over to the manager, who is also my dad, and told him that my knees were hurting. I asked if he could have the back-up catcher, Jill, catch for the rest of the game. He called Jill into the dugout and told her to put on the catcher's gear.

One of the other coaches overheard this conversation and came running over. I could tell that he was mad at my dad's decision because he was steaming like a whistling teapot.

He yelled at my dad, "Are you crazy? Jill can't catch—she has a huge cut on her finger!"

My dad explained to the coach about my knees.

"So what!" The coach rudely yelled at my dad.

Then he furiously walked over to me. His face was red, and I could feel my heart pounding in my chest.

"You'd better get that gear back on and get back out there right now. If you don't, I swear this will be the worst softball season of your life! Every game! Every game you complain about your stupid knees! If your knees keep hurting so much, I don't understand why you even play! You certainly aren't even good enough!" he screamed at me.

I couldn't believe what he said to me. Amazingly, I was able to choke through my tears, "I'm sorry! My knees hurt so bad! If I catch any more I'll collapse!"

"So what! Do you think I care?" he yelled.

By that time I was sobbing hard. The coach stormed off grumbling something over and over, leaving me in tears.

Later that night, I was lying in my bed thinking. Then a very important question came to my mind.

Why should I continue my softball season if I don't even have any respect? I asked myself.

Then, from somewhere deep inside my heart, I found the answer.

It doesn't matter what the coach thinks about me, it only matters what I think about myself. I love softball and I have a right to play, even though I may not be the best catcher in the world. That doesn't make me a loser. But I would be a loser if I believed what he said instead of believing in myself. I would lose my self-respect. No one, even the coach, can make me quit. All I have to do to be a winner is to keep showing up, sore knees and all. And I will.

Amy Severns, twelve

The Yellow Piece of Paper

When you're a young teen, it can seem like your parents have no feelings whatsoever. They don't understand when you just HAVE to get that new CD, even though you don't like the music that much. And that you HAVE to buy the new swimsuit, even though it costs sixty dollars for just two inches of material. Or, that you MUST impress the object of your affection by showing up at the movies, even though you'll dump him after two weeks of boredom. And then you have a huge zit and you need a dermatologist RIGHT AWAY, even though no one else can even see the zit.

These were my sentiments exactly. I never cared about my parents' feelings. I thought they weren't like me and had no idea what emotions were. I didn't believe that they could ever feel the same things I could. How could they? In my mind, they were old and cranky and that was that.

Then all that changed.

Snooping through my mom's purse was sort of a pastime of mine. It was usually for money, which—with my mom's permission to retrieve—allowed me to go to the movies or wherever the hot spot of the evening was. It was like an art form to dig through my mom's purse. Messy was one word for it, but I can think of others! I never found anything too interesting, so I tried to keep my digs quick and to the point, which was getting my money.

One Friday night, while I was looking for ten dollars, I pulled out my mom's black wallet. A piece of yellow paper fell out.

Curiosity killed the cat. . . . Right?

Naturally, I hesitated.

Satisfaction brought him back.

I opened the piece of paper. It looked like a diary entry of some sort. Maybe it wasn't my mom's? That was highly doubtful, considering it was her sloppy cursive. I read it. It hit me; it was about my brother and his friend who died of leukemia. I didn't remember ever meeting the boy, who died when I was barely three.

I was overcome with shock as I read the contents of the letter. I quickly folded up the piece of paper and put it back where I had found it.

The next day, my curiosity overcame me again. Making sure my mom was out of the room, I got out the piece of yellow paper and read it again. It said:

June 3, 1987

I saw grief on my son's face today. He is eight years old. His friend died from leukemia. I've seen hurt, anger and bewilderment on my son's face, but never before have I seen grief on the face of one so young. I wonder what he is thinking. I told him that his friend had become an angel. Even though I had tried to avoid the word "died," he immediately realized what I meant. I'll never forget his look. Somehow I didn't expect such an adult expression of anguish. My angel story could not remove the pain of the passing of his friend. We knew for several months the bone marrow transplants had failed and that my son's friend was on limited time. And yet when the call came, I felt shocked. I had just seen him a couple of weeks before and he looked so good. How could God let life rob us of him so soon?

I keep thinking of his mother's pain. Her son died in her arms on the way to the hospital. Where did he go? How will she survive the loss? The pain must be so great. I see her grasping, trying to find her son. As a mother, it pains me to think of her great agony. There can be no experience worse than the loss of one's child.

For all of us, things will now be different. Next year, in the third grade, there won't be a seat waiting for my son's friend to come back. Our parish won't be praying anymore for that miracle. And his mother will be forever grasping, trying to find her son.

I cried a little, thinking about what my brother had to go through at such a young age. At least he had my mom, dad, sister and a little baby—me—to love him and help him through it.

My mom actually did have more feelings than I thought. Maybe my small problems of needing to have a certain CD, of buying a swimsuit, the need to impress some guy or an invisible zit weren't as important as I thought.

I can't say that, after reading the letter, all of those things still don't cross my mind, but I have a new respect for my mom. I don't ask her for things *as much,* and I don't yell and cry *as much* when she says, "No."

What did change was that I can tell her more about my own feelings, because now I feel that she will understand. I'm glad I found out early enough, before I grew up and left home. I have my mom to talk to, when I need to.

I don't know what would have happened if I had never read that letter. I don't think I want to know. I'm just glad that I did.

Lauren Thorbjornsen, fourteen

Hard Work Pays Off

*The road to happiness lies in two simple principles:
find out what it is that interests you and that you
   can do well,
and when you find it, put your whole soul into it—
every bit of energy and ambition and natural
ability you have.*

John D. Rockefeller III

As a young boy, I grew up with my eight siblings in a tin-roofed shack in Summerfield, Louisiana. I didn't see my circumstance as an obstacle, even though we didn't even have a real toilet in the house. I saw my life more as a card that had been dealt to me and I tried to make the most of it.

I was the youngest of five boys and also had four sisters who had to pull together and take care of each other. Dad wasn't around, so I never knew him well. He committed suicide when I was three years old, leaving Mom with the job of raising and providing for nine kids. She worked at a sawmill running a forklift for fifty dollars a week and had another job at a poultry plant. She was a very hard worker, and in order to make ends meet, she hardly ever rested.

My mom believed in doing all she could do to take care of her responsibilities, so no matter what, she never asked for a handout. You can imagine; we kids didn't get what we wanted, but we always got the things we needed. With my mom as my example, I learned that hard work is the best way to get what you want.

While growing up, I was surrounded with temptations to do negative things like drugs, alcohol and all that. I chose not to go there. Even as a little boy, I knew I was going to be successful. Some people take that to be cocky or conceited, but I wasn't going to let anybody tell me that I couldn't do whatever I set out to do.

Of course, I dreamed about what I wanted to be when I grew up. At first, I wanted be a state trooper, then I wanted to be in the Special Forces. After awhile, I decided that I wanted to drive eighteen-wheelers. There was even a period of time that I wanted to be in construction. I wanted to play football in high school; in fact, I still do. But regardless of what I chose, I wanted to make my brothers, sisters and mom proud of me—not only by being successful in what I chose to do, but also as a person who could be looked up to for the right reasons.

Surprising as it might seem, basketball wasn't in my plans. One day, my mom cut a rim off an old water barrel and then held it up for me to throw an old rubber ball through. By junior high, I started playing basketball on a team. I loved to compete. There was a positive high I got by going out and playing against other people and working hard to win. For me, it paid off. I just let my success in basketball take its course but I always put the effort in, every day.

No matter what I've done, some people wait for my downfall, saying, "Karl Malone can't do it." Instead of letting people like that get to me, they are actually my motivation and I continue to prove them wrong every single day. I try to do the best job I can in a positive way on and off the court. I realize that no matter what I'm dealing with, there's somebody else out there who has it a little bit worse off. I've been there. And I know that without continued hard work, I could be there again.

I am grateful for the life I've enjoyed as a basketball star. But when I see these shirts that say "Basketball is life," I think *Yeah, right!* It is not life. It can be exciting. But the important thing about basketball is that it gives me a way to do good things for others as I move through this journey called life.

Success is really about choosing right from wrong, making a positive contribution to the world around you and valuing the things that are really important—like family and friends.

While everyone else was looking to popular athletes, actors and musicians as positive role models, my mom was my inspiration, and she continues to be all these years later. She taught me that hard work never killed anybody. My mom is my hero. She, my family and friends bring me more joy than anything else in life does.

At the end of my life, I don't want to be remembered as the kind of person who just sat on his rear end and said, "I've made it." I don't ever want to have to say that I didn't give it everything that I've got. Sure there are days that I don't feel like working hard . . . but I do it anyway, 'cause that's who I am.

Karl Malone

Staying True to Myself

This above all; to thine own self be true.

William Shakespeare

I don't know why I believed them after all the teasing and bullying they had put me through.

When the bell rang for our lunch period, once again, the four of them tricked me. "Oh, y'all, we're just gonna go out and play," they said as two of them grabbed my hands.

It was cold outside and there was a lot of snow on the ground. They led me far away from where all the other kids were playing and then, before I knew it, they pushed me down and began hitting me. They said all kinds of mean things to me, like I was the teacher's pet and that I thought I was better than them. Then they dug my head into the snow until I thought I was about to suffocate.

"Stop it. I can't breathe! *I can't breathe!*" I pleaded. That kind of scared them, and they finally got off me, pulled me up out of the slush and helped me into the nurse's office. Scratched, bruised and cold, I listened to them tell the nurse, "We was just playin' and all of a sudden she say she can't breathe." I couldn't wait for those girls to get out of the nurse's office, so that I could tell the truth.

After that, my mother came up to the school and had meetings with everybody she could, but nothing changed. The girls continued to bully me every chance they got.

As a fourth-grader growing up in a small town in Illinois, I didn't have the best of everything, like designer clothes, but Mom made sure my clothes were clean. I was light skinned with long hair, and it could be that those girls thought that I was stuck up because of it. But I was just a kid who enjoyed doing my schoolwork and getting good grades. I always tried to make friends with everybody. As far as I knew, I never did anything wrong to any of those four girls.

After that day on the playground, I was scared every single day. Being at school was a living nightmare. Even after school I was terrified that once I left the classroom to go to my grandmother's car, the girls would jump me. So, I had to have a security officer escort me out every day. My mother had to take me to the doctor's office all the time because there would be something wrong with my stomach, but they could never figure out what it was. Finally, in the fifth grade, I switched elementary schools. School is supposed to be where you learn and make friends—it shouldn't be about having your grades suffer because you gotta watch your back instead of pay attention and do the work.

For the next two years, my school life was wonderful. I made good grades and good friends. Then in seventh grade, I had to face the bully girls again. We hadn't seen each other in several years, so I was thinking that maybe they had grown up some. You know, I actually almost befriended them because I was so scared that if I didn't, they would mess with me again. But I asked myself, *Do I change or stay myself and succeed?* I chose to stay true to myself.

As the year went on, the girls would get into fights all the time and mess with other girls. At one point, some friends of mine that I had grown up with got into it with them. It was one group of girls against the other group of girls. The bully girls were pressuring me to fight on their side. I figured that if I didn't, I would probably become their target of abuse again.

I knew it was about to be blood, sweat and tears in the hallway, and I felt trapped. Then, just as the fight was about to go down, I heard one of the girls say, "Don't mess with her." I was like, *Thank you, 'cause I didn't do anything.* I strongly believe that this was God's protection for me.

I quickly ran into a nearby classroom, and I told the teacher what was about to happen. But before anyone could stop them, the fight began. Girls were screaming, punching, pulling hair and just going crazy. Thankfully, the teachers and principal stopped them before anyone got seriously hurt.

From then on, I knew that God really was looking out for me. I was able to trust him with my life and move forward with less fear of the bully girls. Amazingly, they finally lost interest in me and picked on other girls instead. When high school came, we were zoned to go to different schools. Finally, I had the peace of knowing that I never had to deal with them again.

As I matured and was able to look at those girls' situations, I realized that most of them did not have the love and support of a stable family. I had both parents at home and a very close family. Plus, I was raised in church, and there is something different about people who really are committed to having a Christian life. I had a strong knowledge that I was unique and that the people who really mattered to me loved me. Those girls could never persuade me that being part of a gang could offer me more than that truth. But since they didn't have a strong family or spiritual life, I guess being part of that girl gang gave them a sense of belonging and some security.

My small town hasn't changed much. Over the years, when I go home, I sometimes hear about what has become of the girls who bullied me. One was always back and forth into juvenile hall. I'm not sure what became of her in the long run. All I know is, I wouldn't trade places with any of them.

I'm just so thankful that I stayed on track with my studies and stayed true to expressing my talents and interests. It has taken me to the most amazing places: best-selling records, Grammys, a leading role on Broadway....

From here, my destiny is in God's hands, just as it always has been.

Michelle Williams
Destiny's Child

[EDITORS' NOTE: *For more information about how to deal with bullies, log on to* www.kidshealth.org. *(key word search: "bullying").*]

No, Really . . .
Barney Ate My Report Card!

It is easy to dodge our responsibilities, but we cannot dodge the consequences of dodging our responsibilities.

Sir Josiah Stamp

As a preteen, I felt hopelessly ordinary. When I had to go to a new school where I didn't know anyone, I decided that I was going to make a lot of friends quickly and be really popular. I decided that the only way I could be popular was to make myself interesting, intriguing and therefore, worth knowing. So . . . I decided to tell fibs to get people to like me.

Most of the fibs I told were what my grandmother called "white lies," which are lies you tell people that "won't hurt them." I made up tall tales about celebrities I knew, how rich my family was and exotic places I had visited. I figured that since these lies didn't hurt anyone, that made them only "white lies."

My strategy began to work, and I suddenly became very popular. All my new friends thought I was cool. Of course, none of the stuff I told them was true and eventually, I started to feel a little guilty about it. My newfound popularity was also causing my grades to suffer terribly because being very social was my main focus. I simply didn't have time for homework.

The day our third semester report cards came out, my heart dropped into my stomach. My grade point average went from a 92 percent to a 79 percent. And . . . I had actually flunked English! How crazy was that?

I visualized what kind of torturous punishment my parents would have in store for me because of my bad grades. I figured it would be something like losing my phone privileges, or being grounded until the following semester.

Before I went home that day, my new best friend invited me to her birthday sleepover party. Everyone who was anyone in the school was going to be there. There was no doubt in my mind that my parents wouldn't allow me to go after they saw my report card. There was only one thing for me to do. I would hide my report card until after the party was over.

Weeks went by and my parents asked me every day where my report card was. I kept telling them that I hadn't gotten it yet. They had no reason *not* to believe me, as I had never lied to them before.

The party came and went and I decided that I was ready to face the music about my report card. There was just one little problem. I forgot where I had put it!

One morning at breakfast, Mom finally threatened to call the school. I panicked. I needed more time to try and find where I'd hidden it. If she called the school, she'd find out that I'd gotten the report card almost a month before. Somehow, I talked her out of it.

When I came home from school that day, I glanced at my dog Barney, who was lying on the floor. I noticed a little piece of blue paper sticking out of her mouth and I froze in my tracks. There was my dog, sitting in the middle of the kitchen floor, chewing on *my report card!* My mind reeled. Then, I remembered. I had hidden it in the downstairs closet on the shelf below the dog food. I thought that no one would find it there. Okay—no one with two legs, anyway. With perfect timing, my mom walked into the room, and asked the million dollar question:

"What's Barney chewing on?"

I felt like I was wearing cement shoes as my mother walked over to the dog and pulled the report card out of her mouth. Unfortunately for me, the paper apparently wasn't too appetizing to a dog's taste buds. All of my substandard grades were still as clear as day. So was the date on the top of the report card, which was dated four weeks before.

Needless to say, for lying to them (more so than for the bad grades) my parents grounded me from the phone *and* from going anywhere with my friends until the end of the school year. That really screwed up my social life. Plus, I had bragged to my friends about how cool my parents were because they *never* grounded me.

When my friends called, not only did they find out that the "no grounding" policy was not exactly accurate, but through conversations with my parents, they found out that I had been lying about almost everything else, as well.

It took a long time for me to get my friends' trust back, and even longer for me to regain my parents' belief in me. But I learned the most valuable lesson in my life—there is no such thing as a white lie. Every lie, no matter how small it may seem, is still a lie. Eventually, it will end up biting you in the rear.

Jenn Dlugos

There Is Always
Someone Less Fortunate

Self-denial is painful for a moment, but very agreeable in the end.

Jane Taylor

It's 8:00 A.M., and Mum just called me to get up. I'm lying in bed daydreaming about what I want to do today. I want to stay home and listen to my CDs. I want to work on my tan and then swim in the pool when I get hot. I want to play basketball with my friends and just hang out. I want to watch television and go on my PC and chat with my friends online.

It's 8:30 A.M. now, and Mum is shouting at me to get up. So, I get up, put my swimsuit on and take my CD Walkman outside and lie in the sun for a little bit.

Then my mum comes out telling me that I need to get dressed into some nice clothes that are not going to be too hot for me to walk around in. I ask why do I need to do that—I'm staying home, working on my tan and just chilling for the day. But Mum wants me to go out with her. She tells me a lot about this place called Give Kids the World.

It's a special place for families to spend a vacation when a child has a life-threatening illness. She sometimes goes and meets families at the airport and escorts them to the village. There are several jobs she does there, including serving ice cream and gift giving. I expect this is a very boring job to do, but Mum says I will enjoy it.

So, I get dressed in suitable clothes, get in the car and Mum drives to this place. I think it looks really childlike and silly. There is a warehouse at the back of the village that we go into to do our work. I have to put food into boxes. I don't know why, but I do it anyway. Then I have to put some gifts on the back of a golf cart. Mum tells me we are going to deliver a toy to every child in the village. Mum and I then start off on the rounds. We go to the first villa but no one is home, so we leave the gifts for the children to find when they get back.

We pull up to the next house, and I knock on the door and shout, "Gift giving," and a woman answers the door. She tells me I can come in, so I go in. Sitting in the middle of the living room is a young boy in a wheelchair. I give him the gifts I have for him, and his face lights up with joy. I walk out and think to myself, *That must be a real pain, not being able to jump around or play basketball.*

At another villa a bit later on, I knock on the door, again shouting "Gift giving," and another person answers the door. I go in this villa, and lying on a chair is a little girl with tubes in her nose and one coming from her tummy. Her brother is feeding her through a tube. The food is a milky liquid and looks disgusting. I did the same as before—gave them their gifts and walked out. I suddenly thought that it must really be uncomfortable lying there not being able to feed yourself or to be able to eat anything you want, especially sweets and chocolate.

I get to the third house, and I do the same process again. As I come in with the gifts, it seems a little strange that the child doesn't notice me. Her mum says that she is deaf and only partially sighted, so I need to go and stand in front of her, so she can see the gift. When I do that, she gets very excited and makes a sign with her hands. Her mum tells me this is the sign for thank you. I ask her mum how you say good-bye in sign language. She shows me and I sign to the little girl, and she signs back as I leave the house.

Once back in the cart, I ask my mum what is wrong with these kids. Mum tells me that they all have life-threatening illnesses and that they might not live to see tomorrow. That is shocking to me. Suddenly, I realize that I should be more thankful that I don't have these illnesses—that I am not in the same position as these kids. I no longer want to be at home working on my tan, listening to my CDs, playing basketball or swimming in the pool. I would much rather be doing this, seeing things that not a lot of people really get to see, maybe making a difference in these kids' lives.

My first visit to Give Kids the World was over six months ago, and I now go on a regular basis. I have even taken one of my friends along as well. I do miss spending the time at home and hanging out with my friends, but I wouldn't want to miss the opportunity to make a difference to these kids who are much worse off than I am.

Amy Mallinder-Morgan, twelve

[EDITORS' NOTE: *For information about Give Kids the World, go to* www.gktw.org.]

Thirteen Candles

When my thirteenth birthday came around, I didn't announce the occasion to anyone and made no plans.

"What do you want to do for your birthday?" my mother asked me.

"Nothing," I said.

"Do you want to invite any friends over?"

"What friends?"

My expectations for this birthday were set low. That way, whatever happened, I would be pleasantly surprised that anyone bothered to even take notice.

At school, as predicted, nobody mentioned my birthday except for some old friends whom I'd known since kindergarten. The fact that they actually remembered my birthday didn't earn them any points. I mean, what kind of creepy girls would want to be friends with me? And who would be dumb enough to remember my birthday? I had zits and braces and frizzy hair.

At home, the evening went about the same as any other evening, except that there was cake for dessert and a few presents for me to open. My two younger sisters got me some dumb stuff—stationery sets and candy and hand-drawn cards. There was one big box from my mother. The card read "Love from Mom and Dad," but I knew my dad had nothing to do with it. My dad *never* shopped. In fact, he was hardly ever home. Like most nights, he was still working at the hospital, doing some sort of surgery or something like that.

I reached over for the big metallic-gold Nordstrom box, and when I shook it, I knew there were clothes inside. *Thank you, God,* I thought to myself. *Maybe this birthday won't be so bad, after all.* Being in middle school had made me incredibly insecure about my wardrobe, so I hoped that this package would contain something magical to make me fit in. I opened the box and pulled out a pair of tangerine cropped pants and a matching cotton tangerine striped shirt. *Tangerine!* It was hideous. I'd never owned anything tangerine in my life and wasn't about to start now. I smiled weakly.

"Wow, Mom!" I faked a happy grin. "Thank you so much!"

My mother was onto me right away. "You don't like it," she growled.

"No, I do," I lied. "I really like the outfit."

But I hated it. I'd never received a gift so ugly or so unflattering. Besides, my mother should have known that I couldn't wear tangerine!

She was getting angrier. "You don't like it, I'll take it back," she fumed.

Wallowing further into my low self-esteem black hole, I replied, "Fine, take it back. I don't deserve any presents anyway."

This made her even angrier. "You ungrateful child. Don't you know how much I do for you? I shopped for this present. I cooked you dinner. I have tried to make this evening special, and this is the kind of thanks I get?"

I stared at my mother silently, waiting for her full fury to hit me like a hurricane. My sisters knew the drill by heart now, so they got up from the table and quietly snuck up to their rooms to hide. She continued to yell—about how I ruined her day and how I never thank her for anything or appreciate what she does, and how I never help out around the house, and how bad traffic was this evening on the bridge, and how all I do is take, take, take.

"So . . . take . . . the . . . present . . . back," I said, now with tears streaming down my cheeks, barely getting the words out between my gurgling hiccups and sniffing wet snot back up into my head. My mother always knew exactly how to make me truly miserable.

After she was done yelling, my mother cut half of the birthday cake, about five or six slices, put it on a plate and made her usual Alka-Seltzer evening cocktail. Then she announced to no one in particular, "I'm going to my room and I don't want to be disturbed!"

I carefully refolded the tangerine pants and top, wrapped them back up in tissue paper and placed them inside the metallic-gold Nordstrom box. "There," I announced to nobody. "A perfectly ruined birthday. Just as I expected."

The next morning, the gold box with the tangerine clothes carefully wrapped inside was still sitting on the kitchen table. As I poured myself a bowl of cereal, it occurred to me how ridiculous the box looked, and how even more ridiculous I had acted the night before. I replayed the series of miserable events over in my head. The misery was all mine—I had set myself up for a disappointing birthday because I didn't feel I deserved anything more than that. So, what did I get? Disappointment, *duh!*

I unwrapped the box and pulled out the tangerine clothes. *I could wear these pants with my black top,* I thought. *And I could wear the shirt with jeans.* Nobody said I had to wear a completely tangerine outfit. After thinking it through, I realized that the gift was completely salvageable, and I was much happier about the whole thing.

My mom came downstairs to the kitchen. She was still in her nightgown and her face was slightly puffy. She looked at me, then at the clothes and the cereal on the kitchen table. "I'm sorry about yesterday, honey," she said, groggily.

"I'm sorry too, Mom," I said.

"Can we start over with the birthday?" We said it in unison, then we laughed.

Allison Ellis

Disabilities

What really matters is what you do with what you have.

Shirley Lord

Step by step, Rebekah pulled herself along the sidewalk with her walker on a cold but sunny day. She looked back at me and, laughing, said, "You can't catch me!" She turned around and started to run, fast but stumbling, her walker wheels bumping over little rocks on the pavement. I jumped up and started jogging toward my little sister, and thought about how far she has come since her birth three-and-a-half years ago.

Rebekah was born with spina bifida, a condition in which a baby is born with a hole in its back, and the spinal cord hangs out of it. Right away, she went to the Neonatal Intensive Care Unit where very sick babies are sent. She had surgery to close her spine when she was only twenty-two hours old. I wanted to visit my baby sister, but children weren't allowed in the NICU because doctors were afraid that they would bring in germs.

Rebekah was eight days old before she was well

enough to come home. She looked like a pretzel, because her legs were bent the wrong way, so that they touched her chest. Her feet were both clubbed, so they were turned in toward one another. I was only five, and I didn't know what to think about my new little sister. She was home for only four days before she had to go back to the hospital. Her head was swelling badly and she had to have brain surgery to put in a shunt, which is a tube that drains extra fluid away from the brain.

By the time she was three, Rebekah had already gone through nine operations. She has had bladder surgery, four operations on her feet, and hip surgery too. Recovering from her surgeries was a long and painful process. She usually had to wear casts for six to twelve weeks. After foot surgery, she had to wear braces to keep her feet from going back to the way they had been.

When she was about a year old, she started having physical therapy to make her legs and body stronger. The muscles below her knees don't work because nerves in her spinal cord were damaged. Because of this, the muscles in her thighs have to do all the work. Rebekah was about a year-and-a-half old when she started to walk. She got a walker to help her keep her balance when she walked. Each time she had surgery, she had to learn how to walk all over again, which is very hard to do.

Her attitude is remarkable after all she's been through. Rebekah is determined to not let her disabilities get in the way of the things she wants to do. She does not understand that she is handicapped, so she does the same things as everyone else. She might have to do them differently, but she still does them. She walks, she runs, she jumps, she dances, she kicks balls, and she loves to play outside like most kids do. She has to work harder for everything she does, but she doesn't complain.

For Rebekah, standing and walking is like you or me

carrying someone our own size on our back all the time. She has a wheelchair, but she likes to walk the best. She walks well with her crutches and walker, but she's trying to walk without help. She has taught herself to take five steps without help, and she's still working on it.

I've learned a lot about disabilities since my little sister was born. I used to think it was scary to have a handicapped person in my family. Now I don't think it's scary at all. Rebekah is the same as everyone else. She has taught me a lot of things, but the most important thing I've learned is that if you keep a positive attitude and work hard, you can overcome just about anything that life hands you.

Heather Bradley, eight

The Helpful Stranger

All of us, at certain moments of our lives, need to take advice and to receive help from other people.

Alexis Carrel

With Christmas vacation coming up, I was hoping that we would get a lot of snow, so I could go tobogganing with my friends. I had also asked for a snowboard for Christmas, so I was really hoping for snow to try it out.

On Christmas morning, not only did I awaken to find that it was snowing outside, but I also found an awesome new snowboard under the tree. I begged my mom and dad to take me to the toboggan hill, so I could try out my new snowboard. They agreed, so off we went through snow so thick that we could barely see where we were going.

I got on my board for the first time and made it only a quarter of the way down the hill when I fell off. I became very discouraged and didn't think that I was any good. I made an instant decision that I didn't want to do it any more.

A few days after Christmas, my friend Zachary came over with his snowboard to go to the hill near my house with me. Zachary was very good at snowboarding, and since I could barely do it at all, that made me feel even worse. I wondered if maybe my new board wasn't the right size for me, so I tried riding Zachary's board. I still wasn't able to get very far. Finally I just gave up and said, "I can't do it."

But while I struggled with my new board, Zachary was making run after run down the hill and having a great time. He asked me if we could go to our favorite hill a little farther away to do some more runs, and not wanting to spoil his fun, I reluctantly said I would go.

While out on the new hill, I still struggled to stay up. I had fallen a few times when a teenager that I had never met before noticed that I was getting frustrated. He called over to me to give me some advice about how to snowboard. I don't talk to strangers as a rule, but my mom was with me so I felt safe. So, I listened to what he had to say, and then I tried again. I was able to go farther down the hill than I had before. He watched as I made one more run, and then he came over to give me more pointers, like where to place my feet and what to do with my hands. He also told me that I should lean a little bit forward once I got up. I tried what he told me to do, and I was able to go all the way down the hill without falling! It seemed so much easier with the instructions that he gave me. He continued to help me a number of times and gave me lots of encouragement.

I find it hard sometimes to listen to other people when they are telling me what to do, but this guy was very helpful and nice about the way he instructed me. He could have chosen to make a few more runs for the day, instead of taking time to help me—a kid he didn't even know.

As younger preteens, sometimes when we think of teenagers, we think about those that are "trouble makers," or some who intimidate us. But this teenager was not like that at all. He made me feel comfortable around him and was really helpful and kind to me.

I'm a much better snowboarder now, thanks to a very helpful and considerate teenage stranger.

Alex Judge, ten

8

OVERCOMING OBSTACLES

Lost in dark depression
Not knowing where to turn
I opened the windows to my soul
To see what I could learn
I swept up the depression
Scrubbed the sadness and the hurt
I put it all in trash bags
And set them by the curb
I found stashed in a corner
Tucked high upon a shelf
A treasure chest of knowledge
That I could love myself
And wherever my future takes me
I know that I will win
Because I opened the windows to my soul
And let the light shine in.

Hope Saxton

Annie Wiggle-Do

To live with fear and not be afraid is the final test of maturity.

Edward Weeks

"Look who's here to see you, Brenda," the nurse said. She led a tired-looking woman to the girl's bedside.

Brenda huddled on her side, facing the wall. When her mother touched her shoulder, she pulled her head closer to her chest, as if making her body smaller would help her disappear altogether.

The nurse patted the mother's shoulder.

"Brenda's still not talking to us," she said in a low voice.

Brenda's mother bit her lip to keep from crying. She remembered exactly how bubbly and happy Brenda had been before the car accident that led to the amputation of her leg. She'd been one of the most popular girls in her sixth-grade class.

When Brenda first awakened from her surgery, she had raged at her mother. *Why had this happened?* Now, she felt like a freak. No one would ever want to be her friend. She would never date, never have a boyfriend. Then, Brenda had just stopped talking.

"I wish I could bring her friends to visit her," said Brenda's mother. "It's just too long a bus trip, though, about three hours each way."

The nurse smiled. "Don't worry. We have a plan."

Shortly after Brenda's mother left, two nurses wheeled in a stretcher.

"Moving day, Brenda!" one said cheerily. "We need this bed for someone who's really sick. We've picked out the best roommate in the hospital for you."

Before Brenda could protest, the nurses had rolled her onto the stretcher and whisked her down the hall. The room was awash with light, posters and music.

"Here's your new roomie, Annie Wiggle-Do," one nurse told a dark-haired teenager in the other bed. "She's just beginning to get better, so please don't kill her with your corny jokes."

Fourteen-year-old Annie grinned. As soon as the nurses left, she hopped out of her bed and sat on the end of Brenda's.

"I lost my leg from bone cancer," she announced. "What happened to yours?"

Brenda was so astounded she couldn't even form a word.

"You're lucky," Annie continued. "You've still got your knee. They had to take mine, hip and all, see?"

But Brenda's eyes had already found the raw scar and empty hip socket. Her gaze seemed frozen, like a magnet held it there.

Annie scooted back to her bed. "I'd like to socialize, but my boyfriend's due any time now, so I have to get ready."

As Brenda watched transfixed, Annie reached up and took off her hair! Her head was completely bald.

Annie giggled. "Oh, I forgot to warn you, the stuff they

gave me to kill the cancer also killed my hair. But check this out! My parents, my grandma, my boyfriend and some kids from school all brought me wigs!"

From her bedside stand, Annie removed a tangle of wigs. Brown wigs and blond wigs, short-haired and long-haired wigs, curly wigs and straight wigs.

"That's when I thought up 'Annie Wiggle-Do,' Annie said. "Get it? 'Any wig will do.' Annie Wiggle-Do?"

Laughing at her own joke, Annie chose a curly blond wig and arranged it on her head. She just managed to dab on some pink lip-gloss and powder before a group of boisterous teens burst into the room. Annie introduced Brenda to them all. Her boyfriend, Donald, winked at Brenda and asked her to keep Annie out of trouble.

Before long, Brenda began chatting with Annie and her friends. They didn't make her feel like a freak at all! One girl even shared with Brenda that her cousin wore an artificial leg, played basketball and rode a motorcycle. By the time the nurses shooed all the visitors from the room, Brenda felt more like the old Brenda.

The girls talked into the night. Annie shared her dream of becoming a comedy writer. Brenda told Annie about her secret desire to act in live theater.

"Ladies!"

A night nurse came in and shined her flashlight on Annie and Brenda. "It's after midnight," the nurse scolded. "What do you have to say for yourselves?"

"Nothing, your honor," Annie said. "We don't have a leg to stand on!"

They all laughed, but Brenda laughed hardest of all.

As the nurse's footsteps faded down the hallway, Brenda snuggled under her blanket. "Night, Annie Wiggle-Do," she whispered. "I can hardly wait 'til morning."

Kathleen M. Muldoon

Two Percent Is Enough

From the day I was born, I was a sickly, weak child who never had as much energy as a child my age should. When I turned four, everything seemed to go wrong. I had asthma and for the most part I was in constant pain. Every day, I had a nagging side pain that seemed to never go away and I was in and out of doctors' offices many times, but they could never figure out what was wrong. "Simply growing pains," they told my parents.

One night, I had a fever, high blood pressure, nonstop vomiting and my feet were purple. My parents rushed me to the emergency room, where they were told that I needed my appendix taken out. I lay there that night, getting worse by the minute. Finally, purple feet became numb and my stomach was empty of everything. My parents lost control of their emotions. The next morning, my urine was brown. At that point, the doctors knew it was more than my appendix.

The next day, I was taken by ambulance to Children's Hospital under the care of Dr. Kohen, a kidney specialist. I was diagnosed with a rare form of kidney disease called glumerulonephritis. After two weeks of treatment, I was still not responding. My kidneys were only functioning

2 percent of the time and if something wasn't done, I would die.

My parents were faced with choices they never thought they would have to make: steroids, dialysis or a transplant. They were told that their only daughter was dying and without vast improvement would be put on a waiting list for a kidney transplant.

That night, my dad sat down by my bed and told me that I was going to have to fight harder than I had ever fought before. All of a sudden, I reached up and—mustering all the energy I had—I punched him in the nose! He knew then that I was not going to give up without a fight.

The next morning I was evaluated for a transplant. I was put on a steroid. Within a couple of days, I started showing steady signs of improvement, but my parents were told, "Krissy will never have as much energy as a normal kid, even if she pulls through."

Within four days I was strong enough to return home. For the next couple of months, I was under constant supervision. As a four-year-old little girl, I was taking fourteen pills a day and having my blood taken every other day. Gradually, I was taken off of the medicine and my doctors' visits grew further apart. But still, I was given no chance of a full recovery.

Well, ten years later, I can proudly say, "Look at me now!" I am fourteen years old, I play four sports, I am a member of the National Junior Honor Society at my school, vice president of Student Council, have a 3.5 grade point average, and I am a living miracle to my doctors, family and friends. I thank God every day for giving me my life. Even if you are only given a 2 percent chance of survival, that's all you really need.

Krissy Creager, fourteen

The First Day of Middle School

The transition into middle school will be the hardest change kids experience during their school years. . . . Compared to this, the first day of high school is a piece of cake.

Allan Mucerino, Principal, Ensign Intermediate School

My stomach was tied in knots, and I could feel the sweat soaking through my T-shirt. My hands were clammy as I spun the face of my combination lock. I tried and tried to remember the numbers, and every time I thought I had it, the lock wouldn't open. Around and around went the numbers, left, right, right, left . . . *which way was it supposed to go?* I couldn't make it work. I gave up and started to run down the hallway. As I ran, the hall seemed to get longer and longer . . . the door I was trying to reach was farther away than when I had started. I began to sweat even worse, then I could feel the tears forming. I was late, late, late, late for my first class on my first day of middle school. As I ran, people were watching me and they were laughing . . . laughing . . . laughing . . . then the bell rang! In my dream, it was the school bell. But as I sat up in bed, I realized that it was my alarm clock jarring me awake.

I was having the dream again. I started having the dream around the end of sixth grade, and as the start of seventh grade drew closer, the more I had the dream. This time the dream was even more real, because today *was* the morning of the first day of seventh grade.

In my heart, I knew I would never make it. Everything was too different. School, friends—even my own body.

I was used to walking to school, and now I had to walk six blocks to the bus stop so that I could take the bus to and from school. I hated buses. They made me carsick from the jiggling and the smell of the fuel.

I had to get up for school earlier than in the past, partly because of having to be bussed to school and partly because I had to take better care of myself now that I was in my preteen years. My mom told me that I would have to shower every morning since my hormones were kicking in—that's why I perspired so easily.

I was totally uncomfortable with my body. My feet didn't want to respond to my own directions, and I tripped a lot. I constantly had a sprained ankle, wet armpits and things stuck in my braces. I felt awkward, smelly, insecure and like I had bad breath on a full-time basis.

In middle school, I would have to learn the rules and personalities of six different teachers instead of just one. There would be different kids in all my classes, kids I didn't even know. I had never made friends very easily, and now I would have to start all over again.

I would have to run to my locker between classes, remember my combination, open it, put in the books from the last class and take out different books . . . and make it to the next class all within *five minutes!*

I was also scared because of some stories I had heard about the first day of middle school, like being canned by the eighth-graders. That's when a bunch of eighth-graders pick you up and put you in a trash can. I had also heard that when eighth-grade girls catch a new seventh-grader in the girls' bathroom alone, they smear her with lipstick. Neither one of these first-day activities sounded like something I wanted to take part in.

No one had ever told me that growing up was going to be so hard, so scary, so unwelcome, so . . . unexpected. I was the oldest kid in my family—in fact, in my entire neighborhood—and no one had been there before me, to help lead me through the challenges of middle school.

I was on my own.

The first day of school was *almost* everything I feared. I *didn't* remember my combination. I wrote the combination on my hand, but my hand was so sweaty it came off. I *was* late to every class. I didn't have enough time to finish my lunch; I had just sat down to eat when the bell rang to go back to class. I almost choked on my peanut butter and banana sandwich as I ran down the dreaded hallway. The classrooms and the teachers were a blur. I wasn't sure what teacher went with which subject and they had all assigned homework . . . on the very first day of school! I couldn't believe it.

But the first day wasn't like my dream in another way. In my dream, all of the other kids had it together and I was the only one who was the nerd. In real life, I wasn't the only one who was late for classes. Everyone else was late, too. No one could remember their combination either, except Ted Milliken, the kid who carried a briefcase to school. After most of the kids realized that everyone else was going through the same thing they were going through, we all started cracking up. We were bumping into each other in our rush to get to the next class, and books were flying everywhere. No one got canned or smeared—at least no one I knew. I still didn't go into the girls' bathroom alone, just in case. Yeah, there was laughter in the hallway, but most of it was the laughter of kids sharing a common experience: complete hysteria!

As the weeks went by, it became easier and easier. Pretty soon I could twirl my combination without even looking at it. I hung posters in my locker, and finally felt like I was at home. I learned all of my teachers' names and decided who I liked the best. Friendships from elementary school were renewed and made stronger, and new friends were made. I learned how to change into a gym suit in front of other girls. It never felt comfortable, but I did it— just like everyone else did. I don't think any of us felt very comfortable.

I still didn't like the bus; it did make me carsick. I even threw up on the bus once. (At least it was on the way home, not on the way to school.) I went to dances and parties, and I started to wonder what it would feel like to be kissed by a boy. The school had track tryouts, and I made the team and learned how to jump the low hurdles. I got pretty good at it, too.

First semester turned into second, and then third. Before I knew it, eighth grade was just around the corner. I had made it through.

Next year, on the first day of school, I would be watching the new seventh graders sweating it out just like I did—just like everyone does. I decided that I would feel sorry for them . . . but only for the FIRST day of seventh grade. After that, it's a breeze.

Patty Hansen

Perfect, I'm Not

"Owwww!" Robert yelled, backing away from me. "That hurt!"

"What do you mean? I just hit you with my jacket!" I said, laughing. Robert was the cutest boy in class, and I had a major crush on him. I hadn't meant to hurt him; I wanted him to like me. Besides, it was just a lightweight jacket.

But Robert didn't act like someone who had been hit with a lightweight jacket. He was crying and holding his left shoulder.

"What's going on?" our sixth-grade teacher, Mr. Mobley, asked.

"My shoulder . . . it hurts!" Robert groaned.

The next thing I knew, Robert was heading to the nurse's office. And I, bewildered, was marching back from recess and into our classroom with the other kids.

We started our spelling lesson, and I tried to pay attention as Mr. Mobley read the words for our weekly practice test.

Then someone knocked on our classroom door. When Mr. Mobley opened the door, a student volunteer from the office handed him a note. Every pair of eyes was riveted on Mr. Mobley. A note from the office usually signaled big trouble for somebody. This time, the somebody was me. Mr. Mobley looked up from the note and said, "Julie, Mr. Sinclair wants to see you in his office right away. He says you should take your belongings with you."

Oh, no! I was being sent to the principal's office. What would my parents say? With all eyes now turned in my direction, I dragged myself over to the coat hooks and grabbed the offending jacket. Embarrassment floated around me like a dirty cloud of dust.

How could a stupid jacket hurt anybody? I wondered as the door clicked shut behind me. I slid my arms through the jacket sleeves and slipped my hands into its pockets. *Huh?* My right hand closed over a hard, round object. I pulled it out. I had forgotten that my brand-new Duncan Imperial yo-yo was in my pocket. I felt my legs weaken. So I had hurt Robert not with my jacket, but with my yo-yo. As I crossed the courtyard to the principal's office, I prayed, *Please don't let Robert be hurt too badly. And please don't let Mr. Sinclair call my mom.*

When I reached the office, the school secretary ushered me in to see the principal without making me wait—not exactly a good sign.

"What happened, Julie?" Mr. Sinclair asked. He came out from behind his big wooden desk and sat on a chair next to me.

"We were goofing around . . . and . . . I hit Robert on his shoulder with my jacket. I . . . um . . . I guess I had this in my pocket." I opened my palm to show him the shiny red yo-yo I'd bought with my allowance. "I'm sorry. I'm really sorry. I was only teasing. I didn't mean to hurt him." Little snorting sounds were coming out of my nose now, and my shoulders were heaving with barely suppressed sobs.

"I know you well enough to believe you. But Robert has a knot on his shoulder that's about the size of your yo-yo. His mother is very upset. She's taken him to the doctor."

My head hung so low, it nearly touched my knees. More than anything, I wanted to melt into a puddle and trickle away under the door.

"I'm sure you didn't mean to hurt anyone," Mr. Sinclair went on. "But because Robert was injured, I have to send you home for the rest of the day. Please wait in the outer office until your mother comes to pick you up."

My eyes widened. *Now I'm going to get it!* I thought.

I had plenty of time to think while I waited for my mother. I was always trying to be the "perfect student." Straight A's and praise from my teachers were rewarded with more praise and affection at home from my parents. *What will happen now?* I wondered. I had never been in trouble at school before.

Ten hopelessly long minutes later, my mother opened the door to the office. Her face looked serious. "Come on," she said. "You can tell me about it in the car."

During our short ride home, I told her the whole story. I'd been teasing Robert because I had a crush on him. I hadn't meant to hurt him. We pulled into our driveway. "I'm s-s-sorry, Mom," I said. My body tensed, ready for the punishment I knew I deserved.

Mom leaned toward me, and I sucked in my breath, waiting to see what would happen. *Would she yell? Would she slap me?* I really didn't know what to expect.

My mother put one arm behind me and reached across in front of me with the other. Then she wrapped me tightly in a hug.

"I never told any of you kids this," she said, "but I did something even worse when I was in elementary school. I bit a boy on the arm—on purpose. I got called to the principal's office, too." *What? My mother, who never did anything wrong, had bitten a boy at school?* The thought was too funny. I caught her eye. "I guess we're just a couple of troublemakers, aren't we, Honey?" Mom said with a smile.

"I guess so," I said. In spite of the tears streaming down my face, I started to laugh. Pretty soon, Mom was laughing, too.

The next day, Robert was back at school, recovered except for a little tenderness. As soon as I saw him, I apologized, and our lives went back to normal.

But something important had changed. I had learned that life goes on, even when you make a mistake, and that a child can grow up to become a wise adult even after doing something foolish or hurtful. And to my great surprise and relief, I learned that I didn't have to be perfect to be loved.

Julia Wasson Render

Rediscovery

Believing in our hearts that who we are is enough is the key to a more satisfying and balanced life.

Ellen Sue Stern

Seven. The age of ballet lessons and Barbie dolls, of learning to add and subtract simple numbers; the time when the family dog is your closest companion. Seven. The age of innocence.

I was a typical-looking child. I had long, straight brown hair that fell past my shoulders. My almond-shaped hazel eyes were always full of adventure and curiosity. And I had a smile that could brighten a bleak winter day.

I was a happy child with a loving family, and many friends, who loved to perform skits on home videos. I was a leader in school, not a follower. My best trait was my personality. I had imagination. But what made me special was not seen from the outside: I had a special love for life.

At age twelve, my life had a huge breakdown. It was then that I developed obsessive compulsive disorder (OCD). OCD is a disorder that is the result of a chemical imbalance in the brain. People with OCD don't think the same way as people with chemically balanced brains. People with OCD do rituals. I started to wash my hands ten times an hour to avoid germs, and I constantly checked my kitchen oven to make sure that it was off. This way of life for me continued for four agonizing years, and by then, my OCD had led to depression. I was no longer the happy little girl I had been.

In the tenth grade I finally confessed to my mother that I was suffering from depression along with my OCD. I couldn't take the emotional pain anymore. I needed help if I wanted to continue living.

My mom took me to a doctor the same week. I started taking medicine that would hopefully cure my OCD and depression. Over the course of a few months, the medicine did help the OCD. I stopped doing rituals. I no longer took four showers a day to avoid germs. But one thing didn't change; I still was overwhelmed with depression. I still was constantly sad and I started to believe that my life no longer mattered.

One autumn evening two years ago, I hit rock bottom. I thought that my life no longer had meaning, because I no longer brought joy to other people like I did when I was little. I decided suicide was the only solution to my depression problem, so I wrote a suicide note to all my friends and family. In the note I expressed that I was sorry for deciding to leave them, but that I thought it was for the best. As I was folding the note, my eyes fell on a photograph. It was a picture of an adorable little girl with natural blond highlights in her brown hair from spending so much time in the sun. She was wearing her red soccer uniform and held a biking helmet in her small hands. She had a carefree smile on her face that showed she was full of life.

It took me a few minutes to realize who the girl in the photo was. The photo had been taken one weekend at my uncle's house when I was seven years old. I almost couldn't believe that smiling child was me! I felt a chill go down my spine. It was like my younger self had sent me a message. Right then and there I knew I couldn't kill myself. Once I had been a strong little girl, and I had to become strong like that again.

I tore up my suicide note and vowed that I would not rely only on my medicine to help my depression. I would have to fight the depression with my mind, too. I could make myself happy again.

It has been two years since I "rediscovered" myself. I am OCD- and depression-free. I still take medicine to keep my disorder at bay, but the real reason I am healed is because I took action and refused to let depression ruin my life. I learned a lifelong lesson: Never give up. Life is good. Everyone has challenges in life, but everyone can survive. I am living proof of that. Also, it is important to keep smiling, because in the end, everything will work out.

Of course my life can still be a struggle, but I pull through with a smile on my face. I know I can't give up on life. I am here for a reason. Sometimes, I think it was strange that I had to look to who I was as a little girl in order to regain faith in myself at age eighteen. But I think everyone can look back on their early years and see that it was then that they knew how to live in peace and happiness.

I have plans for myself now. Once I graduate from high school this spring, I plan on going to college to major in journalism. I want to be a writer someday. And I am prepared for whatever challenges life may bring. I have a role model to look up to for strength, and who is guiding me through life. My hero is a seven-year-old girl, smiling back at me from a photo on my desk.

Raegan Baker

[EDITORS' NOTE: *For more information regarding obsessive compulsive disorder, log on to* www.ocdresource.com.]

A Little Coaching

The two important things I did learn were that you are as powerful and strong as you allow yourself to be, and that the most difficult part of any endeavor is taking the first step, making the first decision.

Robyn Davidson

For me, it was normal to feel lost at the inter-camp track and swim meet. Four camps of kids were ready to lead their teams to a blue ribbon and win the day. Not me. I was too little to be a leader and too skinny to be an athlete. I knew this by the time I was twelve, because my camp counselors and the other kids reminded me of it every chance they got. So when our camp needed a fourth runner in the two-mile race around the lake, I knew I was no one's first choice.

I hid in the shade of a maple tree as they called the names of the runners. My body tensed as I heard a counselor call, "Noah! Where's Noah! He's in this race!"

It was Bronto. His name was really Alan Bronstein, but everyone called him Bronto. He spotted me under the tree and lifted me up by my elbows. It was more than just his name that qualified him for his "Brontoism."

"Noah, we need a twelve-year-old who hasn't been in other events to run the two-mile."

"But you've got three guys."

"We need four. You're in."

He gave me a push toward the starting line. Trying to save myself from the humiliation of taking last place as four camps watched, I pleaded with him.

"But I don't know the way around the lake!"

"You're in. Just follow Craig." Bronto smiled.

Craig was my friend and the fastest runner in our camp. And then Bronto said, "When you make it to the last stretch on the field, just throw your head back and run."

At the starting line, I stood next to Craig and trembled.

"On your mark . . . get set . . ." The gun cracked and sixteen of us took off. Kicking up dust on the dirt road leading to the lakeshore path, I was determined not to get lost. I stayed close on Craig's heels. A little too close for Craig, I guess, because he shouted at me, "Back off!"

I did. Two guys passed me but I kept my eye on Craig.

It was tiring. The distance was widening between Craig and me. We made the turn from the dusty road onto the muddy, wooded trail that wound around the lake back to the field. Through the trees I saw Craig slip and fall out of sight. A runner from another camp passed him.

In a moment, he was up again and running. He yelled to me, "Watch the roots. They're slimy!" Struggling to keep my legs moving, I looked down and saw the tree root stripped of its bark. I puffed over it. Fifty yards later I was out of breath, but I turned up the hill into the sunlight again, which shone on the open field. My energy was spent. I scrambled up, ready to see the rest of the pack crossing the finish line and was about to drop to my knees and quit, when I saw not the fifteen guys that I thought would be in front of me, but three. The crowd was roaring, but I could hear Bronto over the rest of them, yelling, "Run!"

I threw my head back and told my legs to go. I never looked ahead and I never looked back for those last hundred yards. I felt free. Nobody was telling me what I was, or what I wasn't. My legs were running a race against my brain and I was winning.

I didn't know when I crossed the finish line. Bronto caught me and I collapsed—winded, but happy that I finished. Then I realized Bronto wasn't just holding me up. He was hugging me!

"You flew! You flew, man! Second! You passed two guys!"

There was a crowd of kids around me patting me on the back, giving me high-fives. I had come in second. Craig had finished first . . . by a step, they said.

They gave me a red second-place ribbon. Even with that and all the high-fives and cheers of the day, the best prize that I walked away with was my confidence. That year I discovered I could do a lot of things if I put my energy into them.

I never got to say thanks to Bronto right after the race. But during the next events, I spotted him over at the lake. He was coaching a reluctant kid who was going to swim in the freestyle relay. I ran over to cheer him on. With Bronto coaching, I had no doubt that this was going to be another good race.

Noah Edelson

The Last Runner

The annual marathon in my town usually occurs during a heat wave. My job was to follow behind the runners in an ambulance in case any of them needed medical attention. The driver and I were in an air-conditioned ambulance behind approximately one hundred athletes waiting to hear the sharp crack of the starting gun.

"We're supposed to stay behind the last runner, so take it slowly," I said to the driver, Doug, as we began to creep forward.

"Let's just hope the last runner is fast!" He laughed.

As they began to pace themselves, the front runners started to disappear. It was then that my eyes were drawn to the woman in blue silk running shorts and a baggy white T-shirt.

"Doug, look!"

We knew we were already watching our "last runner." Her feet were turned in, yet her left knee was turned out. Her legs were so crippled and bent that it seemed impossible for her to be able to walk, let alone run a marathon.

Doug and I watched in silence as she slowly moved forward. We didn't say a thing. We would move forward a little bit, then stop and wait for her to gain some distance.

Then we'd slowly move forward a little bit more.

As I watched her struggle to put one foot in front of the other, I found myself breathing for her and urging her forward. I wanted her to stop, and at the same time, I prayed that she wouldn't.

Finally, she was the only runner left in sight. Tears streamed down my face as I sat on the edge of my seat and watched with awe, amazement and even reverence as she pushed forward with sheer determination through the last miles.

When the finish line came into sight, trash lay everywhere and the cheering crowds had long gone home. Yet, standing straight and ever so proud waited a lone man. He was holding one end of a ribbon of crepe paper tied to a post. She slowly crossed through, leaving both ends of the paper fluttering behind her.

I do not know this woman's name, but that day she became a part of my life—a part I often depend on. For her, it wasn't about beating the other runners or winning a trophy, it was about finishing what she had set out to do, no matter what. When I think things are too difficult or too time-consuming, or I get those "I-just-can't-do-its," I think of the last runner. Then I realize how easy the task before me really is.

Lisa Beach

The Power of the Pen

Woman must not accept; she must challenge. She must not be awed by that which has been built up around her; she must reverence that woman in her which struggles for expression.

Margaret Sanger

The very first speech I ever had to write changed my life more than I could ever have imagined. I was a third-grader when I chose Susan B. Anthony to be the topic.

When I got the assignment, I went to the library and began researching the Women's Fight for the Right to Vote. I learned that Susan B. Anthony led the fight to give women a say in our society. She overcame a lot of obstacles in order to do that. I never really thought about a time when women had no voting rights and that their opinions didn't count.

It was sad that Susan fought so hard for women's rights and never got to vote. She died fourteen years before the passage of the 19th Amendment that gave women the right to vote. But she knew that her goal would be achieved. She said that "failure is impossible," and she was right.

About a week after giving my school speech, my mom read a newspaper article about "The Group Portrait Monument," a statue honoring Susan B. Anthony and other early women's rights leaders. The problem was that few people ever got to see the statue. It was dedicated in the U.S. Capitol Rotunda in 1921, but within twenty-four hours it was taken down to the Capitol basement and stored where it had remained for nearly eighty years.

When I read that article, I was furious! This statue belonged in a place of honor. I felt that it should be in the Rotunda, along with the statues of Abraham Lincoln, Martin Luther King Jr. and George Washington. Do you know that there are *no* statues of women there?

The article asked for donations because it would take $74,000 to move the thirteen-ton statue out of the basement. I decided to write a letter with a self-addressed envelope asking my relatives and friends to send a Susan B. Anthony coin or a $1 bill to me to contribute to the Women's Suffrage Statue Campaign. I really wanted to help get that statue moved out of the basement.

Every day I ran to the mailbox after school. Every night, after my homework, I wrote more letters at the kitchen table. Pretty soon the whole family got involved in the project. My seven-year-old brother, David, licked stamps and envelopes. My mother and grandmother found addresses for people I wanted to contact and my dad drove me around and gave me tons of encouragement when I spoke to big groups. I passed around a piggy bank for donations at the end of each speech. I sent more than $500 to the fund in the first three months. Pretty soon, I had raised $2,000. I began visualizing that statue up in the Rotunda next to the greatest Americans in history.

I was discouraged when I heard that four other times,

in 1928, 1932, 1950 and 1995, people had tried to get the statue out of the basement and had failed. I learned that the House and Senate would have to vote on relocating the statue. More determined than before, I spent three weeks writing to every representative and senator in the United States, urging them to vote yes on the bill to relocate the statue. This was not about politics. It was about respect and responsibility. Susan B. Anthony fought for my rights, and now I was fighting for hers!

The Senate unanimously voted to restore the statue to the Rotunda, but Newt Gingrich, the Speaker of the House, didn't want to use any tax money to pay for the cost of relocating the statue. Even if we raised enough money, the statue couldn't be relocated without a unanimous vote in the House.

There was only one thing to do . . . write more letters! I wrote a letter to Mr. Gingrich *every other week for an entire year!* Boy, did that try my patience! I sent about twenty-five letters to him before I got a reply. He finally wrote a letter saying that a committee would study the issue.

At that point, I figured that I had better write to every member of the House again. By now I had mailed more than 2,000 letters!

My grandmother helped with postage costs by getting her friends and church groups to donate rolls of stamps to help me with the battle. I got writer's cramp from writing letters and discovered that it takes a lot of work to bring about change. But if you believe in something, it's worth the hard work.

My biggest boost came when I was interviewed on radio and TV shows. Then, a bunch of newspaper and magazine articles came out telling thousands more people about what I was trying to do. As a result of all that attention, I was invited to speak at a fund-raising event for the Woman's Suffrage Statue Campaign in Washington, D.C., in July of 1996. I had never flown in an airplane. My whole family got to go and my brother had a great time. He thought that was a pretty good reward for licking all those stamps!

But the best part was getting to see the statue, even if it was in the smelly old basement. I thought it looked really beautiful. I've heard people say that they think that the statue is ugly. To that I say—it was an ugly time! The three women in the statue have their arms pinned in marble because they were trapped by "slavery!"

I spoke from my heart when I talked to all those people and received a standing ovation for my speech!

After I got home, I continued to write letters. I wouldn't give up! It took women seventy-two years to win the right to vote, but they didn't give up until they reached their goal . . . and neither would I!

On September 27, 1996, House Resolution 216, the bill to get the statue moved, passed unanimously. My mom and I jumped up and down in our living room when we heard the news. We just kept screaming, "We won!"

The statue stayed in the Rotunda for a year and then was moved to another place of honor in Washington, where everyone can see it. It will never go back to that awful basement again!

I've learned a lot from this experience . . . mostly about respecting people who fought for rights that too many people take for granted. I've learned to have more patience. If there is a problem, don't say "someone else will fix it." You have to do it yourself.

I'll turn eighteen in a few years and will be able to vote in the year 2005. When I vote, I'll silently thank Susan B. Anthony for her fight and for helping me discover the power of the pen.

Arlys Angelique Endres, thirteen
As told by Carol Osman Brown

Tough, Sturdy and Triumphant

The mind can have tremendous control of the body; very few ailments can defeat focused energy and a determined spirit.

Katherine Lambert-Scronce

Tears filled my eyes as my parents told me why my arm had been in so much pain during the past three months.

"You have leukemia," my dad explained.

I didn't know much about leukemia, but the words still plunged deep into my heart like knives. My parents told me that I had to go into the hospital to have a metal cylinder called a medi-port put into my body. A medi-port has a line through which the doctors would give me medicine to fight the leukemia cells.

I found out that leukemia is a type of cancer that only one out of ten thousand people get. Bone marrow starts making leukemia cells, which take over good cells. *Why did this have to happen to me?* I wondered.

My whole family went with me to the hospital. My parents told me they'd see me after my surgery. Some doctor

hooked me up and made me put on some funky clothes.
Then they rolled me into the operating room.

I was so scared. All of the doctors had on masks. They
attached sensors to me and assured me that nothing
would go wrong. They put a mask over my face, pressed
a button and I fell asleep. When I woke up, the surgery
was over. I had to stay in the hospital for four days. My
doctor told my parents I would have to come to the hospital every other week to stay for four days so that I could
get treatments. I had to do this for one entire year—
twelve months!

When we reached home, I couldn't believe how much I
had missed it. People brought over presents, balloons,
cards and food. My teacher came over and gave me a
stack of letters from my classmates. I read them over and
over. All of them had cried, especially my friends. I didn't
get to see my friends anymore and felt sick practically
every day. But I got tons of letters from them all the time,
and they kept me going!

I have survived this last year, but I still have a lower
blood count than healthy people. I have only two more
years of treatments to go, and from now on, the treatments won't be so heavy.

I have been overwhelmed with support and prayer. My
mom told the Make-A-Wish Foundation how much I
loved castles, and I was granted my wish to see real
castles in England and Scotland. My whole family gets to
go with me and Make-A-Wish is paying for everything!

I know I didn't get through this by myself. My friends
and family have been with me every step of the way. I
look back and see how far I've come. I will fight this and
triumph.

Even though I'm different than most kids because of
the leukemia, I'm as tough as a general leading his men
into battle, as sturdy as a wall and as triumphant as a man

beating an army. I have been able to do this thanks to everyone who has helped me through, and especially to someone in a high position. Where there is life, there is hope for even the most hopeless.

Elijah Shoesmith, thirteen

[EDITORS' NOTE: *At the date of this printing, Elijah is fifteen years old, and is in remission—due in a large part to sheer will and his determination to beat his leukemia. For more information on leukemia, lymphoma and other blood-related cancers, call The Leukemia & Lymphoma Society at 1-800-955-4572 or log on to* www.leukemia-lymphoma.org.]

9

ON CHOICES

Peer pressure is a thing
that every child goes through.
But you have to remember
that to yourself you must be true.
Know that there are times to follow
and there are times to lead.
Do what you think is right,
do things at your own speed.
Don't worry about what others think,
don't worry about being cool.
Focus on friendships
and the grades you get in school.

Jaimie Shapiro, twelve

Forever Stay in My Heart

In loving memory of Cassie L. Sweet

It was late when I heard the phone ring
I didn't know then the grief it would bring.

She was killed by one thoughtless mistake
That a few of her friends decided to make.

I can't understand what they had been thinking
The driver of the car she was in had been drinking.

All I do now is think about her and cry
And ask myself again and then again, *why?*

I cherish all the memories that we shared
And remember how much she loved and she cared.

She is gone now, and yet it's still hard to part
So that's why she will forever stay in my heart.

Jillian Eide, sixteen

[EDITORS' NOTE: *For information about underage drinking, drunk driving and other destructive decisions, contact SADD (Students Against Destructive Decisions) at* www.SADDonline.com.]

Two Tickets to the Big Game

I discovered I always have choices, and sometimes it's only a choice of attitude.

Judith M. Knowlton

Two tickets. Only two tickets to the big quarterfinals basketball game.

Three pairs of eyes all focused on the tickets in Dad's outstretched hand. Marcus, the oldest, spoke the question running through everyone's mind: "Only two tickets? But, Dad, which of us gets to go with you?"

"Yeah, Daddy, who gets to go?" repeated Caleb, the youngest.

"Dad, can't you get any more tickets?" I asked. I might be the in-between sister, but I was just as eager as my basketball-crazy brothers were for a night out with Dad.

"I'm afraid not," Dad answered. "Mr. Williams only has two season tickets. He was thoughtful enough to offer the tickets to Saturday's game to me when he found out he'd be out of town this weekend."

Dad scratched his head. "Caleb, don't you think you're a little young to enjoy a professional basketball game . . . ?"

"Am not! Am not!" Caleb insisted. "I know all the best shooters! I know the team's record! I know..."

"All right, all right," Dad finally had to agree. He shifted his focus and tried again. "Jill, since you're a girl..."

Before I could respond, Mom came to my defense. "Don't you dare say 'because you're a girl,'" she said to Dad. "Jill's out there practicing at the hoop with Marcus and all of his friends, and she's better than quite a few of them, too!"

"Okay, okay," Dad held up his hands in a "time-out" signal. "I guess I'll have to figure out a fair way of choosing between the three of you by tomorrow morning. I'll have to decide who deserves it most. Let me sleep on it—okay, guys ... and girls?" he added quickly before Mom and I could correct him.

The next morning, Marcus hurried into the kitchen and plopped down at the breakfast table. "Where's Dad?" he asked as he reached for a box of cereal.

"And 'good morning' to you, too," I responded in between sips of orange juice.

"Sorry, but you can guess what I was dreaming about all last night," Marcus explained. "So—where is he?"

"He and Mom went to pick up some books from the library," Caleb answered, digging his spoon into a mound of cereal.

"And he said we should all get started on our Saturday chores as soon as we finish breakfast," I added.

"Chores! He's got to be kidding," Marcus said as he set down his glass of milk with a thud. "How can we concentrate on chores when the big game is a mere eleven hours away?"

"Parents! They just don't understand!" I agreed, popping the last piece of English muffin into my mouth.

"I'm going for the morning newspaper," Marcus

announced. "There's probably a preview of tonight's game in the sports section."

"Wait for me!" Caleb added, slurping the last of his milk and dashing after his brother.

The back door snapped shut as the two boys trotted down the driveway. I looked at the breakfast table in front of me: tiny puddles of milk, bits of soggy cereal here and there, a small glob of grape jelly melting in the morning sunlight. *Well,* I thought to myself as I pushed my chair away from the table, *looks like Saturday morning chores start right here.*

A few minutes later, as I was washing off the kitchen countertops, I heard the familiar "thump . . . thump . . . thump" of the basketball bouncing off of the driveway. I glanced out of the kitchen window and saw Marcus practicing his hook shot while Caleb cheered him on. Frustrated, I knocked on the window three times. When the boys looked up, I meaningfully held up a kitchen sponge and dishtowel.

Marcus casually nodded to me and held up five fingers. Taking his cue from his older brother, Caleb did the same.

Sure, five more minutes! I thought to myself. *I'll just bet.* I opened the lower cabinet and tossed an empty muffin package into the almost-full wastebasket. I reached for a twister to tie up the plastic liner bag and carted it out to the garbage container outside the back door.

"He dribbles . . . he shoots! If I make this next shot, I get the tickets to tonight's game," Marcus teased as he shot for the hoop. "Hooray! Two points! And I get the ticket!"

"Do not!" Caleb shouted.

"You guys, Mom and Dad will be back any minute," I reminded them as I lifted the lid on the garbage container and placed the full plastic bag inside.

"Okay, we're coming in to help," Marcus said, dribbling the basketball around and around Caleb, who tried again and again to steal it. "Just one more minute."

"Yeah, just one more minute," Caleb added as he finally managed to tip the ball out of his brother's grasp.

I shook my head from side to side as I began to replace the lid on the garbage container. Then a flash of white on the inside of the heavy black plastic lid caught my attention. A white envelope . . . it must have stuck to the lid by accident. But then I noticed that the envelope was actually taped to the inside of the lid, and someone had written the word "Congratulations!" on the front of the envelope, too.

I lifted the flap on the envelope and pulled out a folded piece of paper. "To the one who deserves to go," the paper read, and inside of it was a ticket to the basketball game!

I don't believe it, I thought. *I'm the one that gets to go! But how did Dad know?*

Then I thought back to Dad's comment last night: "I'll have to decide who deserves it most." I smiled. Leave it to Dad to figure out who the most deserving kid really was.

By now, Marcus and Caleb had worn themselves out. They shuffled toward the back door. "Come on, little brother, we'd better get started on our chores if we want to have a chance at getting that ticket to the game."

I turned in their direction and held up the ticket, the note and the envelope. "It might be a little too late for that," I said with a sly grin.

Marcus and Caleb looked at each other with question marks in their eyes, as Mom and Dad's car pulled into the driveway.

That evening turned out to be as special as I'd imagined: Two seats at center court, and a dad and his daughter cheering their team to victory. It was a long-remembered lesson in responsibility from a dad who let his kids make their own choices and earn their own rewards.

J. Styron Madsen

Fireplug and Dad

You have brains in your head. You have feet in your shoes. You can steer yourself any direction you choose.

Dr. Seuss

I used to play football when I was a little kid. Okay, let's face it. I was never really a *little* kid. I was always chunky, hefty, short for my age, pudgy, stout, tubby, round, robust, portly. You get the picture.

In fact, I was so big that I got to play football a whole year ahead of my friends. Our Mighty Mites football league didn't have an age limit, it had a weight requirement. If you were heavy enough, you got to play. I was heavy enough at eight years old.

The only problem was, by the time I turned eleven I was too heavy. You had to weigh a certain amount to start playing, and if you weighed too much they made you stop.

Not playing would have been just fine with me. I would have been happier sitting at home reading a book.

But Dad was one of the team's big sponsors and friends with the coach, so I figured quitting wasn't an option. I went, day after day, week after week, and year after year . . . until I was eleven and weighed more than two hundred pounds. I thought that would be the end of it, once and for all. And, in a way, it was.

To make sure each kid was under the official weight limit every Saturday, the referees lugged doctor's scales around with them to every game. All of the "chunky" kids had the honor of joining the referees before each game to weigh in.

If the scales tipped past two hundred, off went the unlucky player's cleats. Then the helmet and the shoulder pads. Sometimes the jersey and the pants, and even the undershirt and the socks! Coach knew I was heading for trouble the day I had to step out of my underwear just to make weight. So he came up with a bright idea. The very next practice he presented me with a T-shirt made out of a black garbage bag.

"Put it on," he grunted, pointing out the ragged holes for my head and arms. "Start running around the practice field and don't stop until I say so."

I'd wave at him questioningly after every single lap, while my teammates sat on their helmets and talked—in between laughing and pointing at me, that is.

"Keep going, Fireplug," Coach would grunt around the mushy cigar in his mouth. "Fireplug" was the nickname he had given me. Although no one ever explained it to me, I figured it had something to do with me being shaped like a fire hydrant.

Every day at practice, I had to run laps in that stupid garbage bag. I'd hear it crinkling beneath my underarms as I stumbled through the stickers and weeds lap after lap. My short, stocky legs weren't exactly graceful, and often I'd trip or fall. The other players would laugh, but not as loudly as Coach.

I used to sit in class toward the end of each school day

and dream up excuses why I couldn't go to practice. Nothing worked, and so there I'd be, stumbling around the practice field with the sound of my plastic shirt drowning out my ragged breathing.

When the garbage bag T-shirt didn't exactly work wonders, Coach arranged for me to use the sauna at one of the local high-rise condominiums.

I rode my bike there the next Saturday. Coach handed me my garbage bag T-shirt and wedged me into a cedar-lined closet with two benches and a red metal shelf full of glowing hot rocks. He poured water on the rocks to build up the steam, and then shut the door on me with a wicked smile.

Outside the little porthole window, I could see him chomping on glazed donuts and sipping a cup of coffee. My stomach roared. Since it was a game day, I hadn't eaten since dinner the night before. Nor would I be eating again until after the weigh-in, when, as usual, I would be too weak to do anything much but sit there and pant until Coach shoved me full of candy bars from the concession stand so I could play ball again.

I sat there swimming in sweat and wondering how long this could go on. I'd been trying my best to lose weight ever since I was ten years old. I brought a bag lunch to school and skipped breakfast, but nothing seemed to work. I tried to be strong, tried to be brave, but there I still was . . . teetering on the brink of two hundred pounds and hoping to make it through yet another weigh-in.

Periodically, Coach would pop his bullet-shaped head into the steamy room to see if I was still alive.

I sat there dripping in sweat and realized something was very wrong with this picture. It was Saturday morning, and there I was, sitting in a sweatbox while the rest of the team chomped on Frosted Flakes and watched cartoons. They were still in their pajamas, while there I was in a garbage bag sweat suit! Why?

Was I being punished for something? Wasn't the running, sweating, hunger and pain enough? What more did
they want? I suddenly realized that I'd been knocking
myself out for something I didn't even want to do in the
first place! It was then that I decided that I didn't have to
do it anymore.

My heart fluttered and my stomach flip-flopped, but I
finally stood up on wobbly legs and walked out of the
sauna. At the time, it didn't exactly seem brave. It just
seemed right. It made sense. I had finally realized that there
was no law in the world that said I had to keep knocking
myself out just so Coach would have another strong player
and my Dad could have extra bragging rights!

"Did I say you could get out of there?" Coach bellowed
when he returned from the pool deck a few minutes later
and saw me sipping on a cup of water and enjoying one
of his glazed donuts.

I shook my head, but Coach was waiting for an answer.
So I told him.

"I quit," I said in a shaky voice that had nothing to do
with heat stroke.

"You quit?" he fairly laughed, looming over me. "You
can't quit. What would your dad think? Don't you want
him to be proud of you anymore?"

But that was just it. If my Dad couldn't be proud of me
for just being me, then what was the point? I was a good
kid. I stayed out of trouble, made good grades and even
made him a Father's Day card every year. Did I have to
torture myself, too?

I shook my head and told Coach it was over. All of it. I
wasn't going to starve myself anymore. I wasn't going to
make myself try to throw up anymore, or run around the
practice field in a garbage bag dress while the rest of the
team pointed and laughed.

That was when he called my dad. But it didn't matter to me anymore. I had finally made up my mind. It was time to be proud of myself for a change, no matter what anyone else thought.

After Coach had explained the situation to my dad, he grunted and handed me the phone. Although my hands were shaking, I was glad I wasn't doing this face-to-face!

"Son," my dad said quietly. "Is what Coach said true?"

"Yes," I whispered into the phone.

"You don't want to play football anymore?" he asked simply.

"I never did," I gasped. Well, if I was going to do this, I was going to do it right.

Dad's laughter surprised me. "Then why did you go through with all of those shenanigans?" he asked. "I thought you wanted to be the next big football star!"

I hung up the phone and headed for my bike. Coach just stood there fuming as I pedaled away.

I started carrying myself differently after that. Respecting myself more. I grew a little, shaped up, learned a lot, and eventually, the name Fireplug just seemed to fade with time.

Except for one night, that is. My family and I were waiting for a table in a local restaurant when Coach sauntered in. He greeted my Dad rather coolly and then eyed me with open disdain. "What's the word, Fireplug?" he asked.

Dad looked at me for an instant, and then he finally corrected Coach. "You meant 'Rusty,' right, Coach?"

Coach grumbled something through the mushy cigar in his mouth, but it didn't matter. Our table was ready and Dad kept his hand on my shoulder the whole way there.

And no one ever called me Fireplug again.

Rusty Fischer

Nice Catch!

When I do things without any explanation, but just with spontaneity . . . I can be sure that I am right.

Henri Frederic Amiel

From the moment Kyle heard the loud crack of the Red Sox bat, he was sure the ball was headed over the fence. And he was ready for it. Without ever taking his eyes off the ball, he reached up and pulled it out of the air.

"I caught it!" he yelled to his dad and his grandpa. "And I caught it with my bare hands!"

It was opening day of spring training and they had come out to the ball field to watch the Red Sox play. Kyle's grandma and grandpa lived near Ft. Myers, Florida, where the Boston Red Sox come in late February to prepare for the season.

Later, on the way home to Grandma's house, Kyle kept his head down. He tried to think of a way to convince his parents to stay a few more days.

"Wish we could go back to the ballpark tomorrow," he said. "Maybe I'd catch another ball to put with my Little

ON CHOICES 299

League trophies and stuff. And maybe I'd even get some autographs."

"You know that's not possible, Kyle," his dad said. "We're flying out early tomorrow morning."

"I know, I know," Kyle said, rolling the baseball around in his hand. "I just thought you and Mom might decide to stay a few more days. We don't go back to school until Monday, and tomorrow's only Thursday."

"We were lucky to get that flight!" his dad said firmly. "The airlines are booked solid this week."

That night, a huge snowstorm moved into the Northeast. When they arrived at the airport early the next morning, they were told that all flights into Logan Airport in Boston had been cancelled for the day.

On the drive back to his grandparents' house from the airport, it was obvious to Kyle that his dad was upset. It was definitely not a good time to bring up going back to the Red Sox ball field.

But by the time they were back at Grandma and Grandpa's house, Kyle's dad began to joke about the cancelled flight.

"Another day in sunny Florida isn't so bad," he said. "I'm in no hurry to get back to Boston, where my car's probably buried in snow."

"We could go out to the ball field again," Grandpa said. "Unless there's something else you'd rather do."

"The ballpark's fine," Kyle's dad said with a grin. "I'd never go against the wishes of anyone with so much power over the weather."

It was mid-afternoon when another loud crack of the Red Sox bat sent a ball flying over the fence. Again, Kyle reached up and caught the baseball in his bare hands.

As he rubbed his fingers around the ball, a small voice from behind him called out, "Nice catch!"

Kyle turned around to see a small boy in a wheelchair.

Without a moment of hesitation, Kyle handed him the baseball.

"Here," he said. "You can have it. I already got one."

The grin on the boy's face was a mile wide.

"Thanks," he said. "I never held a *real* baseball before."

Kyle's dad and his grandpa looked surprised—very surprised.

But they were no more surprised than Kyle was himself. He couldn't believe what he'd just done. But he wasn't sorry. He could never forget the happy look on the small boy's face. It was worth a million baseballs.

"I'm gonna get some autographs," Kyle said, rushing off to meet the players as they came off the field.

With three Red Sox autographs in hand, Kyle walked back to the parking lot.

"Think the Red Sox will have a good season?" Grandpa asked.

"They looked pretty good today," Kyle said. Kyle's dad tapped him on the shoulder.

"You looked pretty good today yourself, son."

And three avid Red Sox fans left the training grounds, each carrying with him a special feeling of pride. The proudest of all was Kyle.

Doris Canner

The Gorilla Syndrome

I wouldn't have believed that I could ever be so embarrassed! I was sweating, my heart was pounding like a bass drum in my head and I felt as though the entire classroom could hear it!

Josh, the cute, blonde boy sitting next to me, my secret crush, was looking down at my extremely fuzzy legs! I could feel the heat of his stare. It seemed as though a force field was drawing his dark brown eyes downward to my legs. I swallowed hard and tried desperately to pretend that I was completely enthralled by what the teacher was saying. In reality, she could have been telling me that Martians had invaded the earth, and I would not have reacted. *Oh Lord, please don't let Josh be looking at my hairy legs!*

Time seemed to stand still. The conversation I'd had the previous day with my mother kept whirling through my head like an amusement park ride that wouldn't stop spinning.

"Mom," I said, "Every girl in the seventh grade shaves her legs! I'm the only one who hasn't done it yet! I can't possibly wear a skirt tomorrow unless I shave. I look like some sort of gorilla!"

"Oh, Liz, don't be silly. No one will even notice your

legs. I'm telling you, once you shave your legs, you'll have to shave them forever. Your hair will grow back thicker than ever after you've shaved them, and trust me, shaving is not a lot of fun."

Oh, why did I listen to her?! She couldn't possibly know how I feel!!

It seemed an eternity had passed when at last I could feel Josh's eyes moving away from my legs. Inwardly, I breathed a sigh of relief . . . and then it happened. He said the words that I will never forget as long as I live. "Your mom won't let you shave, huh?"

It was too much. My mouth suddenly felt as though I'd spent forty years in the desert. I couldn't remove my tongue from the roof of my mouth, but somehow I managed a weak smile and shook my head.

He gave me an understanding look of sympathy, but couldn't stop his eyes from, once again, glancing down at my very hairy calves that were now wrapped like giant furry caterpillars around the back legs of my desk.

When Josh looked up, our eyes locked, and the embarrassment I felt nearly immobilized me. Somehow he knew I didn't want to talk about it, and to my great relief, he looked away.

My face felt as hot as a July sun, and I cringed, thinking it had probably turned as red as my hair. My life, as I knew it, was over. My mother had just ruined my life . . . the sweetest guy in the world had noticed my woolly legs, and felt *sorry* for me! *Oh my gosh!!! I can't believe this is happening. He feels sorry for me . . . how embarrassing! How am I ever going to look at him again? How am I going to make my mother understand what this has just done to me? I won't recover!*

I did recover. Slowly, slowly, my pounding heart began to calm down, and little by little I could once again hear the sounds of the classroom around me. I didn't think it was possible, but somehow I made it through seventh period and made it home again.

After slamming the front door, I made a beeline for my bedroom and proceeded to throw myself back dramatically onto the bed. With one arm slung across my forehead, I closed my eyes against the image of the expression of sympathy on Josh's face as he was looking at my legs. *Ughhh . . . was this some sort of nightmare or did he really ask me if I was allowed to shave?!*

I rolled over onto my stomach, crossed my traitorous legs at the ankles, and wished I had about a pound of rich milk chocolate and two cartons of hot, greasy, French fries.

Instead, I thought hard about what my mom had said about shaving, thought hard about the consequences . . . and shaved my legs anyway.

There. I'd done it. My legs were smooth now—except for the half dozen or so cuts. They were shaved though, and I felt extremely pleased with myself.

I did notice, however, that my legs seemed even more pale than before I shaved them, if that was possible. Maybe it was my imagination . . . no, they definitely glowed. Great, that was just what I needed, even milkier white skin that showed my spattering of freckles even more. *Oh well,* I thought, *at least they are shaved!* I would never have those gorilla legs to look at again.

After pulling on a pair of jeans and a T-shirt, I headed for the kitchen for a long-overdue snack and a phone call to my best friend, Krista.

Although I was exhausted from my ordeal, my sleep that night was restless. I dreamt of Josh and gorillas. He was trying to help me shave their backs and legs. It was absurd, and I was very relieved to wake up the next day. I was also relieved that the weather had turned so cold that wearing a skirt was out of the question. I was able to hide my war wounds with jeans.

I stumbled to my drawer and dug out a stuffed-in pair of jeans. They were only a little wrinkled. As I pulled them on, I noticed something weird. My legs weren't even smooth anymore! I ran my hands down my legs, and then I knew. My mother's words came back to haunt me as I stared at my battered-up, white legs with their newly formed stubble.

Closing my eyes, I sighed and tried to pretend that it wasn't true, but to my dismay, my legs were covered with tiny, black whiskers that were darker than I ever remembered my leg hair being.

I threw myself back on the bed in disgust. *Great, now instead of fur-balls on my legs, I have whiskers that feel as sharp as daggers.*

A week later, I found myself standing in a cluster of giggling girls on one side of the gymnasium at school. It was the school's first dance for the year, and the excitement among my friends and myself was at an all-time high.

Of course, the boys were all on the opposite side of the gym, some trying to look bored, others wrestling around and acting tough. Only a few of the most popular kids were brave enough so far to actually have danced, so much to my dismay, the teacher announced a game where *everyone* would have to be asked to dance.

My heart began to slam in my chest as I realized that I could be left standing until the very last, and I found myself panicking at the humiliation of it all. *I think it's time to go to the bathroom.*

I began making my way through the crowd. Suddenly, a faint scent of spicy cologne filled my nose, as I felt a small tap on my shoulder. Fully expecting to turn and find that it was my friend Krista who had done it, I nearly fainted when I discovered Josh standing only inches from me.

Still unbelieving, I turned my head from side to side, sure that I'd made a mistake. *Surely Josh didn't tap my shoulder . . .*

did he? I had no more than formed the thought when he chuckled shyly, and asked, "Do you want to dance?"

Where was my gosh-darn voice when I needed it? All I could manage was a small smile and a nod. Within moments, I was dancing with Josh . . . the sweetest, cutest, best dancer in the whole world.

I was still dancing on air that night while getting ready for bed. My smile was huge as I twirled through the hallway and into the bathroom to brush my teeth. Standing in my nightshirt, I suddenly caught a glimpse of my legs and realized that the embarrassment I thought I'd never survive seemed almost laughable . . . well, almost.

I was better at shaving now. My mom didn't even get mad at me when she found out that I'd shaved against her wishes. She just looked at me and said, "Be more careful next time." I was eternally grateful she didn't make more of a fuss. My dad, on the other hand, was not too pleased that I used his razor. . . . Well, that's another story.

When I went to tell my parents good-night, I hugged them both extra tightly. I was having a hard time falling asleep. My sister was breathing evenly next to me, and I knew she was already out for the night, but I was still so excited that Josh had asked me to dance.

Suddenly, I felt grateful to my PE teacher for making everyone choose a partner, even though earlier that night I'd felt like shooting her when she started the game. I smiled into the darkness at the thought and felt satisfied that I had just survived the worst humiliation of my life. With that thought came the realization that Josh must still like me despite my gorilla legs. After all, he asked me to dance, didn't he?!

My smile broadened, and with a satisfied giggle, I rolled onto my side and fell fast asleep.

Elizabeth J. Schmeidler

Just Desserts

*Do unto others as you would have them do
unto you.*

The Golden Rule

"Great dinner, Hon," said Dad, kissing Mom good-bye,
then giving a kiss to Sherre, Lizzy and me. "Don't wait up,
I won't be home 'til after three."

I was disappointed to see him go. I missed not having dinner together as a family now that Dad had to work nights.
He and Mom ate early, leaving the three of us to eat alone.

"Come on and eat, kids," Mom said after homework was
done. "It's hamburgers tonight."

We slid into the diner-style booth Dad had made last
year before he lost his job as an upholsterer. Little Lizzy
was squashed between Sherre and me. The booster seat
she had given up since becoming a "big four-year-old"
had been replaced with the hips Sherre, now a teen,
seemed to have sprouted overnight.

Mom slid a thin hamburger, one by one, onto each bun
then—plop, plop, plop—three thick spoonfuls of her
tasteless, lumpy mashed potatoes followed.

Our barely audible "Uhhh," was stopped short by a sharp look from Mom.

"Eat all those potatoes, girls," she said. "They're filling and they're good for you." We nodded. Times were tough and potatoes were cheap.

As soon as she left, I took a bite of the hamburger. The smell of heavenly garlic hit my nose. The taste was sheer bliss, juicy and full of flavor. I gobbled it down in four bites.

I risked a forkful of the potatoes, chewed as little as possible and struggled hard to swallow. *Mom must have been absent the day they taught potatoes in her Home Ec class,* I thought.

Sherre and Lizzy were having their share of trouble, too. Sherre gagged and Lizzy looked like she was going to throw up.

I smooshed the potatoes around on my plate trying to make them look less massive. I could dump them in the trash. A pang of guilt shot through me at the thought, knowing how hard Dad worked to put food on the table. Anyway, it'd mean having to pass Lizzy to get to the garbage can, and the little tattletale would tell on me for sure.

Then the idea came to me.

"Look, Lizzy!" I pointed up. "There are footprints on the ceiling!"

"Footprints?" said Lizzy. "Where?" Her gaze followed my finger.

"Up there." I scooped up a spoonful of mashed potatoes. Plop.

"I don't see anything," she said.

"I see them," said Sherre, picking up my lead and a spoonful of her own. "Look, Liz, over the sink!" Plop.

"I don't see them," Lizzy whined.

"Aw, you missed it," I said. "They're gone."

"I hear too much talking and not enough eating," Mom called from the living room. "No dessert till those plates are clean."

Lizzy turned back to her meal. A puzzled look spread across her face. She took her fork and cautiously poked at the huge heap of potatoes now on her plate. Sherre and I snickered quietly, but Lizzy was silent, unable to take her eyes off the swollen blob.

"I'll be in there in two minutes," Mom said in a loud voice. "You girls had better be through."

Sighing, we re-attacked the potatoes again. Lizzy stuffed her mouth full and managed to get them down with a gulp of water. I choked. Sherre chewed and chewed. Gagging, she spit the whole mess into her napkin.

"Look, Liz," she said. "Those footprints are back!" She pointed to the ceiling. Lizzy snapped her head up. Plop . . . plop. Lizzy was still looking up when Mom reached the doorway.

"Elizabeth Ellen Mandell!" she said. "What have you been doing all this time? Your sisters are almost done with their potatoes. Yours have grown!"

Lizzy looked at her plate and gasped. Her lower lip quivered and she began to whimper.

"Never mind the waterworks, Lizzy," said Mom. "There are starving people who would love those potatoes. Eat."

Obediently, Lizzy scooped up another lumpy forkful and tried to eat it. Her face turned red. She sputtered. She tried to swallow. I watched with a lump in my throat as she fought to force them down.

Suddenly I felt clammy and sick to my stomach—and it wasn't because of the potatoes. I opened my mouth to speak, to admit to Mom what was really going on. But remembering the torture Sherre had put me through the last time I confessed for both of us silenced my tongue.

Sherre didn't seem to notice my guilt. As soon as Mom left the room, she was back at Lizzy like a hawk on a chicken.

"Lizzy!" She said pointing to a spot behind Lizzy's head. "There they are again!" Lizzy turned around in her seat. Plop.

I picked up my spoon and filled it up with the last of my potatoes, then stopped. *No,* I told myself. *I'd rather eat Mom's mashed potatoes the rest of my life than to watch my baby sister suffer like this.*

I shoveled the potatoes into my mouth and dropped the spoon. It clattered onto my plate. At the sound, Lizzy looked down at her mashed potato mountain. She turned around again to try to find the imaginary footprints, then looked from Sherre to me, a light of understanding in her eyes.

Grasping a spoon in her pudgy little fist, Lizzy began plopping potatoes onto our empty plates.

"Lizzy, are your potatoes gone yet?" called Mom.

"Almost!" said Lizzy cheerfully, loading on some more. "Better eat 'em all up," she whispered to us with a grin. "Or I'll tell!"

Beverly Spooner

A Chicken-Noodle-Soup Day

Lying is done with words and also with silence.

Adrienne Rich

"I think I should stay home from school today, Mom. I'm sick. Really, I am."

I don't believe my fifteen-year-old sister for a minute. She hates school. This is just another one of her excuses to stay home. Again.

Mom isn't as sure as I am. She's a working mom who struggles with guilt for not being home for us. She gives Sandy the benefit of the doubt. Again.

"You can stay home," she says, "but you have to stay in bed. And I want you to eat chicken noodle soup for lunch."

We always eat canned chicken noodle soup when we're sick. It's the only time either of us likes it.

Mom feels Sandy's forehead as she kisses her good-bye.

"You don't feel warm," she says. "Are you sure you need to stay home?"

My dramatic sister lays one hand across her forehead. "I feel dizzy," she says, "and my head hurts. I must have that bug that's going around."

Mom reluctantly leaves for work.

"I'll call you later, Dear," she says as she closes the door. I have to catch the bus for school.

"Enjoy your day, Sister Dear," I holler over my shoulder, "and get well."

Sandy waves to me from the kitchen window and grins.

She tries her best to look pathetic when I come home from school, loaded down with homework. I hear her scurry into the bedroom we share as I open the door.

"Mom will be home soon. You'd better get your act together," I warn.

Sandy peers at me through drooping eyes.

"I'm feeling a bit better," she sighs.

"Then why are you still in bed?"

"Paying my dues for a day off," she replies.

"Well, save it for Mom," I say. "You're going to need it. I need a snack. What's in the cupboard?"

"Well, I found some donuts, and there's popcorn, and Mom hid a package of candy bars on the top shelf."

"Got you, you little faker. Wait until Mom comes home. This was a chicken-noodle-soup day, remember?"

"Oh, she'll never know."

Famous last words.

When Mom comes home, I'm at my desk doing homework. I open the door a crack so I won't miss anything. Sandy is on the couch, pressing a cool washcloth to her forehead.

"How are you feeling tonight?" Mom begins, in a tone of proper concern.

"Better," Sandy says with only an edge of brightness to her voice. "I think I can go to school tomorrow."

Smart move, Sister, I think.

"The chicken noodle soup must have made you better," Mom says. "Did it taste good to you?"

"Soup always tastes good when I'm sick," Sandy says sweetly.

Liar, I think. *Watch out. You have become an unsuspecting prey.*

"Well, Dear," says Mom, "you just lie there while I get supper. I don't want you to overexert yourself. Are you up to eating your favorite pizza?"

Probably not, I think, *after a day of junk food.*

Sandy manages to say, "I think I could eat a little."

Mom rattles around in the kitchen, stretching pizza dough and filling it with our favorite toppings. I hear her open the trashcan.

I know what's coming next. I think I'll stay right here in my room.

"Sandy, I don't see your soup can in the trash. Where is it?"

If I were you, Sister, I'd confess now. Otherwise, you're done for. But my cornered sister attempts a getaway move.

"I pushed the can to the bottom, so I wouldn't smell the chicken. It was upsetting my stomach."

That's a good one, I have to admit. But Mom's not buying it.

"Poor dear," clucks my predator mother. "I'll get rid of it for you."

"That's okay, Mom. I'm feeling better now. Why don't I empty the trash while you get dinner?"

"No need, Dear. Just relax."

I hear a clatter of cans and bottles in the kitchen.

"Oops," says Mom. "I dropped the trash."

I could help her clean up, but think I'll stay here and begin my essay for English class. I have my topic, thanks to Sandy. I think I'll call it, "What a Tangled Web We Weave."

Mom's voice remains calm and pleasant. Too pleasant.

"That's strange, Sandy. I can't find the chicken noodle soup can anywhere."

There is a long silence. Sandy makes one last attempt to

get out of the trap, but she is definitely the weaker one in this predator/prey game.

"I forgot, Mom. I put the can in the bag on the porch."

I know that there are at least four bags on the porch, all tied up, waiting for trash day—just as I know that Mom and Sandy will play this game to the death.

I have finished a draft about the complications of lying by the time Mom calls me to dinner. We sit at the table in silence. Four bags of trash are strewn on the floor.

Mom and I eat pizza, made just the way I like it, and drink soda. There is a special treat in the oven for dessert.

In front of Sandy sits one solitary mug of chicken noodle soup.

Donna Beveridge

Everything Will Be Okay

The world that we live in is the one that we create. We create our world with every thought that we think, with every word that we speak and with every action that we take.

LeVar Burton

The kitten is a scrawny thing with burrs and bits of wood caught in its coat where it still has fur, and pus coming out its eyes and nose. Its big baby head looks even bigger at the end of such a stick of a body. I found it in the woods at the end of my street where I play most days with my friends. This time I was alone. *Lucky for you I was,* I think. *Otherwise, David or Claude might have decided you'd be good practice for their slingshots. Those two can be mean,* I think to myself. I don't like playing with them really, but they live at the end of the street and sometimes you just play with the kids on your same street, even if they're mean, sometimes, even to you.

The kitten makes a pitiful noise.

"Don't worry," I tell it, stroking its scabby head until the mewing is replaced by a faint purr. "Everything will be okay. I'm going to take you home, and my mom will give you a bath and some medicine."

I tuck the kitten under my jacket and run out of the woods, across the street, down the sidewalk toward my house. I feel the warmth of the kitten through my shirt and start thinking of names.

* * *

I'm only ten, so it will be five or six years before I work for Dr. Milk. My two oldest brothers worked for him part-time and summers when they were teenagers. Now my other brother, Paul, works there. Dr. Milk is the vet out on Ridge Road. He takes care of our dogs, and he will take care of my kitten. I never had a pet that was my very own. A couple of years ago, my father got a new beagle to replace the old one that had died. Patches was his name. He called the new one Bucky and said that Bucky could be mine. But saying a thing is so doesn't mean it is.

Bucky lives in a kennel out back, keeping his beagle smell, which my mother hates, far away from the house. I feed Bucky some days and play with him, but I am not allowed to bring him inside to sleep at the end of my bed or curl up next to me while I do my homework. Bucky is an outdoor dog; he is a hunting dog.

He is my father's dog, really.

* * *

When I am older, I will go hunting with my father the way my brothers have done. I try not to think about this. I want to go, because I want my father to like me. But I don't want to kill animals.

One time when my father and three brothers went hunting, one of my brothers killed a deer. Most times they kill rabbits or pheasants if they get lucky. Most times they don't get lucky. But this time one of my brothers, I don't remember which one, killed a deer.

The deer was hung by its feet from a tree just outside the kitchen. I could see it hanging there when I sat at my place at the table. My father urged me to eat my venison and talked about the slippers he was going to have made from the hide. I couldn't eat. The thought of the venison made me want to throw up.

I could see the deer's eyes, even from the kitchen table. There was life in them still. Only the deer and I knew that there was life the bullet had missed; it was in the eyes.

I pushed the venison away.

My father said, "That's a waste of good meat."

My brothers teased me. One of them called me a sissy.

My mother said, "You don't have to eat it," and took the slab of gray meat off my plate.

* * *

My mother reaches into my jacket and removes the kitten by the scruff of its neck. She tells me to go down to the cellar and take off all my clothes and put them in a pile next to the washing machine.

"This animal is filled with disease," she says. "We can't let it touch anything in the house."

"We'll take it to Dr. Milk," I say. "He'll make it better."

"We'll see," she says, pushing me toward the cellar stairs, the kitten dangling from one of her hands.

I can feel tears welling up. "But that kitten is mine," I say. "I found it and it's going to be my pet."

She doesn't say anything. Looking up from the cellar stairs, I see her shaking her head at the kitten. Its eyes are clamped shut. I can see the pus oozing out of them.

"You are a sorry sight," she tells the kitten in the same soothing voice she uses with me when I'm sick. "A sorry sad sight."

I feel in the pit of my stomach what the future of that

kitten is. The feeling spreads through me like a sudden fever. Down in the cellar taking off my clothes, I cry so hard my body shakes.

When I return upstairs, my mother wraps me in my bathrobe and holds me until I can speak.

"Where's the kitten?" I ask.

"Out on the back porch in a box. Your brother will be home soon."

* * *

Paul will be going to college in the fall. Right now he's a senior in high school. I can't decide if I'm going to miss him or not. He's the brother I know best because he's been around the longest. The others left home when I was even younger.

Paul is the brother who taught me to ride my bicycle and the one who spent an entire Saturday with me and not his friends building a real igloo out of snow and ice. He's the brother who tells me how to be a man.

He is also the brother who plays tricks on me and sometimes the tricks are cruel. When I get angry, he says I don't have a sense of humor. He twists my arm behind my back sometimes until I say I'll do what he wants me to do. He makes promises he doesn't keep.

Paul is seventeen. He shaves every day and kisses girls right in front of me like it was nothing. He works at Dr. Milk's part time and summers.

* * *

I am sitting on the back porch, waiting for Paul to come home and talking to the box next to me.

"Don't worry, Smoky," I tell the kitten inside. "I won't let anything bad happen to you, I don't care how sick you are. My big brother will take you to Dr. Milk's and give you shots and medicine and stuff and you'll get better, you'll see. My big brother can fix anything."

The kitten is awfully quiet. I wish it would make even a pitiful noise.

We sit in silence. I daydream that I am seventeen. I am big and strong like my brother and I can make Smoky better. I see myself driving to Dr. Milk's out on Ridge Road, carrying the kitten in its box into the back room (which I have never seen, really, only heard my brothers tell stories about), giving it some medicine, reassuring it. . . .

"Everything will be okay, Smoky, everything will be okay."

In the kitchen behind me I hear my brother and mother talking in low voices.

* * *

Dr. Milk is not there when my brother pulls the car into the parking lot. It is after hours. My brother has a key. I am impressed by this.

"Come on," Paul says in his take-charge voice, "get that box now. Bring it on in here."

He flicks on the light in the waiting room. "You're coming in back with me," he commands. "I'll need your help."

"What are you going to do?" I ask. I am holding the box tight against my chest. I feel Smoky moving around inside.

"What do you think?" he says. "You heard your mother. That kitten is sick, bad sick."

"She's your mother, too."

"Well, she happens to be right," Paul tells me. "With an animal that far gone, you don't have a choice. It's got to be put to sleep."

I think the tears I jam back into my body are going to kill me. I think if I don't let them out they will kill me. But I won't let them out. I won't let Paul see.

"You do have a choice" is all I say. I hug the box for dear life and move to the door. Paul moves faster.

"Come on now," he says, gently taking hold of my arm, "be a man."

"I'm not a man," I tell him. "I don't want to be."

"You've got to do what's right. That kitten is half dead as it is."

"Then it's half alive, too."

He shakes his head. "You always have to one-up me, don't you?" he says.

I don't know what he means, but I do know that no matter what I say he is going to do what he wants to do.

A few minutes later, we are in the back room. The box is empty. Smoky is inside a big old pretzel can with a hose attached, clawing at the can's sides as my brother pumps in the gas. He is telling me it is good for me to watch this, it will toughen me up, help me be more of a man. Then he starts to lecture me about different methods of putting animals out of their misery, but all I can hear is the scratching. And then the silence.

* * *

At the supper table that night, I don't speak. I don't look at my brother's face or my father's or my mother's. I look at the tree branch outside the kitchen window where the deer once hung. My brother is saying something about taking me to the driving range tomorrow. He will teach me to hit a golf ball.

I won't go with him. I don't want him teaching me anything anymore.

In the fall he will go off to college. I will be eleven. I will be alone with my parents, alone without my brothers.

I get up from the table and no one stops me.

In the living room, which is dark, I sit for a long time thinking. I think about my kitten. I think about the pretzel can. I think about what it will be like not having any brothers around. I feel alone and small and frightened.

And then all of a sudden I don't feel any of those things. All of a sudden it's as if Paul had already left and I am on my own and I know some things so clearly that I will never have to ask an older brother to help me figure them out.

I will never work for Dr. Milk.

I will not go hunting with my father.

I will decide for myself what kind of boy I am, what kind of man I will become.

James Howe

A Silent Voice

If there are people at once rich and content, be assured they are content because they know how to be so, not because they are rich.

Charles Wagner

The situation seemed hopeless.

From the first day he entered my junior-high classroom, Willard P. Franklin existed in his own world, shutting out his classmates and me, his teacher. My attempts at establishing a friendly relationship with him were met with complete indifference. Even a "Good morning, Willard" received only an inaudible grunt. I could see that his classmates fared no better. Willard was strictly a loner who seemed to have no desire or need to break his barrier of silence.

Shortly after the Thanksgiving holiday, we received word of the annual Christmas collection of money for the less fortunate people in our school district.

"Christmas is a season of giving," I told my students. "There are a few students in the school who might not have a happy holiday season. By contributing to our Christmas collection, you will help buy food, clothing and toys for these needy people. We start the collection tomorrow."

When I called for the contributions the next day, I discovered that almost everyone had forgotten. Except for Willard P. Franklin. The boy dug deep into his pants pockets as he strolled up to my desk. Carefully, he dropped two quarters into the small container.

"I don't need no milk for lunch," he mumbled. For a moment, just a moment, he smiled. Then he turned and walked back to his desk.

That night, after school, I took our meager contribution to the school principal. I couldn't help sharing the incident that had taken place.

"I may be wrong, but I believe Willard might be getting ready to become a part of the world around him," I told the principal.

"Yes, I believe it sounds hopeful," he nodded. "And I have a hunch we might do well to have him share a bit of his world with us. I just received a list of the poor families in our school who most need help through the Christmas collection. Here, take a look at it."

As I gazed down to read, I discovered Willard P. Franklin and his family were the top names on the list.

David R. Collins

Walking with Grandpa

The power of choosing good and evil is within the reach of all.

Origen

Grandfather was a wise and honorable man. His house was not far from ours, and I would visit him often going home after school.

No matter how rotten I had been, I could tell Grandpa anything. My secrets were safe. He always understood. He loved me.

I remember a time when a bunch of us were playing baseball in the field behind Mrs. Ferguson's house. I hit one pitch just right and . . . *slam!* It was a home run that soared high and away, and ended up shattering Old Lady Ferguson's kitchen window! We all ran!

Walking home, my best friend, Tom, asked, "How will she ever know who did it? She's blinder than a bat!" He had a point.

I decided to stop by Grandpa's. He must have known something was up by the expression on my face. I felt ashamed. I wanted to hide. I wanted to bang my head

against a tree a thousand times and make the world just
go away—as if punishing myself could undo things. I told
him about it.

He knew we had been warned many times about the
dangers of playing where we shouldn't. But he just listened.

"I was wrong," I told him, with my head down. "I hate
myself for what I did. I really blew it. Is there a way out?
Will she call the police?"

"Well," he said, "she has a problem, just like you. I'll bet
if she knew you cared, she would be sad to know that
you're afraid of her. I'll bet she wishes you would give her
a chance . . . a chance to be understanding. It's your decision," he said, shrugging his shoulders. "Just so I don't
say the wrong thing, is the plan to pretend nothing
happened? Just keep quiet and carry your little secret
around . . . hide what you're not proud of?"

"I don't know," I sighed. "Things might get worse. . . ."

"Let's think it through," he said finally. "If you were
Mrs. Ferguson, what would you do?"

I had been afraid that Mrs. Ferguson would stay mad at
me, so I ran. I didn't know what she might do. On the way
home I imagined that she was a mean witch chasing me,
and the further away I ran, the more gigantic she grew . . .
until finally she towered over the whole town, seeing my
every move with an evil eye.

"Well," I said, taking a deep breath, "One solution is to
tell Mrs. Ferguson I'm sorry and offer to fix her window."

"If you call her," asked Grandpa, "what's the worst that
can happen?" I had to think for a moment. I realized that
even if she did not accept my apology, it could not be any
worse than seeing the disappointment on Mom and Dad's
faces.

Grandpa smiled when he knew I had figured it out.

"Doing what's right is not always easy," he said, hand-
ing me the phone. "I'm proud of you." Grandpa did not

make me do it. It was always my choice. I knew I had found the best answer, just by thinking it through. That's how Grandpa did things. As it turned out, things were not anywhere near as bad as I had first imagined.

"Owning up to what you're not proud of is the hardest thing of all," said Grandpa. "Choosing to be honest, on your own—even when you don't have to be—makes others trust you and respect you."

Besides, it made me feel really good about myself. No one can ever take that away. *Thank you, Grandpa.*

Mrs. Ferguson and I eventually became really close friends. She was so kind and grew to take a real interest in me. I started doing all kinds of odd jobs around her house after school, which eventually helped me to save enough to buy my first car. She once told me, "Fear can make the smallest things look so much bigger than they really are."

Just before he passed away Grandpa asked me, "Who will you turn to when I'm gone?"

Holding his hand I told him, "Honor is its own reward, Grandpa. And a good teacher lives on through his student. Thank you."

After Grandpa died, everyone was sad. So many people loved him and would miss him.

I still talk to him, in my thoughts. I imagine how he would approach things, what questions he would ask . . . what advice he might give . . . whenever there is a problem. His soothing voice is clear and simple.

Grandpa gave me the tools to fix many problems . . . and cut them down to size.

And most of all he showed me I was brave.

Uncle Greg

10

ON TOUGH STUFF

What a child goes through is hard to explain
We've been through stress, anger, hurt, and pain
Adults know what a child goes through
Because you see, they've been through it, too.

What a child goes through is sometimes insane
Sometimes people offer us drugs like cocaine
And now and again on dark, scary nights
We hear sirens and gunshots because of
*   gang fights.*

Death takes family and friends
Divorce takes them, too
Oh, if you only knew
What a child goes through.

Shannon M. O'Bryant, eleven
and Ashley O'Bryant, thirteen

Kelsey

My little sister, Kelsey, was two years younger than me. I can actually remember the day she was born. It was beautiful outside. The sun was out and there was a nice cool breeze. I went into the hospital to see my new sister, but I was too young to hold her.

Four years later, my brother Dakota came along, and by then, I was big enough to hold my new little brother.

Since Kelsey and I were so close in age, we did a lot together growing up. We were typical kids and we sometimes fought like cats and dogs. But there were also days that we were really nice to one another. We used to play games on Nintendo once in a while, but most of all, we loved to play outside.

My sister was the most athletic person in our family. She was a lot faster than me. As we got older, we used to race all the time, but she would usually beat me. We especially loved to swim, so my dad got us a membership at the pool at our nearby church. We loved that pool, especially the lifeguards and the people who would often go there. We would race in the pool, too, and sometimes I would actually beat Kelsey.

My family life was going pretty good but when I was

about eleven, I started to notice that my parents argued a lot. My dad was a hard worker and provided well for us, but he drank too much and my mom had no tolerance for alcohol abuse. The madness never did stop, so eventually they divorced.

I thought things would never be the same without my dad living with us and that it would be the hardest thing I'd ever have to go through. I realized that our lives would never be perfect due to the stress and strain that was created. But I tried to stay positive and remember the good times my father and I had. Mom and Dad seemed happier this way, and I knew we'd be okay.

My family and my mom's family have always been a close-knit bunch. My Nana and Pops were the best! Nana is a really sweet lady and cares for us a bunch, but Pops was my favorite person in the world. He was funny and silly, and he loved me and my brother and sister a lot.

One day, my pops wanted me to come over to watch some John Wayne movies that were on TV. We made popcorn and root beer floats that night. We were up pretty late and had a great time together. I was spending the weekend with them, which I loved to do. The next morning, Pops and I were going to get up early and eat breakfast together. Pops usually woke up at around 6:30 A.M. My Nana was up but Pops still hadn't gotten up, so Nana told me to go and wake him.

I went to get him, but I knew something was wrong as soon as I walked in. My Pops had died in his sleep early that morning of a massive stroke. I was totally devastated. My whole family was numb and in shock. For months we were all in a sad fog. Still, I tried to stay positive. My Pops was in a better place and although I'd miss him my whole life, I knew I'd see him again.

Things were going along all right, but we had our days when it was tough. We did our best to get through them.

Then in November of that year, my mom was diagnosed with an aggressive form of breast cancer. She ended up having a major operation on Christmas Eve. My mom spent her birthday, Christmas and New Year's in the hospital. I was so worried about her. I didn't know how I should deal with it. I guess I just dealt with it by trying to be as much help as I could around the house.

My mom went through several extensive surgeries and a massive amount of chemotherapy. She went away to Omaha for a few weeks to undergo treatment. I was so worried about her through those times. I was lucky to have such strong and supportive friends and family through it all.

Finally, Mom came home and was doing pretty well. We had several false alarms but nothing serious. By July, Mom was feeling good enough to get out with us and have a little fun.

One afternoon, my mom, Nana, brother and family friend Tracy went out to play miniature golf and then we went out to eat. We had a really good day. It was the most fun I'd had in a long time.

When we got home, there were tons of messages on the phone machine. My dad's girlfriend left us an urgent message asking us to call her as soon as we got home. When we reached her, she gave us more horrible news. She told us that my dad had died earlier that day of a massive heart attack. My mind was going in all sorts of directions. I had no idea this could happen to my forty-five-year-old father. It was a total surprise to all of us. I did not know what to do or think.

There was a huge visitation for my dad. Then, as a final good-bye, we spread his ashes in Lake Okobji in Iowa where he always used to say he wanted to be put to rest.

After we got things back on track again and going well, I started back at karate, something that I had always loved doing. Kelsey was excited about starting her first year of middle school and I was going to be in eighth grade. By this time, I'd been through more than most kids had, but nothing would prepare me for what happened next.

On September 3, Kelsey and Dakota begged my mom to let them go to the pool. I didn't go because I was mowing the backyard to earn some extra cash. My mom was not going to let them go, but finally they just broke her down. She was very sensitive to the sun from all of the chemotherapy, so she could not go with them. She said they could go for half an hour—just long enough to come back and get me so that I could go to karate.

My mom had just walked through the door and started to change clothes when the phone rang. It was someone from the church. They said there had been an accident at the pool. Mom came running down the stairs to tell our family friend, Tracy, and me. Tracy left with my mom and I stayed at home. I tried to call my nana and ask her if she knew what was wrong. I needed someone to talk to but apparently Mom called her and asked her to come to the pool. So I waited at home patiently for a phone call or someone to come and get me.

Finally, the phone rang and it was my nana saying she was on her way to pick me up. When she got to our house, she sat me down and told me what had happened.

My sister, Kelsey, had been caught in the pool drain. The paramedics came, but they could not pull her out. She was underwater for approximately twenty-five minutes. Finally, they were able to get her out and they rushed her to the closest hospital immediately. When she arrived, they worked on her and found a faint pulse after about thirty minutes. From there, she was rushed to Children's Mercy Hospital and that is where she stayed on life support. I went in to see her. She was not the same at all; she was not my athletic little sister anymore. She lived for two days, but she passed away on September 5, 1998.

Knowing that I would never see her again, and having to say a final good-bye to Kelsey was the saddest thing that I've ever been through. We had been together through the toughest times our family had ever known and we had helped each other out. Now she was gone forever and I was on my own. I knew I had to learn how to help myself out, and to help Dakota, too. If it weren't for my family and friends, I would never have made it through the experience of losing her.

I think my family and I might have a new start with our lives now. I know it will never be the same without Kelsey, but I think the tragedies in our lives have stopped. Mom is in remission and has gone back to teaching kids with special needs. I'm studying kick-boxing and karate and doing really well in school. As for Dakota, he's following in my footsteps and taking karate, too. So far, so good.

One thing I learned from all this is to treat your family with love and kindness. Always give hugs and kisses to them because tomorrow is not promised to anyone. If you do this, then you won't ever have to wonder if they knew that you loved them.

Shane Ruwe, fifteen

Losing Mom

When I was twelve, my parents separated, and I thought that was hard. Then I realized that something else is even harder: losing someone you love very much.

In my opinion "cancer" is the worst six-letter word in the whole dictionary. My mom was first diagnosed with mouth cancer. She spent Mother's Day in the hospital that year recovering from major surgery. Then, four months later, she was diagnosed with lung cancer. I remember the day so vividly.

When I came home from school that day, my mom's side of the family was there. They were all crying. My mom said, "Come and sit by me," and she started crying, too. My heart began to pound really hard and my eyes filled with tears. I definitely knew something major was wrong. My mom was too upset to explain so my grandpa told me. My mom had cancer in both lungs, and she only had a short time to live. My mom and I just sat there and cried together.

My family had to watch my mom go through so much: chemotherapy, radiation, oxygen treatments and the loss of her beautiful hair. She suffered so much, and we couldn't do anything about it. She couldn't talk without coughing or losing her breath. She was weak, and she was just slowly dying.

We knew it would happen someday, but not as soon as it did. Everything was over in eight months. I came home from school one day, and my mom wasn't there. She was always my first concern when I walked through the door. She had been taken to the hospital in an ambulance. We went up to see her that night. I didn't get my homework done, but I didn't care.

The next day, my brother Robert and I were called out of school because my mom wasn't doing well. I went to my locker and started crying. Two of my friends came out and tried to comfort me. When we got to the hospital, my brother Chris met us at the elevator and told us the grim news. I tried not to cry in front of Mom because it would upset her, and then she wouldn't be able to breathe. I took a deep breath and went in to see her. It was so hard to see her lying there so helpless. I held her hand, and we tried to talk but it was hard for her. I can't even count how many times I told her that I loved her.

When I left her that night, I had the feeling that it was going to be the last time I saw her alive. When I got home, I called her and we talked some more. I remember the conversation word for word. I told her that she sounded better and that I loved her. That conversation was so special.

The next day, Robert and I were called out of school again. I wanted to cry so badly, but I held back my tears. Chris and my dad were in the car waiting for us. I was so scared to face what was in store for us. When we stepped off the elevator at the hospital, I took a deep breath. I just had a feeling that what I was about to hear wasn't going to be good. My sister came out of my mom's room and she was crying. As I got closer, I could see that everyone else was crying, too. I started to shake. My sister came up to me and said, "She's gone. She died." I tried to laugh because I didn't want it to be true. The pain I felt was like no other. My sister asked if I wanted to go in and see her, and I said yes. When it was time for everyone to leave, we went over and gave Mom a last hug. When she didn't hug me back, I knew it wasn't a dream.

Some days I really need my mom. When she died, a part of me died, too. However, I knew that I would have to become an adult very quickly. Sometimes I ask myself, *Why her?* She did not deserve any of the pain that she went through. She fought hard for her children. We meant the world to her, and I know she didn't want to leave us.

I always thought my mom would be here for special things like homecoming, prom, graduation and my wedding day. It's hard knowing she's not going to be. She's never going to know her grandchildren or see Robert and I grow up. I would do anything to have her back. I miss and love her so much.

Very few people consider the true dangers of smoking. They think it is cool because everyone else is doing it. But it isn't. It really isn't.

I'm sure that at least one of you reading this thinks that life would be so much better without your parents. I have a little tip for you: Live life to its fullest and love your parents. It's hard to go on without them.

Diana Carson, fifteen

[EDITORS' NOTE: *For support in dealing with the illness or loss of a loved one due to an illness, call Kids Konnected at 1-800-899-2866, or log on to* www.kidskonnected.org.]

Celebrate the Good Days

Look to your health; and if you have it, praise God, and value it next to a good conscience; for health is the second blessing that we mortals are capable of; a blessing that money cannot buy.

Izaak Walton

Cancer. It sends chills up my spine as I say it. A six-letter word causes so much pain. I didn't think it would happen to anyone that I knew, until it happened to my mom.

It was in April of what seemed to be a great year. I was in fourth grade with the greatest teacher, Miss DeRosear. It was the year everyone looked forward to because Miss D. was the coolest teacher.

I had just come home from school to find Mom at home. That was odd because she never arrived home before me. Mom was sitting on the couch with Dad. A thousand horrible things started flashing through my mind. *What if Grandma had passed away? I did not have the chance to say good-bye. What if my brother was hurt?*

As I crawled up on the couch next to Mom, she gave me

a kiss and a huge smile, so I relaxed and went on with my normal after-school activities. During the TV show that I always watched after school, Mom started getting phone calls. The calls continued for the rest of the night. Each time the phone rang, Mom rushed to her room. I then knew that something bad had happened.

When Mom came back, I asked, "Mom, why do you keep on leaving the room every time you get a phone call?"

She turned to my sister and me and said, "Girls, I have something to tell you. I have a disease that will make me very sick. I have cancer."

As she said that I felt a sharp pain in my heart. I was thinking, *Why is God taking my mom from me so soon? What have I done?* Little did I know that we were just beginning a very long, painful journey.

The next day on the bus I turned to my friend, Kate. "My mom . . ." That was all I could say before I started crying. Kate gave me a big hug and whispered, "I know, and I'm here for you." I knew then that Kate would support me.

As other people found out about my mom's cancer, they all had different ways of dealing with it. When my grandma found out about it, she had a difficult time, because to her, cancer was a death sentence. She had lost her husband, my grandfather, to cancer when my mom was only a senior in high school.

Then the time came for Mom to have chemotherapy. Her hair fell out, and she was always sick. I remember all those nights that she was too tired to eat, or she was sick from the chemotherapy.

During the summer, Mom stayed home. On the good days, Mom, Sis and I went down by the pond and made shapes out of clouds. On these days we talked about what we were going to do the next day, week, month or year with Mom. We never talked about losing her.

Support came from many different people and places.

When school started again, Mom had to have surgery. I stayed with one of my teachers, Mrs. Stephens. Mrs. Stephens made me rainbow French toast. It always made me feel better: it let me know that someone cared and made time to make something for me. I would feed it to the dog if I had too much or if I wanted the dog to feel good also. Mrs. Stephens was always there for me with a smile, a hug or "it will be okay" advice.

Sometimes I lost hope, wondering, *Am I losing my mother just like she lost her father?* I spent hours just ranting at God, telling him that he could not take her away! I needed her! He just could not take her away!

After a long six months of losing her hair and throwing up because of chemo, my mom took a turn for the better. She slowly started to recover.

On April 5, 1999, my mom became a five-year survivor. When that day came, we had a big party. Friends came from far and wide to celebrate how special Mom is and her victory against cancer!

If you know someone who has cancer, you can help by doing little things. You can stay with them for a while and just chat or do some chores.

Dealing with cancer is so hard. Don't bottle up your feelings. Talk to someone. Chat rooms are available for kids dealing with cancer, and support groups help kids and teens deal with cancer, too. Do not give up!

There will be good days and bad days—some more bad than good. But as I have learned from my mother, celebrate the good days!

Leslie Beck, fourteen

Think Before You Act

It was a cold evening, the night before Halloween, when something happened in my town that no one will ever forget. During lunchtime at school, some girls who were my brother's friends told him about a plan that they had to toilet paper a guy's house. They had already been playing pranks on this guy, and they were laughing about what his house would look like when they were through with it. My brother told me later that he knew what they were planning on doing was wrong, but he didn't say anything to the girls. Now, he wishes he would have.

That night my brother's six friends stayed overnight at one of the girl's houses. In the middle of the night, they sneaked out of the house. They piled into one of the girl's small blue car and set off to play their little prank. When they got to the guy's house, everything went as planned—until they got caught. The guy that they were playing the prank on came outside and saw them. Laughing, they all ran to the car and hopped in, hoping to get away. The guy got into his car and chased after them, trying to identify them. He was right on their tail, and it scared the girls really badly. They were not sure what he would do to them if he caught them, so they went faster.

Then, when they were turning on a blind curve in the road, they lost control of the car and hit a tree head-on. Three of the girls were ejected from the car and were killed instantly. The other three girls were seriously injured. One of the girls had just enough strength to get out of the car and go to a nearby house. The people who answered the door were afraid of her and didn't even believe that there had been an accident. They said, "Yeah, right, you really got into a wreck," and they would not call the police.

The three girls that died were all honor-roll students and were looking ahead to doing something great with their lives. But all of their dreams were shattered when they hit the tree on that cold night. Only one of my brother's friends was wearing a seat belt, and she was one of the survivors. Now whenever I get into a car, I think about the accident and put on my seat belt.

The guy that chased them went to court. All he got was a ticket for running a stop sign and for speeding. I often wonder if he feels anything at all about the death of the girls in that car that he chased. My brother feels bad that he didn't say anything to his friends that day when they told him what they were planning on doing. They still might have gone on their mission regardless of what he said, but he might have saved his friends' lives. We'll never know. So many people have suffered because of a stupid act that was never meant to go wrong.

The only good thing that came from this tragic event is that the mother of one of the deceased girls is setting up a teen center in town in memory of the girls that died. Now there will be a place for teens. Maybe that will keep some of them from getting into situations like this by providing a place to hang out and have fun, to talk to each other and hopefully give them a chance to help them think before they act.

Lauren Wheeler, twelve

Getting Better

I was a nine-year-old girl beginning a journey to a whole new place. My mother and I were saying good-bye to our family, and were on our way to Kent, Washington, where we were going to live. My sisters, brother and dad were staying in Billings because my parents were divorced. My parents divorced when I was around two, and my dad remarried when I was four years old.

My mother and I were moving to Seattle because she had been offered a job as a special ed teacher. The only reason that I went with my mother was because she had told me so many bad things about my father, and I was too scared to live with him. I didn't even really want to leave because I wanted to stay with my sisters, but I didn't know what to do about my dad.

Let me tell you, it was incredibly scary to be all of a sudden moving to a whole new place, where I didn't know anybody. My mother and I moved into an apartment. Just after we arrived and we were unloading our things, a somewhat nice-looking guy came walking down the stairs. He introduced himself as John and offered to help us unload our belongings. He seemed quite nice, so we said yes and just kept on unloading. We finally finished unloading so we began to unpack our things.

Pretty soon, my mother and John began to date, and after about three months, John would come over to our apartment all the time. To me it began to feel like they were married. He would stay until really late, and he loved to tuck me into bed. I was not sure how to deal with all of this because something about him scared me really badly. My mother and John decided to get married. I didn't get excited about it.

After the wedding, John started to come into my room more and more, and would stay for a long time. He began to touch me in very uncomfortable ways and I would get extremely scared. I didn't say anything, because I was too scared. Sometimes I would put my hands over my chest and roll over so that my back was facing him. During this particular time, my mother would usually be in her room watching TV, and I did not want to scream. I knew that if I did he would immediately stop and pretend to be innocent, and my mother would think that I was crazy.

A few months after the wedding, my mother and John found a new house. I was given the opportunity to live with my dad again, and based on what was going on with John, I decided to move back to Billings.

My family in Billings was extremely excited to have me back, but when I got home it was hard for me to get close to them. I found myself having a hard time showing any physical affection toward my dad and stepmom. John had confused me as to what was normal and what was appropriate. Any physical contact made me pull away.

My sister and I would go see my mother during every vacation. Sometimes neither of us wanted to, but we were expected to. I used to cry and beg my parents not to make me go. Every time I was there, John would touch me and I would get more scared about what was happening and whether or not anyone would believe me if I told.

At one point, I told my best friend Lindsey what was happening and she told me to tell my parents. I didn't think that they would believe me so I made her swear to keep quiet, and I didn't take her advice.

My dad and stepmom began to wonder if there was something going on that I just wasn't able to talk about. Then one day, my stepmom decided to have a school counselor come to the house to see if she could help me break through the awkward silence. Rather than tell a stranger what had been happening, I finally burst out and told my stepmom the truth.

At last, I had the courage to tell my family what John had been doing to me. My stepmom, Jean, pulled me close to her and we cried for a long time together.

Soon after that, we contacted an attorney who got in touch with the police in Washington. John was arrested, but it took nine months before we actually went to court. It was really hard on me to face my mother during the trial, but I got through it. All that I have to say is that it was one of the hardest times of my life.

John was found guilty and went to jail, but immediately he hired a new lawyer to appeal the case. Just before he was to be sentenced, he was granted a new trial. He decided to accept a plea bargain and was freed from jail after only five months. As unbelievable as it sounds, he was able to return to his job with the government and is living with my mother. As I suspected, she didn't believe me, even after a jury of twelve adults found John guilty. The family has not had any contact with her in nearly three years.

After the trial, I felt that the attorneys had taken such care with my case and treated me so wonderfully, I wanted to become a lawyer. I want to defend little kids, or anyone else, who is unfortunate enough to be in the same situation that I was.

I always have hope that one day my mom will see how much she has missed and get back in touch with us kids. There are days when it saddens me and I cry and get furious. I will always love my mother no matter what, and hopefully someday I will be able to accept the choices she has made and the person that she is.

I now live my life the best way that I possibly can. I know who I am inside, and that took a lot of counseling. I also don't think that I would be who I am right now if it weren't for my stepmom and dad and their intuition that something was terribly wrong in my life back then. I can't imagine what my future would have held. Now, it's better than it's ever been, and getting better.

Tiffany Jacques, fifteen

[EDITORS' NOTE: *To get help with child abuse issues of any kind, call Childhelp USA at 800-4-A-CHILD.*]

For the Best

It is not only for what we do that we are held responsible, but also for what we do not do.

Moliere

It was two days after the tragic school shooting in Colorado, and I was feeling bad about what had happened to the students there. My school began having a lot of bomb threats and it seemed that police cars were there often. I was standing with my friend, Amberly, and her boyfriend when he casually said, "I'm gonna blow up the school and kill everyone." I asked, "Why would you want to do that?" and he said, "I just do," and walked away.

I was scared because no one had ever said anything like that to me before. I found out when talking to other friends that he also bragged about this to other people. My friends told me that I should tell an adult what he had said, but I was too scared and I made them promise not to tell anyone either.

One day, Amberly and I were talking about what he had said when the teacher overheard our conversation. She took me out into the hallway and made me tell her who had said it and what they had said. At first, I refused to say a word. She told me it really was for the best, so I told her. I felt awful for doing it. I was angry with her for making me tell who said it. I wasn't sure he really meant it and didn't want him to get into trouble.

He got suspended for two days and had two days of in-school detention after that. I sometimes wonder if I had not told, would he have done what he said he was going to do? The guys in Colorado seemed pretty normal to a lot of people. The bottom line is, you should never joke around about something as serious as killing people. If you do, responsible people have no choice but to have you checked out to ensure everyone else's safety.

After he was suspended, the whole sixth grade had an assembly. The principal and counselors told the students that there was a kid who was making threats and that he was suspended. I decided later to tell him that it was me who told on him so he wouldn't speculate about who did it. I was surprised to find that he was not angry with me for doing what I did. He was able to get help for his feelings and behavior.

Many people are in the same situation that I was in. If your friend is saying threatening stuff like my friend was, then they obviously need help—soon. It seems like when one school shooting happens, then another one occurs not too long after that. If there were any way that you could prevent one school shooting it could perhaps save your own life and many others as well. If I had to do it over again, I would—because it really was for the best.

April Townsend, twelve

[EDITORS' NOTE: *If you are aware of dangerous or illegal activity that has happened or is going to happen at your school, tell this information to a trusted adult, or in case of an emergency, call 911. If you would like information on starting a student-led safe school initiative (S.A.V.E. chapter) contact the Center for the Prevention of School Violence at* www.ncsu.edu/cpsv/. *If you would like to report your concerns about an act or potential act of violence, contact WAVE America [Working Against Violence Everywhere] at* www.waveamerica.com. *You do not have to give your name.*]

A Smile Can Save a Life

The day that changed my life forever started out like any other day for me. I have been a professional speaker for the last four years, since I was eighteen. I travel around the country speaking to middle and high school students about self-esteem, goal setting and helping others. On that day in 1999, I was speaking to a group of students near Fort Worth, Texas. The auditorium was full of applause, hugs and smiles. Such a love-filled morning did not prepare me for the tragedy about to unfold.

After my speech that day, I went back to my hotel room. It was then that I received the emotional phone call that I will never forget.

"There was a tragedy at a youth event, right near where you spoke. Most of the victims were kids. I don't know what their conditions are."

For once, I was speechless. I was also afraid. *Were any of the kids I spoke to today involved?* I wondered. Even though I didn't really know them, I felt a strong connection with the young people who had been in my audience only hours before.

I immediately hung up the phone and turned on the

radio to find out more. A middle-aged man had walked into a youth rally at a local church and started shooting. In only minutes, he had ended the lives of several pre-teens from the church's youth group.

I bought a map, and drove the few miles to the scene. When I got there, it was a horrible scene. Helicopters were circling overhead, and parents were screaming and calling the names of their children. Everyone was crying. I didn't know how to help, or what to do. Then I noticed a group of young people sitting on the street corner and I walked up to them.

To this day, I don't remember exactly what I said. I do remember that we hugged one another and did our best to comfort each other while the crying and screaming was going on all around us. I will never, for the rest of my life, forget sitting on that street corner with those kids—feeling their pain and confusion—and crying with them.

I knew from that moment on, that my life work would be about preventing youth violence.

I began asking questions during my speeches and listening to the students, tens of thousands of them from all over the country. I learned from them what they thought causes violence and especially what they thought could prevent it. Having the students sharing their opinions, and working with them to shape their schools has become a moving experience for me.

I will never forget the eighth-grade girl, Jenny, who told me she was more afraid of sitting alone at lunch than being physically hurt, and that no one ever smiled at her. Or looking into the teary eyes of Stephen, who had sat next to another boy for an entire year—a boy who later shattered his school and many lives. He hung his head as he told me, "I never once said hello to him. I never once asked him how his day was. I never once acknowledged him." I started to realize that these kinds of behaviors are the seeds that can later create violence. My belief was confirmed when I got word about the man who had shot the kids at the event in Fort Worth. He had opened fire on those kids just to get attention, and because he had felt that this was a way to get back at people who had ignored him.

The most important thing that I have learned is that young people are amazing. I am always so frustrated that the media often depicts teenagers as lazy, unintelligent and violent. They rarely discuss the millions who work hard to get through school, hold steady jobs, support their families and stay clear of trouble. They overcome all kinds of obstacles, limitations and fears every day, in order to move forward with their lives. Such as Maria, the blind girl, who is a star on her school's track team, or John, the school bully, who turned his life around to become one of my best volunteers. Thousands of students put forth an effort every day to help others, and they never even expect to be acknowledged.

Together we can work to respect all different types of people. We can learn what behaviors can hurt and what behaviors can help. Ignoring others or calling them names can create an atmosphere that fosters violence. And, something as simple as a smile can truly save a life.

Young people do have the potential to make their own schools and communities safer. Most of all, we can sincerely value ourselves and others for who they are. Together, we can connect and end the hurt.

Jason R. Dorsey

[EDITORS' NOTE: *With the help of mentors and young people across the country, Jason founded the nonprofit Institute to End School Violence, whose goal is to take student solutions for preventing violence and use them to build stronger school communities. Learn more at* www.endschoolviolence.com.]

My One Regret

Don't ever slam a door. You may want to go back.

Don Herold

Even though my mom and dad still loved each other, my dad's lifestyle came between them and us. Dad always picked his friends over his family. He owned a bar, rode a Harley, and had other hobbies that I do not feel too comfortable talking about.

My mother and father had been divorced for five years when I went to live with my dad. My mom and I were not getting along. As it turned out, I spent most of my time with my twenty-six-year-old brother. My brother took me to school, picked me up and dropped me off at Dad's house because my dad was still the same and spent all of his time either at work or with his friends.

Pretty soon, I started to miss my mom, so I wanted to move back to live at her house. My dad was really upset with me for wanting to leave, even though I hardly ever saw him. I went ahead and moved back in with my mom anyway. Three months went by without my dad and I

speaking a word to each other. It didn't really bother me
too much, because my mom and I were getting along, and
we had even moved into a new house. Then my whole life
changed with just a single telephone call.

My ten-year-old sister and I were the only ones home
when a woman called. She did not tell us what was going
on, only that my mom should call when she came home.

When Mom returned a few hours later, she called and
was told that my father had been in a motorcycle accident
and that she needed to call the hospital. When she called
the hospital they told her to contact my dad's family. My
mom became hysterical and started yelling that *we* were
his family and that she was his ex-wife and she had his
children with her. They still would not tell her anything,
except to contact my brother.

I knew that we were too late. I started to cry, but then I
stopped. I guess part of me just wanted to hold on to the
small chance that maybe I was just overreacting. Deep
down I knew that I was not, I just did not want to believe it.

All of us piled into the car and drove to my father's
house as quickly as possible. My brother was sitting outside on the picnic table with people all around. When I
saw my brother sitting there, I panicked. Right then I
knew that he did not have good news for us. My brother
squeezed into the car and told us to drive. I can still
remember the exact words my brother said—I don't think
that I will ever forget them. He said, "Kids, I hate to be the
one to have to tell you this, but Dad is dead."

The next few days are still a blur. Everybody tried to act
strong. I would catch my older sister locked in the bathroom crying. My younger sister would write messages in
her notebook about how she wished that she still had her
daddy. I think that I suffered greater than they did. My
father and I never had a chance to resolve our problems. I
cannot remember the last time we told each other how

much we loved each other. He was mad at me when I left his house, and I never had the chance to work things out with him.

The only thing that kept me from going insane was my mother. She told me about dreams that she has had about my father. He talked to her in her dreams. He told her that he is watching over us, and that he loves all of us very much. I want to believe that with all my heart.

I often think about how things could have been different if I had just picked up the phone during those three months and broken the silence between us. I guess I just thought he'd always be there.

The greatest advice that I can give anyone is to always forgive each other—don't let your differences linger over time. You never know what the future will hold.

Angelia Lee Swift, seventeen

The Perfect Figure

I am as my Creator made me, and since He is satisfied, so am I.

Minnie Smith

"Oh my gosh, it looks sooo good on you," exclaimed my best friend. "That color flatters you, and I'm getting it for you for your birthday. After all, it's in two weeks!"

I had gone bathing-suit shopping with my best friend. Since we were going into the seventh grade we needed to look cooler. We tried two-piece suits in hopes that we would get more attention from the guys. We wound up purchasing them, and the topic of conversation came up about going on a diet. The only reason for going on one would be to lose a little bit of our "baby fat." I thought all the guys would like me if I was pretty and thin.

So I decided to stick to the diet, even though it would be hard because I am a chocoholic. I had always been a big girl. Not necessarily fat, but tall with a solid build. All the courses in school I took were advanced placement and I played many sports. I thought, *A thin, pretty, smart, athletic girl—everyone will love me.* When I would come home I wouldn't snack, and I cut down on my dinner portions. I had cravings for ice cream, but I just looked at beauty magazines and my bathing suit. The craving dis-integrated quickly.

My mom noticed when I dropped five pounds. She told me to stop because I could hurt myself. I promised her I'd stop, but I couldn't. My best friend lost about ten pounds and stopped because she knew she looked good. I started getting complimented by my peers at school. I wore my same clothes which kept getting baggier and baggier. Some people would ask me where my lunch was. I lied to them and made up excuses.

Since I lost weight by dropping lunch, I did the same with breakfast. I tricked my dad into thinking that I ate my bagels, but I fed them to the deer. My weight dropped drastically, and my best friend would threaten to tell my parents if I didn't eat. I fooled her so she thought I was eating, but I wasn't. When I looked at myself in the mirror every day, I saw bulgy thighs that had to go.

My gym teacher confronted me about my immense weight loss. I told her I was losing weight, but that it was all through exercise.

Finally, dark circles formed under my eyes, and I stopped physically developing. It was a struggle for me to even walk up my driveway. I couldn't sleep at night, and I wore layers of clothing in eighty-degree weather but I was still cold. That didn't matter. I still needed to be thin-ner, and I started wondering how many calories were in toothpaste and communion wafers.

About a month and a half after I had bought the bathing suit, I tried it on again and it fell right off me. My mom told me to look in the mirror. I could see my eye sockets, my transparent skin, the dark circles under my eyes, and my cheekbones popping out of my skin. That was the day I realized how skinny I was.

I went to our family doctor and a psychiatrist. My total weight loss was about twenty-five pounds in one month and a week. It took one year for my body to start working normally again.

Sometimes I want to go back to being thin, but I would *never* do what I did again. It's not worth it. Please don't go on diets when you're young. You will regret them. I know I do. Get help right away because you'll slowly kill yourself and suffer greatly. Don't judge and compare yourself to others. Try to love yourself for who you are, not for how you look. Besides, you probably look fine just the way you are.

Nikki Yargar, fourteen

[EDITORS' NOTE: *For information regarding eating disorders, log on to the Eating Disorders Awareness and Prevention Web site at* www.edap.org *or for information and referrals call the hotline at 1-800-931-2237.*]

Pale Dawn of a New Day

Recovery is a process, not an event.

Anne Wilson Schaef

I had always had a feeling of dread deep down within me. When it happened, it hit me with such surprise that you would never know that I predicted it.

At the time, I did not know how lucky I had been. I would lie awake at night before falling asleep, hearing my parents fight and yell at each other. Although neither hurt the other, it always ended up with my mother crying . . . and that always scared me. I suppose they never thought I could hear them, and they hid their tension from me as much as possible.

One afternoon, my mother told me she needed to talk to me. I never thought of the obvious. My mother sat down next to me on our gray couch with my father on the other side. My mother calmly explained that they no longer enjoyed each other's company and that they would be getting a divorce. As I fought back tears, my mother continued to tell me how they had tried so hard to make it work—for me. They said they never wanted to hurt me. They could never know how much it did. They said that even though they no longer loved each other, it did not affect how much they loved me, and that my dad would move to an apartment nearby, close enough for me to walk to.

I could no longer hold back the tears, and I ran sobbing to my room, slammed the door and collapsed on my bed. I clutched my pillow to my chest. Everything flashed through my head, everything I could have done to make it work. I lay there, never wanting to leave the safety of my room, not wanting to accept my new reality. I stared for hours out my second-story window, not really thinking . . . not really looking, just sitting out of the reach of my own mind.

I woke up the next morning and trudged to the bus stop. At school, my friends comforted me and I hated it. I was trapped, and everyone made it worse. My friends tried to make me feel better, but they always reminded me of how it had been before. I began to associate the pain of the situation with them and it hurt. I pushed them away, enjoying the solitude.

I found I loved writing, though I shared my compositions with no one. Everything had been turned upside down. No one knew. I only suffered internally. I hid inside myself, remaining the same person externally. My parents, in separate places, acted as though nothing had happened, and that outraged me even more.

My father did not move to an apartment nearby. Instead, he stayed in our house. It was my mother who left and moved to the other side of town.

I was informed my father had fallen in love with a new "companion." It hurt immeasurably to watch my father preferring to hold her hand instead of mine. My mother had found one as well, and moved in with him. I would spend long hours at her house waiting to leave, feeling alone and ignored. I thought I would die.

My writings began to be terrible stories of girls in far worse situations than I, making me feel more fortunate. I moved back and forth between homes every week, and when anything went wrong, it was always the other parent's fault. I woke up every morning to meet the dawn, which seemed to be paler and more frail than ever before. Alone, not allowing anyone into my reality, I cried.

Now, two years later, I almost never cry, for I feel that I have cried my share. I have accepted and moved on. I've become closer to both of my parents, and throughout the trials they go through, I now feel involved and helpful. My mother's companion recently left her and she came to me in friendship, looking for support.

But it still hurts quietly somewhere inside of me. I will never forget, and I will always miss how it was. Even though they fought, we were together and I never appreciated it when we were. As for now, I realize that there is nothing more beautiful than the dawning of a new day and that I must go on.

Katherine Ackerman, twelve

11

ON CHANGES

*Change is the only absolute
in the world,
the only thing
that you can depend on.
Nothing stays the same.
Tomorrow will come,
bringing with it
new beginnings and sometimes
unexpected endings.
You can hold on to the past
and get left in the dust;
or, you can choose to
jump on the ride of life
and live a new adventure
with perseverance and
an open mind.*

Irene Dunlap

My Very First Kiss

I was in the seventh grade when I fell in love at the school-bus stop.

"Who's that?" I hissed to Annie, my best friend.

"I dunno. New kid. Let's find out," replied Annie. Then she approached him. "Hi!" she dimpled.

Annie never just smiled at boys. She dimpled. She had the cutest, roundest cheeks with a dimple in each cheek. I was so jealous.

"I'm Annie. Did you just move here?" Annie lowered her head and looked up at him through her lashes.

"Yeah," he answered.

"This is my friend, Patty."

He looked at me.

I had never seen eyes so blue . . . eyelashes so long . . . a gaze so intense. . . .

I FELL IN LOVE.

Everything you have ever heard about falling in love came true for me at that instant. My legs started to quiver and my kneecaps turned to jelly. I felt like I couldn't breathe very well. I couldn't walk, I couldn't talk, I couldn't even see very well. I just stood there, like the skinny geek that I was, looking at him.

His name was Jerry. He had moved into a house only four blocks from mine. Jerry was shorter than me, but that didn't matter. He didn't have much to say, but that didn't matter either. I was truly in love.

I started riding my bike past his house every day, gliding past the big picture window in the front, afraid he was looking out, yet praying and hoping that he was.

I was miserable and ecstatic all at the same time. I didn't want to share my feelings about Jerry with Annie, because if I made him look too desirable, she would probably want him. And if she wanted him, she would get him.

Then one Friday I got an invitation to a party. I couldn't believe it. It was a boy/girl party. My first. And my parents said I could go. And Jerry was invited.

The party was at Phyllis's house, and her parents had a room for parties that was separate from the rest of the house. Her parents wouldn't be watching us all the time. Annie told me that meant that it would be a kissing party. Perfect. The sweat was already forming under my armpits.

After two hours of eating potato chips, drinking Cokes and listening to our favorite music, someone suggested that we play Seven Minutes in Heaven. Someone else suggested Spin the Bottle. Spin the Bottle seemed much less threatening than spending seven whole minutes making out in Phyllis's garage. We all voted on Spin the Bottle, but you had to really kiss, not like some kind of kiss you give your grandma.

We all sat in a circle: boy-girl-boy-girl. Whoever had the tip of the bottle land on them had to go into the garage with the spinner of the bottle. If you were a girl, and you landed on a girl, you got another turn until you landed on a boy. Same for boys. Couples went into the garage and came back out, some looking weirded out, and some totally grinning.

Then the bottle landed on Jerry. He went into the

garage with Charlene. Then, it was Jerry's turn to spin the bottle. It landed on Brian. Jerry spun the bottle again. It landed on me.

I thought I would die, right then and there. I couldn't even breathe. I tried to untangle my legs and stand up, but everything was jelly. I felt every pair of eyes on me. Somehow, I managed to get up and walk into the garage with Jerry. The door shut behind us.

It was pitch black. I could hear him breathing, somewhere in the darkness.

"Patty?"

"Huh?" Nice. Real smooth.

My eyes were getting accustomed to the darkness, and I could see the outline of his face. How was this supposed to happen? Was I supposed to close my eyes or keep them open? If I closed my eyes, how would I know where his face was? If I kept them open, would I look cross-eyed to him when we got close—sort of like the Siamese cats in *Lady and the Tramp*? What if his eyes were closed and my eyes were open? Or vice versa? Should I pucker up my lips, or just let them relax? Was I supposed to breathe, or hold my breath? Was I supposed to move my face toward him, or wait until he moved toward me?

I decided to keep my eyes open until the last minute, then close them as we got close enough to kiss. I took a breath, moved forward and closed my eyes. Unfortunately, so did Jerry. He must have had his eyes shut, too.

KLUNK!!!

"Ow!" we both said in unison. My front teeth and Jerry's front teeth had collided with the force of both of us moving forward toward the other.

"Ow, I think I chipped my tooth," I whispered.

"I'm sorry, I couldn't see you," said Jerry.

"It's okay. I'll live." I ran my tongue over my front tooth.

There was a definite chip right in the front. It wasn't very big, but it was there.

"How do we explain this one?"

"I don't know."

All of a sudden I felt like laughing. It had been too much for me: the nervousness of my first kiss, being with Jerry in the garage (in the dark, alone), my chipped tooth. I started to giggle.

Jerry started to laugh, too. Then we heard someone from the other side of the garage door yelling, "What are you guys doing? You're taking too long!" For some reason, that was even funnier than the collision. Then they started pounding on the door.

"Okay, let's go." Jerry grabbed my hand as we opened the door and walked into the room. Jerry and I smiled at each other. Annie looked upset. I was in heaven.

The next day, Annie tried to get me to tell her what happened, but I just smiled. I think she was jealous of me for the very first time.

I'd like to say that it was the beginning of a boyfriend/ girlfriend relationship, but that just wasn't the case. For some strange reason, I started feeling differently about Jerry. I now saw him as he really was: a short boy with bright blue eyes who was my friend. In the eighth grade, I fell in love with someone else.

But every once in a while, when I least expect it, I'll run my tongue across my front teeth and feel the chip in my left front tooth. That's when I remember Jerry—the cutest boy in the seventh grade—and my very first kiss.

Patty Hansen

A Life Once Lived

Every second brings a fresh beginning, every hour holds a new promise, every night our dreams can bring hope, and every day is what you choose to make it.

Jessica Heringer, fifteen

When I was thirteen, I found myself at home alone after school every day while my parents worked until seven or eight o'clock each night. I was bored and I felt somewhat neglected. So I started hanging around with other kids who were at home unsupervised after school.

One day, I was at my friend's house and she had some other friends over as well. There were no parents at her house and mine were in Nashville; we had total freedom! As we sat there doing nothing, one of the guys pulled some marijuana out of his coat pocket. In this crowd, I was the only one there that had never tried it, so, under pressure to be cool, I did.

As the weekend approached, everyone was talking about a party at my friend's house. I ended up partying with people I didn't even know and had my first experience of being drunk *and* high. I was now ruining my life, but as far as I knew, I was making more friends and hanging with a different crowd. The only thing that concerned me was partying on the weekends and looking for something to give me a better high.

One day, when I was in the eighth grade, my best friend and I were bored out of our minds. We thought that it would be really cool to go to my house where no one was home, find the keys to my dad's car and drive all over town showing off to our friends. When we ran a stop sign with a cop car right behind us, we were taken in for stealing my dad's car.

Things at school were equally as bad. I was suspended from school twice for fighting. The second time I was out for three days. I no longer cared about my grades and was literally failing school. I never looked at my parents' opinions as being important anymore. It seemed like I was always grounded, but I would sneak out of the house at night to see my friends. When my parents discovered that I was sneaking out, my dad no longer had any type of trust for me. I had put myself into a position of having no freedoms whatsoever. No matter what, I was never happy, and my parents and I argued constantly. My life was falling apart.

No longer was I the girl who was getting good grades, no longer did I have parents who trusted me, or friends that really even cared. I lost all that; it was gone.

So one night I sat with a bottle of prescription pills, sure these pills were going to get rid of all my pain. It was late at night so I thought, *No one's at home so who's going to stop me?* I stared at the pill bottle with a deep feeling of hate toward myself. I never thought that an emotion like this could take over my life.

I began sobbing and tears were rolling down my cheeks. I wondered if anyone was going to care. I told myself that they didn't care now, so why would they care when I'm gone?

Then I heard a car door shut, and I knew my parents had come home. I quickly took as many of the pills as I could with a couple drinks of water.

I sat on the couch with my dad, stepmom and one of their friends. They had no clue as to what was about to happen. We were watching my favorite TV show. Then, the weirdest thing happened. I laughed with my dad for the first time in what seemed like forever. Suddenly, I no longer wanted to die. I realized that I loved my family and that they really loved me. Now what was I to do? I ran to the bathroom and made myself vomit up all the pills.

I lay awake all night thinking. I realized that my priorities were all wrong and if I kept up this behavior and kept hanging around the same people, my life would never improve. I recognized that I was the one who made my life what it was, so I also had the power to change it.

The first thing that I did was stop taking drugs and hanging around that crowd. Within days, I noticed a huge improvement in my self-esteem. Then, right after the first of the year, I switched schools so that I could get away from my "friends" who only cared about partying all the time. It wasn't long before I had made new friends and my grades improved. (I now have a 4.0 grade average—straight A's!)

The new choices I've made totally beat waking up with hangovers and not caring about where my life was headed. I made cheerleading this year and I'm having so much fun. Drugs never made me feel this high.

I'll never know if I was going to die that night, but I do know one thing; I'm glad I didn't. I learned from my mistakes and found that ending life completely is not the way to go. It is *never* too late to change your direction. Every day, every hour is a new opportunity to begin again.

Brandi Bacon, fifteen

Papa

When you get to the end of your rope, tie a knot and hang on.

Franklin Delano Roosevelt

Papa died last night. He was my mom's dad, and I knew him for as long as I can remember.

He told me that if I studied hard and got good grades he'd buy me my first car. He promised. I'm twelve now and the oldest in my family.

I bet he was thinking that the thought of my own car would keep me focused on school. And, of course, if I really buckled down it would take the pressure off Mom.

Mom always said I was born with one foot out the door. Papa knew that. And my quest to grow up quickly and dash out that front door had always been hard on Mom. Papa knew that too, and that's when his voice roared like a lion, "Education, Brian. That's the key!"

Yet, as if he knew what I was feeling, he shook his head back and forth and pretended to whine, "I know, I know, I didn't want to study either." He put his arm around me and whispered, "But you have to do it," as if he were telling me a secret. Our secret. I think he was just trying to help make growing up easier.

I'll never forget the look on Grandma's face. "Your grandfather," she said, rolling her eyes, almost like she knew what he was going to say before he said it.

But once her eyes stopped rolling, she looked right at him, the way Mom looks at us when she wants us to hear her words. She told him to calm down. "Don't get Brian's hopes up," she said.

But Papa wasn't like a lot of people. He meant what he said.

I think his promises sometimes worried Grandma a little. So he just did what Papa always did. He purred like a kitten and snuggled up to Grandma and pinched her cheeks. Then he made a kissing sound with his lips over and over through the air, the way I'd seen him do it a thousand times before. And then he told her how much he loved me.

He used to kiss my brothers, sister, Mom and I that same way. Mom said Papa came from a long line of cheek pinchers. She said it was a family tradition. His father and grandfather did it too. I think it was the Italian in him.

Papa showed me that you can love people in front of others. He was always kissing us and pinching our cheeks. He didn't care who was watching. I remember how all that squeezing used to hurt at first, but we got used to it. I could tell Grandma got used to his way a long time ago. I think Grandma knew that Papa needed to love his family up close.

When Papa came to visit he always wanted to be near us. And he brought us books and magazines because he said we should read every day.

He would sit with us and we would read together. I think he liked to hear our voices. He brought over lots of puzzles, too. He said they were important for exercising our mind. I think he liked to see us learn.

I always felt good about my family after Papa came to visit. His hugs were stronger than anybody's and he liked to laugh out loud with us. He didn't seem to mind our noise. He said we were just being kids. I think he remembered what it was like.

I won't forget the last time Papa was here with us. He came over to hang a fan with a light on it, outside, in our patio. I remember how he worked all day, climbing up and down the ladder, exchanging one tool for another. I helped him for as long as I could, though after awhile I got tired. But he kept on working.

He wanted us to be able to eat outside during warm summer nights. He said the fan would help, but it needed to be put in right. And of course, it couldn't squeak.

Last night, the last night I would see him, we all ate dinner together under the light and the quiet breeze from the fan. And not a thing squeaked. In fact, nothing ever squeaked when Papa was around.

Papa always said his tools were his treasures. He never went anywhere without them. I guess he just liked to fix things. I know Mom's going to miss his help around here.

I'm sad that Papa's gone. Today the phone keeps ringing. Lots of people are calling to say they're sorry that Papa died. Mom has put me in charge for awhile. She wants me to watch my brothers and sister. She has arrangements to make because Papa died.

Now my littlest brother is looking to me. He says he didn't want Papa to die. He wants to know if he keeps eating those healthy apples, does that mean he won't get old and die?

I don't have an answer for my brother. I'm sorry. He has so many questions. "You're so smart, Brian," Papa used to always tell me. I think I'm not so smart right now.

"Does everybody get old and die?" my brother asks.

"No," I tell him, "that's not the way it always goes.

Sometimes people die sooner than that, from other things. That's why Mom holds your hand when you cross the street and makes sure we're buckled up when we drive in the car."

"Then I don't ever want to let go of her hand and I want to live in the car where I'll be safe," he cries.

"I'm not sure that's the right way to live," I tell him.

"Then I want to be a cowboy. Do cowboys die?" he asks.

"Yeah, cowboys die," I say.

"Then I want to be the president. Do presidents die?" he asks, still crying.

"Yes," I nod. "Even presidents die, I learned that in school. It's better to think about living. It's the right thing to do."

Those words just fall out my mouth. Suddenly I realize what Mom means when she talks about doing the right thing. It's kind of like you really only have one choice. I think Papa would say so too.

My brother asks me one more question. "Brian, is Papa going to come alive again and be a ghost?"

"No," I answer sadly, wishing I could still see Papa. "But maybe we'll see him again up in heaven."

"Is that a long drive?" he wants to know. I start to laugh. I feel like jumping up and down, but instead I hug my brother tightly. He feels so small.

"It's a very long drive," I almost shout, "but when we get there and the gates to heaven swing open, I promise you, they won't squeak."

All of a sudden I feel a lot better. I let go of my brother and I can see he feels better too.

I think you can be both happy and sad at the same time.

Brian Normandin, fifteen
As told by Mary Normandin

Loving Equally

We are taught you must blame your father, your sisters, your brothers, the school, the teachers—you can blame anyone, but never blame yourself. It's never your fault. But it's ALWAYS your fault, because if you wanted to change, you're the one who has got to change. It's as simple as that, isn't it?

Katherine Hepburn

My parents had been married for eighteen years and dating since my mother was fourteen. Their marriage had been on the rocks for as long as I can remember. They had talked about divorcing many times but never went through with it for the sake of their only child, me.

One of their last fights that I can remember was very physical. My parents destroyed all of each other's belongings, and it soon came to the point where there was nothing left in the house that wasn't demolished. There were holes in the walls and just pieces of everything covering the floor.

My father shoved my mother around and bruised her

pretty badly, and I had to witness it all with my fourteen-year-old eyes.

Before I knew it, we were in court and I had to make the decision of whose hands to put my life into. I had to choose which parent I would live with every day. I felt like my heart was being cut out of my chest and my parents were tugging at each end of it. I loved both of my parents, and I knew one way or the other I was going to hurt one of them. After I thought for a while, I decided to live with my mom even though I knew my dad would be upset.

But it was much harder than I thought it would be. My mom was always talking about my dad and how terrible she thought he was. She still held a lot of anger inside of her heart, and she wanted to get back at my dad through me. I felt like she wanted me to love only her and to despise my father. Because I loved my dad, too, I was upset a lot and we started to argue all the time.

Nine months later, I went to live with my dad because my mother and I could no longer stand each other. I was blaming her for my feelings of confusion and anger. At first, it was better with my dad, but after only a week he started the same thing that my mother had been doing—only in reverse. My dad seemed to want me to have a lot of feelings of hatred towards my mother. I stuck it out at his house for a while. Then I began to see that he wasn't as interested in me as I thought that he would be. He never asked me when I would be home or who I was hanging out with. I had pretty much all the freedom I wanted. Without any curfews or rules, I began to feel like he didn't even care about me. I began partying too much, and my life was getting completely off track.

After I had a few fights with my dad and spent many nights alone, crying myself to sleep, I realized that I had to figure out what to do.

I recognized that there were ups and downs about living with both of them. They both had their faults and made mistakes. Neither of them wanted to admit their own mistakes, and they were both quick to point out the mistakes of the other. There was no way for me to decide who was right or who was wrong. I couldn't love one of them more than the other and leave the other one behind. I decided that I had to love both parents equally.

I could no longer let them influence me and take control of my feelings so easily. I began by asking them to please keep their feelings for each other to themselves. I think that they tried, but it didn't work. When that failed, I realized that I would have to do this myself. I'd just have to try and be strong and ignore what they said about each other. As soon as I made that decision, I felt more in control and my life began to change.

My mom and dad still say things out of anger about each other and they don't speak to one another. But do you know what? That's *their* problem. Not mine. I'm just doing the best I can to be fair to both of them. In my life, it has been a welcome change to not get caught up in their personal battles, but to focus on loving them instead.

Nicole Peters, fifteen

Just Do It!

The shortest answer is doing.

English Proverb

My vision is getting worse. I can't even see what is five feet away from me without squinting. I know I need to get glasses, but I refuse to. I'm afraid they will make me look dorky. Besides, I can manage without them. These were my thoughts two years ago, when I was in the sixth grade. An embarrassing experience taught me that what I was thinking was wrong.

School had been out for two months. I was going to go to junior high school shortly, where I was sure that appearances are everything. So the question still remained. *Should I, or should I not, wear glasses?* The question was still in my mind when my family and I attended a wedding late in the summer.

During the wedding, I don't know why, but I felt as if I were ready to explode. Maybe it was the excessive amount of soda I drank prior to the wedding. Immediately after the ceremony ended, I walked quickly to the bathroom. Since it was an emergency and I couldn't clearly distinguish which door was marked boys, I just opened the nearest door and entered the restroom.

Unfortunately, I had entered the wrong restroom. I didn't know this though, at the time, because all I could think about was to accomplish what I had gone there to do.

After I was done, I went to the faucet to wash my hands. *That's awkward,* I thought, after looking around the squeaky-clean restroom. *How come there are only toilets in here? Could I be in the girls' bathroom?* Abruptly, as if to answer my question, I heard a shrill scream coming from the direction of the entrance to the restroom.

After that incident, I decided to wear the dorky-looking glasses. I didn't really care about what people thought of me anymore, as long as I never, ever, entered the wrong bathroom again.

On the first day of seventh grade, instead of making fun of me, I received compliments from my friends. They thought the glasses made me look more intelligent—more like a grownup.

So if you know something is right, just do it! Don't make premature assumptions the way I did. You can avoid unnecessary embarrassment. It doesn't matter what others think of you. All that matters is what you think of yourself—and that you can see where you are going!

Son Truong Nguyen, fourteen

I Love You, Lindsey

Time is a dressmaker specializing in alterations.

Faith Baldwin

My heart drooped as I forced my unwilling body into the car. It would be miles and miles until we reached our painful destination, where we would have to leave Brandy, my oldest sister. Brandy was leaving home to serve as a volunteer in the Americorps.

My dad revved the car engine and we left the house. Soon, the streets turned into highways, and we were closer to having to say good-bye with every mile. My heart continued to sink lower.

All of the bittersweet memories of growing up with my sister flowed into my brain . . . from when I was young and Brandy telling me that my troll was evil, to when I copied her every move because I admired her so much, to when the painful teenage years came and her life was too busy for her younger sister. The anger came back to me too: the anger that came when suddenly my life was too immature for hers.

I didn't understand how come my old companion only

talked to me when I did something wrong or when I annoyed her. *Why did her new clothes make my childish apparel look babyish?* These questions and many more stayed in my head.

Now I knew that my time with her was very limited. Throughout the ride she made wicked remarks that hurt, but this time I knew what they meant. They still hurt me even though I knew that this was the agonizing way that she pulled herself away from us, in preparation for her leaving us at last.

When we reached the place where Brandy was to stay, we did everything that we could to stall the painful good-byes that awaited us, until all that was left were the good-byes. The tears began to stream down my cheeks as she hugged me and told me the words that I hadn't heard in a long time.

"I love you, Lindsey."

I sobbed an answer in response. The family was all tears. We all piled into the car and pulled away. Brandy, still crying, turned her back and walked off. In that one moment, I loved her more than anything in the world. She looked like an adult as she walked away, but as the light from the headlight lit her face, I saw the little Brandy that still wanted to be my friend and still wanted to be a part of the family.

On the long drive home that night I felt as though I had left my heart with Brandy. I couldn't imagine life without my big sister or the endless chatter that Brandy always supplied. Would life ever be the same?

It has taken some time, but now I know that life goes on, even though Brandy isn't here. She is always with me because a part of her is in me and always will be.

Lindsey Rawson, twelve

My Best Friend

We had been best friends since fourth grade. Me and Patty. Patty and me. Just about everywhere we went, people knew we were best friends. She taught me how to play pool in her cool, dark basement, and I taught her how to play basketball on my asphalt driveway. But the best part about having a best friend was taking turns sleeping over on Friday nights, sharing secrets over popcorn and soda, year after year after year.

Then in eighth grade everything changed. Or, I believe I changed and Patty didn't. Suddenly, boys became more than pals to me and my interest in make-up and clothes surprised even my mom. I couldn't believe Patty started the first day of school wearing the same pigtails she had worn forever. I had the latest hair fashion. I felt so confused and guilty at the same time. What was happening? Other girls seemed more interesting than Patty, and I wanted their approval. I felt restless and bored every time I went to her house now.

I started avoiding her and making excuses. Finally, during the middle of the year, as we were sitting on my front lawn, the words burst out. I said, "Go home, Patty, and don't come back." I ran into the house crying and sobbing.

Mom sat me down and I told her everything. I'll never forget her words. She said, "Friends will come and go in and out of your life forever. You are changing and it's okay for both of you to make new friends. What's happening is hard but perfectly normal." Hearing the word "normal" was just what I needed.

The next day, the word was out at school and classmates picked Patty's side or mine. The rest of the year was tough—I missed having a best friend but I also started enjoying the new "me" that was emerging. Patty became captain of the girls' basketball team while I got the lead in the eighth-grade spring play. We spoke to each other but only on the most superficial terms.

Time healed a lot of the awkwardness, and over the next few years we clearly went down separate paths. Still, when I saw her in the halls of high school, I felt a strange sadness and longing. I thought if I went back and "fixed" everything between us, we could somehow start all over as friends. But that was a fantasy. Our differences were too great, and I could only hope she understood.

I'll always remember the years Patty and I were best friends, but Mom was right. Friendships can change, and we have to let them go when it's time.

Tamera Collins

You Know You're Growing Up When . . .

You can't fit in the baby swing at the park.

Kirsten Gunderson, eight

You manage to squeeze yourself into your old hiding space but you can't get back out.

Rachael Pavelko, twelve

You can go on the roller coaster because you pass the height mark.

Kelsey Gunderson, ten

You realize the world does NOT revolve around you.

Lindsay Carlson, fourteen

You start getting more phone calls than your mom.

Kim Riddle, eleven

Instead of getting up at the crack of dawn to watch cartoons on Saturdays, you sleep until noon.

Lauren Aitchison, eleven

Food tastes just as good with a lot less ketchup.

Amanda Long, ten

You realize it's YOUR underwear that your mother is hanging on the clothesline for all the neighbors to see.

Janelle Breese-Biagioni

You go to the movies and you can see something not made by Disney.

Alex Blake, nine

Boys and girls no longer have cooties! (I don't know if I'm there yet.)

Amaelia Macoritto, twelve

The goofy-looking neighbor kid who plays football with your brother comes over and asks if you're home, not your brother, and he has suddenly transformed into a handsome prince!

Ashton Howe, thirteen

You stop giggling at the word "kiss."

Katy Coleman, thirteen

You no longer crawl in bed with your mom and dad during thunderstorms.

Annie Barkley, thirteen

You tell your mom that you're too old to be holding her hand while walking in the mall.

Emily Skees, thirteen

You won't take a bath with your younger sibling anymore.

Keley Katona, fifteen

The waitress no longer assumes you want crayons and a kid's menu.

Kaleigh Cronin, ten

You are trying on thousands of clothes just to go to the skating rink (acting like your big sister).

April Randes, sixteen

You are asked to say the blessing at a family gathering.

Craig Lee Watrous Jr., ten

Your daily vitamins switch from Flintstones to vitamin C.

Jennifer Luptak, eleven

You get grounded instead of getting a "time-out."

Allie Thrower, fifteen

You start spending an hour in front of the mirror.

Erin LeSavoy, ten

You totally flub your first kiss, and you still think that it was wonderful.

Ellen Lloyd-Reilley, twelve

Your friend who is a boy becomes your "boyfriend."

Kendall Nixon, eight

You have to watch your younger brothers so that your mom can get her first real rest in twelve years.

Gregory Neel and Morgan Neel, twelve

Your mom says she'll give you some privacy in the bathroom.

Faith Khan, thirteen

You start getting deodorant in your Christmas stocking.

Tim Robine, eleven

Silence

You can't turn back the clock. But you can wind it up again.

Bonnie Prudden

It hits like a tornado hits. And, just like the changes in the atmosphere that signal that there is a tornado on the way, there are signs in a home that a divorce is in the air. There is yelling, crying and arguments, but the worst is the silence. During the silence, even if you try to tell yourself it's not true, you know in your heart that your parents are drifting apart. Then, just like a tornado . . . after it's over you have to step back and inspect the damage.

The damage that hurt the most was not leaving my friends, school or home. The worst damage was that my parents didn't love each other the way that they did when they were first married, had their four kids, bought a home or sent each kid to their first day of school. Now it was a different love, a love that had been forced way over the line . . . a tie of love that started thinning out at a slow pace but rapidly became more strained through the years of their tense relationship. The tie finally broke and they got a divorce.

The first few months after the divorce were hard. My relationship with my dad totally changed. Right after the divorce, the calls started . . . calls from my siblings and me to my dad. After his usual questions like, "How is school?" and "How are your friends?" came the worst question . . . "How is your mom?" There would be this terrible silence that made me run to my room after each call, to cry my heart out for hours.

My whole life had suddenly changed with one word. *Divorce.* It was hard to start over. It was hard on us all— my brother, my two sisters and me, but especially for my mom. She still loved Dad, not the same as before, of course, but you have to have some remainder of love for a man you spent almost twenty-three years of your life with.

My dad tried to come to see us every month, but he worked on the railroad, and vacations and time off for him were scarce. I can remember how we would get excited when he said he could come and see us, and be so disappointed when he would have to cancel if someone at his work got sick and he had to cover for them. I never told anyone . . . but I was a little glad when he had to cancel. I wouldn't have to deal with the awkward conversations . . . and the silence.

Then my mom met someone. His name is Shawn. At times I hated him when they first started dating. I had been secretly hoping that somehow my parents could get back together again, and things would be like they were before . . . when we were happy. Shawn became the reason why that would never happen . . . and I resented him for that.

It has taken a while, but now I see that Shawn is a good man. He was the one who took in a woman with four kids and never complained. At first, my dad hated Shawn and constantly reminded us kids that he still loved our mom.

But now, after three years, my dad has released his grip and moved on just like my mom did. It's amazing, but my dad now works for my stepdad, so we get to see him more than we used to. He often eats supper with all of us. I think the silence has slowly turned into a new life for us all and we are finally happy again.

Elisabeth Copeland, thirteen

The Best Brother
in the Whole Wide World

A brother is a friend provided by nature.

Legouve Pere

In your life, a lot of people will come and go. Friends betray you, pets die and parents get divorced. But in my life, one person I've always remembered being there for me is my brother, Bear.

Bear was seven years old when I was born. That's a pretty big age gap, and anyone would think that we wouldn't be close. But we were. When I was five years old, my parents got a divorce and we both had to deal with a hard change. My mother remarried a sergeant in the Army, so we moved to Fort Bragg, North Carolina. Even at the age of six, I was very, very upset. I cried a lot, I had a hard time fitting in at my new school, and the quarrelling between my parents had discouraged me. But Bear made me feel safe and accepted.

During that summer, we would play together: trap insects, watch *Blues Clues* and do all sorts of crazy, mischievous stuff that normal brothers and sisters should do.

Even though my brother was fourteen and I was only going on seven, we had the best time hanging out together. But, as time went by, things started to change.

Bear began to lose interest in playing with me—or spending time with the rest of the family, for that matter—and started to do normal "teenage" things . . . hang around girls, head-bang to rock music and tack posters of girls on his walls. Oh, yeah, and he spoke to me every once in awhile. But I missed the way we used to spend time together. I found myself missing him *a lot*— and we were living in the same house!

The trends changed, and so did he. He started to get into rap music and wanted so much to fit in. He laughed out loud at the thought of ever watching *Blues Clues* with me, and he was too busy socializing to even think about making me laugh the way he used to, or trapping insects, going on expeditions or bike rides. I felt lonely again.

I wasn't sure if things took a turn for the worse or the better when I received some news one day in July. I was coming home from my dad's house. My mom picked me up at our meeting place, and then she told me what had been going on since I'd been gone. What she said shocked me: Bear and his girlfriend, Elizabeth Anne, were going to get married.

All sorts of things raced through my mind. *Bear was only eighteen. He was my brother—brothers aren't supposed to get married! Did this mean that I would never see Bear again? Would he pull away from me permanently? Would he be too busy with his new family to even remember me?* While I was excited, I was also worried.

Bear, who was then working at a restaurant buffet down the street, had nowhere to turn for a career. He didn't want to go to college, so he joined the Army. Now it was my mother's turn to worry. Bear was gone, in Fort Knox, Kentucky, in basic training for almost three months until Christmas. I wrote him whenever I got the chance, and he wrote me back a couple of times. He was gone for another two months and then went to Alabama until April. Then more shocking news came: Bear was assigned to a military base in Hawaii!

In April, Bear and Elizabeth Anne got married. The wedding was very small, and I was the only bridesmaid. I wore a purple dress and almost cried when I watched Bear making his vows, giving himself away. When the wedding was over, I could not hold it in any longer. I broke down and bawled.

My brother acted shocked when he found me crying. He asked me why, and I just shook my head. I knew the reason—I would miss him *so much* but I could never tell him that. Even though I hadn't said a word, he understood. I threw my arms around him and hugged him very tight. He hugged back, and we stood there for a moment thinking about everything, until finally he broke away. He stood there looking at me and smiled. I was so proud of him at that moment, in his Army greens, smiling that same mischievous smile that he never outgrew. I looked at him and wondered for the final time if our relationship would ever suffer. *Would he neglect me again, this time for his new family? Would he forget about me? Would he ever begin to comprehend how much I would miss him?*

And then, as I hugged him one last time before he left for Hawaii, I rested my head on his shoulder and smiled. Because standing there with him, I knew the truth. A lot of people will come and go in my life, but no one else will ever be the best brother in the whole world to me . . . except Bear.

Katie Beauchamp, thirteen

[EDITORS' NOTE: *As* Chicken Soup for the Preteen Soul 2 *goes to press, the best brother in the world, Bear, is serving our country, stationed in Iraq.*]

The Board

They won't last long, school days and childish
*   things.*
We're moving up, going our separate ways.
Enjoy your future, all the changes and shifts.
And remember these years were precious gifts.

Maria Lamblin

"We were the cutest babies in the world!" I smiled as I put up the picture of me riding a horse and pretending I could fly.

"I know, look at this one!" Rachel pointed to a picture of us at age five, dressed up in our mothers' clothing and wearing so much makeup that you could hardly see our skin. We both giggled and shook our heads. We couldn't believe that we would be graduating in a week.

As a way of celebrating our childhoods, we had been asked to bring in pictures of ourselves growing up. The board took up the space between the eighth-grade classroom and the bathrooms, and every square inch was now covered with pictures. As I looked from photo to photo, from kindergarteners to fourth-graders to sixth-graders, I began to look at my classmates around me.

First I looked at Rachel, and I remembered the first day of school. I was a scared little five-year-old, clinging to my mother for dear life. Then the unimaginable happened, she left me—she just set me down and *left* me! Having been abandoned by my mother in a room filled with books and crayons, I didn't know what else to do but cry. I was so busy crying that I didn't notice the twenty other kids around me that had been left to a similar fate. Then I felt a hand on my shoulder. Expecting to see the scary woman who would be in charge of us each morning, I turned around and saw Rachel. Her hair was darker than midnight, and her skin had a beautiful olive tone. But what was most beautiful about Rachel was her voice. It was the kind of voice that made you just want to listen for hours. It was the kind that was meant for the radio, the kind that captured people's attention. Even in kindergarten, her voice captivated me, and the first words she spoke remain in my mind. "Why are you crying?"

"My mommy left me," I sobbed.

"What's your name?" she asked with confidence.

"Sarah," came my soggy reply.

"Well, Sarah, wanna play Chutes and Ladders?"

That got my attention. I loved board games. I started to play and after a few minutes I wasn't crying anymore, I was actually enjoying myself so much, that I cried when it was time to leave.

I looked back at the board and my eyes landed on a picture of TJ. TJ lives right next to me, and we have always been close. I was a bit of a tomboy until about fourth grade and I remember how much fun I had playing with the boys, and how it wouldn't have been allowed if it weren't for TJ.

"C'mon, she's a girl—she'll make you play Barbies or somethin'," one of the boys on our block had said to TJ.

"Let's go, TJ," I said. I turned and started to walk away, tears welling up in my eyes, when I heard TJ answer the other boy.

"Nuh-uh, I wanna play with Sarah. She's more fun than you anyway. We're gonna play basketball."

After that day, people started to join our basketball games; first just a few boys brave enough to get beaten by a girl, but pretty soon we had the whole neighborhood on the court. And you know what? I was beating all of them. "Sarah, Sarah! Earth to Sarah!" I snapped out of my day-dream to see Rachel waving her hand in front of my face. "Why are you crying?" she asked, just as she had on that first day. I felt my face, and sure enough, there was a tear rolling down my cheek. Pretty soon, I was pouring out my heart and soul and my face was damp with tears. I was thinking about the million memories that I had collected over the past nine years, and how I was leaving. I was leaving this school. High school would be different. I was afraid that we weren't going to be as close. I couldn't imagine how that would feel, and I didn't even want to.

When I told Rachel this, she just smiled. "We are growing up. We may make new friends, but we will still have each other always."

She always knew what to say.

As I stood up to leave, I looked at the board once more and noticed how, in every picture, each of us were at different points of our lives, but we were always smiling. We were all okay, even through all the changes. We had grown up in those pictures, as we were growing up in real life.

I took one last sniffle and a deep breath.

I was finally ready for high school.

Sarah Kessler, thirteen

12

ECLECTIC
WISDOM

Life is given as a gift,
So wonderful and new.
We need to live it day to day,
Being careful as we do.
For life can give us many years,
Or only months or days.
Each moment must be savored,
And used in special ways.
Stop and take a moment,
To help the poorer man.
Or teach a child something,
Lend a helping hand.
Small things take but minutes,
And one thing is plain to see:
Great rewards return to you.
Give the best of life; it's free.

Meghan Beardsley, sixteen

Redsy

When we begin to take our failures non-seriously, it means we are ceasing to be afraid of them. It is of immense importance to learn to laugh at ourselves.

Katherine Mansfield

Redsy was not only the class clown, he was the class terror because he was fearless. He was always in trouble with Miss Farley, our first-grade teacher. Miss Farley couldn't punish him enough to change his behavior. He did whatever he wanted to do, no matter what. He was also the smartest kid you ever saw. We were at the beginning of our first year of school, and Redsy could already count all the way up to one hundred.

But Redsy had a little problem. He couldn't say the *th* sound. He couldn't say the word "three"—it came out as "free." It drove Miss Farley crazy because she thought that he could do it right if he only tried harder. Every time Redsy would get caught doing something wrong, Miss Farley would keep him after school and make him practice his *th*'s.

One Friday afternoon, Miss Farley announced that we were all going to count up to one hundred the following Monday. Sure enough, when Monday rolled around, Redsy was the first one to be called on by Miss Farley to come to the front of the class and count.

As he passed her in the aisle, Miss Farley grabbed his sleeve and their eyes met. She was a mean old woman who strictly insisted on having things done her way. I remember not ever wanting to look her in the eye. We were all terrified of her, except for Redsy. He wasn't afraid of anything.

Redsy started counting fast and furiously the instant he reached the front. "One, two, FREE, four, five . . . " The class snickered and Miss Farley started to get red in the face. Redsy got a little flustered too, because he realized what he had just done. He had told us in the schoolyard, before class, that he was going to do it right. On he went: "Ten, eleven, twelve, FIRTEEN . . . " The rest of us began to giggle and stifled laughter broke out here and there. Miss Farley stood up and glared at the class. We all stopped and became quiet as Redsy flew on into the twenties.

Then the magic moment arrived. Redsy got to twenty-nine and when he did, the class held its collective breath in unison. Redsy met Miss Farley's stare with utter disregard and cried out, "TWENTY N-I-I-I-I-I-I-NE . . . FIRDY!" Then Redsy flew on in a continuous, nonstop torrent, "Firdy-one, firdy-two, firdy-free . . . " with a huge smile on his face. The entire class exploded in laughter. We were seeing Redsy at his best—he knew just exactly what he was doing! Our laughter was much more important to Redsy than was Miss Farley's wrath. Miss Farley lunged at Redsy to get him to stop, but he dodged her as easily as a rabbit and continued, "Firdy-four, firdy-five . . ." to a rising din of uncontrolled laughter.

The laughter continued through the forties. When he

reached the fifties, the laughter began to subside, and Redsy slowed his pace as he continued to dodge Miss Farley's now-feeble attempts to grab him as he ran back and forth in front of the class. She finally gave up and sat down at her desk, and Redsy picked up the pace. As he flew past "Ninety-free . . . " no one uttered a sound because we all were afraid of what would happen when he got to the end.

"Ninety N-I-I-I-NE . . . one hundred!" he bellowed. Then silence.

Miss Farley remained at her desk with her head lowered, her face in her hands. She was shaking uncontrollably and we became alarmed. After a long moment, she lifted her head and laughter burst out of her like the breaking of a dam. Then the entire class joined in, including Redsy.

Miss Farley finally agreed, for the first time in her long teaching career, that she had been had by the best.

Barry Fireman

Tippy

I was late for the school bus and rushing to get ready. My dog, Tippy, ran past me. *What's your big hurry?* I wondered, annoyed. It wasn't like *he* was late for the school bus like I was. When he got to the front door, he laid down in front of it—his way of asking to be petted. I ignored his shameless begging for affection, hurdled over him and sprinted for the waiting yellow bus.

That afternoon, I jumped out of the bus and dashed up the driveway. *That's odd,* I thought. Tippy was usually outside, barking an entire paragraph of "hellos" as soon as he saw me come home. When I burst through the door, the house was quiet and still. I dumped my coat and backpack on the floor. Mom silently appeared. She asked me to sit down at the kitchen table.

"Honey, I have some sad news that I need to tell you. This morning, while you were at school, Tippy was hit by a car and killed. He died instantly, so he didn't suffer. I know how much he meant to you. I'm so sorry," said Mom.

"NO! It's not true!" I was in shock. I couldn't believe her. "Tippy, come here! Come on, boy!" I called and called for him. I waited. He didn't come. Feeling lost, I wandered into the living room. He wasn't on the couch, so I had no pillow for my head while I watched cartoons. Mom called me for dinner and I rambled to my place. He wasn't hiding under the table, so I had to eat all of my dinner. I went to sleep that night, but I didn't cry. I still couldn't believe that he was gone.

When I got off the bus the next day, the silence grew deafening. Finally, my sobs bubbled up and erupted like lava from a volcano. I felt like I was also going to die from having my insides shaken apart, and I couldn't stop crying or end the thoughts that kept going through my head. *I should have trained him better. If I had been home, I could have called him away from the road. I didn't even pet him when I left. How could I have known that was my last chance?* I cried until I felt hollow inside.

My parents bought a new dog named Tinker Belle. I didn't care. I was busy giving hate looks to people speeding in their cars. *They shouldn't drive so fast that they couldn't stop when they see a dog in the road.* My parents still got the silent treatment from me. *Why hadn't they made sure that Tippy was tied up?* I was mad at Tippy for getting killed, and I was mad at the entire "dog kingdom" for not knowing enough to stay out of the road.

I didn't share my dinner with our new dog. She was too small to be my pillow for television, and her bark was squeaky. When she begged for attention, I pushed her away. I spent a lot of time alone, feeling sorry for myself and wondering, *Why did this have to happen to me? What am I going to do now? Why did Tippy have to die?*

Time passed, and against my will, I started to understand some things. It felt like waking up a little at a time. I realized what little control any of us have over what happens to a dog. Sure, we can train them and tie them up and do everything right, but bad things can still happen. And, in spite of us, good things can happen too. That's life. The best way to deal with the hard times is to figure out what I need to do for myself to get through them when they come, and to remember that hard times pass.

I also discovered that my capacity to love didn't die with Tippy. I became awfully lonely when I was trying to harden my heart. I began to realize that there were good things about Tinker Belle that were different from the good things about Tippy. I couldn't rest my head on her little body, or pretend to ride Tinker Belle the way I had done with Tippy, but I could fit Tinker Belle into my backpack and carry her around.

I learned that I need to pet my dog whenever I can—and to really enjoy my time with her! Now I pet my dog slowly when I have the chance and quickly when I'm in a hurry, but I never leave the house without petting her.

I now deeply understand the "Circle of Life." Everyone is born, everyone dies, and that's the way it is. If dogs never died, there would be no room for others like Tinker Belle . . . and her five cute puppies!

Best of all, I realize that Tippy left behind all of my good memories of him. And they come to me every time I call!

Christine Armstrong

What's a Miracle, Granddad?

Decisions determine destiny.

Frederick Speakman

"What's a miracle, Granddad?" asked five-year-old Sam. He looked up at me with his innocent, wide eyes.

I did know of a miracle. It happened to a friend of mine named Bart.

One day, Bart decided he wanted to have a dog. Bart's parents agreed to let him get a dog from the animal shelter, but they wanted to help pick it out. Bart agreed.

The next morning, Bart and his parents drove to the local animal shelter. There were two dogs that Bart liked. It was very difficult, but Bart finally picked one. He named him Scruffy. Scruffy looked exactly like his namesake; he was a small, terrier type with hair going in all directions. His color was sort of brown and sort of red, and there was even gray in there too. He was a very energetic dog, never still for a second. He just wanted to play and run around.

Bart's parents did not like Scruffy at all. Scruffy was too energetic for them. He was not a good-looking dog. The other dog, called Lady, was a very pretty dog. Lady had quiet manners and was a handsome beagle.

Bart agreed that Lady was a much prettier dog, and gentler. Since his parents insisted, he agreed to adopt Lady and not Scruffy.

Bart held Lady all the way home. She slept in Bart's room that night and the next night, too. Bart liked having her near him. He started to love that sweet dog.

On the third day, tragedy struck. For no apparent reason, and with no warning, Lady quietly died in her sleep. It was a tragic moment for the family.

Bart cried and cried. His mother did, too. His father cried a little, also. Bart felt heartbroken. Lady had become the love of his life.

The next morning, after they had laid Lady to rest, Bart said, "Mom, Dad, I really liked the other dog, Scruffy. I know he liked me, too. Can't we go back and get him?"

His parents told him to forget Scruffy because three days had gone by, and it would be too late.

"Too late? Too late for what?" he asked.

They explained that the animal shelter only keeps stray dogs for three days, and if they are not adopted the shelter has to do something about it.

"Like what?" asked Bart, not wanting to hear the answer.

"They have to put them to sleep," said his mother gently. His father put his arm around Bart and added, "There are just too many dogs and cats in the city, Bart. The shelter only has so much money, and so few volunteers to take care of them. The animals do not suffer at all. A veterinarian just puts them to sleep. It is done very quietly and painlessly."

"I guess they have no other choice," Bart said. "But let's go back anyway. Maybe we can save Scruffy."

Bart's parents argued against going back. They said it was too late. There was no way that Scruffy could still be in the shelter. They warned Bart not to expect anything but disappointment.

But Bart's parents drove him back to the shelter. Bart's dad parked the car and sighed. He had seen the veterinarian's car parked in the official's spot. He did not want to tell Bart that this was the veterinarian who put the animals to sleep.

The three of them entered the shelter. They went directly to the wire cage that had held Scruffy three days before. It was empty!

"Scruffy is gone," said Bart. "Mom, Dad, he's gone."

"We tried to tell you. Try to understand," said his mother.

"Can I help you folks?" said a voice.

Bart whirled around and saw a young woman in a white coat.

"Were you looking for a dog to adopt?" she said.

"Yes," said Bart. "I want the dog that was here, in this cage. The dog is gone. I want *that* dog."

"The veterinarian was late getting here today because of car trouble. What you want is in that room over there." She pointed to a door.

Bart bolted past her and raced through the door. It was marked "PRIVATE—KEEP OUT." In the middle of the room, on a cold steel table was Scruffy. He was strapped down. His legs were kicking. His big brown eyes were wide with fear and his tongue was hanging from the side of his mouth. Standing over him was the vet, an ugly hypodermic needle in his hand.

Bart jumped into the room. He screamed at the veterinarian, "Stop! Stop, please," said Bart. "I want that dog. Don't kill him!"

Bart got his dog, and Scruffy still lives with Bart today.

Do you know what a miracle is now, Sam?

Lew Talmadge

Never Put Rocks in Your Mouth

When I was in the sixth grade, my teacher asked our class the question, "What does 'doing the right thing' mean to you?" She asked us to think about that question over the weekend, and to talk to our parents or anyone else we thought might have a good answer. By Monday, we were to turn in an essay on what "doing the right thing" meant, and be prepared to live up to our answers.

The entire weekend, I wracked my brain trying to come up with something that would impress my teacher and be easy to live by. I talked to my parents, called my grand-mother and asked my next-door neighbor. I even asked the mailman! Everyone had good answers, but I didn't feel like I could live up to them.

By Sunday afternoon, I hadn't written my essay. To make matters worse, my parents said we were going to my Aunt Cindy's house. That usually meant that I would have to entertain my cousin Andrea while my parents visited after dinner. Andrea was four and a major pest.

Just as I predicted, my parents told me to play with Andrea while they visited. I turned on the television and found a Disney movie for Andrea, and then I sat down and started to write my essay. I still didn't know what I was going to write about, but it was due the next morning and this was my last chance.

Soon I felt a pair of eyes on me. It was Andrea.

"What are you doing?" she asked.

"I have to write an essay about what doing the right thing means to me."

Andrea laughed. "That's easy," she said.

"Okay," I said, thinking, *What could this smart aleck four-year-old possibly know that all of the adults who I had asked hadn't already come up with?*

"Tell me the answer," I said smugly.

Andrea cleared her throat and stood up.

"Doing the right thing means being nice to your family and friends. Doing what your mommy says. Never lie. Eat lots of fruits and vegetables. Don't eat dog food. Take a bath when you're dirty and wash your own private parts. Don't watch icky movies with kissing and stuff. Don't waste water and electricity. Don't scare the cat. Don't ever run away. And never, never put rocks in your mouth."

I stared with astonishment at my little cousin. Then I jumped up, grabbed Andrea and gave her the biggest hug I could. Not only had Andrea answered a very tough question for me, I could easily live by all of her rules. All I had to do was be nice, not lie, keep myself clean and healthy, not scare cats, and never, never put rocks in my mouth. Piece of cake. So when I wrote my essay, I included the story about Andrea and how she had answered my question.

Two weeks later, my teacher returned everyone's essays. I received an A+ along with a little note my teacher had written at the top: "Always do the right thing—and give Andrea an A+, too!"

Shirley Barone Craddock

The Moment I Knew I'd Never Be Cool

From their errors and mistakes, the wise and good learn wisdom for the future.

Plutarch

My older sister was born to be liked. She came out of the womb with a cute face, blonde hair, a sense of humor, athletic ability, and what my mom called the "gift of gab." She went through her childhood with lots of friends, lots of parties and lots of attention. I wanted what my sister had: popularity.

I studied her for years and never came close, so I turned to kids my own age for role models. Jen, the girl I always sat next to in school, threw her blonde hair around, showed off her dimples, put her head to one side when she asked for favors and was easily voted most popular in class. *Okay*, I thought, *I'll try her tactics.* I threw my brown hair around, smiled without dimples, put my head to one side and asked my teacher for a pass to the bathroom. She looked at me and said, "Why are you doing that with your head? Don't you feel well?"

That was my cue to try for cool instead of popular. I'd

do anything to escape my lack of social status. Cool kids always acted as though they had the world under control, maneuvering around obstacles and adults with ease, and never cracking under pressure. My big chance came when a new girl moved to town and into my class. Nothing seemed to ruffle Tiffany. She was cute, trendy, and best of all, she liked me.

Our friendship lasted four weeks—just long enough for me to learn that Tiffany took European vacations, went skiing in Aspen and bought clothes at Nieman-Marcus. I'd never been outside of Illinois, on skis or anywhere but the Sears preteen department. We were only eleven and she'd already picked out the car she'd get for her sixteenth birthday. Tiffany was way too much for me. I crawled back into my familiar invisibility. . . .

Until I met Mandy. Mandy's middle name was "rebel." She and her brother, Kevin, smoked cigarettes and stole money out of their mom's purse. *If popularity and cool are out of reach,* I thought, *I'll take rebellion over facelessness.* I was soon hanging out at Mandy's house, where no adults were ever around to notice what we were doing. I puffed cigarettes, pretended to shoplift and felt powerful for the first time in my life. I did crazy things my parents never suspected, and had a great time bragging about it to other kids. I could feel my status rising. Then Kevin was arrested and sent to a detention center. Never wanting to end up like him, I pitched my cigarettes and headed back into obscurity.

By eighth grade, I was desperate. I tried out for cheerleading at my small school, and by some miracle, made it onto the squad. My head swelled like a melon. *I must have absorbed popularity and coolness without realizing it,* I thought. I took this tiny piece of status and ran with it.

At first, being popular and cool seemed to be easy. I tolerated, agreed with or laughed at the nasty comments of the cool girls who stayed that way by pointing out the uncoolness of others. Things like, "Look at Dana's hair. Think she used a hedge trimmer?" or, "Can you believe those shoes Lauren wore last night? She must have borrowed them from her grandmother." Guys weren't spared. "Oh, Tyler. What a crater face!" and, "Yeewww. Bryce actually thought I'd be seen with him in public!"

The better they were at cutting people to shreds, the faster those girls seemed to rise above the masses. Like stand-up comics, they pointed out other people's flaws and made the crowds roar. *Why,* I wondered, *were putdowns cool? They made my stomach cramp. Was it who said them? The way they were said?*

Okay, I decided, *I can say nasty things about other people for the sake of personal success.* I picked a time and place for my initiation. A budding friendship with the Faris twins gave me a stage. Sara and Shauna were way cooler than I'd ever be. They'd been hanging with guys since seventh grade.

My debut came after church. The three of us were standing around waiting for rides home. I listened to them rip first on girls and then on guys. One guy in particular took the brunt of their hits: first his clothes, then his voice, then his brain, then his looks.

"I know what you mean," I volunteered, as Shauna turned up her nose at the mention of the poor guy's hairy arms. "Some guys are real apes. . . ."

As the words left my mouth, a not-so-good-looking guy drove past in a blue convertible. *Perfect opportunity,* I thought. I pointed to the driver, ". . . like that guy—red-haired and u-g-l-y." I made chimp sounds as I watched the car turn into a nearby driveway. Instead of agreement, I heard nothing from the twins. It was like I was standing on the ocean bottom with my ears plugged. I turned slowly to see Sara and Shauna with necks stiff and eyes impaling me on an invisible stake.

What? What? my confused brain was pleading. *What'd I say?*

The answer slithered out of Sara's mouth as the twins turned their backs and walked toward the blue convertible. "That red-haired and u-g-l-y ape is our brother."

The rest, as they say, is history. My journey to cool stalled right there in front of church. With face burning and ears ringing, I'm sure I heard an otherworldly voice whisper, *You'll never be popular, cool, or anything else your heart won't let you be. Start looking inside, instead of out.*

It took me a while to get what those words meant. But once I stopped trying to be like other people, life got a whole lot easier. I'm even growing up to be someone I really like.

D. Marie O'Keefe

Lost

One afternoon, when I was five, my mom and I went shopping at a very large grocery store. While we were in the dairy department, something caught my attention and I became distracted. When I turned, expecting to find my mother, no one was there. My mother had moved on, thinking I was behind her. I panicked! I spun around several times, desperately searching for my mother but to my dismay, no luck. I started running up and down every aisle, with my eyes darting in every direction. I passed the cereal, green beans, spaghetti sauce and pork chops.

Then I spotted someone, wearing a similar outfit to my mom's, with her back to me. I had found her! I sprinted as fast as I could toward the woman. I was running so fast that I could not stop myself and planted my face right into her rear end. As I fell to the floor, the lady spun around screaming. After a quick look at the woman's face, I realized it was NOT my mom! I picked myself up as fast as I could, turned around and ran the other direction.

Not watching where I was going, I stumbled right into a cardboard shelf containing several bags of potato chips. I was so scared, I was crying profusely as the chip bags tumbled down around me.

Fortunately, my mother was standing at the end of the aisle and had seen the whole thing. Laughing hysterically, she came running to pull me out of my grave of chip bags. She hadn't been as far away from me as I had thought.

I learned a valuable lesson that day. From then on, if I ever thought I was lost in a grocery store I asked the person behind the counter to help me find my mom.

Casey Veronie, thirteen

Kindness Is a Simple Gift

In this world we must help one another.

Jean de La Fontaine

My family and I were taking a well-deserved vacation to Disneyland. I had never been there before and was eagerly anticipating experiencing the magic.

There was another reason that this trip was special. My father was a workaholic who worked long hours. I longed to spend time with him. I wanted to be able to sit down with my father, who I loved more than life, and just talk. It always seemed like there was never time.

The day finally arrived when I was allowed to pack my clothes. I chose only my favorite outfits. I threw in my autograph book and then muscled the suitcase zipper around the overflow of clothes. I set my suitcase on my comforter and smiled. I was ready.

I didn't get any sleep that night. I lay in my bed and stared out the window. I knew that my father's work was going to be left at home, finally.

After a brief breakfast we hit the open road. It was all smooth sailing for the first couple of hours until I unexpectedly felt a sharp jerk. We coasted to the side of the road, and my dad said something about the engine being shot. We were in the middle of four lanes of traffic, so he decided the easiest thing to do would be to flag someone down and get a ride into town.

An hour later, my dad was still waving his hands at each and every passing car but it wasn't doing any good. Not a single soul would stop to assist my helpless family. Finally Father gave up and decided to walk into town. I was certain it was a very long distance. I pleaded with him to stay and try again, but he was deaf to my pleading. He just said that he wouldn't let anything ruin this trip for me. My heart ached as he put on his coat and began to walk away from our car. My dad has a back problem, and he was too stubborn to admit that he wasn't in any condition to even walk a couple of miles.

Then I saw a figure out of the window. It was a lone trucker. I looked around for his rig. I didn't see it until I realized that his truck was parked on the other side of the road. He had walked across four lanes of traffic to get to us. The feeling I felt at that moment is indescribable. I was truly touched that this man cared so much. Not one other person had taken time out of his or her own selfish life to stop and see if everything was okay, but this man was different. He didn't even know us, and he didn't expect anything in return.

Father got his ride back to town, and our car was repaired. My visions of Mickey were rekindled, as was my faith that angels do exist. Because of that man's actions, my father and I had the opportunity to grow close again, and I still cherish my genuine Mickey Mouse autograph.

None of this would have been possible if that man hadn't given us the gift that he did—the gift of kindness.

Michael Oknefski, seventeen

Our Christmas Secret

Admitting errors clears the score and proves you wiser than before.

Arthur Guiterman

It was Christmas Eve when my sister and I decided to open our presents before our mom got home from work. She usually came home about an hour after we got home from school, which we thought was plenty of time to sneak a peek at the gifts under the tree. Since my sister was older, and that put her in charge, she opened the first gift while I was ordered to stand guard at the big picture window in our front room. I was to report any suspicious activity or persons, namely our mother.

I was so excited that I could barely stand still. I also couldn't keep my eyes on the window very long. My head moved from the window to my sister and back to the window again. I felt like I was watching a Ping-Pong match.

"All right!" my sister shouted. She pulled out a jewelry box. "You know what that means, don't you?"

I jumped up and down. "Yeah, it's my turn!"

"No," she said. "It means that there must be some jewelry

under here." I watched my sister rummage through the presents under the tree trying to find one she thought was small enough to be a necklace or earrings.

"Hey, that's not fair!" I whined, stomping my foot.

"Are you watching for Mom?" is all that she said. I couldn't do anything except stand guard as she opened present after present. Finally, when my sister's curiosity was satisfied and she had finished wrapping her last present back up, we traded places.

My heart hammered so hard that it felt like my chest was moving in and out. My sister reminded me to be careful so I wouldn't tear the paper, and to wrap the present back up the same way that I had found it.

After unwrapping a few presents, I found it faster to open one end of a present and peek inside. "Cool! Mom and Dad got me headphones for my stereo!"

I pulled the headphones out of the box and was about to put them on when my sister shouted, "Quick! Wrap it back up! Mom's coming!"

My heart hit the floor along with the headphones when I heard what sounded like glass crushing. I knew it was my mother coming down our gravel driveway. My body was as frozen as a snowman.

"Come on!" My sister's face was as white as the paint on the wall.

I shoved the headphones back in the box but my hands were shaking so much that I tore the paper trying to wrap it back up. My sister was yelling at me, which only made my hands shake more. I heard the jingle of keys and the doorknob rattle. I thought I was going to wet my pants! My heart pounded harder as I tried to get the tape to stick.

"Just shove it under the tree and put some presents on top of it!" my sister shouted as she ran to stall my mother.

I had just finished burying the package with my headphones in it when my mother came into the front room. I jumped up and said, "Hi, Mom!" She smiled at me and said, "Hi," back, but didn't appear to suspect a thing. My heart began to slow as I took a deep breath. That was close. Too close!

On Christmas morning, my sister and I smiled for pictures and gave award-winning performances when we opened our presents—again. "Headphones!" I exclaimed. "Thanks, it's just what I wanted." After everything had been opened, my sister and I looked at each other, and our eyes met. Our secret was safe, but somehow Christmas morning didn't feel the same.

My sister and I never opened our Christmas presents early again. I don't know if it was that opening our gifts for the second time just wasn't as much fun as the first time, or if we came too close to getting caught and didn't want to think about what our mother would have done to us.

I also learned something that year about my mother. I found out that she wasn't as dumb as I thought she was. Maybe it was the lack of squeals on Christmas morning or the torn wrapping paper that tipped her off. For some reason, all of the packages for our birthdays, which she usually hid at the top of her closet shelf, never appeared. I never did find out where she hid them.

Lori Menning

What I've Learned So Far

Never try to get corn off the cob with a fork.
When playing in the gym, beware of steel beams.
Never let guys in your room on an overnight school trip.
The condiments at meals are not toys.
Before you give a kid Listerine, make sure that he knows not to swallow it.
NEVER throw up in a vent.

Melissa Amyx, fourteen

Don't try to baptize your neighbor's cat, especially with a hose.

Marleigh Dunlap, thirteen

Some teachers are there to teach and that's all, but others are there to watch and help you grow.

Janne Perona, thirteen

Everything you do in your life cannot be taken back.
Family is the most important gift of all.
Be true to yourself and it won't matter if others aren't true to you.

Nikki Chance, fifteen

Don't be afraid to make new friends and expand your relationships with other friends.

Reanna Grissom, twelve

Don't trust anyone who knows how to give a wedgie.

Sylvia Lares, nine

If you have something bad to tell your mom, tell her when she's on the phone.

Brennan Shaw, eleven

Never let a stain from the past make a mark on your future.

Jillian Graham, twelve

Read lots of stuff written in the 1700s, it'll make you smarter.

Dena Soffer, ten

Never put your tongue on a really cold metal pole.

Joshua White, twelve

Never eat unsweetened chocolate. Yuk!

Dylan Dudley, seven

If you give your enemy a second chance they might turn out to be your best friend.

Mandy Tallant, twelve

Always pretend you understand what the Spanish teacher is saying.

Tarek Audi, fifteen

Never trust your fifteen-year-old uncle to make dinner.

George Preston, fourteen

Never eat prunes, no matter what your grandma says.

Melanie Hansen, twelve

Never fall asleep during a field trip if your friends have toothpaste with them.

Filipe Romero, thirteen

Don't use words that you don't understand to impress someone. It can be very embarrassing.

Chastity Sezate, thirteen

Make sure to look at yourself in the mirror before you leave the house, especially if you're going somewhere important.

Carol Rodriguez, thirteen

Don't let older siblings get the best of you; that's just what they want.

Gladys Lau, twelve

You can't run away from your fears, unless it's a wasp.

Michael Betancourt, twelve

If your dad asks you, "Do you think I'm an idiot?" carefully consider your answer.

Liz Hansen, fourteen

Your food ends up in your lap when you sit too far away from the table.

Cory Price, nine

With my wheelchair, I can run faster than anyone else in my class and I can write faster than anyone with my computer.

Becca Yurcek, ten

When your parents yell at you they still love you.

Santana Hubert, ten

Pay attention in class. That way, when the teacher calls on you, you won't make a goof of yourself and have to ask, "What was the question?"

Courtney Stewart, twelve

Sometimes it's nice to be important, but it's always important to be nice.

Kaleigh Cronin, ten

Never play with a baby right after it finishes eating.
Don't bother your cousin when she is on the phone with a guy.

Jade Mason, thirteen

When something bad happens to you, think about someone out there who may have a bigger problem.
Never underestimate the power of love and friendship.
Never laugh with a piece of chocolate in your mouth.

Melissa Quincosa, thirteen

Don't eat noodles when you are wearing your retainer; they get stuck in there and it's really hard to get them out.

Ashley Fannon, thirteen

Even if dinner looks disgusting, it doesn't mean it will taste that way.
Have boys for friends, not just for boyfriends.
No matter how much I learn, there is always stuff I don't know.

Chelsey Rice, eight

Having had over nine surgeries by the age of fourteen, I will never again take for granted the gift of walking.

Vanessa Cupo, fourteen

If you want to make a difference, get off your butt and do it.

Danielle Relue, thirteen

Begging works, but don't rely on it. You don't always get what you want.

Melissa Lansford, thirteen

Play the hand that God has dealt you to the best of your ability. You never know what the next card will be.

Jacqueline Christy, thirteen

When you are waiting for your mom to finish her haircut, don't spin on the chair or you'll throw up your lunch.

Lorin Padgurskis, ten

Never play basketball by your parents' new car.

Kaitlyn Sweeney, twelve

Don't flush the toilet when your older sister is in the shower getting ready for a date.

Weston Dunlap, ten

It takes years to build up trust, and seconds to destroy it.

Dijana Atikovic, twelve

When you are cleaning your room, don't shove stuff under your bed, in your closet or under your dresser. You just end up cleaning those places, too.

Eddie Holtz, eleven

Who I am is not what I have but what I try my best at.

Julie Lundgren, eleven

When you are sick or sad, laughter is the best medicine.

Aaron Snyder, eleven

Keep dreaming and you may be writing the next *Chicken Soup* book.

Jason Trusso, eleven

Covered

*One important key to success is self-confidence.
An important key to self-confidence is preparation.*

Arthur Ashe

The day began like most days; I was running behind. After wolfing down breakfast, I ran out the door and down the street to my friend Teresa's house, only to find she wasn't going to school that day.

I knew if I went back for Mom, I would be late for school, so I ignored her warnings about the dangers of being at the bus stop alone. If I'd had a clue as to what was in store for me, I would have chosen to be late.

As it was, the bus itself was late, so I sat on the grass under a tree and opened a book. I got so into what I was reading, that I didn't pay much attention to the men in the pickup as they passed by, or when they stopped up the road and backed up. They caught my attention when they spoke to me, but I didn't understand what they said. I stood up and asked, "Pardon me?"

The truck held two men who were in their mid-twenties. The driver had dark hair and a tattoo on the arm he had hanging out the window; the other man had long blond hair.

I knew not to speak to strangers, but I asked again, "Pardon me? I didn't understand what you said."

The driver asked, "Have you seen a black lab running loose? He disappeared out of our yard last night, and I can't find him anywhere."

While he was talking, something in the back of my mind told me I shouldn't be having this conversation at all. Finally, a bell went off in my mind and I remembered Mom and Dad having Mr. Jay come into our karate class and act out this very same scenario with all the younger students.

It was like déjà vu. The man in the truck uttered the very same words Mr. Jay had used during our self-defense class, "How about coming over here so I can show you his picture. That way you can let me know if you see him. Maybe you will see him while you're on the bus, or something."

Under the tree, I was well away from the road, but I still began to back up.

"Come on, it will only take a minute to look. What if it was your dog, wouldn't you want somebody to help you find him?"

My emphatic "No! You look for your own dog" wasn't the answer he was looking for, and when the driver first opened his door, I was shocked. No one in class had ever said someone would actually get out of their vehicle and come after me. They did always have a saying in class though, "He who runs away, lives to fight another day."

I ran.

When I looked back, the blond guy had slid over to the steering wheel and was driving on the road parallel to me while the other guy was gaining ground behind me. It was then that I really started to get scared.

I tried to pray, but all that would run through my head was, *Oh God! Oh God! Please don't let him get me!*

When the man latched onto the neck of my T-shirt and pulled me backward, I couldn't scream, claw, bite, punch or kick, because I froze.

It was only when he let go of my shirt and grabbed my wrist that I was once again able to move. We had covered wrist grabs many times, and thankfully, lessons that had been repeatedly practiced became instinctual.

I stepped back and executed the twisting yank against his thumb that also caused my upper body to twist away from him. When I realized it had worked, I almost froze again, but instead, I finished the technique they had taught me.

Using the torque of my twisted body, I swung back around at the man and landed a back fist to his face. Between the torque, the adrenaline and my height, I made a solid connection that made his nose bleed. I allowed my body to continue on past with the back fist and gave the strongest spinning back kick I could to the man's knees.

With blood running down his face and hopping on one leg, the guy began to curse me, but I didn't wait around to hear much. I ran across the field, crawled through the fence of a horse farm, ran past the horses and on to the closest house. Luckily, I knew the people who lived there. From there, I called the police and then my mom.

When Mom heard what had happened, she began to cry and shake. It wasn't until we got to the sheriff's office and I told them my story that I began to cry, too.

Two weeks later, the paper reported the abduction of a twelve-year-old girl not far from our home who was taken by two men in a truck that matched the description I had given the deputy. I often wonder if some martial arts training could have helped to save her.

Later on I heard Mom and Dad discussing what had

happened. I heard my mom say to him, "All those years of karate really helped her defend herself when she really needed it. But, knowing what happened to that other girl, I think Victoria had a little extra help that day. I believe that God covered her back, too."

Victoria Perry, twelve
As told by Tenna Perry

Pyramid Surprise

People seldom refuse help, if one offers it in the right way.

A. C. Benson

Nellie and I have been best friends for as long as I can remember. We were born only a few days apart, so every year we plan a combined birthday party. The year we were in seventh grade, we were especially excited. Our moms said we could finally invite boys. Our theme, we decided, was "Discover the Pyramids."

Nellie was writing out the invitation list when my mom came up and peered over her shoulder.

"What about inviting John?" Mom asked.

John had been in our class for only a few months, but he was already getting better grades in math and science than anyone else in class. He was a loner, though, and hadn't made very many friends.

I wrinkled my nose. "Mom, he wears the same pants to school every day. How could he even afford a costume?"

Mom frowned. "The same pants?"

"Yes. Brown corduroy ones." I felt a twinge of guilt. My family didn't have a lot of money either, but my mom was a whiz at bargain shopping. I never had to wear the same thing twice in one week.

"Hmm," said Mom. Her office phone rang, and off she went.

After school the next day, as Nellie and I were cutting paper for party decorations, Mom waltzed up and handed me an envelope.

"What's that?" I asked.

"Nellie's mom and I thought it would be nice for you two to give this to John," Mom said as she headed back to her office.

I opened the envelope delicately and gasped. Inside was a gift certificate for our favorite department store.

"Wow," said Nellie. We both knew how many cute clothes that would buy.

I stared at the certificate in awe. "So, are we going to just hand it to him?"

"How embarrassing would *that* be," Nellie scoffed.

She was right. John would be totally humiliated if we gave him money for clothes. "What if we slipped it into his desk when no one is looking?"

"He'd probably give it to the teacher, and then we'd have to say it was for him in front of the whole class." Nellie rolled her eyes. *"Triple embarrassing.* We have to think of something else."

"Hmm. What if we ask our teacher . . ."

"Wait a second. *Stop everything.* I have an idea." Nellie snatched the envelope and started hopping up and down.

"What? What?"

Still bouncing, she sang, "I'm not going to tell you!" I pestered, I wheedled, I glowered. But Nellie wouldn't budge.

For days I watched Nellie and John carefully. No new pants.

Maybe he's saving them for the party, I thought. *Or worse, maybe Nellie was going to give them to him there!* For just one tiny second, I wondered if she might have confiscated the gift certificate and used it herself.

She wouldn't do that, I told myself. But I watched in vain for new pants to appear.

On the day of our party, kids arrived dressed in white sheets, black wigs and snake bracelets. John arrived in a dingy sheet, with—no surprise—the brown corduroy pants underneath.

Nobody seemed to care, though. We danced, ate Mediterranean snacks, and divided everyone into teams for a mummy wrap contest and a hieroglyphic scavenger hunt.

"And now for the grand prize game," Nellie announced.

Grand prize? My mouth dropped. This was not in the plan.

"Get your pencils ready! The grand prize game is the following riddle: Osiris and Isis were building pyramids. Osiris' bricks were 4 feet cubed, and he worked at the rate of 8 bricks per hour. Isis' bricks were 3 feet cubed, and she worked at the rate of 12 bricks per hour. They both started with a base 60 feet square. If their pyramids had to be 60 feet high, who finished first?"

A math game. *Of course!* Nellie winked at me. Neither one of us was surprised when John came up with the answer way before anyone else and walked off with the envelope.

Everyone ooohed and aaahed when our moms brought out an enormous chocolate pyramid cake. I noticed John took particular delight in slicing off the very top.

The next week, he wore a new pair of pants every day, and even a couple of new shirts. The whole time he had a big grin on his face.

And so did we. I have never been more proud to be Nellie's best friend.

Holly Cupala

Initiation

Do not do what you would undo if caught.

Leah Arendt

"I'll bet you won't do it," Tiffany whispered.

"Shut up and leave me alone," I said.

"Wimp!" Tiffany said. "I do it all the time. We all had to do it. You won't get caught. You're just chicken!"

"I am not!" I said hotly. "I just need a minute to figure out which one I want."

"Hurry up! Just stick it in your pocket. She's not looking. Do it now!" Tiffany ordered as she walked out of the store.

I stood in front of a nail polish display in a costume jewelry shop at the mall, nervous as I could be. Sweat popped out on my forehead. I felt my underarms getting sticky. I checked once more to see if the girl at the register was looking at me. Confident that she wasn't, I quickly jammed a bottle of the nail polish into the pocket of my jeans and walked out of the store.

I hurried to the food court where my friends were waiting. Still sweating profusely, I held my head up high and smiled. "I got it!" I exclaimed proudly.

"I don't believe you. Let me see it," Tiffany demanded. Tiffany was the unofficial leader. You did what she said, or else. I was the new girl, so I had to be initiated. My job was to steal two different things from the same store, two separate times. Up to this point in my life, I had never stolen anything. I lived with my grandparents and I knew that they would be disappointed in me if I ever got caught stealing.

"Ha!" I said, pulling the polish out of my pocket. All the girls nodded approvingly when they saw the polish.

"Give it to me, now!" Tiffany commanded. "And go back in there and get something else."

"I don't want to go back in there right now," I said. "Can't we eat lunch first?"

"I guess. Honestly, DeAnna, you are such a baby," Tiffany said as she headed for Arby's.

She's so mean to me. Why do I even want to hang out with them, anyway? I thought to myself. It only took me a minute to remember why. Tiffany was the baddest girl at school. Nobody messed with her or the girls who hung out with her. If they did, she took care of it after school.

We ate, and then she announced that it was time for round two. We all headed back to the store. They left me by the entrance and made their way toward a different store.

"There are some earrings down there that I want and Jen is going to get them for me. By the way, we're leaving in ten minutes. You'd better hurry or we'll leave without you," Tiffany said.

I took a deep breath and walked back into the store. I felt a little less guilty, because Tiffany now had the nail polish and my pockets were free. *Tiffany wouldn't know if I just bought something instead of stealing, would she?* I made up my mind. I wanted more than anything to be accepted. If I were one of Tiffany's friends then nobody would pick on me—nobody would call me names. Nobody except Tiffany.

I kept thinking about my grandparents and how proud of me they were. I knew how hard they worked to teach me right from wrong. They just didn't know what it was like at school. I was in the seventh grade, and I had no friends. Tiffany wasn't really my friend. I knew that. The more I thought about it, she wasn't really *anybody's* friend.

I decided right then and there that she wasn't worth it. I wasn't going to let her use me like she did Jen and Katie. I picked out a key chain and stepped up to the register to pay for it. I saw the nail polish display and I started to sweat again. "Are you alright?" the girl asked me.

"Yeah, I'm fine. I'm just a little tired," I lied, grabbing a bottle of white nail polish. I put it with the key chain on the counter and paid for them. It was one way that I thought I could help to make it right.

I went to the store where they had gone but Tiffany, Jen and Katie weren't there. After looking throughout the mall for about half an hour, I concluded that they had left me. It was kind of weird, but I felt relieved that I didn't have to deal with them anymore. I realized that I'd probably get it when I got to school on Monday, but I just didn't care. Who I wanted to be was more important than being so-called friends with them. It would be worth what they would put me through just to be free of them.

I used the pay phone to call my grandmother and asked her to pick me up. As I sat outside the mall waiting, I clutched the bag containing the polish and the key chain that I had bought and thought about the decision that I had made. Then I smiled, because I knew it was the right one.

DeAnna Doherty

My Dad, the Superhero

When I was only seven my family took a road trip to San Francisco. My father was driving our family car along the highway during an intense rainstorm. The rain was drenching the entire road and each drop of rain felt as if it were going to break the windshield. As soon as the windshield wipers would sweep the water off, a fresh blast of water would already be there, making it very difficult to see.

I wasn't scared. The downpour mesmerized me. My brother, who is three years older than me, was asserting his power over me in the backseat. He was inflicting me with some sort of older brother torture that is apparently essential for all older siblings to do to the younger ones. Every time I tried to block his hits, he would outwit me by hitting me someplace else. And each time I tried to grab his arm, his other hand would strike like a venomous snake. My only defense was to complain to Mom.

I complained to her in detail about the injustice going on in the backseat, but it was relatively ineffective. My father, who was driving, knew that the only way to get us to stop fighting was to distract us. So he said, "Spencer, do you know that I have learned magic?"

I was stunned at first, and both my brother and I stopped immediately. "What?" I asked for clarification.

My father replied, "Do you want me to show you some magic?"

I got excited. It was every child's dream to have a superhero father. Even my brother was curious about what Dad was saying.

"I have the ability to stop the rain from falling. It's only for short periods of time, so you have to pay close attention," he instructed.

I was speechless. This seemed to be an incredible feat, even for a superhero. All I could do was stare at him through the rearview mirror in suspense.

"Are you ready?" he asked.

"Yes!" we both answered.

"Okay. Let me summon my powers." There was a short pause. "Okay. First, I have to say the magic words, 'Abra Cadabra.' Here we go . . . *Abra Cadabra!*"

And just like THAT, for one split second, the rain stopped! The great drops ceased to fall from the heavens. It was a miracle! I was shocked. My dad really was a superhero. How could I not have known? For years, his powers had eluded me. He must have hidden his gadgets and weapons in the garage. I bet his old Ford was just a cover so that the villains wouldn't know who he *really* was.

"Wow!" I said to my brother, who seemed to be just as amazed as I was.

"Wow . . ." was all he could say, too.

Then our car drove under another overpass.

Spencer Westcott

Grandma's Pearls

When the heart grieves over what it has lost, the spirit rejoices over what it has left.

Sufi Epigram

Two weeks after Grandpa died, Grandma came to live with us. Every day, she sat in a rocker in the living room, staring out the window and fingering a small red pouch that she kept with her always. I would try to joke with her and make her laugh like she used to, but she would just nod sadly and continue rocking.

One day, I noticed Grandma looking out the window. I stood up, stretched my cramped legs and walked over to her. "What are you watching, Grandma?" I asked.

Grandma's head jerked, like she was waking up from a nap. "Nothing, really. Just looking into the past."

I didn't really know what to say. Grandma stared at me, seeming to really see me for the first time in the weeks since she'd moved in. I pointed to her lap. "Why do you keep that red bag with you?"

Grandma's skinny, bent fingers moved lovingly along the bright velvet. "Everything I ever learned is in this bag," she said.

I pulled up a stool and sat by her knees. "What do you mean?"

"I'll show you." Grandma gently pulled the worn ribbons that held the bag closed, then reached in and removed a strand of large, silvery-white pearls.

"It's beautiful!" I said. Leaning closer, I realized the huge pearls were strung on a slender length of leather.

"Your great-great-grandmother gave this to my mother, who gave it to me." Her eyes glistened. "I remember it like it was yesterday. She gave me this piece of leather, with one pearl strung on it. She called it a pearl of wisdom. She gave it to me because I ignored the stories everyone was telling about a man who had moved into town with his two daughters. I made friends with the girls, even though I lost my old friends for awhile. And she gave me this one when I didn't ask Jim Redmond to the Sadie Hawkins dance, even though I was terribly in love with him, because my best friend Penny wanted to ask him.

"She gave me another pearl each time she felt I'd done something special, learned some kind of lesson, or had done something she felt was wise."

"So, every pearl is a pearl of wisdom," I whispered, running my hand over the cool spheres.

"That's right," she said, slipping the pearls back into their bag. She pulled the ribbons tightly and smiled at me. "Your grandfather gave me the last one, on our fiftieth wedding anniversary, because he said marrying him was the wisest thing I'd ever done." We both laughed.

Grandmother died that fall. After the funeral, my mother gave me a round jewelry box of polished dark wood, with cut glass set in the top. "Your grandmother wanted you to have this."

I lifted the lid. Inside the box rested the red velvet pouch with a note written in my grandmother's crooked scrawl. "I should have given these to your mother a long time ago, but I always felt like I still had things to learn. I hope you'll keep these pearls safe, and continue the tradition with your own child."

Angry and sad, I stuffed the box with its contents into the very back of my dresser's bottom drawer. *All the wisdom in the world didn't keep you from dying,* I thought.

Three years later, I was fourteen. The last thing I wanted was to start high school with glasses so thick you couldn't see my eyes. I wanted contacts, but my parents couldn't afford them.

I mowed every lawn in the neighborhood that summer. I pulled weeds, painted garage doors and washed cars. Two weeks before school started, I picked up the contacts I had been able to order with the money I had earned.

I took the hated glasses and stuffed them in the very back of my bottom dresser drawer, and there was the box. I took it out and opened the lid. Smiling, I untied the leather and let all but one of the pearls fall into the pouch. "I'm not going to continue the tradition with my own child," I whispered, "I'll continue with me."

I had worked hard for something I wanted instead of expecting someone else to hand it to me. I added one more pearl, retied the ends and put the box on my dresser, where it should have been all along.

In those few moments, I felt I had learned something important. In my memories, and in those pearls, my grandmother and her wisdom lived on.

Catherine Adams

13

LIFE HAPPENS

Bad hair days and mixed up romance
Told that there's gooey stuff stuck to your pants
Getting a sister when you wanted a brother
Finding that "Life Skills" is taught by your
*   mother*
Slipping and falling and ripping your jeans
Discovering your sister has ruined your things.

Sometimes life gives us days full of laughter
And then we have some that are filled with
*   disaster*
Some things that happen aren't part of our
*   plans*
We have to roll with it and just throw up our
*   hands*
What life will bring next is predicted by none
Which makes it exciting and often more fun.

Irene Dunlap and Patty Hansen

Klutz Dust and Puberty

Life is a roller coaster. Try to eat a light lunch.

David A. Schmaltz

Have you ever had one of those days that seem normal at first, but little by little, you realize that you're out of sync with the world around you? On the way to the bus I tripped over a crack in the sidewalk, making me drop my English report onto the road, just in time for it to be run over by the bus, then it hit me! (No, not the bus.) The realization that this was one of those days.

In math, I found my little brother's homework folded neatly inside my book, instead of my own. Try explaining *that* to a teacher who already knows that math is not your best subject.

"Let's not make this a habit," Mr. Barner said, tapping his pencil on his grading book for emphasis. *Like I could even think up this excuse for not doing my homework.*

"Since you claim to have already done this assignment, you shouldn't have any difficulty reproducing the answers for me during your lunch hour." *What? No trouble reproducing the answers? It took me one hour and all my dad's patience to produce them the first time.*

My English teacher accepted my crumpled and tire-treaded report, but not without delivering a lecture on the importance of the proper presentation of my work. "I do expect better from you in the future." *Future? What future?* I re-did my math homework and made it to the cafeteria with a few minutes to spare. A lot of good that did me. The only food choices left were liver and onions (like onions are supposed to be some big bonus) and spinach.

All through my geography speech on "The Greening of the Earth," my best friend, Kara, kept showing me her teeth. I thought she meant for me to smile more, so I grinned bigger.

It wasn't until I sat down after my presentation, in front of the whole class, that Kara told me I had spinach stuck in my teeth.

"I know," I joked, trying to sound like I wasn't humiliated, "it was a visual aid for extra credit."

I got unstoppable hiccups in science, started out on the wrong note in choir . . . well, actually, it was the right note—but, for the wrong song, and I slammed my finger in my locker.

When the final school hour came, I thought for sure that I had it made. My mother was the trained volunteer presenter for the Life Skills unit that month. I knew at least she had to be kind to me.

Laughing and talking as we took our seats, my mother asked for our attention.

"Welcome class," she smiled, "our subject during this unit is puberty." She paused and looked around the table. *WHAT!!!!! No, no, no, no, NO! Not that! Not here! Not my mom talking about puberty and hormones in front of my friends! With diagrams! And boys in the room!!!!*

She calmly stood there as though she was only discussing the weather. I guess in a way she was discussing the weather—whether or not I'd live through this.

What if I accidentally made eye contact with someone? What if it was a boy? I safely stared at the floor. The hands on the clock moved in slow motion. I tried to force time along by thinking of places that I would rather be.

Allergy shots. Detention. At home cleaning the bathroom. Tick. . . tock . . . Tick . . . tock. *Does she have to tell us absolutely everything she knows? Does she know absolutely EVERYTHING?*

My mother finally wrapped it up. "Are there any questions? Don't be afraid to ask!"

Right! And don't be afraid to walk through a tornado, or tease a hungry pit bull or jump out of an airplane with a hole in your parachute.

Silence.

"Go to my happy place. Go to my happy place," I said under my breath, frantically trying to calm myself.

Tick . . . tock. Tick . . . tock. Tick . . . tock.

My mother just kept smiling, "Well, next week you will have a chance to write your questions on a piece of paper and we will go over them together."

Next week! Maybe if I slept without covers and left my windows open all night I could be in the hospital with pneumonia by this time next week. Would it be wrong to pray for something to happen to prevent my mother from being here? Nothing bad or anything. How hard can a flat tire be for God?

It was only when the bell rang that I could breathe again. The class hurried out before I dared to look up. My mother was smiling down at me.

"Sweetheart, you handled yourself very well. I realized by your reaction that I should have made sure that you understood what our topic would be today." We pushed the chairs back under the table. "I was so concerned about Kara's mother this morning that I wasn't as sensitive as I should have been."

"Kara's mother? What's wrong? Kara didn't say anything."

"Kara doesn't know. She had already left for school

when her mother was rushed by ambulance to the hospital with severe diabetic shock."

My heart froze. "Diabetics can die from shock, can't they?"

"Yes. It was very serious but she made it through." My heart beat with relief.

We headed out the door into the golden light of late afternoon filtering through the autumn-colored trees that umbrella the sidewalk. My mother seemed to glow with the light around her.

"How was your day, Sweetie?"

"Well, Mom, it was a rough one," I paused, "but now, after knowing that Kara almost lost her mother today, little things don't seem to matter all that much."

My mother put her arm around my shoulders and we headed off for the car. "Sweetie, there's something that I have wanted to tell you since you came into class."

"Yes," I answered, feeling the near magic of our closeness.

"Sweetheart, you have a big wad of gum stuck to the seat of your pants."

"I what?" I twisted and turned, but I couldn't see behind me. I gave up.

What's a little klutz dust in the grand scheme of things? Life is beautiful, after all.

Cynthia M. Hamond

Jimmy, Jimmy

Mistakes are the usual bridge between inexperience and wisdom.

Phyllis Therous

When I was in the seventh grade, I broke my leg skiing. The doctor described my injury as serious—a spiral fracture of the tibia that was fragmented in three places—and just barely spared me the surgery to put pins in my leg. The tradeoff was that I had to wear a cast from hip to toe for four months, the first of them in a wheelchair. The weather that winter alternated between snowy blizzards and mucus-freezing-in-your-nose cold, so Mom or Dad had to drive me anywhere I wanted to go. Since sledding, skating, going to the local McDonald's and hanging out were my friends' favorite pastimes, I didn't get out much.

That left plenty of alone time for me to daydream and develop the biggest crush on a new boy in my class. His name was Jimmy, and he was *gorgeous.* He had thick brown hair, dreamy dark eyes, a perfect complexion and a great body. His slight Texas accent could charm anyone, and he was *sooooo* nice. *If only he would notice me!* But how could he? I hardly ever got to see him outside of the class-room, and he seemed to like one of my girlfriends, Kim. Besides, boys tended not to "like me" like me, because I was taller than all of them. I hoped Jimmy wouldn't notice my height thing since I was sitting in a wheelchair or slouching over crutches all the time. I didn't dare tell any-one about my crush, not even my best friend. I wanted to spare myself the misery of being teased. The crush on Jimmy was my big secret.

Then one Saturday evening, I got the phone call of my life. It was my best friend, Jodie, calling to say that some-one in our class liked me and wanted to ask me out, but he wanted to know if I liked him first.

"Well, who is it?" I asked Jodie.

"Jimmy," was the unbelievable reply.

I felt goose bumps crawl up the back of my neck to the top of my head. I nearly dropped the phone.

"Well, do you like him? Would you go out with him if he asked you?"

Then doubt quickly crept its way into my thoughts. Paranoia set in. Perhaps this was some cruel trick by my friends to find out who I liked. After all, how could Jimmy like *me*? We'd never even spoken so much as a word to one another.

"I guess so," I tentatively replied. My stomach was get-ting queasy. I waited for the teasing to begin.

"You guess so? Well, do you or don't you like him? It's got to be one or the other," Jodie pressed.

"Yes, I like him," I replied with a little more enthusiasm this time, my secret finally out.

"Great! Can we come over now? Jimmy wants to ask you out tonight!" gushed Jodie.

"Uh . . . sure. Come on over."

When the doorbell rang about fifteen minutes later—an absolute eternity—I answered the door to find my friends on the front porch. The guys were around the corner, waiting to send Jimmy over. I stepped out on the porch with the aid of my crutches and closed the front door behind me. My friends were smiling at each other, celebrating their roles as matchmaker, so excited to be a part of getting me together with my first boyfriend.

The girls left me alone on the porch so that Jimmy could ask me to go out in private. I waited there for him. I was anxious, nervous and excited. My stomach uneasy, part of me still wondered if this could be some big joke. For the first time since I broke my leg, I was thankful to have crutches to support me.

I was as white as a ghost, more nervous than I had ever been. Jimmy rounded the corner and stepped up onto the front porch. *Oh, no.* I wanted to hobble back inside and shut the door behind me. *What have I gotten myself into? How could I be so stupid?* I was so caught up in Jimmy dreamland that I had neglected to ask Jodie, "Jimmy who?"

There stood Jimmy, so sweet, with a nervous smile and a love-struck look. His red-freckled face seemed a little redder than usual. This wasn't *my* Jimmy. Not my big-crush Jimmy. Not Jimmy of my dreams and daytime fantasies. It was the *other* Jimmy in my class, who I liked as a friend but most definitely did not "like" like.

I heard myself mutter a feeble, "I guess so," when he asked me to go out with him. *What else could I do? How could I turn him down after he had prescreened his proposal through Jodie?*

We didn't hang around very long on the front porch. As soon as I could, I made some lame excuse about how I had to go back inside the house because my parents would wonder where I was.

Once alone inside the house, I worried about what to do next. I certainly couldn't tell anyone about the mix-up. I'd never live it down. I decided to hide behind the excuse of my broken leg and my life as a social recluse, until I could figure things out. And there was the solution! I would only have to see Jimmy in school, and only in the classroom where we couldn't really talk, and most definitely could not kiss. How on earth could we go out under those circumstances?

I waited what seemed to be an appropriate length of time (about three days), offered my excuse to my girlfriend, Jodie, and asked her to break up with Jimmy on my behalf. I figured that since she helped me get into this mess, she should help me get out of it. Jimmy confronted me, flushed with anger, to confirm the breakup after Jodie told him. Slouching down lower on my crutches, I said something like, "Sorry. I hope that's okay with you." *Lame. Lame. Lame.*

Rumors floated around about me only agreeing to go out with Jimmy so I could say I had had a boyfriend . . . and about me breaking up with Jimmy because I was too afraid to kiss a boy. I suffered their laughter in silence and never told anyone about the case of mistaken Jimmy. My big crush remained my big secret, my first true love.

Karen Lombard

The Mummy Returns

Let there be more joy and laughter in your living.

Eileen Caddy

Here we were, standing at the entrance of the ride, "The Mummy Returns," at Universal Studios, in Hollywood. My mom, dad, brother, and best friend, Stephanie, were there with me. My heart started beating fast and as we walked in, I began thinking about what crazy things might happen in there.

The shadows crept silently over us as we glanced at ancient Egyptian artifacts. A chill of excitement immediately ran up my spine. We walked deeper and deeper into the mazelike cave, entering a world of the unknown. The creepy walls started narrowing into a small hallway, where we were spinning and turning in circles. We timidly approached the aisle, dizzily grabbing the railing on either side of us.

As we walked on and on, things started popping out at Stephanie and me. Scared to death of this place from the beginning, Stephanie started frantically running in the opposite direction, back the way we came in. Wanting to pull me along with her, and not realizing what she was doing, she grabbed some lady's purse thinking that it was mine. When she realized that it wasn't mine, she returned it to the person then ran to catch up with us.

Looking at the spidery cobwebs and dead bodies all over the place, we were led to a vast bridge. Dangling from a rope was a man! (Fake, of course!) Stephanie got the living daylights scared out of her again, and literally threw my mom completely off the bridge because she was so scared.

Worse things started to happen. As I was holding on to Stephanie frantically, in the rush of people on the bridge, my brother Gianni tried desperately to get my attention.

"Turn around, turn around," Gianni yelled repeatedly. Finally realizing what he was saying, I turned around. There, to my surprise, was a big mummy standing right there! He was covered in a white wrap from head to toe. He looked at me through those ancient eyes of his, staring at me and giving me a dirty look. As he went past me, he walked impatiently, sternly, strictly and seriously, like an army general. He must have been trying to get past me to get to Stephanie, but he couldn't. I have a feeling that he radioed his other mummy friends to watch out for our group after that, because worse things started to happen, like scary things jumping out at us from the walls.

Stephanie and I screamed, yelled, pushed, shoved, and dodged everyone and everything in our way, to get out of there. In the process of doing so, we created a domino effect—Stephanie pushed into me, I shoved into Gianni, and Gianni rammed into my dad—which was a big mistake! Losing his balance, my dad desperately flayed and waved his hands in the air, trying to grasp onto something—anything—in the pitch-black darkness. Yes, my dad did catch his fall, but with something very peculiar.

His hand touched a gushy, blubbery thing, and he grabbed on to it for support. It turned out to be some lady's left boob! The lady must have been too embarrassed to respond, because she didn't even scream.

Trying not to laugh too hard and make any other accidents happen, Stephanie and I calmly walked on. As we did, another mummy popped out at us. We couldn't help but scream our brains out again. It happened to Gianni, too. "Aaaawww!" The mummy screamed at Gianni. Then Gianni screamed back. The confused mummy attempted to try to scare my brother one last time. He came at it a different way. "You need to brush your teeth," the mummy commented. My brother quickly responded, "You need a shower!"

Later on, mummies were falling out of the walls, and one just happened to bump into my mom. The ridiculously haunting mummy got my mom so freaked out, she screamed and peed her pants!

We all piled out of the haunted house, out of breath, laughing hysterically and holding our stomachs tightly. We all had the same thought running through our minds: *We had just experienced the funniest moments of our lives!* A lot of crazy things can happen in one little haunted house.

Chiara Cabiglio, thirteen

Whose Room Is It, Anyway?

Who could deny that privacy is a jewel?
In each civilization, as it advanced, those
who could afford it chose the luxury of a
withdrawing-place.

Phyllis McGinley

I dreaded coming home from school and going into my room. Every day it was something different. The hours away at school were long enough to cause a drastic, terrible change to my peaceful haven. Today was no different.

As I entered the house, Mom called out a cheerful, "Hello!" and greeted me with a smile. It seemed like nothing was wrong. She asked me how my day had been, if I had any homework. . . blah, blah, blah. I was still suspicious. Mom could be so unaware! Yesterday, I discovered a chocolate chip cookie smeared around the mouth of my favorite figurine, a porcelain angel with glittering gold wings and beautiful long blonde hair. She had the prettiest pink lips, which were now covered in chocolate. Obviously, Callie had enjoyed the cookie so much she wanted to share it with my angel. *Not funny.*

I looked around for my little sister, Callie, who had just turned three. I didn't see her, but I heard the TV blaring in the other room. She loved to sit and watch the afternoon cartoons, turning the volume up and then back down, up and down. As I scanned the family room, I noticed it was pretty messy. There were toys all over the floor, but none of them seemed to be mine. There were a few headless dolls, some blocks, a few juice-stained stuffed animals, the remains of a green grape crushed into the carpet and videos strewn all over the floor. My hopes were slowly rising. If Callie had focused on destroying only the family room, well, maybe . . .

I peeked around the corner into the extra room, and there she was, sitting on the couch with her chubby legs stretched out in front of her, clutching the remote with sticky hands. Her long, thick blonde hair was all tangled, and it looked as though she had specks of sand or crumbs in it. Her pink and blue outfit was still remarkably clean— that was truly amazing. I figured that Callie must have gotten her clothes so dirty that Mom had recently put a clean outfit on her. That seemed much more reasonable than assuming that she had kept this outfit clean all day. No way. Not my sister, the destroyer. Not my sister, the three-year-old terror. Not my sister, the menace of my life.

She looked up from gazing at the TV and saw me. A huge grin broke out on her face, and she laughed in delight, clapping her hands. I was surprised that they didn't stick together.

"Sissy!!" She leaped off the couch and ran to me, squeezing my knees and almost tipping me over.

"Hi, Callie," I said, with the slightest hint of a smile. I ruffled her hair, and white crumbs drifted like dust to the floor. "Yucky, Callie," I said, pointing to the crumbs that had settled onto the carpet. I turned around and started the dreaded climb to my room.

Up the stairs I trudged. *What was it going to be today? Grapes shoved into my CD player? My treasured collection of ceramic bear figurines colored with Magic Markers? Or maybe smashed into a million bits and shoved into the CD player?* My door was still closed, which was a good sign. Maybe she hadn't been in here today after all. Maybe Mom had been able to keep her out. I was so hopeful that I breathed a sigh of relief.

I pushed open the door . . . .

And saw destruction! Covering the floor was more of the same substance that I had just seen in Callie's hair! It was *everywhere*—on my bed, on the floor, on my bookshelves and desk, and yes, even coming out of my CD player! I bent down and touched it, wondering what it was. Then I saw an empty can thrown in the corner. *Parmesan cheese!* She had poured Parmesan cheese all over my room! I ran downstairs as fast as I could, almost tripping a few times, and came face to face with my bewildered mother.

"She did it again!" I screamed, my face red and hot with rage.

"Oh no, now what?" My mother covered her face with her hands, as if dreading what I was going to say.

"Parmesan cheese," I replied through clenched teeth.

"What? How . . ." And then Mom's face registered understanding. "I made spaghetti for her lunch and I must have forgotten to put the cheese away," Mom sighed. "Don't worry," she said, "I'll clean it up, and then we'll get your dad to put a Callie-proof lock on your door tonight."

I felt better, now that I knew that soon my room would truly belong to me once again. But I was still angry at my little sister so I went into the family room to tell her how bad she had been.

"Callie . . ." I started.

"Sissy!" she cried, her big brown eyes lighting up with joy. "Hooray!" She leaped off the couch once again, and hugged my knees with such happiness that I could only look down at her and smile. After all, she was only three and experimenting with the world. It was sort of nice to feel so loved by someone younger than me and I guess that's why she always chooses my room to explore and destroy—because she looks up to me, her big sister.

Mom kept her promise and cleaned my room so that it was spotless. Dad put a lock on my door that very evening. And . . . they bought me a new CD player that was even better than the old one Callie had jammed with Parmesan cheese!

Aidan Trenn, eight
As told by Melinda Fausey

Gabriella

Life is 10 percent what you make it and 90 percent how you take it.

Irving Berlin

I was so excited when I found out that my mother was pregnant. The sonogram showed that she was going to have a little girl.

I was five years old, and all I could think about was having a little sister who looked up to me. In my mind, I formed the image of what my perfect little sister was going to look like. She was going to have curly gold hair that cascaded down her perfect little shoulders like a waterfall and perfect heart-shaped, berry-stained lips that were always smiling. Her cheeks were going to be a rosy red color, she was going to have eyes that looked as if they came from the heavens because they were such a bright, beautiful shade of blue, and her skin was going to look like it was carved from porcelain because it was so pale and flawless. She would be quick-witted and always fun to be around. I couldn't wait until she was born.

My mama and daddy even let me choose her name. She was going to be called Gabriella. I thought that was the most beautiful name in the whole world. I went clothes shopping for Gabriella with my mama and I picked out the tiniest and most beautiful clothes I could find, all sorts of pink, fluffy dresses and outfits. I didn't think that I could wait nine whole months until she was born! Nine months is an eternity to a five-year-old.

Well, finally the day came. I rode to the hospital with my grandma. We were both so excited! I chattered nonstop about how Gabriella and I were going to be inseparable.

When we got to the hospital, I wasn't allowed to go into the labor room, so I sat outside and waited, forever . . . it seemed. Finally my grandma came out. She was smiling from ear to ear. She said, "Tiffany, come and meet your brother, Christopher."

BROTHER!?! What!! I didn't want a brother—I was going to have a sister! They were just going to have to put him back because I didn't want any smelly little brother. I followed my grandma into a little room, crying because I didn't want to see him.

She placed him in my arms, and I looked at him. He had scrunched-up little blue eyes that were sparkling with happiness. His nose was perfectly rounded. He opened his mouth and stuck out his tiny pink tongue, tasting the air. *He was beautiful.* Then I knew, right when I looked into his eyes from heaven, that I loved him just as much as I would have loved Gabriella.

Thirteen years later, I still love Christopher with all my heart—even though he can be a pest sometimes. He has grown up to be tall and good-looking. At thirteen, he is becoming a young man. The best part? He looks up to me—just like I had wanted my little sister to.

Tiffany Clifton

The Big Slip

I was getting ready to walk out the door after my usual morning routine when my mother yelled for me to get out to the car—as she often had to do just to get me moving. I grabbed my book bag, threw on some shoes, and walked through the door to the garage with no idea what was going to happen that day.

The morning went off without a hitch: math class, English, social studies. Finally it was 11:30, time for lunch.

I went to my locker, grabbed my lunch, and walked to our gym/cafeteria with the rest of my friends. The lunchroom was always a mess when it was our turn, because we were the last ones in the school to eat—after the kindergarten through fifth-grade kids were done. We had a very small school and it was used as both a cafeteria and a gym. Dust and dirt often collected on the floor from students' shoes—not to mention spilled milk, drinks and dropped food.

I sat down at a table with my friends, ate my lunch and sat back to talk with them for the remainder of the lunch period. We got up when it was finally time for recess. During recess there was never anyone eating in the gym, so we had the option of using it. We started playing a game of half-court basketball.

The game was about halfway through, and my team had the lead. I was outside of the key, guarding an opponent, when he shot the ball over my head. I jumped to block but missed. Michael, a teammate, got the rebound and was immediately covered by Andrew. Seeing that I was open and that he had a clear passing lane, he threw the ball to the ground for a bounce pass. I remember the ball hitting the floor only to come back up and hit me in the chest. Then my memory just goes blank. Just like when you fall asleep. You never see it coming—it just happens and there is a gap of memory between that instant and when you wake up.

It turns out that I caught the ball, slipped and bounced on my head. Maybe it was the wet floor or the shoes I was wearing. But either way, I was headed to the hospital.

The next part of this story is a little sketchy because I don't remember it at all. What you are reading now is what I've heard from various sources. I was lying on the ground with blood coming out of my nose, and Jarred asked me, "Are you all right?" There was no reply. The lunch aides ran to my side as I suddenly sat up and began hitting away or waving my arms at anyone who came close to me. I said that I had a really bad headache and the aides suggested that I lie down on the couch in the teachers' lounge. Our principal came into the gym and started to ask me questions. When I hit her with my fist, she realized I wasn't myself and yelled for someone to call an ambulance.

The paramedics arrived and took me to St. Luke's. The doctors, noticing I was going to need an emergency CAT scan, called and told them to rush the person out to make it available for me. Such a call is uncommon. Usually they simply rush the patient up there, hoping it's open. They rushed me to the CAT scan and took the pictures of my brain. The doctors found that I had ruptured a blood vessel inside my skull. I was bleeding inside my head, and the growing amount of blood was applying a lot of pressure to my brain.

The doctors had to surgically relieve the pressure, so I was rushed to surgery where Dr. Shinko would operate. He told my mother that there was a 75 percent chance he could relieve the pressure. My father, who was away in Chicago on business, was frantically awaiting a flight home after hearing about what had happened to me. As I headed into surgery, I have a vague memory of saying to my mother, "Tell everyone that I love them."

Inside the operating room, I have another vague memory of about six people around me, very busy doing things. I remember yelling, "My head hurts like heck, my head hurts like heck!" Then a female nurse kindly said to me, "We're doing everything we can." That's where the memory ceases.

Dr. Shinko had to shave the side of my head to make a clean incision, which begins at the front side of my ear and ends about a centimeter away from my left eye. He cut through a lot of nerves, but he knew they would grow back. He was able to relieve the pressure and close the incision using staples instead of stitches. Then I was taken to a hospital room where the doctors and my parents awaited my awakening.

I remember slowly raising my eyelids. My eyes half open, I heard someone whispering, "He's awake." Then another person saying the same thing. I remember thinking, *What is going on?* There was a machine to my right displaying my heart rate and other information. To my left was an IV bag hanging on a rack. Sitting on a chair to my left was my mother and standing behind her was my father. I asked in a soft voice, "What happened?"

They explained what had happened, and they asked me if I remembered the basketball game. I remembered every detail of it—even who was on my team and who was on the opposing one—everything, that is, except the accident. I stayed in the hospital for about a week, really groggy most of the time. I did more sleeping than anything else.

I woke up one day to find my room showered with cards. A few of my friends visited me to tell me how all the girls cried after it happened. And they asked if I could play in our upcoming tournament basketball game. I knew I wouldn't be able to, no matter how much I wanted to.

After some more tests, I finally left the hospital in a wheelchair, all the while insisting I didn't need one. But I didn't get my way.

It was weird going to church the following Sunday and hearing my name on the sick list to be prayed for. My punishment, as I call it, was that I couldn't run for two months and worse, couldn't play contact sports for six months. It stunk having to be tied down like that, but I got through it.

Dr. Shinko say he fixxxed everythiiing but for ssomme eason me dont realllly belive himm.

Scott Allen, eleven

Confessions of a Four-Eyes

Assumptions allow the best in life to pass you by.

John Sales

I made it all the way to fifth grade before anyone (besides me) realized that I couldn't see twenty feet in front of me. Our school had vision screenings every year, but somehow I had managed to fake good vision and pass the tests.

But then in the fifth grade, I got busted. It was my turn to go into the screening room, and I nervously took my seat in front of the testing machine. The nurse told me to look into the little black machine and tell her which direction the letter E's legs were pointing. Barely able to make out the black blob of an E, I strung together a guess: "Right, left, left, up, down, up, left, right." I looked up at her.

She squinted her eyes and studied my face for a moment. Then she said, "Could you repeat that?"

I panicked. I'd never been asked to repeat it. And I hadn't memorized the guess I'd just made up. I was trapped. So, I peered into the machine again and made up another sequence of guesses. I glanced over at the nurse,

who was leaning forward with a stern frown on her face.
"You have no idea which way they're facing, do you?"
she asked.

"Not really," I confessed.

"Can you even see the E at all?" she asked.

"Sort of . . . no," I admitted.

"Then why didn't you just say so?" she demanded.

I didn't respond. I thought the answer was obvious. Glasses in the fifth grade were a social death sentence. I assumed she knew this, but apparently it had been a very long time since she had been ten years old.

So, she sent me home with a note for my mother that said I needed to visit the optometrist because I'd failed the vision test. The trip home that day was very slow.

My mother (who wears glasses) said it would all be just fine. It wouldn't hurt a bit, she said. But I wasn't worried about pain—I was worried about looking like Super Geek.

The next day, my mother dragged me to the eye doctor's office, where I flunked with flying colors. I picked out a set of frames and tried to believe my mother when she said they looked really good on me. The doctor said the glasses would be ready soon. But I wasn't ready, and I didn't think I ever would be.

When the glasses arrived, the eye doctor put them on my face and walked me out onto the sidewalk in front of his office. When I looked up from my shoes, I was born into a whole new world—a world filled with crisp images, bold colors and sharp detail everywhere I looked. Suddenly I noticed the beautiful outline of crimson leaves on trees. I could see the details of people's faces long before they were standing right in front of me. I could see my mother smiling, as she watched me see the world in a whole new way.

"Glasses aren't so bad, are they?" Mom asked.

Not bad at all, I thought to myself. On that first day, they were a miracle.

Then Monday morning came, and I had to face the kids in my classroom. And it happened, just like I feared it would. A mean kid pointed at me in the middle of math class and yelled, "Four eyes!" But at that same moment, looking through my new glasses, I could see all the way across the room that the kid who had said it had an awfully big nose.

Life has a way of balancing itself out sometimes.

Gwen Rockwood

14

BUSTIN' DOWN WALLS

I did not struggle as invisible hands pulled
me down.
I just waited for someone else to pull me
out. I wondered why no one did.
Finally, I realized others were reaching
They just couldn't reach far enough.
And no rope was long enough for me to
grab.
So with all my strength, I started to climb
the mountain.
Because I began to realize that I was the
only one
With a rope long enough to pull me out.

Jennifer Lynn Clay, fourteen

To a Different Drummer

*If a man does not keep pace with his compan-
ions, perhaps it is because he hears a different
drummer. Let him step to the music which he
hears, however measured or far away.*

Henry David Thoreau

"Come on—put up your hands and fight!"
I groaned. *Why was this happening to me?* My mother had
said, "No fighting," right before I left the house. After coming from London, England, to Kitchener, Canada, to live
with her, I was starting a new life. During recess, this kid
wanted to scrap with me, and now it looked like I wouldn't
even be able to get through my first day of school and
keep my promise to my mum.

"Naw," I replied.

"You're just chicken," he yelled. "Is that it? Are you
chicken?" The kid's red hair blazed in the winter sun and
his freckles seemed to jump out of his pale skin. At twelve,
I was tall for my age, but I was kind of skinny and lanky.
He was taller than me, and with his heavy parka on, he
looked heavier than me, too.

"No. I'm not chicken. My mother just told me to stay
out of trouble."

"I don't care . . . I want to fight with you, anyway." He pushed me in my chest. Then he put up his hands. "Come on!"

So, I hit him. Down he went into the snow. Other kids on the playground started to circle around us. He got up. He put up his hands—and I hit him again. He went down for a second time. All the kids were yelling, "Fight! Fight!" This time, I kept my hands up just in case someone else in the circle of kids wanted a taste of me, too. I waited, and the kid got back up again.

He walked toward me, stuck out his hand and said, "Shake. I just wanted to see how tough you are. Wanna be friends?"

I heaved a sigh of relief and shook hands with him. I figured that I would need a friend. The snow, strange country, new school, the way that people spoke—different from my London street slang—and being the only black kid for miles around, all of this added up to being a weird new world for me.

I was born in London, England, and lived there with my mother until I was about eight years old. My mum wanted to find a better life for us, so she went to Chicago, in the United States. She left me with friends in London until she got settled enough to send for me. Mum ended up not staying in Chicago but moved to a small town in Canada because she had a friend there who helped her get a good job.

Meanwhile, back in England, I was getting into trouble. I had always felt like an outsider, different from the other kids. They didn't want to play with me. That made me mad, so I got into fights and ended up getting expelled for being a danger to the other kids at my school. The people I was staying with were upset with me and felt they couldn't manage me. So, after living with them for almost two years, they sent me to a home for kids—kind of a boarding school. I lived there for a year. I felt alone and bored, the food was gross, and I really missed my mother. Finally, she sent for me.

My mum met me at the airport in Toronto with a smile on her face, a warm hug and huge parka to put on. When we went outside the airport, there was snow all over the ground, the cars—everything! I didn't know what it was. I asked my mum, "What is this?" I touched the snow and was amazed by how cold and fluffy it was. It was different from anything I had ever seen before.

The weather was different, my school was different, the country was different, but some things were still the same—I was still getting into fights. Other kids picked on me about my accent, the color of my skin, my grades or whatever. I was different, still left out. It didn't matter; I hated getting picked on, and I let them know it—with my fists. All through grades seven and eight, I was sent to the principal's office so often that he and I became friends. Instead of punishing me, he would counsel me. He told me that I would be better off using the energy I had in more positive ways and encouraged me to play football and basketball after school. He also suggested that I check out boxing—maybe I could learn to use my fists in a constructive way instead of being on the destructive path I seemed to be headed for.

Even though I was an outsider and a loner, I liked going to school dances. At one of the dances, some of the guys wanted to fight a group of guys from another school. We agreed to meet them on neutral ground—the police boxing gym downtown. We showed up, but they didn't. While we were hanging around waiting for them, one of the boxing trainers called out to me, "You, come over here."

I walked over to him and he asked me, "Do you want to go a few rounds with him?" He pointed to a guy getting into one of the rings. I was pretty full of myself and figured I could take him because he was small, so I said, "Sure, why not?"

I just couldn't hit the guy. He danced all around me while I tried to hit him. Then that little guy really connected with my nose. Not only did that make my eyes water, but it bruised my ego and made me realize that there was more to the sport of boxing than just swinging my fists. The coach put me into the ring with another fighter who was about my size, and I did pretty well. That was a moment of decision in my life. I remembered what my middle school principal had told me and everything clicked. The boxing ring was where I belonged.

All through high school, I played football, basketball and soccer, and I was on the track team. But from that day on, boxing was the sport that I liked the most. Because it's an individual sport, it's more challenging and exciting to me. I found that I enjoyed the thrill of one-on-one competition. I also liked the fact that it was up to me whether I won or lost—that I was the determining factor. I think I've always been a competitor, and winning would give me a glow of satisfaction and a good feeling about myself. There was always a bad feeling if I lost, and I didn't like that. I wanted to win—every time.

I started training with the man who got me into the ring that first time. He became my boxing coach, friend, mentor and a father figure for me to look up to. I learned that boxing is a sweet science where I could use my brain as well as my strength and size. I used my ability to focus under pressure. Under his training, I went from being a street fighter to a gold medal-winning Olympic champion.

Though I was basically an outsider, even as a little boy I wanted to be first in whatever I set my mind to. Once I went professional, I worked hard and got what I wanted. I have earned millions, but for me, it's not just about the money. I made my dreams come true. I did it my way. I stayed away from bad promoters and bad managers and upheld my integrity. Throughout my career, I have gained, regained and retained the WBC and IBF heavyweight belts, the most prestigious in the boxing world. I want my place in history, and I know I will have it.

A couple of years ago, I was given the title, Member of the Order of the British Empire, an honorary title bestowed by Queen Elizabeth II for distinguished achievement. I have come a long way from being a brawling London street kid to the man I am today—the man that my mum raised me to be.

Lennox Lewis
Undisputed WBC Heavyweight Champion of the World

Life Rolls On

In three words I can sum up everything I've learned about life. It goes on.

Robert Frost

I was about nine the first time I got on a board. Something inside of me connected to surfing unlike any other sport. I had played a bunch of different sports, like baseball, soccer and hockey, but surfing became my true life passion. I never regretted walking away from all other sports in the pursuit of surfing.

By the time I was eleven or twelve, I began to compete in surfing. Before long, I was rated number one in the Juniors level of the Pacific Surf Series. I was featured in surfing articles and magazines, and companies began sponsoring me.

I began traveling to surfing competitions to some of the most beautiful places in the world. Things were really looking up. My lifelong dream of becoming a professional surfer was finally on the verge of becoming a reality. Then came the day when my life changed forever.

I woke up like on any other day. I watched a little bit of a surf movie to pump myself up for my surf session. I was excited; the waves were going to be so good. I called my friends. When I pulled up to the beach at Zuma, the waves looked great. I put my wetsuit on and surfed for a while; then I caught this one perfect south swell peak. I stood up backside and pulled in the barrel. As I came out of the tube, the wave hit me in my back so fast that I didn't have time to put my hands up. I hit my head on a sandbar beneath the surface of the water. My whole body went numb and tingly, then I was floating face down—unable to move. When the next wave flipped me over, I yelled for help. At first nobody came to help me, then finally my best friend, Brad, came over to me. I told him, "You gotta keep my head out of the water or I'm gonna drown!"

With the help of another friend, Brett, Brad was able to get me out of the water and onto the beach. I *knew* I was paralyzed. As I lay on my back, my dreams of becoming a pro surfer, of having a wife and kids, and my hopes of being in a big surf movie flashed in front of my eyes. *What was going to happen to me? What kind of a life would I have if I was paralyzed forever? This can't happen to me!* Guess what? It did.

I was taken by helicopter to UCLA Medical Center where it was determined that I had suffered a severe spinal cord injury, just like Christopher Reeve. With the flip of a wave, I had become a quadriplegic with no sensation or movement below my mid-chest. In that split second, my surfing days as I had known them were over. With only limited use of my arms and hands, I spent most of my time in intensive care units and rehab hospitals instead of in the water surfing. My worst nightmare had come true, and I was forced to deal with it.

As bad as it was, and it was very bad sometimes, I surprised myself by maintaining the will to live. I can't really say what made me go from not wanting to live if I couldn't surf—to embracing life without surfing—but by some miracle, it happened. Instead of being angry or afraid, I realized how fortunate I had been the first seventeen years of my life. I realized that I was still better off and more fortunate than some others. I had surfed the world—more than many could ever say.

That fall, I returned to school. I was elected Homecoming King, which was pretty cool, and ended up graduating on time. Shortly after my high school graduation, I enrolled at San Diego State University, stayed as busy as I was before the accident and graduated. I've got to say that I'm living my life to the fullest.

Every year, I speak to thousands of students in schools across the country. I really want kids to know that dreams can change and life can turn out different from what we sometimes expect. At the start of an assembly, I show a video of me surfing in competitions, rippin' on the waves and everything. They expect to see this high-profile surfer coming to speak to them, and then I come out in a wheelchair. They just don't anticipate that at all. I talk about the fact that my life has really just begun. I explain to them about the importance of family and friends. I tell them about how, since the accident, I've gone out on wave runners, gone waterskiing and inner tubing, played wheelchair tennis and ping pong, competed in a billiards tournament—playing pool with the best of them—and have even jumped out of an airplane skydiving!

I've traveled to places like Australia, France, Mexico, Spain, Italy and all over the United States. So many people have gotten behind me. Celebrities have helped me raise public awareness of the need to find a cure for spinal injuries, and I've also hung out with some very cool, great musicians.

But the highlight of my life since my injury came nearly four years after that fateful day. It took surfers like world champions Rob Machado, Kelly Slater and my brother

Josh, and the guys from the Paskowitz Surfing Camp to figure out just how to get me back on a board again—and they did it.

I finally got back in the water that I had missed so much—on a surfboard. They rigged a board so that I could hold on to something and ride the waves. I ride lying down, more like a body boarder would, but hey, it's still surfing to me. It's different—but I'm in the water.

Some people kind of freak out, thinking about me out in the water surfing again, but I don't even think about the danger. I've got a lot of trust in my abilities and the people around me. I make my own path, my own decisions. I'm the last one who wants to get hurt. Still, if it weren't for the help of my buds, I might not have ever had the chance to get back out there. I don't know of another quadriplegic in the world who surfs.

I believe that someday I'll regain some use of my paralyzed limbs. It is no longer a question of if, but *when*. I'll be ready, when the time comes, to take advantage of the breakthroughs in modern medicine. I know I'll never achieve my dream of being the world's greatest surfer, but dreams are abundant. I still have so many that are just as worthy and exciting—so many dreams that I have yet to achieve. I know that I've got a lot of living left to do. Life rolls on, waves continue to roll on and I'm rollin' and surfing right along with it all.

Jesse Billauer

[EDITORS' NOTE: *To find out more about Jesse and his organization, Life Rolls On, log on to* www.liferollson.org.]

Kindness Is More Powerful

As the sun makes ice melt, kindness causes misunderstanding, mistrust, and hostility to evaporate.

Albert Schweitzer

"Is she coming?" my shaky voice cracked. I didn't dare look behind me. My sister, Kayleen, turned to see the front of the middle school where eager seventh- and eighth-graders were pushing their way to carpools or making their way down the sidewalk toward an evening of television and homework.

"No," she whispered, "but if we walk faster, maybe we'll miss her completely. I'll bet she's still waiting for you outside the gym door."

I walked faster with my head bent down because tears were stinging my eyes and my nose had started to run. My heart was beating furiously and I had a sick feeling in my stomach.

Who was "she"? you might be wondering. Her name was Sabrina, and she was a bully. We were in gym class together, and I was less than athletic—more like pathetic! I didn't run very fast, and I was afraid of being hit by a ball, so I was a ducker not a catcher.

That day during gym class, we had played soccer. I not only embarrassed myself, I also made Sabrina mad—basically because she was on my team, and we didn't win. So, in the shower, she threatened me! "I'll meet you after class," she sneered, "and you will wish you and I had never met!"

I didn't need to wait until after class, I already wished we had never met!

As soon as class was over, I snuck out the teacher's entrance and ran to my locker where Kayleen was already waiting for me, so we could walk home together.

"What's up with you?" she asked, noticing the look of panic in my eyes. "Sabrina!" I choked. "We lost the soccer game in gym and it was my fault. She was on my team."

"Oh," Kayleen simply stated, but she patted my back in understanding. "Well," she said, "we'll walk down Seventeenth South instead of Harrison. It's out of the way enough that Sabrina won't have a clue."

Kayleen and I lived straight down the hill about a mile from Clayton Middle School. Sabrina lived somewhere in the middle. She had followed us most of the way chanting harassments since the first day of school. I couldn't figure out what I had ever done to her. She couldn't have had an idea of how bad I was at sports on the first day of school!

My mother said it was because I was quiet and kind and nonconfrontational that made me an easy target for bullies. I just felt like a loser! I was grateful for Kayleen, though. I always knew I could count on her. I think because she was my older sister, she felt like she needed to be my protector, and she was, always thinking of ways to avoid Sabrina or any of her sidekicks who enjoyed harassing me on a daily basis.

"Slow down!" Kayleen gasped. "You're practically running. We're far enough away now to be safe."

I looked up and Kayleen noticed my tears. "What about tomorrow?" I sobbed. "She'll just make it worse tomorrow!"

Kayleen stopped dead in her tracks, causing me to stop,

as well. I turned to look at her. She stood there with her hands on her hips. "Well, then," she said in her favorite grown-up voice, "I guess you just might have to tell someone, then!"

"It will just make it worse," I mumbled.

The next day arrived in record time. As Kayleen and I made our way up the steep Harrison Avenue hill, I felt sick. "I still think you should tell somebody," Kayleen chirped every few minutes.

I never replied until she had said that at least ten times, and then I burst out, "Tell somebody *what*? That Sabrina is mean and scary and just creeps me out? She's never actually done anything! Am I supposed to just tell them I am a big, fat baby who can't handle seventh grade because she is in it, too? What am I supposed to say?" Kayleen didn't respond. We walked the rest of the way in silence.

In homeroom, Sabrina's best friend passed me a note that stated, "At lunch, you will pay for running away!" I didn't even look up, but I accidentally swallowed my gum and choked until Mr. McKonkie excused me to go and get a drink.

Walking down the hall, I felt a slight sense of relief and freedom. Still, the note had me scared, and I ducked into the girls' bathroom and just cried. When I calmed down enough, I washed my face so I could go back to class without it being totally obvious. As I made my way down the hallway, I had a sick feeling that I was being followed.

Suddenly, someone kicked me in the back of the leg, hard. I almost fell over. "You little chicken!" Sabrina's voice sneered. I didn't turn around, I just walked faster. *Why wasn't she in class?* I wondered in my panic. I turned to go into Mr. McKonkie's class, but Sabrina blocked me. I turned again and started running down the hall. I had no idea what she was going to do, but three months of constant harassment was weighing heavily on my mind, and I was really freaked out.

Sabrina was now chasing me. At last, she caught up with me enough to kick the back of my legs, trying to knock me down. In a panic, I swung around to the staircase that led to the science and math department. Sabrina was so close to me by then that my sudden shift in direction knocked her off balance and she toppled down the stairs. I stood there watching her fall.

At first, I felt a sudden independence and victory. I turned to walk away from her when I noticed she hadn't stood up yet. Instinct took over, and I suddenly wasn't afraid of her anymore. I practically jumped down the stairs and touched her shoulder. "Can I help?" I asked. When she looked up, I could tell she was in pain. "I can't walk," she moaned. I helped her into a standing position, put her arm around my shoulder and together we hobbled to the nurse's office.

Sabrina never harassed me after that. We never became friends, but from that moment at the foot of the stairs, I knew I had earned her respect. She still hated being on my team in gym class, but things were different. Her best friend would still start in on me sometimes, but Sabrina would shake her head and quietly say, "Leave her alone."

And she always would.

Janalea Jeppson

[EDITORS' NOTE: *For more information about how to deal with bullies, log on to* www.kidshealth.org *(key word search: "bullying").*]

Bully Girl

For a while now she's teased me
I've learned to ignore it
But some things she's said
Just stay in my head
The looks and the faces
Mean and unkind
Bugging me, bothering me
Scaring my mind

My life will get better
In the end she will see
Those things that she said
Brought the strength out in me
To stand up to her
Make her leave me alone
Then I'll finally shine
A light all my own.

Alex Estey, twelve

Anything Is Possible

When your heart is in your dream, no request is too extreme.

Jiminy Cricket

When I was a little kid, I would always come in last when my friends and I ran races. I was never fast at running. I also had a hard time playing basketball because I couldn't jump well. It's hard to jump when your ankles don't move. So, I was always picked last to be on a team. I used to get so frustrated and would be really upset about my "fake legs." But I made up for it all when I got my first pair of Rollerblades.

I was born with a condition that caused me to have to be fitted with prosthetic legs and feet. I got my first ones when I was eight months old. Also, my fingers on my left hand were joined together. I had to have surgery to separate them, and as a result, I now have only eight fingers. But for those of you who think that a person with no feet and only three fingers on one of his hands should be in "special ed" classes—well, you've got me way wrong.

At first it was pretty hard to learn to skate—I kept

falling. But I liked the way I felt; while I was on skates, I felt like I was able to move just as fast as the other kids. So, I kept practicing—and I learned how to get up. Soon, I got better and faster. Then, when my friends were running races, I would put on a pair of Rollerblades and skate the race with them. Win or lose, I was able to keep up. Since skating had become my favorite thing to do, I signed up for the local roller hockey team and then the ice hockey team. I began playing hockey year round.

When I first joined, I thought I would just skate up to the net and take a shot. But I soon found out it wasn't so easy. I didn't score one single goal that whole season.

So, I trained hard in the off-season and the next year I signed up again. When I got through with the tryout, I was actually put into an older age bracket. The problem was, the kids in the older group were *huge,* and I quickly became intimidated. They actually stole the puck from me during the first game, and I didn't know what to do. I remember thinking, *Aren't we on the same team?* It made me feel like quitting, and I didn't show up at the next game. But my parents and my younger brother encouraged me to get back in there and keep trying.

On the next game day, late in the game, we were losing four to five and I was playing right wing. Finally, a pass came to me and I took the shot. To me, everything went in slow motion. I saw the puck fly into the net just as the buzzer went off. My goal tied the game. When my team came skating over to me with excitement, I realized that I really could become good at this game. It would be the first of many goals.

Now, at thirteen years old, I have played in three all-star games for ice hockey and roller hockey, all on able-bodied teams, and I don't even know how many goals I've scored in my entire career. I play for the American Amputee Hockey Association as well. We play all over the country and we have even played in Canada and Russia. Recently, I got sponsored by Nexed, an inline-hockey skate company. I get free shirts, hats, skates—anything that has to do with inline hockey. And just think, all this stuff started with one little two-second goal—and an awesome prosthetist named Eric.

Eric makes my prosthetics and knows exactly what I want and need. He's always looking for ways to make them function better. Before this year, my prosthetic legs had no bendable ankles. I had to grow to a certain height—and this year Eric made them for me. Now I know what it's like to have my feet on the ground while my legs move around. These new prosthetics with ankles that bend are good for running, jumping, hiking, and golf, which I recently took up. However, the old style where the ankles don't bend, is great for hockey—and, as a matter of fact, creates an advantage for me over other kids, whose ankles can get strained or even broken during a game. Now, I can choose which prosthetic I want to wear, according to the sport I'm playing!

I can also decorate my legs any way I want. I bring Eric a T-shirt or patches and he laminates them right onto the legs. I used to have the Rangers and Yankee logos—once I even had the American flag. Now I have them with tie-dye and Green Day and Nirvana patches. Everyone thinks they're pretty cool.

I've had some pretty funny things happen, like the time that I joined an out-of-town roller hockey team. Most of the guys on the team and their parents didn't know that I wore prosthetics. (You can't tell with all my equipment on.) So, you can just imagine everyone's faces when one of my legs came flying off during the game, as I was trying to shoot a goal. My leg kept going toward the net almost scoring a goal! There was dead silence in the arena. I think everyone was in shock! The two coaches came to get me off the rink. One coach carried me, the other coach carried my leg.

When I got off the rink, everyone just started clapping and whistling—they were flipping out! I don't think anyone who was there will forget seeing that! My mom helped me get my leg back on and all we could do was laugh at what had just happened. When the game was over, people kept coming up to me and shaking my hand like I was the "most valuable player" or something.

I have never thought of myself as handicapped. I'm definitely differently-abled. I began skiing when I was only seven, and now I am a black diamond skier. I go to ski camp every year with my amputee friends and for the whole week we ski and hang out. Maybe some day I will train for the Paralympics, which is like the Olympics, only it's just for people who are physically challenged. Whatever I decide to do, I know I would have to train hard to be one of the best—just like any other pro.

As I get bigger, my prostheses get even better, and it gives me more courage to get out and try new stuff. One day, after I had run in a six-mile race, one of my friends asked me where I'd been all day. When I told him that I had just finished a six-mile race, he said, "I couldn't do that!"

Someday, I want to go to a good college and eventually play for a team in the National Hockey League. I also want to be on the All-Star Team. But more than anything, I want to beat Wayne Gretzky's record. My philosophy is, you just have to go for it. You'll never know until you try.

Hey, as they say, "Anything is possible!"

Danny Stein, thirteen

A Skater's Determination

The man who can drive himself further once the effort gets painful is the man who will win.

Roger Bannister

It was just a simple request. I went to get Mat, "my Mat," as I call him, his iced tea. I would never regret anything more than that.

My brother is a skateboarder through and through. He always has been and always will be, and along with that comes determination. Anytime he has fallen down, he gets right back up and tries it again. If he has broken something, he just keeps on skating. He has always been such an inspiration to me, because he is so determined. Sometimes that determination is good, but on this particular day, it was a curse.

We were out in the front of my grandparents' house. Mat was determined to "ollie" over a chair that he had placed in the street. I was watching him try and try, over and over again. Deep down, I was thinking, *If he really wants to jump over that chair so badly, why doesn't he just put down that board with wheels on it, and do it?* If you knew my brother, you would know that he wouldn't have stopped until he jumped on his skateboard over that chair many times.

I could see him sweating. As usual, it was a hot Texas day. I was worried that he would get heatstroke. Even though I was only about five, I had heard grown-ups talking about people dying of heatstroke, and I kind of understood what it was. I really didn't want my living, yet hardheaded, brother to get it.

So there I was, my chin cupped in my hands, sitting on the porch of my grandparents' house, worrying about my Mat and thinking of ways to keep him cool.

"Hey Brit, could you get me my tea?"

I snapped out of my thoughts and back to the heat of the day. I replied to his request with a nod and stood up to go get the iced tea. Even through my plastic pink sandals, I could feel the extreme heat of the concrete steps. It was burning my feet, so I quickly went inside the house.

I headed through the hallway toward Grandma's kitchen, on a mission. I was thinking of how sweet and delicious her iced tea is, so I didn't see Wetta, Grandma's Chihuahua. On my way, I tripped over her.

As I entered the kitchen, my nose was filled with the sweet smell of tea and cinnamon toast. It was in the early afternoon, but my grandma knew how much I loved her cinnamon toast, so she made it whenever I came over. As I was walking toward her, hoping to surprise her, she turned around. As she did, I heard the most bloodchilling sound I had ever heard in my short life. "What was that?" Grandma said. "Did you hear that? Did Matthew scream?"

"I dunno. I'll go see."

As I ran though the house toward the front door, I had one thing on my mind—HEATSTROKE. I wish I could say that was what happened. Instead, I saw something that will forever be burned into my mind.

My image of my Mat, my big brother, my protector was shattered. He lay, motionless on the pavement. I ran to him to see what was wrong. My grandma was far ahead of me, running as fast as she could. When she got there, she told me to go wait inside for her. People started to come out of their houses to see who screamed. Mat's friend, Jeffrey, was the first to call 911. When the paramedics got there, they took my brother to the hospital. I didn't get to see Mat for at least a month.

Finally, it was Easter, and I was going to get to see my brother. I couldn't have been happier. I had missed him so much. I made sure that my dress was straight and my shoes were buckled. I wanted to look my best for Mat. When we got to the hospital, I saw a giant bunny that was passing out candy to the patients. Mat gave me his candy.

After a few more weeks at the hospital, Mat came home. He wasn't supposed to get out of his wheelchair and walk around. The doctors said he wouldn't be able to walk after the accident.

But Mat did. He was determined to walk again. He would get up out of his wheelchair and try to walk around on his crutches. After awhile, he didn't even use his wheelchair. If he wanted to go somewhere, he would walk. Soon he didn't even need his crutches. He couldn't run yet, but he was really trying to become the guy he had been before the accident. He could play with me, and finally he went back to school. It didn't take long before Mat could run and play, like any other kid, but he knew what he wanted to do.

Mat was determined to skate again. He was so determined to get better at skating, that he turned his whole life around. He went from not being able to skate—or even walk for that matter—to being one of the best board-skaters that I know.

That changed my outlook on life. I now look at everything as a way to help me skate better and help me in other ways. I am always looking on the bright side. That is what I have learned from my brother—a skater's determination.

Brittany Nicole Henry, twelve

The Fall and Rise of a Star

I was sure everyone in my junior-high drama class saw the paper in my hands shaking when I stood up to audition for a lead role in the annual Christmas play. I was there, not by choice, but because the teacher wanted each of us to try out for a part.

As a "good" student, I did what I was asked, even if it was scary. I was small for my age, wore secondhand clothes and cried easily. At school, I was often the brunt of jokes and taunts and had no friends. I wanted desperately to shrink back into my seat and be invisible. But there I was, onstage. Reading was, at least, something I loved. So, I read.

Within moments, the fear was gone. I entered the beautiful world of make-believe. *So much better*, I thought, *than the real and cruel one.* I was reading the part for the main character, "Star." She was poor—like me. But unlike me, she had a positive outlook on life even though she was an orphan. I wasn't an orphan, but I felt like one. My dad had disappeared. My mom worked days, went to school at night and spent her weekends doing homework. I ached for more time with her. In the play, Star was a lonely child who longed for parents, a few kind words and a home. It was easy for me to feel that her words were also mine. I finished reading and rushed back to my seat. The spell was broken. I was just me again, wanting to curl up and disappear. When the teacher read the cast list and called my name, I wasn't paying attention. No one ever chose me for anything.

"Patty," she repeated, "you are Star. Come and get your script."

This is impossible! How can it be? With a pounding heart and cold, moist palms, I felt nearly faint, but incredibly happy. I stumbled up to get the papers.

The cutest boy in class was playing the other lead. I didn't know him, but I wanted to. I was even hoping a little that some of his popularity might rub off on me. I was eager to learn my lines and wanted to do my best. So, I practiced every day—while walking to school, at lunchtime, before bedtime, even on weekends. At first, I was worried about forgetting parts of a long monologue that took place in one scene, but I managed to memorize it. I felt more confident after that.

Then we started to work on blocking, which is when the actors must touch, move and learn to use the props— in other words, really "act." The cute boy played a Scrooge-like character who refused to spend even a dime to put a candle in his window, so that the light would show passersby the slippery ice on the path below. On Christmas Eve, Star comes along, falls on the ice and sprains her ankle. The "Scrooge" finds himself helping her up, and in gratitude, she kisses him on the cheek.

One day, right before our drama class started, some of the kids were standing in front of the blackboard, snickering and looking at me. When they moved away, I saw a grotesque, cartoon like drawing of a girl with a huge behind and enormous, ugly lips. Above it were the words, "Falling Star."

I had been teased so often in the past that I had a sort of shield over my heart, which I tried to keep up in order to shut out the pain. But I wasn't very good at it, and this time, I was taken off guard. It really hurt. I was too embarrassed to even cry. Calmly, the teacher erased the picture. "Who did this?" she demanded. No one answered . . . of course.

We started to rehearse. I said my lines, but my heart wasn't in it. At the end of class, the teacher pulled me aside and told me not to pay any attention to the silliness. It probably wouldn't happen again. But she was wrong.

Every single day after that, a "Falling Star" picture, each one uglier and more embarrassing than the last, appeared on the board. Our teacher, who always had to rush from another class to ours, never caught the culprit. Each day it felt like I was entering a torture chamber. My dreams of being liked by my classmates were shattered. They all laughed at the pictures. I was sure that each and every one of them hated me as much as the person who drew the picture did.

In spite of that, at first, I refused to give up. I had worked too hard. Then I began to forget my lines, and I started to have nightmares about being onstage and unable to make a sound, while the audience laughed at me. Finally, I told the teacher to use my understudy for the part; I felt like I would be a terrible flop. She said, "No, you won't. You can do this. I know you can. I'll help you. If you want to, we'll use the auditorium, so you can feel comfortable there."

After that, we met several afternoons each week after school. She taught me to use my voice to show the emotions I was feeling and to fall without hurting myself. I had never worked so hard in my life at anything so terrifying . . . yet so much fun.

At last, it was the day before the show, time for the dress rehearsal. I was excited, even confident. I really felt and looked like Star when I had on my stage makeup and the old-fashioned, long, soft-flannel green dress. With the full skirt, thick petticoats, knit hat and muff, the transformation was complete.

Everything went smoothly at the dress rehearsal until the scene where I slip on the ice and Scrooge helps me up. When I kissed him on the cheek, a loud, ugly noise sounded from behind the set, like someone farting, followed by loud laughter.

I ran to the stairs, dashed down the aisle into the empty auditorium, collapsed into a seat and started to cry.

"I can't do it. Get someone else!"

Suddenly, I felt gentle hands on my arms. I heard voices and a soft, warm hand took mine. I looked up through my tears to see concerned faces. Four girls, my classmates, had come after me.

"Please, don't drop out," they said. "You're really, really good! Don't pay any attention to that scum, Peter. He's an idiot!" So, *he* was my tormentor . . . the boy that everyone said was a bully. No one even liked him very much.

"You've got to go on," the girls said. "Our play will be a flop without you!"

One of them handed me a tissue. I wiped my eyes and blew my nose. "Okay," I said, giving them a shy smile. I went back onstage and finished the scene with no further interruptions.

The following day, two performances were scheduled for the whole school plus an evening show for families and friends. During the first show, everything went perfectly, and people even applauded in the middle of the play after my monologue! I was flying, dancing, filled with the greatest joy you could imagine.

During the second show, in the first act, part of the scenery fell down. The audience laughed, but I didn't care. I knew they weren't laughing at me. Applause was tremendous at the end of that performance—but the crowning event was the evening show when the parents attended, and my mom got to see me perform.

In the weeks that followed, kids at school came up to say, "You were good," even "great" or "terrific." Although frustrations and failures have come my way since then, along with them, I have also had great joy and success. At times I've felt discouraged, and I still do. But it helps to remember that I was once a fallen star who managed to rise and sparkle, through my own efforts, with the loving guidance of a great teacher and the help of a few unexpected friends.

Patty Zeitlin

Panic

What life means to us is determined, not so much by what life brings to us as by the attitude we bring to life; not so much by what happens to us as by our reaction to what happens.

Lewis L Dunnington

One October day, in eighth-grade English class, I sat taking notes while my teacher explained prepositional phrases for what felt like the eightieth time. Suddenly, my forehead and fingertips became numb, as if a crazed dentist had injected them with Novocain. I tried to concentrate on the teacher's lecture, but his words sounded garbled, like he was speaking through a long cardboard tube. My heart raced, and I couldn't breathe. I was either going to throw up or pass out.

It seemed like I was having a dream. *Was I really sitting in English class?* I turned my head to look at my classmates. They were moving slowly, like a film being viewed frame by frame. I touched the smooth Formica desk and squeezed my pen. I wasn't dreaming. *What was wrong with me?*

My friend touched my arm. "Are you okay?" she asked. "You're completely pale."

I raised my hand; it felt detached from my body. "Can I go to the nurse?" I asked. The voice came from my throat, but I didn't recognize its sound. Our teacher had told the last guy who asked for a pass to the nurse to wait until the bell. Before that could happen, he had hurled into his desk.

"Sure, go ahead," the teacher told me.

I rushed out of the room. The hallway's spotted floor seemed to slant under my feet. I rested my forehead against the cool turquoise tiles of the wall. *What was happening?*

The nurse had me lay down on her fake leather couch, and she popped a thermometer in my mouth. I prayed that I had a fever and could go home. After a few minutes, the nurse read my temperature. "No fever. Better go back to class," she told me.

"No, I can't," I nearly shouted. "Please, send me home," I begged.

The nurse frowned at my urgent tone. She paused a moment, then telephoned my mother.

Once I was home, I felt fine. I cuddled under my down comforter, read one of my favorite horror novels and then watched a soap opera on TV. My mother served me strawberry Jell-O and sliced bananas for dinner. I was an only child, and my mom spoiled me. She gave me a hug. "You'll be up and around tomorrow," she assured me. At home, I was safe.

The next day, I convinced my parents that I was too weak to return to school, but I was really just afraid. "Okay, just one more day of rest," my mother told me, "but make sure you do the homework. You don't want to ruin your A average."

The following morning, my mother said, "Get up and get dressed, have a bit of breakfast and see how you feel." I knew this trick. She'd been using it on me since I was a kid. Once I had pulled on some clothes and had eaten, she'd say, "If you're healthy enough to be out of bed and keep cereal down, you're well enough to go to school." And, that's exactly what happened.

One afternoon a few days later, one of my classmates asked me to her house for dinner. Supper at her house was a foreign experience for me. She had a big family, and they all talked at the same time, fighting to be heard.

Suddenly, the hum of the kitchen lights became loud and drowned out their voices. Their faces looked too clear in the unnatural light. My cheeks began to go numb, and I felt like the floor was caving in under my feet. It was happening again. *Maybe one of the blood vessels in my brain is slowly leaking blood,* I thought. I had to get out. I had to find help. I mumbled, "Excuse me. I feel sick," and I bolted from the house.

I ran all the way home. I slammed the front door behind me and collapsed on the family-room sofa. "What in the world are you doing home so early?" my mother asked.

"I don't feel well, again," I told her. I felt tears well in my eyes. "What is wrong with me?"

My parents were concerned about me, but not as worried as I was about myself. They scheduled an appointment with my doctor. I explained the scary episodes to him. He ordered a test for diabetes. I had to swallow this super sweet, cola-flavored glucose drink, and I had blood taken from my arm. I went for stomach X rays, where I had to drink a chalky barium milkshake. Finally, he sent me for a full neurological exam.

When the test results were in, the doctor telephoned.

"I'm glad to say that you are perfectly healthy," the doctor told me. My parents thought that was great news, but I wasn't sure.

The next morning, I couldn't face going back to school and the frightening possibility of another episode. I lied and told my mother that my stomach hurt. "The doctor said you are healthy," she reminded me. "He didn't test me for the stomach flu," I insisted. That nonexistent stomach virus bought me two more days at home.

When the third morning arrived, I just couldn't drag myself to class. For two weeks, I refused to go. Each day, I cried, screamed and begged. At first, my parents tried to reason with me; then they threatened to punish me. My father yelled, and my mother dissolved into tears. Again, they turned to my doctor for help, and he suggested that I see a psychologist. *Oh, great, I am totally insane after all.*

I was queasy with nerves at my first appointment with the psychologist. He was an old guy, but he was funny. He told me about a time that he was giving a speech at the local high school. "My microphone wouldn't work, so the janitor hopped up on the stage to check out the equipment. After a bit of fiddling, the janitor shouted, 'There's a screw loose in the speaker!'" I giggled and the knot in my stomach disappeared.

He listened quietly as I told him about my problem. "Your racing heart, tingling hands and your need to escape sound like classic symptoms of a panic attack," he told me. "In a panic attack, your body reacts like someone just jumped out of the closet and scared you, but, really, no one is there. Many people suffer with panic disorder. With some work on your part, and courage, it is a condition that can be overcome."

I leaned back into the chair's overstuffed cushion. I felt so relieved to have a name for what was happening to me. I was having panic attacks, and I wasn't the only one in the world, either.

The next few times I met with my therapist, he taught me relaxation exercises. He told me to close my eyes and picture a calm place. "I'm lying on the beach on a sunny July Fourth day," I told him. "Just leave before the fireworks," he joked. Then I had to imagine that my muscles were so relaxed and heavy that they were sinking into the warm sand. I was supposed to breathe deeply and slowly. We talked about how to use these techniques until a panic attack ended.

When I mastered these exercises, the psychologist took me to a 4 P.M. field trip to my school. I sat at my desk in the empty classroom and practiced my relaxation. We walked around the school until I felt comfortable.

"Tomorrow, you'll have to try a full classroom," he said.

My stomach tightened. "What if the teacher won't let me leave the class if I have to? What if the nurse won't let me go home?" I asked.

"We can take care of those fears," he assured me. My therapist made special arrangements with my teachers. They agreed that I could leave the room without asking for a pass, and the nurse would let me call home, no questions asked.

I was shaking the first morning when I entered homeroom, but my friends gathered around me and told me how great it was to have me there. "I've missed you guys," I told them. I was glad to be back.

It wasn't easy, though. The panic attacks were still the scariest things I'd ever experienced. Sometimes, I could stay in the classroom and relax through them. Other times, I slipped out the door and sat in the hall until they passed.

The popular kids made a warped game of trying to gross me out so I would leave the class. They would make disgusting vomiting noises or stare at me with their eyelids turned inside out. I was so mad that I forced myself to stay in my seat. In a twisted way, their being mean actually helped me.

My real friends stood by me, though, and every day got a bit easier. Before my eighth-grade graduation, there was a school talent show. I played the piano in front of a full auditorium. When the judges handed me the first-place trophy, my parents and friends gave me a standing ovation. I felt so proud of myself, not because I'd won, but because I'd beaten the panic attacks. I couldn't wait for high school.

Marie-Therese Miller

Believing in My Strength

*What lies behind us and what lies ahead of us
are tiny matters compared to what lies within us.*

Oliver Wendell Holmes

I am different from a lot of other kids. I have cerebral
palsy, which happened to me before I was born. I was
born really early, and I had an injury to my brain; because
of this I am not able to use some of the muscles in my
body in a normal way. Kids like me who have CP may not
be able to walk, talk, eat or play the same way as most
other kids do.

One of my legs is shorter and smaller than my other leg.
I don't have very much control over that leg and foot; for
example, I can hardly bend my toes. When I try to move
that foot, I get a tingly kind of pins-and-needles sensation,
like it has fallen asleep. I have to wear a brace on my leg
to keep it from curling up, and that makes it hard for me
to balance. I bump into things a lot. You may think it is no
big deal to have a weak leg and to come in last in all of the
races you compete in . . . but it is. When you are growing
up, you don't want to be the one who always lags behind.

Because I walk differently and wear a brace, kids call me "retard" and other names. People even imitate the way I run. You honestly don't know how cruel kids can be unless you experience it. I try to rise above it, but sometimes I just have to cry my feelings out. Sometimes I come home with my eyes red from crying. It's not fun to be made fun of over something that I can't control.

CP is not an illness or a disease. It isn't contagious. It will never go away. I will never grow out of it; I will have CP for my whole life. Over the years, I have learned to rise above the people who don't understand my situation. I have learned to look for my strong points and not be pulled down by my weaker ones. One of my strong points is singing, and I try to focus on that. I try especially hard at whatever I do. I think that is something that keeps me going every day.

If you have some kind of disability, I encourage you to start today to do something that makes you happy. You can do whatever you believe you can. Talk to someone who may struggle with the same thing that you do, because it may help you a lot.

I hope my story inspires you to take a better look at life and to let you know there are kids just like you who have a hard time, too. Just don't let your hard times take the place of your dreams, and keep reaching for the stars.

Kelsey Peters, ten

[EDITORS' NOTE: *For information on cerebral palsy go to* www.cdc.gov/ncbddd.]

More Chicken Soup?

Many of the stories and poems you have read in this book were submitted by readers like you who had read earlier *Chicken Soup for the Soul* books. We publish at least five or six *Chicken Soup for the Soul* books every year. We invite you to contribute a story to one of these future volumes.

Stories may be up to twelve hundred words and must uplift or inspire. You may submit an original piece or something you clip out of the local newspaper, a magazine, a church bulletin or a company newsletter. It could also be your favorite quotation you've put on your refrigerator door or a personal experience that has touched you deeply.

To obtain a copy of our submission guidelines and a listing of upcoming *Chicken Soup* books, please write, fax or check one of our Web sites.

Chicken Soup for the Soul
P.O. Box 30880 • Santa Barbara, CA 93130
fax: 805-563-2945
To e-mail or visit our Web sites:
www.chickensoup.com
www.clubchickensoup.com

Just send a copy of your stories and other pieces to any of the above addresses.

We will be sure that both you and the author are credited for your submission.

Who Is Jack Canfield?

Jack Canfield is one of America's leading experts in the development of human potential and personal effectiveness. He is both a dynamic, entertaining speaker and a highly sought-after trainer.

He is the author and narrator of several bestselling audio and videocassette programs, including *Self-Esteem and Peak Performance*, *How to Build High Self-Esteem*, *Self-Esteem in the Classroom* and *Chicken Soup for the Soul—Live*. He is regularly seen on television shows such as *Good Morning America*, *20/20* and *NBC Nightly News*. Jack has co-authored numerous books, including the *Chicken Soup for the Soul* series, *Dare to Win* and *The Aladdin Factor* (all with Mark Victor Hansen), *100 Ways to Build Self-Concept in the Classroom* (with Harold C. Wells) and *Heart at Work* (with Jacqueline Miller).

Jack is a regularly featured speaker for professional associations, school districts, government agencies, churches, hospitals, sales organizations and corporations. His clients have included the American Dental Association, the American Management Association, AT&T, Campbell's Soup, Clairol, Domino's Pizza, GE, ITT, Hartford Insurance, Johnson & Johnson, the Million Dollar Roundtable, NCR, New England Telephone, Re/Max, Scott Paper, TRW and Virgin Records. Jack is also on the faculty of Income Builders International, a school for entrepreneurs.

Jack conducts an annual eight-day Training of Trainers program in the areas of self-esteem and peak performance. The program attracts educators, counselors, parenting trainers, corporate trainers, professional speakers, ministers and others interested in developing their speaking and seminar-leading skills.

For further information about Jack's books, tapes and training programs, or to schedule him for a presentation, please contact:

The Canfield Training Group
P.O. Box 30880 • Santa Barbara, CA 93130
Phone: 805-563-2935 • Fax: 805-563-2945
To e-mail or visit our Web site: *www.chickensoup.com*

Who Is Mark Victor Hansen?

Mark Victor Hansen is a professional speaker who, in the last twenty years, has made more than four thousand presentations to more than two million people in thirty-two countries. His presentations cover sales excellence and strategies; personal empowerment and development regardless of stages of life; and how to triple your income and double your time off.

Mark has spent a lifetime dedicated to his mission of making a profound and positive difference in people's lives. Throughout his career, he has inspired hundreds of thousands of people to create a more powerful and purposeful future for themselves while stimulating the sale of billions of dollars worth of goods and services.

Mark is a prolific writer and has authored *Future Diary*, *How to Achieve Total Prosperity* and *The Miracle of Tithing*. He is coauthor of the *Chicken Soup for the Soul* series, *Dare to Win* and *The Aladdin Factor* (all with Jack Canfield), *The Master Motivator* (with Joe Batten) and *Out of the Blue* (with Barbara Nichols).

Mark has also produced a complete library of personal empowerment audio and videocassette programs that have enabled his listeners to recognize and use their innate abilities in their business and personal lives. His message has made him a popular television and radio personality, with appearances on ABC, NBC, CBS, HBO, PBS and CNN. He has also appeared on the cover of numerous magazines, including *Success, Entrepreneur* and *Changes*. In 2000, Mark was a recipient of the prestigious Horatio Algier Award for his humanitarianism.

Mark is a big man with a heart and spirit to match—an inspiration to people of all ages who seek to better themselves.

For further information about Mark write:

MVH & Associates
P.O. Box 7665
Newport Beach, CA 92658
Phone: 949-759-9304 or 800-433-2314
Fax: 949-722-6912
Web site: *www.chickensoup.com*

Who Is Patty Hansen?

Patty Hansen is coauthor of *Chicken Soup for the Kid's Soul*, and contributor of some of the most loved stories in the *Chicken Soup for the Soul* series. She is also the coauthor of *Condensed Chicken Soup for the Soul* and *Out of the Blue: Delight Comes into Our Lives*.

A third-generation native of California, Patty was raised in Pleasant Hill where her mother, Shirley, still lives. Her sister, Jackie, lives in Oregon.

Prior to her career as an author, Patty worked for United Airlines as a flight attendant for thirteen years. During that time, she received two commendations for bravery. She received the first one when, as the only fight attendant on board, she prepared forty-four passengers for a successful planned emergency landing. The second was for single-handedly extinguishing a fire on board a mid-Pacific flight, thus averting an emergency situation and saving hundreds of lives.

Patty has been her husband Mark's business partner during their twenty-one years of marriage. Currently, as president of Legal and Licensing for *Chicken Soup for the Soul* Enterprises, Inc., she has helped to create an entire line of *Chicken Soup for the Soul* products.

In 1998, Mom's House, Inc., a nonprofit organization that provides free childcare for school-age mothers, chose Patty as Celebrity Mother of the Year. In the spring of 2000, the first annual "Patty Hansen Scholarship" was awarded by Mom's House.

Patty shares her home life with her husband, Mark; their daughters, Elisabeth, fifteen, and Melanie, thirteen; housekeeper and friend, Eva; and three rabbits, one peahen, three horses, four dogs, five cats, five birds, three hamsters, twenty-five fish, twenty-seven chickens, a haven for hummingbirds, and a butterfly farm.

If you would like to contact Patty:

Patty Hansen
LifeWriters
P.O. Box 10879
Costa Mesa, CA 92627
Phone: 949-645-5240 • Fax: 949-645-3203
e-mail: *Patty@PreteenPlanet.com*
www.chickensoup.com or
www.PreteenPlanet.com

Who Is Irene Dunlap?

Irene Dunlap, coauthor of *Chicken Soup for the Kid's Soul*, began her writing career in elementary school when she discovered her love for creating poetry, a passion she believes she inherited from her paternal grandmother. She expressed her love for words through writing fictional short stories, lyrics, as a participant in speech competitions and eventually as a vocalist.

During her college years, Irene traveled around the world as a student of the Semester at Sea program aboard a ship that served as a classroom, as well as home base, for more than five hundred college students. After earning a bachelor of arts degree in communications, she became the media director of Irvine Meadows Amphitheatre in Irvine, California. She went on to co-own an advertising and public relations agency that specialized in entertainment and health-care clients.

While working on *Chicken Soup* books, which she absolutely loves, Irene stays involved with her children's music, theater and sports activities, carries on a successful jazz singing career and continues to be an active member of her church's music team.

Irene lives in Newport Beach, California, with her husband Kent, daughter Marleigh, son Weston and Australian shepherd, Gracie. In her spare time, Irene enjoys horseback riding, painting, gardening and cooking. If you are wondering how she does it all, she will refer you to her favorite bible passage for her answer: Ephesians 3:20.

If you would like to contact Irene, write to her at:

Irene Dunlap
LifeWriters
P.O. Box 10879
Costa Mesa, CA 92627
Phone: 949-645-5240
Fax: 949-645-3203
e-mail: *Irene@PreteenPlanet.com*
www.chickensoup.com or
www.PreteenPlanet.com

Contributors

Several of the stories in this book were taken from previously published sources, such as books, magazines and newspapers. These sources are acknowledged in the permissions section. However, some of the stories were written by humorists, comedians, professional speakers and workshop presenters as well as kids. If you would like to contact them for information on their books, audiotapes and videotapes, seminars and workshops, you can reach them at the addresses and phone numbers provided below.

The remainder of the stories were submitted by readers of our previous *Chicken Soup for the Soul* books who responded to our requests for stories. We have also included information about them.

Kim Aaron is a braille specialist working with blind and partially sighted children. She has been married for seventeen years to a television news reporter and has one son, Adam, who is an honors student. She volunteers in her community, and in her spare time, rides an eleven-year-old mule named Bob. You can reach Kim at #3 Maple Tree Ln., Cross Lanes, WV 25313; 304-776-0403; *Jaaron2255@aol.com.*

Denise and Rett Ackart live in California. Denise is currently working on a series of children's books and enjoys spending time with her husband and two sons, Rett and Rhys. Rett is an active twelve-year-old who enjoys soccer, basketball, snowboarding and drumming for the junior high school jazz band. They can be reached via e-mail at *mongo@tco.net.*

Katherine Ackerman is a thirteen-year-old from Florida. She enjoys traveling, writing, painting, drawing and sculpture. Katherine is also involved in many different sports including canoeing and backpacking and is on her school swim team.

Andrea Adair is a mom to three girls, a children's librarian assistant and a freelance writer. She has been published in *Horizons, The Toastmaster* and *Signatures* and is currently writing a mystery.

Catherine Adams received a bachelor of science in medical technology from Texas Christian University and works as a clinical laboratory scientist. She's recently been published in multiple genres and enjoys reading, writing and spending time with her family. Send e-mails to *rachbo03@yahoo.com.*

Max Alexander is now fourteen. Even though they passed away four years ago, at times it is still hard for Max to deal with the death of his grandparents; but he enjoys remembering the good times.

Scott Allen was twelve when he wrote "The Big Slip." He is currently attending classes at the University of Michigan working toward an engineering degree. He enjoys golfing, running, playing piano and spending time with friends. Please e-mail him at *allensc@umich.edu.*

Laura Andrade has over ten years experience as a teacher and administrator. With a doctorate in educational leadership and B.S. in biology, it's clear that she is passionate about education. Laura shares her California home with her husband, two cats, two dogs and two horses. Contact her at *mandrade29@cox.net.*

Christine Armstrong is an attorney who lives with her husband Roger and their son Randy in a farmhouse in the Minnesota woods. In addition to writing, her hobbies include reading, making handmade books, jewelry and quilts. Christine has continued to open her heart to a variety of animals over the years including ducks, hamsters, parakeets, dogs, cats, a chinchilla and even a goat. Reach her via e-mail at *Chris99337@aol.com.*

Brandi Bacon is a sixteen-year-old sophomore in Kentucky. She is a cheerleader and has recently returned from Germany where she was a foreign exchange student. Brandi has been writing since she was in the second grade and hopes that her story will help other kids who are facing difficult situations.

Raegan Baker is a freshman in college majoring in communications. She enjoys reading, writing and spending time with friends and family. Raegan loves children and would like to one day work with children and teenagers who suffer from OCD. You can reach her via e-mail at *RWB7and18@aol.com.*

Whitney M. Baldwin is a thirteen-year-old from New York. She is a dance competitor and loves to read and write poetry. Whitney would like to thank Mr. Sherry for being the first to inspire her to write.

Miriam Bard is a first-year student at Sarah Lawrence College where she majors in English literature. She volunteers teaching English as a second language at a local public school and enjoys traveling, art history, creative writing and camping. She plans to be a travel journalist. E-mail her at *mbard@slc.edu.*

Shirley Barone Craddock is the published author of two children's books and several magazine stories. She is an artist and has received the People's Choice Award from the North Valley Art League. Shirley loves to write in such a way that will stimulate a child's mind and entertain them to silliness and surprise. She can be reached at 1703 Victor Ave., Redding, CA 96003; 530-223-2584; *tigerknot@thegrid.net.*

Lisa Beach is an instructor at Indiana University East in Richmond, Indiana. She is the author of a children's book, *Building a Bridge*, and a short story, *Taking Baby Home*. Hard at work on a novel, Lisa lives with her husband David and their children Jon, Traci, Richard, Alaina and Blair. You can reach her at *Beachwriter@aol.com*.

Leslie Beck is a high school sophomore in Missouri. She enjoys playing the flute and running track. As a freshman, she was Rookie of the Year on her softball team. Leslie aspires to be a veterinarian and own her own practice. She dedicates her story to her grandmother who was not here to see Leslie's mother win her fight against cancer.

Katie Beauchamp is an eighth-grader who serves as a Beta Club officer, chief editor of her school's literary magazine, is captain of the Affirmative Team in Debate Club; and is in her fifth year of studying the viola. She has won awards with the Young Authors Competition and Future Problem Solving program at state and national levels.

Donna Beveridge is a primary literacy specialist. She loves early mornings, sing-alongs, children's books, new journals, her grandchildren and family stories. Her first children's book, *Henry*, was published in 1999 for the educational market. She has also published books for teachers. Donna can be reached at P.O. Box 1635, Windham, ME 04062, or via e-mail at *DLBeveridg@aol.com*.

Jesse Billauer was born in Pacific Palisades, California. At the age of nine, he found his true passion in life—surfing. He began traveling the world surfing in competitions when he was twelve years old and was named one of the top 100 up-and-coming surfers in the world by *Surfer Magazine*. After suffering a spinal cord injury from surfing, Jesse was left quadriplegic, but continues to surf and travel, and has become a motivational speaker. He has helped raise money and awareness to find a cure for paralysis through his nonprofit foundation, Life Rolls On. Jesse continues to inspire people with his message to "live life to the fullest and never give up on your hopes and dreams."

Heather Bradley lives with her mother and two sisters in Southern California where she is currently in seventh grade. Heather enjoys writing, reading, horseback riding, camping and just hanging out with her friends.

Kyle Brown, a high school senior from California, lives with his parents and younger brother, Jack. He enjoys theater and is involved with drama at his school. An avid sports fan, Kyle likes to watch and go to professional sporting events. Writing is a hobby, as well as computer graphics, video games and cars.

Judith Burnett Schneider, a former research organic chemist, is the mother of three. She is the author of *Write Well & Sell: Changing Life's Simple Stories into Sales* and is a contributing author for the book *Plastics Recycling*. Judith is also host of Critique Retreat for Writing Women. She teaches workshops at bookstores,

CONTRIBUTORS

her local community college and through her Internet writing classes. Judith welcomes feedback via e-mail at *jbswrites@sgi.net*, or mail P.O. Box 207, Ingomar, PA 15127.

Emily Burton, age twelve, loves art and creative writing. She enjoys all sports, especially basketball and soccer. Emily wants to give a big "HEY, I'M IN A BOOK" to her friends Leah, Kate, Clair, Bevan, Sierra, Chelsea, Miranda, Frani, Jeff, Luke, Mike and Meaghan, who is her best friend, and to her mom.

Nicole Buckner is twelve years old and attends middle school. She enjoys reading, writing stories, poetry and horseback riding. Her story "Dapples" tells about the loss of her beloved horse. This tragic event, and her love for horses, has inspired her to become a veterinarian one day.

Chiara Cabiglio has always had a passion for writing. At thirteen, she has already written over forty songs and hopes to become a famous singer and songwriter. She loves to snowboard, sing, shop, play basketball, and travel (especially to Italy since she's of Italian descent).

Stephanie Caffall, age thirteen, was inspired to write "Friends at First Sight" because of her friendship with Jesse, whom she still considers a true friend. She'd like to thank Jesse for being able to count on him. Thanks, Jesse! Love, Steffie. By the way, Jesse, now fourteen, would still rather escort a spider outside than kill it. He is currently working on his Eagle rank in Boy Scouts.

Courtni Calhoun, a thirteen-year-old eighth grader from Texas, is a GATE student who plays alto sax, holds first chair in her school band, won second chair in an all-region competition and has been a majorette for the past two years. Winning fifth place in a state writing competition and being published is proof of the impact that her teacher, Mrs. Barrow, has had on her life. Courtni is a dedicated Christian and is active in her church.

Doris Canner has three grown sons and four grandsons. She resides with her husband in New Hampshire on Lake Winnipesaukee. When she's not surfing the Internet, Doris enjoys reading and listening to music. Her love for children and for the written word has been the motivating force behind her passion for writing children's stories. Currently, she's working on a biography for young readers. Doris can be reached at 9 Campfire Cir., Alton, NH 03809.

Danny Cannizzaro, age sixteen, created the cover artwork for *Chicken Soup for the Preteen Soul.* In addition to regular high school, he attends the Orange County High School of the Arts where he takes classes in drawing, painting and graphic design, all fields in which he hopes to someday have a career. When not in school, he spends time hanging out with friends, playing with his brother, Joey, and his sister, Diana.

Mel Caro received her bachelor of science in finance from New York University and works in New York as an equity trader. She began writing as a hobby and is now in the process of working on several short stories on a variety of topics. Mel is a certified personal trainer and enjoys running, yoga and painting.

Diana Carson is a sixteen-year-old from Pennsylvania who loves to write and with a few poems already published and her story in *Preteen Soul*, it shows. Diane enjoys playing volleyball and would like to major in journalism and minor in theater in college.

Tiffany Clifton graduated from the Academy of Career Sciences in 2003. She works as a secretary at a manufacturing company and hopes to pursue a career in writing. She enjoys reading, writing and spending time with her family and fiancé, Timmy Oliver. Contact her at *peachy_172002@yahoo.com*.

Mel Ann Coley received her bachelor of science in education from the University of North Texas in 1976. A loving mother to two preteens, she taught developmental writing at Richland College and was teaching writing courses for elementary school students at the time of her passing on November 29, 2003. She will be missed.

David R. Collins combined two careers, teaching English in Moline, Illinois, for thirty-five years and writing books for young readers. Many of his articles and stories sprang from his classroom experiences, as did "A Silent Voice." Named "Outstanding Illinois Educator," Collins has won recognition from the American Legion, the Veterans of Foreign Wars, the PTA and the Junior Literary Guild. A prolific biographical writer, he now writes full-time and makes author visits to schools. He can be reached at 3404 45th St., Moline, IL 61265, by e-mail at *kimsuess@aol.com*, or by calling 309-762-8985.

Tamera Collins is a busy mother of two, ages six and seven. This is her second published piece; the first, a children's story, *Emily's Coat*, was featured in the literary review, *O' Georgia*. Tamara is a former mathematics teacher who enjoys golfing with her husband, tennis, reading and her cat, Cleo. She can be reached at 14290 Morning Mountain Way, Alpharetta, GA 30004.

Elisabeth Copeland is a freshman in high school in Tennessee. She hopes to move back to Alabama where she was born. She likes acting and making people laugh. Elisabeth wrote her story about her experience when her parents got divorced.

Krissy Creager is a sophomore from Arizona, where she lives with her parents. She likes playing basketball, soccer, running track, writing stories and poetry and doing normal teen stuff like hanging out with friends. She enjoys listening to and giving advice to friends. Krissy hopes to either become a physical therapist or a counselor, in order to make a difference and help others.

Holly Cupala paints, writes and lives with her husband and new baby in Seattle, Washington. She loves traveling to exotic places and imagining the stories of the people she meets. Her advice to budding writers is to write down your ideas and read everything! See her Web site at *www.hollycupala.com.*

MaryJanice Davidson has written several critically acclaimed novels, but this is the first time that she has been able to write about the fire. She lives in Minnesota with her husband and children, about twenty miles from the site of the fire. "The Best Christmas I Never Had" is her first published short story. For information on her books, visit Mary's Web site at *www.usinternet.com/users/alongi.*

Justin Day is a sixteen-year-old from Oklahoma who lives his life playing soccer and is interested in playing for a pro club. He enjoys going on dates and playing video games. He also enjoys writing poems and short stories in his spare time. Justin wrote his true story "April Morning" because he wanted to write something that came from the heart.

Jenn Dlugos is a comedy writer and stand-up comedian in the New England area. She has a book coming out in 2004 entitled *Public Health Disturbance.*

DeAnna Doherty has a bachelor of science in psychology. She is a stay-at-home mom with a two-year-old daughter, Ayden and a six-month-old son, Conner. She enjoys writing children's stories and reading.

Jason Dorsey is the founder of the not-for-profit Institute to End School Violence and president of Golden Ladder Productions, LLC. Jason authored *Graduate to Your Perfect Job* which is now used as a course in over one thousand schools. Utilizing the input of over 100,000 students, Jason authored *Can Students End School Violence? Solutions from America's Youth* to provide a student's perspective to preventing violence. Annually, Jason speaks to over 100,000 educators, students, parents, and administrators across America. He may be reached at 512-259-6877 or at *www.jasondorsey.com* or *www.endschoolviolence.com.* Jason's life mission is to help youth shape their world.

Noah Edelson is a director/writer/producer for television and film. His credits include producer/writer for Nickelodeon and NBC, among others. His short film, *78,* premiered at the 1997 Sundance Film Festival. An award-winning poet for his children's verse, Noah is also founder of Mighty Oak Press, committed to publishing "books for kids to grow on." He lives in Sherman Oaks, California, with his wife Valerie, his daughter Hannah and his cat, Mister. Contact Noah at *MightyOakPress@aol.com.*

Jillian Eide is a sixteen-year-old junior living in California with her parents, big brother, Jeff, and little sister, Jolene. She is a varsity cheerleader and spends a lot of time with her family and friends. Her poem is dedicated to the loving memory of her cousin Cassie Loraine Sweet, who was killed in a car accident in 1996.

Allison Ellis is a youth media specialist and editor and writer for teen fashion Web site, *www.BPnordstrom.com.* Prior to that she was the vice president of *www.FoxKids.com/FoxFamilychannel.com*. Allison is the founder of *FreeZone*, a collection of youth-driven publications. In her free time, she writes middle grade fiction. E-mail her at *allison.ellis@comcast.net*.

Arlys Endres, thirteen, enjoys synchronized swimming, softball, old music, old movies and hanging with her friends. She also plays violin, clarinet and the piano. Arlys loves animals and has four cats, two dogs and a hamster. She is also a member of the United Neighbors Association, a community watch program that includes painting over graffiti and taking down Christmas lights for the elderly.

Alex Estey is fourteen years old and lives in New Brunswick, Canada, with her family. She hopes to be a professional author someday. Her hobbies include basketball, drama, writing and spending time with friends and family.

Melinda Fausey received her bachelor of arts in 1995 and currently is a stay-at-home mom of three children. She enjoys writing and has made recent sales. Melinda is a Florida native and enjoys traveling, jet-skiing, surfing, swimming and spinning. She is currently working on several children's books.

David Ferino is a thirteen-year-old living in Illinois. His favorite pastimes include playing the guitar, skateboarding, golf, soccer, basketball, theater and art. He is involved in speech tournaments, where he has received several first-place medals. David has also had his artwork hung in a college art museum but feels that his greatest accomplishment is being published in this book.

Barry Fireman has been married for thirty-five years and has three adult children. His hobbies are woodworking, golf and reading. When he retires, he plans to devote time to writing. He loves telling stories and was encouraged by friends and his children to write Redsy. Barry recently saw Redsy again at their forty-year high school reunion. You may reach Barry at 434 Warick Road, Wynnewood, PA 19096; 610-649-2210; or via e-mail at *bfireman@worldnet.att.net*.

Jaime Fisher is fourteen years old and lives in Texas. She enjoys being with friends, talking on the phone and going to the movies. She plans to go to college at LSU and become a pediatrician.

Christine Fishlinger is seventeen and lives in New York with her parents and brother. She enjoys reading, writing, soccer, track, working on school plays and hanging out with friends. She looks forward to being a senior, and to going away to college.

Kelli Frusher is seventeen and from California. When not at home singing, dancing or reading you can find her hot-air ballooning, white-water river rafting, dirt biking, snorkeling or horseback riding. She has written mininovels about her experiences, as well as poems. Kelli would love to make it on Broadway or the radio.

Eugene Gagliano is the father of four children, a published author and teacher who shares his love of reading and writing with his second-grade class at Meadowlark School in Buffalo, Wyoming. He lives with his wife, Carol, at the base of the majestic Big Horn Mountains. His fiction book, *Falling Stars*, will be released this year. You can reach him at 20 Hillside Dr., Buffalo, WY 82834.

Kerry Germain writes and publishes children's picture books on the island of Oahu, Hawaii. She enjoys island activities with her son and his friends, telling stories of when she was a kid, surfing, shell hunting, sailing and diving with sharks. Check out her Web site at *www.surfsupforkimo.com*.

Barbara L. Glenn is a writer, horseback riding teacher and 4-H Horse Project leader. She began her freelance writing in 1989 and has published articles in magazines such as *Horse Illustrated, Horse Power, Stable Kids* and *Children's Playground*. She owns three horses, a Great Dane and two cats. Barbara enjoys art, traveling, photography, music and the company of her two girls, Ginny and Amy.

Uncle Greg is Greg Hall, a father, uncle and businessman living in Los Gatos, California. He is the author of numerous stories for kids of all ages. You can visit his Web site at *www.unclegreg.com*, or call 408-366-9812.

Mia Hamm is widely recognized as the world's best all-around soccer player. In the 1996 Centennial Olympic Games, she proved it by leading her team to Team Gold in front of eighty thousand screaming fans in Athens, Georgia. Never in history had so many spectators come out to watch a women's sporting event. Then in 1999, Mia's team won the Women's World Cup while more than 40 million viewers watched in the United States alone. Mia was the youngest player ever to play for the US National Team at age fifteen and has been U.S. Soccer's Female Athlete of the Year for five consecutive years. Her awards and accomplishments tell only part of the story of this remarkable athlete. Through the Mia Hamm Foundation, she supports two causes: promoting women's athletics and raising funds for research and awareness of bone marrow diseases. Each year, Mia hosts the "Garrett Game" in honor of her brother, whom she lost to complications from aplastic anemia, a form of bone marrow disease.

Elisabeth Haney is a twelve-year-old who has never been published, until now! She enjoys reading, playing basketball and playing outdoors. She has an eight-year-old little brother who drives her crazy. Her mom home schools Elisabeth and her brother, and her dad is a pastor at a bilingual church.

Laurie Hartman is the director of licensing of *Chicken Soup for the Soul* Enterprises, Inc. She loves writing, reading, horseback riding and her job with the "best people to work for on the planet." Laurie is also the mother of one incredible son, Connor, who shares her love of writing at the tender age of ten, hoping to be a contributing author to *Chicken Soup* one day himself. You can reach Laurie via e-mail at *laurieh@chickensoup.com*.

Hannah A. Heninger is a freshman in high school and an honor student. She takes voice lessons and partakes in the drama department at her school. She plans to go into medicine and hopes to inspire young people all over the world.

Brittany Nicole Henry is a fifteen-year-old who enjoys skateboarding, writing, drawing and hanging out with friends.

Lauren Elizabeth Holden, age thirteen, lives in Georgia with her parents, kitten and dog. She enjoys reading, writing, tennis, boating and hanging out with her best friends, Leslie, Lauren and Salley. A very special teacher, Joi Cox, helped Lauren develop her love for writing. Lauren continues to write and has submitted numerous entries for her school's writing fairs.

Christa Holder Ocker is a freelance writer with a special interest in rhyming picture-book stories. "This Old Chair" makes her a three-time contributor to the *Chicken Soup* books. Her story "Merry Christmas, My Friend" *(Kid's Soul)* appeared on the *Chicken Soup for the Soul* television series. Contact Christa at 55 Royal Park Terr., Hillsdale, NJ 07642.

James Howe is an award-winning author of more than sixty books for children, including the popular *Bunnicula* series. His other books for middle-grade readers include the Sebastian Barth mystery series, *A Night Without Stars, Morgan's Zoo* and the highly acclaimed *The Watcher.* In addition to fiction, James has written many picture and chapter books. He lives in a small town north of New York City with his daughter Zoey, and a cat named Freckle.

Marieta Irwin is wife to Steve and mother to three daughters. She is the oldest daughter of a Christian minister and has always had lots of creative energy. She is the director of the Ecumenical Youth Program at her church and works at the Sac Community Elementary School. Her writing comes out of personal experience as a kid and now as a mom. You can reach Marieta at 630 S. 10th St., Sac City, IA 50583; 712-662-4084; *irwins@pionet.net.*

Tiffany Jacques is a high school sophomore in Montana. She is very close to her family. The things she loves most are children, the color yellow, butterflies, and having fun with her friends and boyfriend. Tiffany plans to go to college and would like to be a physical therapist, get married and have lots of beautiful children.

Megan Jennings is a high school student from Kentucky. She enjoys writing poems and true life stories. Megan is a straight-A student, the secretary of her local FFA chapter and an employee of an auto parts store. Megan loves animals and owns four dogs, two horses and two donkeys. She loves the outdoors, horseback riding and hiking.

Janalea Jeppson was born and raised in Salt Lake City, Utah, and is a graduate of the University of Utah. She currently works as a customer service specialist for a major wireless carrier. Janalea enjoys spending time with her large extended family, working with children and serving in her church. Janalea writes short stories and poetry and especially enjoys writing for children. E-mail her at *giggles2263@juno.com.*

Lance Johnson is currently a sophomore in high school. His hometown of Mammoth Lakes provides a wonderful environment for skiing and mountain biking. He enjoys writing and hopes to be a professional author when he grows up to be an old wise man.

Alex Judge is an eleven-year-old who lives in Ontario, Canada. He likes reading, riding his bike and playing computer games with his friends. He has a green belt in Tae Kwon Do and enjoys swimming.

Lou Kassem was born in the mountains of East Tennessee and inherited a talent for storytelling. In 1984, she put her talent on paper, publishing the first of eleven novels. Being an author is a career that she loves. Her hobbies are reading, traveling, golfing and mountain hiking with her husband. You can reach her at 715 Burruss Dr. NW, Blacksburg, VA 24060, by phone at 540-552-2241, or e-mail her at *Lmk1931@aol.com.*

Michael Kavalinas, sixteen, swims, does karate, works part time and loves science. He is a lifeguard and has done volunteer hospice work. Michael still misses his dad and thinks about him all the time.

Ryan Kelly, age eleven, lives in New York with his parents, sister and maternal grandparents. When not in school, where he is on the wrestling team, he likes to play Playstation and swim, and he is a huge Pokémon fan. Ryan would like to thank his parents and Miss Finnegan for the inspiration they gave him in writing his story.

Kathy Kemmer Pyron is a devoted wife and mother of four children, three dogs and two cats. When time allows, she writes children's stories for picture books and magazines. Kathy has been published in *Highlights for Children* and *The Flicker Magazine.*

Sarah Kessler, thirteen, enjoys attending high school in Wisconsin. She loves basketball, acting, writing and reading. She thanks all of her family, friends and teachers who have encouraged and believed in her and feels blessed to have such incredible people in her life.

Mridu Khullar is a freelance writer from New Delhi, India. She is the editor-in-chief of *www.WritersCrossing.com* and has been published in hundreds of national and international magazines including *New Woman* and *Business World.* She is currently completing her studies in information technology from Delhi University.

Erin K. Kilby received her bachelor of science in education and English from Bowling Green State University in 1994. She teaches English at a high school in Texas and enjoys writing freelance, crochet and spending

time with her husband, Michael, and son, Tyler. Please contact her at
erinkilby@hotmail.com.

Ashley King is an eleven-year-old who plays on her school's soccer team and
participates in band, choir and drama. She likes to express her feelings
through writing. She would like to thank her friends and family, and especially, her mom. A special, heartfelt thanks goes to her sixth-grade teacher, Ms.
Oderman, who encouraged her to write to her fullest extent. But most of all,
she wants to thank God for putting the words in her heart.

Cheryl Kremer is married to Jack and is the mother of Nikki, twelve, and
Cobi, nine. She is a "soccer mom" who cares for infants and toddlers in her
home and church nursery. When she isn't watching her kids play soccer,
she can be found crocheting, cross-stitching and writing inspirational
stories of her everyday life as a wife and mother. She lives in Lancaster,
Pennsylvania, and can be reached at *j_kremer@msn.com.*

Amber Kury, age twelve, is a poet who leads a physically active life and
likes to help others. She handles difficult situations with a positive
demeanor and fun attitude. To her sister, brother and father, she exempli-
fies hope, love and caring. Amber plans to attend a university and graduate in a field where she can use her knowledge to help others deal with life.

Barbara Lage is a library media specialist for an elementary school in Omaha,
Nebraska. She has been a media specialist for a middle school in Iowa and
worked as a librarian for a Japanese college in Honolulu, Hawaii. She likes kids
and books. She has three children, Jo Anne, Mark and Amy, with her husband,
Pete. She can be contacted at 759 N. 130th Plaza, Omaha, NE 68154.

Dakota Lane has had her work published in a variety of publications, including *Interview Magazine, Village Voice* and *L.A. Weekly.* She is the author of the
young adult novel, *Johnny Voodoo,* for which she won the 2000 American
Library Association Popular Paperback of the year award. She has two daughters and lives by a river in Woodstock, New York. You can contact Dakota at
Dakota@netstep.net.

Veneta Leonard lives in Crown Point, Indiana, and enjoys raising her family. She's an avid reader and plans to go back to college next year to get
her teaching degree. Veneta also enjoys playing bunco, Skip-Bo, bowling
and going to the show. She lives a happy and blessed life and wishes
everyone lots of happiness and peace. God bless.

Lennox "The Lion" Lewis is a man who has made history. Capping an
impressive amateur boxing career, Lewis earned a gold medal by knocking out future heavyweight champion Riddick Bowe as a member of Team
Canada during the 1988 Olympics in Seoul, Korea. In 1993, only a few
years after turning professional, Lewis was officially crowned WBC
Heavyweight Champion of the World and went on to defend the title

three times. His scientific approach to boxing along with a stiff jab and blistering overhand has secured his place as the preeminent boxer of his generation. Refusing to rest on his laurels, Lewis has consistently and vigorously defended all of his titles and in his quest to succeed at whatever he puts his hands to, "The Emperor of Boxing" continually grows from strength to strength.

Karen Lombard holds a Ph.D. in economics from the University of Chicago and has a broad range of consulting, research and teaching experience in the areas of antitrust, industrial organization, labor economics and applied microeconomics. Her current passion is writing for children and entertaining her two-year-old son, Geordie.

J. Styron Madsen writes to make kids laugh, think, feel, and most importantly, to realize that they can make choices. She writes in front of her antique Macintosh surrounded by seven dogs, all adopted from local animal shelters. You can e-mail her at *mad03@execpc.com*.

Colleen Mahoney got a scholarship from Take Stock in Children in the sixth grade. She is currently in the seventh grade and her hobbies include singing, acting and anything that involves performing. She would like to major in fine arts.

Lauren Maffeo, a fifteen-year-old, has been acting since the age of eleven and has appeared in numerous local films and theater productions. Her biggest role to date has been a voice-over in the independent feature *Little Erin Merryweather,* which was screened at the Hollywood Independent Film Festival. As a writer, she has been published in *Teen Vogue, Teen Ink* and *Spire* magazines. Lauren enjoys skiing, traveling, shopping, listening to music, and spending time with her friends and family. Being published in her favorite book series is a dream come true, and her poem is dedicated to her dad.

Amy Mallinder-Morgan, fourteen, was born in England and now resides in Windermere, Florida. She enjoys music, horses and her PC. Her volunteer activities inspired her writing and she was selected in the top ten for Disney Dreamers and Doers at her school for her piece on Give Kids the World.

Karl Malone is a ten-time NBA All-Star player and the 1997 Most Valuable Player in the league. He was also the co-MVP in the 1993 All-Star game with teammate John Stockton. Voted one of the fifty greatest players of all time, he has truly earned his famous nickname, "The Mailman," for Karl Malone never fails to deliver. He was a member of the original "Dream Team" that won the Gold Medal in the 1992 Barcelona Summer Olympic Games. Malone lives in Utah with his wife and six children. He enjoys hunting, fishing, camping and riding his Harley in his spare time. A giving man, Malone supports the Special Olympics and many charitable causes through the Karl Malone Foundation.

Caleb Mathewson enjoys playing basketball and baseball. He is an avid fan of the St. Louis Cardinals and has an extensive collection of baseball memorabilia. Caleb appreciates playing catch and hoops with his dad, his brother, Jordan, and his sister, Allyse.

KeriAnne McCaffrey is a sophomore in New York. She is a goalkeeper for the varsity soccer team and a member of Leader's Club. Keri enjoys music, movies and sharing laughs with her friends and family. Her writing began receiving attention after winning an essay contest in 1996.

Karli McKinnon is a sixth-grade student living in Ontario, Canada. She loves creative writing and wants to be a journalist when she grows up. She has been swimming competitively for eight years and playing piano since she was five. She likes reading, writing, skating and spending time with her friends and family.

Lori Menning is a preschool teacher, mother of twin boys and author of *One Was Not Enough,* a children's picture book published by *TWINS Magazine.* She lives with her family in Memphis, Tennessee.

Carol Miller is a freelance writer who lives in New Jersey with her husband, Jack; daughters, Stephanie and Lauren; and beagle, Tapper. Her work has appeared in *Chicken Soup for the Mother & Daughter Soul, FamilyFun, The Christian Science Monitor* and many other publications. Contact her at *miller_carol@usa.net.*

Marie-Therese Miller earned her M.A. in writing from Manhattanville College. She pens a humorous family life column for the *Taconic Press* newspaper and writes about family issues for the *Poughkeepsie Journal* and *Hudson Valley Parent.* She, her husband, John, and their five children live in Salt Point, New York. E-mail her at *thisisthelife@hvc.rr.com.*

Sydney Jane Miller is a sophomore from Southern California. She loves photo booths, sushi and receiving mail.

Beverley Mitchell was discovered by a talent agent when she was only four years old while throwing a tantrum at a mall. She booked her first job acting in a commercial for AT&T and the rest is history. Aside from working on the hit television show, *7th Heaven,* Beverley enjoys hanging out with her friends, shopping, going to the beach, snowboarding, photography and making scrapbooks. She has two dogs, Dakota and Trixie, and two cats. Beverley is the winner of the Young Artist Award for Best Actress in a Television Drama Series *(7th Heaven)* in both 1996 and 1997.

Jordan Mitchell, fourteen, is the youngest of four and lives in California. She is a creative artist and passionate writer. Jordan enjoys playing soccer, watching movies and being with her friends and family.

Kathleen M. Muldoon has written for children's magazines for many years. She is the author of one picture book entitled, *Princess Pooh.* When she is not writing, she enjoys reading, taking long walks and playing with her cat, Prissy. She can be reached at *mink@texas.net*.

Marisol Muqoz-Kiehne was born in Puerto Rico and lives in the San Francisco area. She is a clinical psychologist who works with children and families, teaches child psychotherapy, and is the host of *Nuestros Niños*, a radio program on parenting and child development. She can be reached at: *marisol@nuestrosninos.com*.

Son Truong Nguyen, age seventeen, loves to write. He encourages everyone to pick up a writing instrument and "just write for the sheer enjoyment of it," and go out there and live your life to the fullest.

Aubrey Nighswander lives in Ohio, on the south shore of Lake Erie. She is active in her junior high Pen program and an editor for the school newspaper. Aubrey enjoys a wide variety of activities and is very competitive in soccer, swimming and sailing.

Brian Normandin is a sophomore in California. In addition to hanging with his friends, he spends his spare time collecting and trading basketball cards and working a part time job.

Mary Normandin began writing four years ago and draws the inspiration for her stories from her family life. Mary resides in Southern California with her husband and four children, where she volunteers at her kids' school and chauffeurs them to their various activities.

Pier Novelli is twelve years old and the youngest in a family of six. He enjoys talking with friends, listening to music, playing sports and taking care of his three pets. Pier enjoys making people laugh and hopes to continue his writing to reach out to others.

*NSYNC, which includes Lance Bass, J. C. Chasez, Joey Fatone, Chris Kirkpatrick and Justin Timberlake, have obtained global stardom. Their self-titled 1998 debut album sold more than ten million copies and yielded four number-one singles: "I Want You Back," "Tearin' Up My Heart," "God Must Have Spent a Little More Time on You" and "Drive Myself Crazy." Even while touring nonstop and doing more than three hundred concerts in the last year, they recorded hits with other artists including Gloria Estefan and Alabama and released a Christmas EP, "Home For Christmas." *NSYNC has won numerous awards including a 1999 American Music Award for "Best New Pop/Rock Group," embarked on some solo projects and recorded a new album, "No Strings Attached" for Jive Records.

Colleen O'Brien, age thirteen, wrote her story for *Preteen Soul 2* after reading about other people's experiences much like hers. It is her hope that those who read about her experience of loss at a young age will find comfort. Colleen's hobbies include reading, writing and hanging out with friends.

Ashley O'Bryant is a fourteen-year-old honors student. Some things she likes to do for fun are reading, shopping, spending time with family and friends, but especially talking on the phone. She is always willing to lend a helping hand and enjoys serving others. Her career goal is to be a psychologist.

Shannon O'Bryant, age twelve, loves to play soccer. It is her favorite sport because it keeps her active and it's fun. Her favorite foods are pizza, barbeque ribs, artichokes and corn. She enjoys expressing herself through poetry and making home videos.

D. Marie O'Keefe, a Wisconsin freelance writer and former librarian, now knows that it's way cooler to give time and energy to family and friends than to becoming what others think is cool. Her passions include dogs, parrots, fly-fishing, protecting endangered plants and animals, and collecting books. She also enjoys photographing wildlife, encountering wild grizzlies and wolves, digging for dinosaur bones and riding in hot-air balloons.

Michael Oknefski is a senior in high school who plays on the school golf, basketball and baseball teams. He is a member of the National Honor Society and has been nominated to "Who's Who" among high school students for three consecutive years. Mike will major in engineering at Penn State University in fall 2000. You can e-mail him at *davo@ncentral.com.*

Jennifer O'Neil has a master of fine arts in screenwriting and has over ten years experience in film. She is a writer, producer and director in San Francisco and creator of gala-event scripts for Columbia/Tristar, Sony, and Discovery Networks. Jennifer and her sister Kitty's first book, *Decorating with Funky Shui,* hits bookstores in June of 2004.

Daphne M. Orenshein is a full-time kindergarten teacher in Los Angeles, California, and a distributor for DKFL publishing company. Her hobbies are reading, basketball, photography, dance, singing, event planning and keeping her husband on his toes. She has three terrific book-loving, Lego-building, cooking-helping, Marco Polo–playing, in-your-face little boys.

Carol Osman Brown is a freelance writer and photographer whose work has been published in many magazines and newspapers. She speaks at writing conferences and teaches writing at Arizona State University and Rio Salado College in Phoenix, Arizona. You can contact her at *cobrown@aztec.asu.edu.*

Susan Overton was born and raised in Denver, Colorado. She resides in Seattle, Washington, and is a manager at Andersen Consulting, where she specializes in the area of international e-commerce. Susan enjoys biking, snowshoeing and running. She continues to be an advocate for child literacy by supporting programs that put books in the hands of children. She credits her parents and siblings for always providing guidance, eternal optimism and patience in her many crazy ideas. You can reach her at *v-acsuso@microsoft.com.*

Tenna Perry has black belts in American Freestyle Karate and Bushido Kai. She has taught martial arts to students of all ages for ten years. Tenna focuses a great deal of her writing on self-defense, all forms of child abuse and rape. Please e-mail her at *midnightwriter@ev1.net.*

Victoria Perry is a high school freshman and a junior karate instructor who enjoys teaching other children the importance of self-defense. Victoria participates in as many karate tournaments as possible in her area where she has consistently won in both sparring and katas.

Kelsey Peters is an eleven-year-old who enjoys reading *Chicken Soup* books, writing and playing with her dogs, Lilli and Dottie. She is in fifth grade and loves to sing for her church.

Nicole Peters is a sixteen-year-old from Oklahoma. Her goal in life is to continue writing and earn a master's degree in psychology so that she can help others. She is active in her Christian youth group and enjoys being a teenager.

Jonathan Piccirillo is a junior in Pennsylvania. His hobbies include soccer, drama, music, debate, travel, creative writing and spending time with friends. Jonathan became interested in writing from his creative-writing teacher, Mrs. Aiello. He plans on pursuing an English or arts degree in college.

Michael T. Powers is a high school girls' coach, youth pastor, founder of *www.Heart4Teens.com,* and author of his own book, *Heart Touchers.* To read more about his writings, which appear in nineteen inspirational books, or to join the thousands of worldwide readers on his inspirational e-mail list, visit *www.Heart4Teens.com* or e-mail him at *Heart4Teens@aol.com.*

Rachel Punches grew up in Muskegon, Michigan, and is a soldier in the Army National Guard. She now lives in Kalamazoo, Michigan, where she is attending college. In her spare time, she enjoys movies, reading, singing at the top of her lungs and dancing when no one is around. She draws inspiration for her writing from family and friends. She dedicates her poem to her friend, Kerry, whom she loves and misses very much.

Lindsey Rawson, age thirteen, enjoys writing poetry and short stories. She spends much of her time dancing, acting in plays, helping people and hanging out with friends. Lindsey hopes to make the cheerleading squad next school year.

John Reiner was born in 1956 and raised on Long Island. He met *Mad Magazine* artist Mort Drucker in 1974, who encouraged him to pursue cartooning as a career; and in 1984 hired Reiner to work on King Features' comic strip *Benchley*. In collaboration with Bunny Hoest, Reiner took over production of the classic comic panel *The Lockhorns,* created by the late Bill Hoest. They also took over *Bumper Snickers, Howard Huge* and *Laugh Parade.* Reiner won the 1994 National Cartoonists Society award for gag cartoons.

Michelle Richard is a sixth-grader in Louisiana, where she lives with her parents and three younger brothers. Her interests include reading, visual arts, acting and composing songs. She is also an active member of the Girl Scouts. Michelle would like to thank all of her friends for their support, especially Amber and Brittany.

Nicole Ritchie is a ninth-grader from Texas. She belongs to two dance groups and has been jazz dancing for nine years. She plans on attending college after high school.

Alexandria Robinson, twelve, is an excellent writer who loves to express her feelings, thoughts, emotions and life experiences on paper. She likes to do normal girl stuff like hang out with friends and talk on the phone. She still can't believe that one of her poems was picked to be in *Chicken Soup for the Preteen Soul 2!*

Gwen Rockwood received her English degree from the University of Arkansas. She writes a humor column called "The Rockwood Files" for newspapers in Arkansas and Missouri and is currently working on a compilation book of her columns. E-mail her at *rockwood@cox-internet.com.*

Nadine Rogers has been writing picture books, magazine articles, educational material and chapter books for eight- to twelve-year-old children for ten years. Current educational titles coauthored include a set of three books called *Directives* (Humanics Publishing Group) and a book of Constitution puzzles (Royal Fireworks Press). She writes a monthly column in a local newsletter called *Grammargram*. Nadine enjoys playing duplicate bridge and tennis in her free time. She can be reached at 2403 Greenhorn Rd., Yreka, CA 96097-9467.

Cynthia Ross Cravit is a freelance writer who has written primarily for children's magazines. Recently, she completed several chapter books and is working on a middle-grade novel. She resides in Northern Michigan with her husband and three children, all of whom have enormous influence on her writing.

Shane Ruwe is a fifteen-year-old from Missouri. He is a black belt in the martial arts and enjoys bow hunting, football, baseball and golf. He likes writing mostly nonfiction stories and also writes some fiction. Writing "Kelsey" helped him express his feelings about his family's tragedies.

Jessica Sagers is in eighth grade in Utah. She is boy crazy, loves hanging out with her friends and enjoys seeing Orlando Bloom movies. Jessica likes writing poetry and fictional stories and plays tennis, water-skis and snow-skis.

Mary Ellyn Sandford is a happily married mother of seven. She has been published in several magazines, *Chicken Soup for the Kid's Soul* and is currently working on a middle-grade novel. She is the head director of Ministering Metacarpals, a traveling puppet performance team. When teachers didn't encourage her desire to write, she spent lots of time with heroines like Anne Shirley, Jo March and Laura Ingalls. You can contact Mary Ellyn at 4507 Chelsea Ave., Lisle, IL 60532 or via e-mail at *wfkig@quixnet.net*.

Mary Saracino lives in Denver, Colorado. She is the author of two novels, *No Matter What* (Spinsters Ink, 1993) and *Finding Grace* (Spinsters Ink, 1999). Her memoir, *Autobiography of a Voice*, will be published by Spinsters Ink in spring 2001. In 1991, Mary won a Loft Mentor Series Award for fiction writing. Her work has appeared in a variety of literary magazines and anthologies including *Hey Paesan!, Writers Who Cook, Sinister Wisdom, Voices in Italian Americana* and *Italian Americana*.

Hope Saxton lives in Ontario, Canada, with her husband and two sons. She began writing stories and poetry as a child, and her love of writing has carried her into the present. Her work has appeared in many magazines, as well as *A 6th Bowl of Chicken Soup for the Soul*. Hope is currently working on her fourth novel. She can be e-mailed at *hope_saxton@hotmail.com*.

Elizabeth J. Schmeidler is happily married to her husband, Gary, and feels blessed to have her three sons, Jerome, Paul and Roy. She started writing three years ago and since has written a Christian romance mystery entitled *Forget Me Not*, as well as a collection of poetry and three children's books. Her second novel is in the works. She also enjoys singing at church and at weddings and funerals. Elizabeth can be reached at 508 W. 32nd St., Hays, KS 67601.

Bunny Schulle has more than fifty published stories, articles and plays for children and young adults and has received several writing awards. She taught English as a Second Language through adult education and has volunteered in the Listen to the Children program. Currently, she is writing a preteen mystery novel and enjoys spending time with her granddaughters. She can be contacted at 106 N. Dory Rd., North Palm Beach, FL 33408.

Mark Schulle is a classical guitar instructor in Florida. He is the owner of the Gainesville Guitar Academy where he shares his love of music with children and adults. Mark also enjoys boating, reading and hiking.

Amy Severns, age fifteen, has enjoyed writing for many years. Her poetry can be found in the International Library of Poetry's Anthology entitled *Seasons of Happiness*. She is also an active softball player, musician (playing the bass guitar and the clarinet), and Web site designer. More of Amy's writing is available on her personal Web site located at *www.manifest-angel.com/roses*.

Jamie Lauren Shapiro is fourteen years old and lives in Virginia with her large family and dog named Max. She loves writing poetry and often uses it as a way of expressing herself and communicating with others.

Elijah Shoesmith is a freshman in high school who enjoys writing adventure stories, reading action books and playing computer games. He aspires to write adventure books for teens. He would like to thank God, his family, the Oraras, the Boyds, Jason, Josh and Rachel for their support.

Jaimee Silber is an eighth-grade honor student from Michigan. Her interests include cheerleading, dance and, of course, writing. She has a dog, a cat and a sister, Alexis. This is Jaimee's first published work and she would like to thank her Nana for buying her her first *Chicken Soup* book.

Samantha Slaughter, age twelve, has been surrounded by people who read her entire life. She loves to write and includes her personal feelings in her pieces. Her favorite color is purple and she likes playing basketball and spending time with family and friends.

Makenzie Snyder is a nine-year-old from Maryland who enjoys gymnastics, ballet, drawing and making things. She has been twirling baton since she was four years old and won first place in Dance Twirl competition at the national championships. She has two older brothers, a dog and two cats. She can be reached at Children to Children, 3262 Superior Ln., PMB# 288, Bowie, MD 20715, or at the Web site, *www.childrentochildren.org*.

Beverly Spooner wanted to be a writer since the age of seven. Throughout her preteen and teen years, she was an avid journal writer and poet. In her late twenties, she became a contributing writer for *The Topanga Messenger*, a local newspaper. She is now a freelance writer living in Illinois with her artist/husband Michael, son Philip, and dogs, Snowy and Rembrandt.

Danny Stein enjoys hockey, golf and skiing, as well as playing guitar. He believes that you can do anything you put your mind to!

Monte Stewart is a journalist living in Calgary, Canada who became a *Calgary Herald* staff writer in 1987 and has covered sports (including the National Hockey League and the 1998 Winter Olympics). He serves as president of Falcon Press, the publishing company that produced his critically acclaimed book, *Carry On: Reaching Beyond 100*, the inspirational autobiography of centenarian Tom Spear. His freelance articles have appeared in such publications as the *Toronto Star, Profit Magazine, The Hockey News* and *San Jose Mercury News*. He enjoys hockey, golf, reading and traveling. You can reach him at *monstr@telus planet.net*, or phone him at 403-284-4292.

Craig Strickland is married with two kids. He likes bodysurfing and going to movies. He has had numerous stories published in magazines and anthologies. His two books for middle-readers are *Scary Stories from 1313 Wicked Way* and *Scary Stories for Sleepovers #8*. You can e-mail him at *Strickland-4@cox.net*.

Angelia Lee Swift is a freshman at Tennessee Technological University who enjoys creative writing, reading and hanging out with her friends. She looks forward to contributing to society by becoming a published author. You can contact her at P.O. Box 2490, Cookerville, TN 38502, or via e-mail at *aLs9514@tntech.edu*.

Lew Talmadge, a retired Chief Warrant Officer, U.S. Army Intelligence, has been writing for thirty years. He is a polylinguist (German, Albanian and

Romanian) who enjoys photography, volunteer reading at a local elementary school and playing Santa Claus. He lives with his wife, Vivian, and cocker spaniel, Caycie. He can be contacted at 1714 View St., Athens, TN 37303, by calling 423-744-7227, or via e-mail at *Ltalmadg@icx.net.*

Stephanie Taylor, age eleven, enjoys skating, shopping and talking on the phone with her friends. She owns a dog named Ginger and two cats named Tiger and Mittens. Her favorite subjects in school are history and science. Her Web site is *www.dogvest.com.*

Quinn Thomas lives in Georgia with her husband and one-year-old daughter. After a twelve-year career in social services, she is now a stay-at-home mother and loves spending time with her daughter and writing children's stories.

Lauren Thorbjornsen is a freshman at her high school where she serves on student government. She is a member of the swim and soccer teams and enjoys traveling, shopping, music and being with her friends.

April Townsend is thirteen years old and likes reading and writing. She wants to be a middle-school English teacher or a psychologist because she enjoys listening to people and helping them with their problems.

Aidan Trenn is a nine-year-old girl who loves to draw, make crafts and play with her friends. She was born in Maryland and has lived in Florida, Oklahoma and New Mexico. Aidan also enjoys inline skating and boogie boarding. She is in Mrs. Jones' third-grade class and is a member of the Math Superstars Club.

Mike Vallely, skateboard legend and East Coast rebel-punk-poet, changed the face of skateboarding in 1986 with his innovative and artistic approach to street skating. Eighteen years later he is still making an impact with his unflinching individuality and his aggressive and expressive skating. A touring machine, Mike V. has covered more ground than any other professional skater in the history of the sport, spreading the gospel of skateboarding around the globe. Lead singer of the hardcore punk outfit Mike V. and the Rats and star of ESPN's Tony Hawk's Gigantic Skatepark Tour and featured in the Tony Hawk Pro Skater video game series, he is on a mission to live his life to the fullest each and every day, which means plenty more relevant and impassioned skating and music is yet to come from this man.

Casey L. Veronie is a sophomore who plays the trombone in his high school band. He is active in his church high school youth group and has achieved an Eagle Scout ranking in Boy Scouts.

Julia Wasson Render is a former elementary teacher who now works for a company that helps very young children build literacy skills. In her spare time, she contributes to *Partners for Schools* and *Partners for Parents,* two newsletters just for parents of preteen kids. Her inspirations are her daughter,

Lindsay, and sons, Aaron and Jake. Julia can be reached at 1916 Grantwood Dr., Iowa City, IA 52440.

Megan Weaver is a thirteen-year-old from Georgia who has been writing and illustrating short stories since she was eight. She is active in her church and loves art, sports, tap and jazz, and playing the piano. Megan plans to write a book someday and maybe become a doctor or veterinarian.

Lauren Ashley Weilbacher is a high school freshman. Her hobbies are ballet, pointe, jazz and tap. She is a pom-pom girl and also teaches ballet and tap.

Spencer Westcott was seventeen when he wrote "My Dad, the Superhero." He is currently studying political science at the University of California, San Diego. Spencer is the president of the Poker Society, the Secret Society of Pirates; a member of the Associated Students; and enjoys playing golf and guitar. You can contact Spencer at *spencer@ucsd.edu.*

Lauren Wheeler is twelve years old and enjoys going to camp, hanging out with her friends and playing tennis. She loves making new friends online with people from diverse backgrounds. She is on a swim team that has been undefeated for two years.

Michelle Williams joined Destiny's Child, one of the bestselling female groups of all time, with steely determination to learn. That same fearless, faith-driven quality came in handy while jump-starting a solo career as an inspirational/gospel recording artist with her 2002 release, *Heart to Yours.* Her tireless work ethic motivated her to conquer a starring role on the Broadway stage as the love-crossed Nubian princess, *Aida.* And in January 2004, Michelle excitedly delivered *Do You Know,* an inspirational and contemporary urban-gospel style, set to everyday life-based testimonials of self-doubt, questions of faith and bad relationships.

Kristi Yamaguchi is skating's best and brightest; a dominant force and major star in the world of figure skating. Her professional career is marked by numerous major championship titles and critically acclaimed performances earning her accolades from major sportswriters as the "best female skater in the world." Following a tremendous amateur career, in 1992 Kristi won the U.S. National Championship, fulfilled a lifelong dream by winning the Olympic Gold Medal in Albertville and defended her World title in her hometown in Oakland. In 1998 Kristi returned to the U.S. National Championships to be inducted into the U.S. Figure Skating Hall of Fame. She has recently finished her tenth year of touring with Stars on Ice along with fellow Olympic medallists Katrina Witt, Ilia Kulik, Todd Eldridge and Tara Lipinski.

Nikki Yargar, age fourteen, plays lacrosse, softball and basketball and loves swimming in the summer. Music and her friends are important to her. In her free time, she likes to write in her diary and work on her scrapbook. She is very close to her parents, three brothers and two sisters.

Megan Youpa, fourteen, enjoys playing softball and hanging out with her friends. She started writing poetry to express her feelings to the world and to show others how she feels. Megan would like to thank her English teacher, Mrs. Always, for introducing her to poetry.

Julia Yorks is a fifteen-year-old high school freshman who loves to write, although her ambition in life is to be an actress or news commentator. Julia has appeared in M. Night Shyamalan's *Unbreakable,* and on the CBS television show "Hack," among others. Her favorite pastimes include singing, being with friends and playing sports.

Patty Zeitlin is an author, poet, playwright and songwriter with recordings for young people and adults and an M.A. from Pacific Oaks College in human development. She teaches classes in Compassionate Communication (NVC). Patty enjoys dancing, reading and Hawaii. She just finished writing a fantasy-fiction novel for young adults. Contact her at *patty@psncc.org.*

Xiao Xi Zhang, age eighteen, moved to the United States from China at the age of twelve. His experiences of sadness, loss and success in this country led him to write his story for *Chicken Soup for the Preteen Soul.* He can be reached at *xzhang2000@aol.com.*

NOTES